COPYRIGHT AFRICA

First published in 2016
Paperback edition published 2019
Sean Kingston Publishing
www.seankingston.co.uk
Canon Pyon

British Library Cataloguing in Publication Data
A catalogue record for this book is available from the British Library.

ISBN 978-1-912385-04-1

Copyright Africa

ⓒⓒⓒⓒⓒⓒⓒⓒⓒⓒⓒ

How intellectual property, media and markets

transform immaterial cultural goods

EDITED BY UTE RÖSCHENTHALER AND

MAMADOU DIAWARA

Sean Kingston Publishing

www.seankingston.co.uk

Canon Pyon

Preface and acknowledgements

This book is about shifting norms and rights with respect to immaterial cultural goods in African countries. It grew out of the research project 'Norms and Media in Africa' carried out by Mamadou Diawara and Ute Röschenthaler. The project was affiliated with Research Area 2 'Historicity of Normative Orders' in the Cluster of Excellence 'The Formation of Normative Orders' at the Goethe University Frankfurt, Germany, funded by the German Research Council (first period 2007–12). In this framework we organized two conferences in the Forschungskolleg Humanwissenschaften (Institute for Advanced Studies in the Humanities) in Bad Homburg, with international junior and senior scholars from different disciplines. The first of these conferences, in December 2010, served to elaborate the topic and the second, in June 2011, to present and discuss the individual chapters of this volume.

The principal question which motivated us to engage in this project was: why has the application of norms and rights to immaterial cultural goods gained so much importance, especially since the 1990s? In different African countries, we observed how the international discourse on global rights and norms has become increasingly influential over the past couple of decades. Mamadou Diawara, who has been working on the recycling of tradition in Mali since the 1970s, noted mounting concern about the loss of effect of spoken words and music as ever more modern artists began to stage 'tradition' on the global music scene. Similarly, Ute Röschenthaler, who in the 1980s began to study the development of local rights in cult and dance associations in south-west Cameroon and south-east Nigeria from pre-colonial times until the present, noted that the conceptions of the ownership of immaterial goods have in the past couple of decades diversified, and are no longer imagined to belong to clans and later cult associations only, but increasingly also to entire ethnic groups and single artists.

Scholarly work that discusses the impacts of globalization largely focuses on the repercussions in local cultural contexts of Western-induced financial flows, diffusion of commodities, technologies and habits of consumption and the reception of these in different local cultural contexts. We felt that this discussion would greatly benefit from a study that explores what happens, from a local African point of view, to immaterial cultural goods when they are confronted with large-scale commodification, globalized mediatization and divergent judicial systems, institutions and cultural norms.

We want to encourage the taking of a closer look at the intersections of these globalized norms, technologies and products with local normative standards and concepts of rights which have their own history. In addition to this, we stress the importance of studying the practices of the actors on the ground. To understand, for example, what copyright is about and how it is discussed in Africa, we must keep in mind that it has become a global phenomenon which emerged in the specific historical context of one part of Europe, from where it developed into different 'traditions', following its origin. Thus, rights to creations should also be conceptualized as cultural constructions with specific purposes and local characteristics which, according to the circumstances, privilege one or the other aspect of these constructions, be it the rights of a single 'author', purely commercial considerations or the 'common good'. The same applies to other normative standards in the domain of immaterial culture, such as literary genres or aesthetic concepts.

The Cluster of Excellence 'The Formation of Normative Orders' provided us with the opportunity to consolidate the results of individually conducted studies by bringing together an international and interdisciplinary team of anthropologists, jurists and literary scholars for a fruitful exchange on the topic. This broad-based intellectual interchange enabled us to overcome the dichotomies oral/literary, ideation/materialization and improvisation/fixation (of performance). It also enabled us to comprehend the complexity of cultural expressions as mediated representations – in performance, songs, music, books, and tapes – in addition to the normative frameworks of ownership rights connected with their use.

We are grateful to the many individuals and institutions that helped us to realize this project. The Cluster of Excellence and the Centre for Interdisciplinary African Studies, both at the Goethe University Frankfurt, Germany, have contributed substantially to what we consider the success of this undertaking. They have financially underwritten the two conferences as well as the editing of the book. Special thanks are due to Andreas Fahrmeir, the Speaker of Research Area 2 of the Cluster of Excellence, for his moral support, to Peter Siller, who facilitated the unrolling of the project as its Scientific Manager, and to Stefan Schmid, Director of the Centre for Interdisciplinary African Studies. Thanks are also due to the Anthropology Department (Institut für Ethnologie) at the Goethe University for its support in the organization of the conferences. We wish to extend particular gratitude to Ingrid Rudolph, the Director of the Forschungskolleg Humanwissenschaften in Bad Homburg, which hosted our conferences, and to her entire team for their warm welcome and the congenial atmosphere essential to the success of any symposium.

We also wish to acknowledge the efforts made by the authors to get themselves together to participate in this inspiring project, many of whom travelled twice to Bad Homburg, most often quite far from their homes, for the purpose. We are very fortunate to have had the expertise and moral support of Karin Barber and Alexander Peukert at both conferences. Their presence, as well as that of Elisabeth Mudimbe-Boyi, was invaluable for the realization of the undertaking. Two participants, Rosemary Coombe and Monika Bruss, have not contributed directly to this volume, but unstintingly offered their input. Veit Erlmann joined us at a later stage. We also wish to acknowledge the important stimuli we owe to our participation at the conference 'Tuning in to African Cities' at the Centre of West African Studies at Birmingham in 2010, and to the other audiences to which we presented the topic at lecture series and anthropology conferences in Europe and North America. We also greatly benefitted from conversations with many more scholars who readily discussed the topic with us but who are too numerous to list here.

Finally, we thank our students Kathleen Witt and Tom Simmert for their untiring help in organizing both conferences and in welcoming the participants. Tom Simmert also efficiently assisted in the editing of the volume. We are particularly grateful to our late copy editor Elliot Klein for his outstanding efforts not only to edit the English language but also to translate long passages from German and French and, after all, to make the text readable and put the finishing touches to the July 2012 draft of the manuscript.

Mamadou Diawara and Ute Röschenthaler

Frankfurt am Main

Contents

List of contributors

Karin Barber: Professor of African Cultural Anthropology at the Department of African Studies and Anthropology, University of Birmingham.

Mamadou Diawara: Professor of Anthropology at the Goethe University Frankfurt; Principal Investigator at the Cluster of Excellence, Deputy Director of the Frobenius Institut; Founding Director of Point Sud, The Center for Research on Local Knowledge, Bamako, Mali.

Veit Erlmann: Endowed Chair of Music History at the University of Texas at Austin.

Matthias Gruber: Research Fellow in the project 'Africa's Asian Options' (AFRASO) at Goethe University, Frankfurt.

Alessandro Jedlowski: Post-doctoral fellow in anthropology at the University of Liège.

Caroline Mose: Post-doctoral independent researcher.

Elisabeth Mudimbe-Boyi: Professor Emerita of French and Comparative Literature, Stanford University.

Neo Musangi: Fellow at the Institute of Social and Economic Research (Wiser), University of the Witwatersrand, Johannesburg.

Patrick Oloko: Senior Lecturer in the Department of English, University of Lagos.

Alexander Peukert: Professor of Civil Law, Commercial Law and Intellectual Property Law, Faculty of Law, Goethe University; Principal Investigator of the Cluster of Excellence 'The Formation of Normative Orders'.

Ute Röschenthaler: Professor at the Johannes Gutenberg University of Mainz; Scientific Collaborator in the Cluster of Excellence 'The Formation of Normative Orders' and the project 'Africa's Asian Options' (AFRASO) at Goethe University, Frankfurt.

Dorothea Schulz: Professor in the Department of Cultural and Social Anthropology at the University of Cologne.

Alexie Tcheuyap: Professor of French and Francophone Studies at the University of Toronto.

Ibrahima Wane: Senior Lecturer in the Department of French at the University Cheikh Anta Diop of Dakar.

INTRODUCTION

African intellectual worlds in the making

©©©©©©©©©©

UTE RÖSCHENTHALER AND

MAMADOU DIAWARA

Africa is known worldwide for its multi-faceted immaterial culture, manifested in its highly original music, oral texts, artistic performances, textile designs, literature and its local knowledge applied in interaction with plants and the environment, or in the construction of earthwork architecture. With the increase of knowledge about Africa's cultural heritage came a growing unease about how to treat and consider these forms of cultural expression and artistic production. The question of its ownership and use have become to an ever greater extent the object of legal regulations and commercial interests which go hand in hand with its global distribution through the media. Joost Smiers (1999) quite accurately observes that everywhere in the world all domains of cultural life – music, literature, performance, video, sports – and all expressions of lifestyle, and the human body itself, have been affected by these processes.

Many scholars are disconcerted that it is no longer just in consumer societies, but even in the furthest reaches of the planet that all cultural expressions are now increasingly regulated by intellectual property (IP) rights (Coombe 1998; Cowan 2001 *et al.* 2006). Also, IP has moved from its formerly exclusive location within legal discourse into much wider public prominence (Hirsch and Strathern 2004:3). Jean and John Comaroff attribute this to the prevalence of the neoliberal order (2000, 2009; see also Coombe 2003), which appears to favour the appropriation and control of artistic products by big companies that earn a fortune from the rights to immaterial property (Benthall 1999; Smiers 1999). Thomas and Nyamnjoh (2007:14) wonder whether increasing privatization is the inevitable fate of a connected world.

These trends can in any case be clearly read as indicators of swiftly changing 'normative orders' (for more on this concept see Forst and Günther 2011).

Scholars have also noted that the intensified attempts at control have provoked civil disobedience, spurred local creativity into circumventing the rules (Roitman 2005) and produced hotly contested illicit trade and piracy. Ravi Sundaram suggests that both tendencies are intrinsically connected, inseparable companions: piracy is the twin sibling of the increasing control of IP rights. Extensive endeavours to make the (Indian) city more transparent and safe have only contributed to rendering it more opaque (2010:175–6). This is also true for Africa. As Mbembe and Roitman (1995) note, promises and dreams of modernity develop their own underground lives in the (African) city. Which side to take is, however, far from self-evident. Do the deprived artists, whose art is their only way to survive, require more support, or do the laws intended to help them only hinder them and constrict the production of art forms (Anon. 2005)? Should we sympathize with the small pirates who question these laws, arguing that they deprive the public of access to 'common goods' (see also Goldhaber 2000; Raustiala and Sprigman 2006)? Is the real battle even between artists and pirates, or does that rather serve to distract us from the underlying reality that governments in need of taxes or other significant income support the exploitative monopolies of big companies at the expense of the creators of artworks and the local owners of cultural expressions? Arriving at such an uncomplimentary interpretation, Philip (2005) interrogates the intricate complexities of this economy and Chang (2004) points to the increasing impossibility of distinguishing originals from fakes in global (Asian) markets.

Many scholars, including those from Africa, call for more protection and better implementation of IP laws (Brush and Stabisky 1996; Dutfield 1999; Globerman 1988; Hewitt 2007; Mills 1996; Ouma 2006; Strathern *et al.* 1998), with good arguments to acknowledge tradition-based art as the heritage and property of the community of its creators or of an ethnic group. Other scholars are worried by the intensified enforcement of rights and advocate the copyleft movements[1] that propose free access to immaterial goods and creations so that all can profit and benefit from innovation, provided it remains free (Anon. 2005; Benthall 1999; Guillebaud, Stoichita and Mallet 2010; McLeod 2005; Rowlands 2004; Vaidhyanathan 2001).[2] Others criticize

---

1   The copyleft movement is a growing alliance of artists, authors, activists and legal theorists who are building an alternative to the current restrictive regime of IP controls.

2   Guillebaud, Stoichita and Mallet (2010) dedicate an entire issue of *Gradhiva* to the topic, entitled *La musique n'a pas d'auteur: ethnographies du copyright.*

the IP norm as a Western notion that does not coincide with African cultural conceptions (Boateng 2011; Geyer 2010; for Asia: Lehmann 2006; Yung 2009; and more generally: Strathern 2006). This criticism can also be found in many African contributions to the topic, although their dominant focus is to censure their own malfunctioning state institutions.

These reflections raise basic questions about how to treat and regulate immaterial goods. Who should have access to them, who should be permitted to make what use of which specialized knowledge, who should be considered their author, discoverer or owner, and who should have the right to profit from their sale? The responses to such questions also differ at the local level. Many local actors have a growing sense of competition and crisis linked to the loss of free access to, and control over, immaterial goods, whereas others see such perplexities themselves as an opportunity to create a new self-consciousness and recognition of their culture (see for example, Comaroff and Comaroff 2009; Geschiere 2009). These developments also encourage entrepreneurial activities, be they legal, illicit or illegal.

Two basic tendencies can be observed. On the one hand, individual local actors appropriate cultural expressions in their locally practised forms, then transform them and amplify them with new elements, declare the results to be their own creations and market them as their intellectual property. On the other hand, ethnic groups proclaim certain cultural forms of expression and local knowledge as their cultural heritage, to be intrinsically linked only to their group from now on, often essentialized and declared to be an ancient legacy from their own earliest ancestors. Endeavours to implement the new IP legislation are promoted by non-governmental organizations and the global art market. Thus both local and international actors contribute to the emergence of new 'invented traditions' (Ranger 1983, 1993).[3] The global distribution of IP norms also represents what Appadurai (1996) calls an 'ideoscape' (Goodale 2009:2–3).

Yet, we still do not know enough about these intricate interconnections in Africa. We need to know more about what transpires, from a local perspective, among pirates, artists, governments and international organizations. What happens to the art forms, the music, performance, inventions, oral literature, local beauty ideals and sports activities when they become media products, confronted with international norms and regulations, and practices of

---

3   Ranger's primary intention, when he wrote *The Invention of Tradition* (1983), was to the draw attention to the distortion of local history by colonial officials in order to make it coincide with their own construction of African culture as one which existed within narrowly defined ethnic boundaries and without a noteworthy history.

sanctioning them? How are oral art forms and ritual performances transformed when they are fixed on paper or on modern sound carriers and video media, which then become commodities, when sport is converted into a commercial event and bodies are increasingly mediatized and normatized?

Little is still known of the complexity of local norms and rights to intangible goods, and what happens to these local regulations when international IP rights are introduced. Are they simply replaced by Western norms and regulations, or do both continue existing side by side, and, if so, what are the consequences of their co-existence? In whose interests are the copyright laws applied? Under what circumstances do they inspire people to create new cultural productions and market them globally, or rather invent strategies to circumvent the laws? To what extent do they determine the outcome of art? Whose norms are they? Were art forms, cultural expressions and knowledge already owned before they became subject to copyright law, and, if so, were the owners an entire ethnic group, a community, a family or an individual? How do cultural expressions become the property of individuals and collectivities? How is the immaterial staged in Africa, which rights and norms are disputed and which new styles and performances are emerging as a result?

In this book we intend to explore these questions to gain a better understanding of the processes involved, from a local point of view, when immaterial cultural goods face globalization and technological innovation. We want to know more about the transformation of cultural expressions when confronted with international regulations and processes of commodification and mediatization. The understanding of these transformations – one of the most challenging questions in this book – also requires knowledge of the forms of ownership, technologies of mediation and degrees of commercialization that existed pre-colonially in different African societies.

The contributors to this volume all focus on one or the other aspect of these transformations. They investigate in which way local and international norms have, at a specific time and in a particular place, encouraged the transformation of orally transmitted stories and plots, ritualized speeches, praise poetry, music, performance, sports or other corporeal practices. They explore what happens to them when they are fixed and turned into written documents, when they are commercialized and broadcast in the media or become subject to legal regulations such as the IP rights regime.[4] We argue that these transformations result not only from the introduction of legal regulations by the so-called West, nor always from that of technologies such as the printing press and electronic media. The process is more complex. The

---

4   The book deals with legal regulations such as authors' rights and copyrights, but
    not with patents, brands or trade secrets, which could easily fill another book.

local regulations, media and forms of commerce in these goods have to be understood before we can grasp their confrontation with varying Western legacies of immaterial property regulations. Most important, it is only when the local actors begin to embrace them in a specific historical situation that these technologies and regulations become influential forces for change and provoke various transformations, including the development of piracy. The question is thus less whether international IP norms conform to African practices or whether media impose a Western style, but rather what local actors do with these regulations and how they appropriate, implement and make use of them, and how both local and Western practices and technologies have an impact on each other.

In the realm of copyright and piracy: impacts of law, technology, media and market

Property has been described 'not as a thing but a relationship' (Murphy 1980), and rights to property define this relationship between people with respect to certain things (see, for example, Hann 1998; May 2000; C. Rose 1994; M. Rose 1993; and in the African context Chanock 1985; Lentz 2006). This perception also applies to intangible property, but its immateriality further complicates the definition of rights in terms of relationships between people. These rights can be passed on, but what is subject to the rights can be kept and given away at the same time (Röschenthaler 2011a; see also Weiner 1992). Rights to intangible property can be acquired and sold, but immateriality encourages clandestinity, as it is far more difficult in respect to immaterial than to material goods to define exactly what one has a right to, how this intangible product came into being, and consequently, how ownership can be secured and imitation and the production of copies prevented.

Any researcher interested in immaterial cultural goods in sub-Saharan Africa will quickly realize that the subject has been relatively little studied, quite contrary to the case of material goods, especially art objects.[5] Working on intangible goods requires one to take a detour through the laws that treat

---

5   For works – just to name a few important ones – focusing on the material aspects of African art and performance, see, for example: Arnoldi 1995; Boone 1986; Fardon 2007; Fischer 1984; Kramer 1993; Ranger 1975; Strother 1998; for textile patterns: Arnoldi, Geary and Hardin 1996; Asmah 2008; Boateng 2011; Picton 1995; Rovine 2001. Other monographs focus more on immaterial cultural goods and expressions, and some also discuss claims to ownership. For example, see for music, Charry 2000; Dorsch 2006; Erlmann 1991; Goodman 2005; Hoffmann 2000; Ntarangwi 2009; Schulz 2001; Stewart 2000; White 2008; for oratory: Barber 2007; Diawara 1990, 2003; Fabian 1990; Finnegan 2007; Furniss 2004; for cultural heritage: De Jong 2009; De Jong and Rowlands 2007; Probst 2011.

authors' rights and which serve as the matrix of the principles governing the management of all intellectual property, including immaterial goods, especially music, dance and rituals, and their public performance.

The present situation can be understood only from a diachronic perspective. The laws which have spread through the world originated in Europe, and have become innate to the West. We will examine this history, for at least two reasons: first, to see the diverse ways in which intellectual property can be protected and in which profit can be derived from it; second, to take note of the rifts deriving from the practices enshrined in IP law that divided, and still continue to divide, the very same people who have globally imposed this judicial system on other countries. We also have to take a critical look at the object under study and the terms and concepts used to describe and shape it. The jurist, for example, expresses himself in legal terms with respect to a 'work' (*œuvre*) (see Peukert in this volume). It is necessary to locate these terms in the contexts in which they were developed before entering into arguments about them with respect to sub-Saharan Africa. Against this background, we can see the particular path they took in Africa and contextualize the property rights in force there.

Most works on IP begin their account with the invention of the printing press. There is agreement that in one way or another it was print technology that enabled large-scale copying and necessitated copyright as an attempt to 'control the flow of knowledge' (Altbach 1986:1643). Print technologies also inspired ideas of ownership, authorship and the right to make copies. The printing press as a mechanical means of producing an unlimited number of copies was invented by Johannes Gutenberg in Germany around 1445, but it took at least 250 more years until the first substantial regulation of the production of copies was established with the Statute of Anne in 1709 (in Britain), which addressed what was at the time a state monopoly, implemented by the British Stationers' Company (Briggs and Burke 2001; Johns 1998). It would take over a century more for regulations concerning music to be included, in 1842 (Goehr 1989; Toynbee 2006).

In the epoch in which printing and multiplying a manuscript required the granting of a privilege, the state proceeded to codify the ownership authors could claim to their work. From now on, they would have the right to take part in a market flourishing from its ever-increasing self-liberalization (Edelman 2004:201–5). This transition was effectuated in England in the eighteenth century, in France following the revolution of 1789, in Germany in the eighteenth and the beginning of the nineteenth centuries, and in the USA after independence in 1776 (Löhr 2010:37, 41).

In Europe, the institutionalization of cultural goods was a matter treated at a national level. At the time, bilateral agreements regulated the relations

between states. Lazar (1971:5) succinctly summarizes the basic principle in
these terms: 'We shall treat you as you treat us.' That was the rule, including
among the various German Principalities in the period preceding unification
(1832–7). The situation in Italy was analogous in the 1840s, before its own
unification. The goal was to avoid, by means of inter-state treaty, the illegal
reproduction of works produced in the north by the southern regions of both
Germany and Italy (Löhr 2010:41, 43–4). We can already see the extent to
which the territories were divided by their coverage by the law.

In 1858 the first literary congress was held, in Brussels, in which authors
and publishers broached the issue of the inadequate protection accorded to
authors' rights. This was the initiation of a series of meetings, culminating
in 1886 with the signature of the Berne Convention, which regulated the
protection of artistic and literary properties in a world opening to a market
until then completely unknown. The nations constituted a union to sign this
Convention. Lazar (1971:5) correctly observes the transition from the principle
of reciprocity to one of 'national treatment'. The number of signatories to this
accord grew from nine to fourteen at the end of the century. When the First
World War dawned, they were seventeen. The members in 1914 included
Great Britain, France, Germany, Belgium, Spain and Switzerland. They had
the clear objectives of assuring their dominance of the market, guaranteeing
the revenues of their actors in the trade in cultural goods and imposing the
recognition of their rights, with all derivatives and appurtenances (Löhr
2010:73, 75). The Berne Convention gives, however, a false impression of
the unanimity of the states that fostered it, masking, at this level, the very
strong and real interests which separated the partners. Nor did the national
delegations allow themselves to be encumbered by the customary *politesses*.
Lobbyists intervened violently in the work groups to defend their interests
(Löhr 2010:121).

At the end of the nineteenth century, what Löhr (2010:19) terms 'the
global expansion of the protection of authors' began. To graft the made-in-
Europe notion of authors' rights onto the American conception of copyright
turned out, however, to be complex, because of the profound difference of
interests. Moreover, aside from the Convention of Montevideo signed in 1889,
all the others (the Convention of Mexico of 1902, the Convention of Rio de
Janeiro of 1906, the Convention of Buenos Aires of 1910) were the exclusive
reserve of American states, one outcome of which was that these granted
themselves the right to reproduce European works on an industrial scale. A
typical example is the USA, which extended copyright only to US citizens and
permanent residents. As a predictable result, American publishers authorized
themselves to print British works massively, and with impunity. The USA did

not adhere to the Berne Convention until 1989 (!) (US Copyright Office 2010; see also Löhr 2010: 77, 132, 140–1); the USSR, at long last, ratified it in 1995.

One of the central principles of the Berne Convention of 1886 had been to bond the colonies into the same juridical framework as their respective metropoles (Lazar 1971:4; Löhr 2010; Peukert in this volume). Thus French colonies, wherever they were, were assimilated to France, just as the British colonies were to Great Britain. This reality perpetuated itself without encountering any significant resistance until 1967, the date at which the long-standing crisis of confidence of the ex-colonies with respect to the Convention reached its culmination. On 14 July 1967 a protocol was adopted in favour of developing countries. Monsieur Tournier, General Director of the Société des Auteurs, Compositeurs et Éditeurs de Musique (SACEM),[6] and the officially recognized spokesperson for the exporters of authors' rights, emphatically refuted the point of view of India as follows:

> Since, as we know, the *Convention of the Berne Union* is entirely based on the principle of *the author's exclusive right* it is to be wondered *what India is doing in that Union*. We should hope rather to see that country *depart from the Union as soon as possible, together with all the other countries sharing views that are totally incompatible with the Instrument* with which they mistakenly associate themselves.
>
> (Tournier 1967 in Lazar 1971:4; our emphases)

We now have to ask ourselves several questions essential to our enquiry. For example, considering the reluctance of some Western countries (the USA) to submit to the Berne Convention, and also such eloquent responses of defenders of the Convention to their detractors as the one just cited, what were the constraints placed on African actors in particular once the Convention had been imposed on them, after independence, and how did they react and respond to these? What was the Convention's itinerary from the first moment that the colonial powers that had promoted it compelled their colonies to adhere to it? In addition to the relations between the post-colonial state and the metropole, we also have to take into account the often conflicting relationships between the local actors themselves. What relations develop between those local actors who enthusiastically support authors' rights and their compatriots, who either know nothing about them or knowingly ignore them?

Let us return to the divergent European notions of intellectual property. Different traditions of authorship and copyright were developed in the various

---

6   SACEM was founded in Paris in 1850.

European countries. British law (much later adopted by the USA) stresses the legal rights of the author and views copyright through a commercial lens: creations are to be widely disseminated to stimulate creativity for the profit of all. Frith (1988:60) critically concludes that '[t]he whole point of copyright is to ensure that the author of a work, its "absolute owner", is duly rewarded for other people's enjoyment of that work – without such rewards there would be no economic incentive to make musical or literary works in the first place'. Artistic works are created within a market system through which artists of various kinds expect to gain financially from their endeavours. Altbach (1986:1644) points out some of the ambivalences and reversals, above all that the USA, now perhaps the strongest proponent of prosecution for piracy, itself did not accept copyright until 1954, when it joined the UCC, but not yet the Berne Convention which it ratified only decades later, as earlier mentioned (for more on Anglophone copyright see Samuels 2002; Saunders 1988; Stokes 2004; Yung 2009; on music Frith 1993; Seeger 1992).

In France, copyright was adopted after the revolution (1793), with the emergence of the concept of the Romantic author. The French copyright stresses the moral right of the author to control his work. This reflects a then new conceptualization of the author as a sole and 'original creator' of a literary and artistic work, his rights to it largely based on the labour invested. This author concept has been criticized and deconstructed by French philosophers, such as Roland Barthes (1967) and Michel Foucault (1984), as an invention, a historical, social and cultural construction by Romanticism that does not adequately represent the process by which an artist creates art, in which innumerable identifiable or unknown individuals have participated over generations. Foucault argues, even further, that since, finally, it is the readers who create the meaning of a work, they should be considered as its true authors. Elisabeth Mudimbe-Boyi (in this volume) discusses the French legacy in African literature (see also Sherman and Strowel 1994 for a critical view of the author concept).

A third way of dealing with immaterial cultural goods was practised in Socialist countries. This approach prioritizes social content and accessibility over the claims of individual authors and commercial gain. According to this approach, immaterial cultural goods do not belong to any single person, but rather to the collectivity, and the state chose to manage them in the name of the community (Altbach 1986).

In the course of time, more countries developed their own IP laws, all more or less variations of these three approaches. They were valid only in each respective country, until bilateral and multilateral international agreements were signed to seek mutual protection of 'the work' in member states. Within

Europe copyright displays remarkable diversity, whereas, viewed from Africa, it is rather perceived as a uniform, universal law.

Let us now take a look at what is meant by 'a work'. Although most often taken for granted as self-evident, the concept is, nevertheless, a cultural construction. The philosopher of music Lydia Goehr (1989) provides an excellent history of the concept. She puts its usage into perspective, even in the West, its cradle. A 'work' is obviously intimately linked to its author. Goehr defines it as follows, pointing out that the concept dates only from the eighteenth century, and cannot be unreservedly applied to all types of music:

> A musical work is held to be a *composer's unique, objectified expression,*
> a public and permanently existing artefact made up of musical elements
> (typically tones, dynamics, rhythms, harmonies, and timbres). A work is
> fixed with respect, at least, to *the properties indicated in the score* and it is
> repeatable in performances.
>
> (Goehr 1989:55; our emphases)

Though the concept emerged in the eighteenth century, it is, however, the outcome of a long process set in motion in the sixteenth century. In other words, it took two-hundred years to be adopted in the West. Goehr pertinently insists that this concept of 'work' has long neglected, and even excluded, folk and popular music. To underscore this, she invokes and advocates the relevant criticism addressed to the topic by Czerniawski, the translator of Ingarden (1986), who was a resolute elitist and defender of this concept of 'the work' (Goehr 1989:63). Goehr is quite rightly adamant about the problems posed by the concept, as soon as one considers even avant-garde music, and cites the abundant bibliography on the subject. Likewise, she demonstrates the relativity of the notion by referring to well-known European musical genres such as flamenco. Goehr (1989:65 n.5) dwells at some length on a specific concert given by the famous flamenco guitarist Carlos Montoya, noting that it ended in an artificial way. Indeed, at a given moment in his show, the artist simply stopped playing. The audience applauded. But then the artist continued his concert by improvising, in his manner, various melodies from his own repertoire. Where, then, is 'the work' in all this? We will ask this same question as it applies to artists in African countries. Their music is far more exotic than flamenco with respect to the Western canon. The problem becomes ever more urgent to resolve when copyright, drawing in particular on Berne, crams the artists and authors into this format, which defines 'author' in individualistic and exclusive terms. Both 'author' and 'work' remain elusive concepts, deceptively simple 'trick questions'. Moreover, it is the function of 'writing' that makes an author. But how should we think of this when considering the African artists?

What is most often either overlooked or deliberately masked is that prior to the development of the printing press and, subsequently copyright, concepts for the regulation of ownership and copying existed almost everywhere. For example, in south-west Nigeria only certain families have the privilege of performing certain genres of songs (Barber 2003, 2007), or, in Mali, of reciting history and praise in public (Diawara 2011). In south-west Cameroon such privileges were already alienable in pre-colonial times, so rights in the ownership and performance of cultural institutions could be acquired, and transfers were accompanied by regulations to protect the acquired immaterial good from illegitimate appropriation (Röschenthaler 2011a). Most of the contributions in this volume refer to the existence of such earlier regulations in African societies. Local regulations also existed early on in Europe, defining what people were allowed to do with valuable immaterial goods and to what extent and in what ways they could make use of knowledge and skills as resources. These regulations were, however, not (yet) implemented centrally by a state, but rather determined and defended on a local level alone (Long 1991; Somers 1996).

Wherever such regulations of the use of valuable goods existed, we also encounter plagiarism (Theisohn 2009) and piracy (Jones 1994). Walter Benjamin (1970) discusses the similarities and differences between hand-copying of texts and paintings and their mechanical reproduction. Hand-copying of books was a normal practice in the Middle Ages before the invention of print, whereas copies of artworks were considered fakes. The early regulations appear to have been at least as well able to cope with the complexity of local practices as the state-controlled laws accompanied by a series of definition problems, in particular how to protect works which build on those of prior generations, which they complete, vary, reconstruct, reconfigure and mix in multiple ways, making it impossible to distinguish between identifiable and perceptible constituents (see Anon. for Jazz; Mose in this volume for rap; and in the areas of speech and language, Goldhaber 2000; Pennycook 1996; Scollon 1995). These artistic practices entail borrowing, quoting and modification, and also move among different genres, media and formats, a phenomenon which has been variously described as intertextuality, intermediality and remediation (McLeod and Kuenzli 2011). Musical genres such as jazz and rap, the very basis of which is improvisation, inevitably come into conflict with copyright regulations that prevent musicians from improvising on other artists' music, but which is unable to protect the artistic achievements of improvisation until these are, somehow, 'fixed,' and so in this way impede artistic freedom (Anon. 2005). Similar multi-layered complexity occurs in oral literary practices the very art of which may consist precisely in the citation, modification, blending and variation of other literary works (Barber 1999). In anthropology, it is above all Karin Barber (2003) who has pointed out that all texts are made from other texts (oral or written), and always build upon existing ideas and interpretations (see also Barber 2007; Finnegan 2007:137). Property-right jurisdiction faces immense difficulty when it has to distinguish ownership from piracy given such multifaceted interconnections and artistic creations with entangled genealogies. The way these activities are considered greatly depends on which side of the fence the decision-makers and observers are positioned.

National legal regulations have been created by politicians in reaction to the diversity of practices that have emerged from new possibilities of copying and selling artistic products. The establishment of these legal regulations by bureaucratic authorities appears to be an attempt to bring 'order' to the wild growth of artistic creativity and the multiplicity of forms it can assume. IP norms completely neglect the complex creative processes which produce artistic works in different environments and performance contexts, in which – as Karin Barber argues – the active participation of audiences plays a major role (Barber 1997). This also applies to other, only apparently straightforward artistic domains. Elizabeth Bigham (1999) states that even in the production of a portrait photograph – her example is the Malian artist Seydou Keïta – many individuals are creatively involved, including the person photographed, but only one person is considered 'the artist'. This is further complicated when the images are acquired by a collector, who becomes their owner, as can the author of a book in which they are published, the publishing house or an image bank. In most societies, the judicial and public discourses often do not coincide with the complexity, practices and usages involved in the production and management of artistic property (Benda-Beckmann 2000; Geisler and Daneker 2000; Singer 2000:4).

As we shall see, copyright issues became virulent in Africa mainly from the 1980s on, a decade which ended with a proliferation of media reforms, market liberalization and the foundation of numerous state-independent media (Bourgault 1995; Hydén and Leslie 2002). Beginning in the 1990s, the markets were also swamped with all kinds of cheap electronic and other products imported from Asia (see, for example, Sachikonye 2008). The widespread introduction of new technologies facilitated the recording of cultural expressions, their broadcast in the media, and the appearance of unlimited copies of such products on the market (Chang 2004), now affordable for large audiences and clienteles. Such media products are available as originals, but more often as pirated copies (see Tcheuyap for music and Jedlowksi for videos, in this volume; see also Larkin 2004, 2008).

Increasing numbers of African authors have addressed copyright questions in recent years (Boateng 2011; Shyllon 2003; Sodipo 1997). Many also criticize the inadequate implementation of the relevant regulations or argue that African practice and copyright are intrinsically incompatible (Asmah 2008; Mills 1996; Ouma 2006; Boateng 2004, 2011 with respect to Adinkra and Kente textile design in Ghana). Others suggest that 'rights' serve better to exploit artists and indigenous peoples than help them (Lunsford and West 1996). The questions remain as to why piracy is proliferating and why governments are reluctant to fight it. This apparently has to do with inequalities in the world market and with particular entanglements of the political and economic sectors (Roitman 2005), but Veit Erlmann (in this volume) also shows that governments can indeed successfully fight for their citizens' rights.

There is a widespread conviction among international organizations that immaterial cultural expressions are ethnically or communally owned in African societies.[7] A number of scholars and organizations argue that there was no such thing as 'individual author' and 'exclusive proprietor' previous to the introduction of these notions from the so-called West, and that it is therefore difficult, if not impossible, to adopt Western copyright and patent laws which recognize one single person as the exclusive owner of creations and inventions, in order to 'protect' them. Michael Brown (1998, 2003) points to the inappropriateness of the international law as a means of protecting the cultural expressions and knowledge of ethnic groups and communities from exploitative appropriations by large companies (see also Rose 2005). Scholars therefore suggest protecting immaterial cultural goods and folklore by designating them the communal property of specific ethnic groups, just as cultural heritage is attributed to ethnic groups or regions in the framework of the nation-state (Brown 2004, 2005).[8] But these attempts underestimate the dynamics of ethnic groups, and overlook their having been formed at specific times to achieve particular objectives. While, in the West, immaterial cultural expressions, inventions and knowledge become only temporarily privatized and are returned to the public domain after a certain lapse of time, cultural expressions and heritage remain the property of ethnic groups forever. However, even the 'public domain' is a judicialized concept which provides free access to cultural goods under certain conditions. As already mentioned,

---

7   Hirsch and Strathern (2004:6) also are of the opinion that stereotypes of communal and collective forms of ownership have little to do with local realities in Papua New Guinea.

8   For a discussion of the relationship of heritage to property, see Rowlands 2002; of heritage and memory in Africa, see De Jong and Rowlands 2007; and of cultural heritage generally, see Kockel and Craith 2007.

this has not always been the case, as families and specialists were endowed with privileges or acted as the custodians of knowledge (Boateng 2011; see also Hirsch and Strathern 2004 in Melanesia).

Creatively coping with increasing judicialization, commercialization and mediatization

The focus of this volume is on studying the ways in which local actors participate in the transformation of Africa's rich artistic cultural practices in their grapple with international regulations, new technologies and global networks, or, more specifically, increasing judicialization, commercialization and mediatization. These tendencies, which intensified with the reforms and liberalization of African markets and media beginning in the mid-1980s, are the subject of a growing body of literature focusing predominantly on the introduction of print and electronic media, the impact of these on societies and the roles played by their respective audiences. To grasp the full effect of the new media it is useful, however, to work with a broad approach which stresses the common ground shared by all types. William Mazarella complains that most of the literature on media overlooks that mediation itself is a crucial foundation of social life. A medium is not only a framework that both enables and channels expression, it is also a reflective and reifying technology that makes society imaginable and intelligible to itself in the form of external representations (2004:346).

The most basic medium is the human voice, often amplified by performance with the body, manufactured instruments such as drums and institutions such as rituals or festivals. Electronic media have broadened the range of these pre-existing practices (Diawara and Röschenthaler 2013). Media, in a wide sense of the term, are essential to all the forms of performance and cultural expression examined in this volume. Media render skills and messages visible and audible, and these messages are shaped by the medium in its materiality, its production formats and the varying actors involved, as well as by the regulations applied to them and their consumption by audiences. Performances have always been, in most societies, embedded in economic activities and exchange networks. New techniques for recording and storing performances increase their opportunities for commercialization, which brings regulation and taxation in its wake.[9]

When we were searching for concepts to describe the impact which copyright laws, technology, media and the market had on immaterial

---

9   For a recent anthropological approach to media see the contributions in the special issue of *Social Anthropology* (2011), edited by Patrick Eisenlohr, and entitled *What Is a Medium? Theologies, Technologies and Aspirations*.

African cultural expressions, and the transformations this implied, we discovered that major incentives for this discussion arose in the 1980s, when such transformations were observed on a large scale in Asia. Of particular importance was the work of the Indian anthropologist Arjun Appadurai, who coined the phrase 'the social life of things' (1986, see also Kopytoff 1986). His approach was pioneering because of its actor-centred conceptualization. From then on, 'things' could no longer be viewed monolithically in terms of the particular function for which they had been designed. Appadurai emphasized that the purpose of things was ascribed to them by both their producers and their users, and that in the course of their 'social lives' their value and meanings could shift, especially while changing hands, according to the context and historical circumstances. Appadurai (1996) extended this approach to 'things' to the movements of people, techniques, stories, ideologies etc. in a globalized world. He did not, however, study these processes in detail in what remained a programmatic outline. Appadurai inspired numerous works, perhaps most notably a collective work edited by Van Binsbergen and Geschiere (2005) which provides detailed case studies demonstrating how we can conceive of material things in circulation in a new way, with a critical focus on the impact of commodification on local cultures.

In response to the huge body of literature on the diverse impacts of globalization, anthropologists have primarily sought for defences against a possible homogenization of culture (Eriksen 2003; Featherstone 1990; Featherstone, Lash and Robertson 1995; Van Binsbergen, Van Dijk and Gewald 2004). Studying the reception of globally disseminated material goods in different local cultural contexts, they have emphasized the creativity that independent local actors have displayed in appropriating these goods according to their own ideas, needs and values. They found that objects assume, in often unexpected ways, a wide range of new meanings and uses (Probst and Spittler 2001; Spittler and Hahn 2001; Strang and Busse 2011; Ziff and Rao 1997). In this entire discussion, however, and in particular with respect to Africa, intangible cultural expressions have remained largely understudied.

The debate on creativity, innovation and improvisation is related to our central concern and object of our enquiry, but has a different focus. A collection of studies edited by John Liep explores the interconnectedness of culture and creativity in a changing globalized world and its relation to the notion of entrepreneurial success (2001:1–13). It assumes that innovation and novelty are created through the recombination or transformation of existing cultural practices and forms in a way partly reminiscent of Lévi-Strauss' concept of *bricolage* (Röschenthaler 2004). In their collection of essays, *Creativity and Cultural Improvisation* (2007), Hallam and Ingold focus on improvisation rather innovation in the creation of cultural production (2007:2). They challenge the polarity between novelty and convention, i.e. between the dynamics of innovation and static tradition. Their approach is close to that of Edward Bruner (1993), who sees culture as constantly under construction through an ongoing process of improvisation rather than as the result of the purposeful transformation of a body of existing traditions. Jonathan Friedman (2001:48, quoted in Hallam and Ingold 2007:3) also pointed to the necessity of studying processes in a world which is always in the making (Jackson 1996:4).

Close to our topic is also the collection on Melanesia edited by Hirsch and Strathern (2004; see also Aragon and Leach 2008). They also employ an interdisciplinary approach – law and anthropology – intended to open a comparative perspective on intellectual and cultural property rights in Melanesia (2004:5). The editors show that property concerns in Melanesia are shaped by motives different from those of Euro-American origin, but this regime of IP has apparently foreseen possibilities to protect artefacts, performances and repositories of wisdom that identify a 'culture' and make it distinct from others (2004:3). Cultural expressions have long been perceived in local contexts as important economic and symbolic resources, but the IP regime encourages the 'creation' of property from something culturally significant, and questions of creativity are pertinent to what is or is not transacted, creativity and innovation having become the basis of ownership claims. The issue disputed by Melanesians is not the loaning or sharing of their immaterial culture but rather the exclusive rights to its ownership and to the benefits this might confer (2004:1–2). The editors also point to a range of limitations on ownership, for example, custodians of culture may well have to be consulted before an owner can dispose of anything connected to ancestral values and therefore an integral part of the group's identity. Concerns about maintaining the distinctiveness of their cultures have also led local actors in African societies to appropriate and naturalize their cultural expressions as something innately belonging to them alone and/or to their group's ancestral past, and such efforts have been encouraged by the introduction of international norms and programmes (Geschiere and Nyamnjoh 2002; Röschenthaler 2011b; Rowlands 2002).

This volume is interested in such on-going transformations, in cultural components constantly renewed and reshaped by different actors with different interests. We are, however, less concerned with reflecting upon concepts such as creativity, novelty, innovation, improvisation or transformation of culture as such, but rather, like Hirsch and Strathern, attempt to offset and counterbalance the international IP rhetoric. We study the confrontation of local actors with the new norms which have come to frame their everyday lives and which, precisely because they inspire creative ways to deal with them, open the way to transformations. We argue that it is individuals who shape and modify elements of the culture into which they are born and live. But this should not be seen as a dichotomy between individual creativity and the conventions of society; all individuals contribute to culture, but their interests do not necessarily coincide. It is in accordance with these that they give different contours to different aspects of a culture, which can then be conceptualized as fluid and diffuse. Some strive to preserve older traditions in the name of the ancestors, others acknowledge the culture of the elders but modify it, and yet others opt to copy and multiply it, most often intending no harm but only to enable the survival of their families. A performance artist might well consider the wide illicit dissemination of his or her music as a loss, but no less justifiably as free promotion, spreading his or her fame and resulting in many new invitations to perform (see also Panzacchi 1994:201).

Staging the immaterial: rights, piracy and performance in sub-Saharan Africa

This study has four parts and comprises fourteen chapters by scholars of law, anthropology and literature. They investigate developments in the cultural expressions of oral and written texts, music and recordings, performance and video, sport and beauty contests broadcast in the media. Some of them follow an interdisciplinary approach, combining ethnography, history, literature, law or media studies. Part 1 presents issues of IP in Africa from the viewpoint of the disciplines of law, literary studies and anthropology. The chapters in the following three parts pursue these topics in individual case studies of the local perspectives of actors in South Africa, Kenya, Cameroon, Nigeria, Mali and Senegal. All the authors demonstrate historical continuities between older and more recent cultural expressions, and describe the experiences artists have had with the new media formats and legal regulations, and how these, in turn, have left their impression on them.

There are of course many other important cultural practices that are subject to transformation but could not be included in this volume. Some of them have been well studied, notably the issues involved in marketing and protection of pharmaceutical and other local knowledge (see for example, Mazonde and Thomas 2007), the identity branding and marketing of cultural expressions for tourism (Comaroff and Comaroff 2009) and the effect that nomination by UNESCO as cultural heritage has had on various cultural forms (De Jong and Rowlands 2007; for heritage and IP norms see Röschenthaler and Diawara 2011; for the commodification of heritage more generally Nic Craith 2007).

Part 1, 'Protecting immaterial cultural goods: authors, artists and the law', deals with the history of IP rights in Africa (Peukert), questions their applicability to African literatures (Mudimbe-Boyi) and provides insight into the complexities of musical practice and into the inequalities African artists face in the global market (Erlmann). These authors discuss the topic in its global context: how the law arrived in Africa, the criticism of the author concept from literary and philosophical perspectives, and how the copyright law has figured in precedent-setting lawsuits. It explores the problematics of attributing a creative work to a single individual as its sole author and of the inequities implicit in the global application of the copyright concept.

Alexander Peukert surveys the history of IP rights and their transfer to African countries from the perspective of a jurist. He summarizes the development of the copyright and author concepts in Europe, their extension to the colonies and their continuation by post-colonial governments. He shows that these IP laws were primarily intended to protect European rights holders, not the colonized. This exclusion continues in the TRIPS agreement, which has been widely touted as a major step toward multilateral cooperation, but whose principal thrust is to regulate trade-related aspects of IP for WTO members. He emphasizes that African interests in protecting cultural expressions and heritage have not been taken into account by any of the international copyright conventions.

Elisabeth Mudimbe-Boyi questions the applicability of the concept of 'the author' to African oral texts. Following post-structuralist philosophers who have deconstructed the author concept, she examines Francophone novelists from Senegal, Mali and the Congo, and their differing degrees of moral obligation to acknowledge the literary genealogy of their texts. Enquiring into the differences between oral and written texts, she notes that such rhetorical strategies as variations in rhythm, gestures, certain kinds of word play and repetitions are denotative techniques difficult to incorporate into a written text. She argues that writers whose work is based on existing oral literature should be termed '*auteurs au second degré*', as they are only one link in the chain of creators in an African community.

Literary work did not until recently become an issue in African copyright debates, most likely because both producing and reading books long remained the pastime of a small elite. This is quite different to the music and video sectors, which quickly reached global proportions and have spurred controversies over copyright in many African countries since the 1980s.

Veit Erlmann analyses the landmark lawsuit in which the South African artist Solomon Linda (more precisely his family) won a judgment against an entity no less powerful than the entertainment industry giant Disney Enterprises Inc. Erlmann shows that much of the reasoning employed in both the litigation and the subsequent debate was couched in racial terms, as were constructions of authorship and originality which neglected the polyphonic texture of the song and many parameters of musical organization. This lawsuit encouraged South Africa to find a way to become perceived as a serious player in the global IP regime, protecting both individual artistic creations and communal cultural expressions such as knowledge systems and folklore.

Like Mudimbe-Boyi, Erlmann questions the concept of 'the author' and suggests looking at the genealogies involved in artistic production, but, going a step further, argues that musical works involve such a multiplicity of processes that none can be termed 'originals' (as many works on music and IP do). He even questions the distinction between original and copy, and sees 'appropriation' as key to the production of normative concepts of musical substance, authority and ownership.

Part 2, 'Creating norms and genres by modelling, quoting and mixing', further elaborates the issues of authorship and of drawing dividing lines between original and copy, one work and another, by documenting the interconnections on which artistic work is based and from which genres emerge.

Karin Barber examines the relationship between oral and written literature but, to the contrary of Mudimbe-Boyi, emphasizes their continuities. Newspaper journalists in the earlier phases of Yoruba-language print culture in Lagos, Nigeria, were well aware of copyright laws, but only appealed to them selectively, when their publications seemed likely to be suitable for republication as booklets. In their other writings, they did not insist on named authorship, but rather alluded to shared popular knowledge and often concealed their identities behind pseudonyms and nicknames. The owners of these early newspapers enhanced their prestige and prominence by drawing on a wide diversity of sources, much in the same way as skilful performers of *oriki*, the Yoruba praise poems which are based on the borrowing and sharing of textual resources. Barber demonstrates that the two options – either to claim copyright as a named author, or to participate in an anonymous print sphere characterized by extensive quotation and recycling – coexisted for many years. The choice of one or another option was controlled by the writers' particular interests and projects. It was not simply a matter of an external legal regime that originated in Western print culture being imposed upon and displacing older African oral modes. Writers exercised aesthetic, social and economic choices about how they (re)presented their texts.

Patrick Oloko examines print culture in a later stage, analysing what it takes to transform a manuscript into a publishable novel. He explores the early post-colonial period when Heinemann began, in close conjunction with Chinua Achebe, its Nigerian flagship author, to publish Nigerian novels. Achebe established the criteria according to which authors, genres, topics and approaches were selected, and by which they would be deemed publishable and likely to sell. Oloko shows that many manuscripts remained unpublished because they did not conform to the norms that defined, in a particular period in literary history, what a novel should be and how Nigerian literature should be presented internationally. Questions of the genealogy of texts and of the ownership of plots, canons and genres were implicit in this context too, but, in legal terms, only the designated author's rights to a specific text were taken into overt consideration.

Caroline Mose studies hip-hop in Kenya and the production of this musical genre from the multiple components which comprise it. The musicians who create the lyrics regard a song as theirs because they are the authors of its text. The musical beats which forms the integral background for their freestyle improvised oral performance are, however, assembled from bits and pieces of other chants, beats, speech and sounds from very diverse sources, creatively mixed into a hybrid known as 'sampling'. She shows that hip-hop is a genre that by its very nature pirates or plagiarizes music from other sources, but also argues that sampling should not be seen as 'theft' but rather as 're-contextualization'. IP issues arose only when media laws obliged radios to broadcast local music, which in turn encouraged the commodification of music and the growth of the local music industry.

Barber, Oloko and Mose demonstrate that it was neither the introduction of a specific technology nor the copyright law that transformed artistic practice, but rather that it was the commodification of certain formats (such as the book and the individual music album) that raised the issue of authorship. Oloko and Mose show how literary canons and musical genres are created in a specific market situation that influences and even determines how artists fashion their products.

Karin Barber shows how local actors in the incipient print culture made it all but impossible to identify most writers, just as today, hip-hop musicians and producers blur the provenance of background beats, so that both sectors inherently challenge the acknowledgement of individual creators. These authors also examine, as do Mudimbe-Boyi and Erlmann, a fundamental question to which there is no single answer, namely how the artists themselves conceptualize the provenance of their products, i.e. whether they attribute them to an entire community, to a group of people in this community, to an individual, or to no one in particular, and how they believe their own work should be used by other artists.

Part 3, 'Transformations of cultural goods: imitation, appropriation and piracy', explores how individual artists and cultural groups cope with growing mediatization, commercialization and the resulting relevance of the copyright law. It also deals with transgressions of the IP law by traders in order to satisfy consumers' desires to gain access to artistic products.

Ute Röschenthaler studies the transformation of performances in south-west Cameroon using the example of an artist involved in dance, music and video production. Analogously to sampling in the music sector and oral literary practices, this performance artist quotes from other performances, modifies and re-contextualizes music, songs and (masked) dances, and – despite his stated objective of 'reviving' these performances – he endows them with new meaning and appeal. He combines elements drawn from village performances and popular urban styles, mixing ancient, contemporary and foreign dances, and he has to deal with both local rights of ownership and international copyright legislation when he records and sells his productions.

Neo Musangi traces the genealogy and evolution of the Ngqoko Cultural Group, how it first came to perform on stage, and the origins of its performances. She shows that the conceptions of rights and ownership embedded in IP regimes cannot be reconciled with local articulations, because, at the village level, songs were not regarded as 'entertainment', but were rather always integral to a specific ritual context in which they had power, not market value. She enquires into what happens to cultural expressions when they become cultural goods that can be marketed and sold, copyrighted, but no longer 'embodied', even – or especially – in the context of 'cultural preservation'. Like other authors in this volume, Musangi concludes that local conceptions of cultural ownership and international IP regimes are largely incompatible.

Mamadou Diawara explores how music has been handled in successive generations in Mali and how ideas of music, media and authorship have been modified with the introduction of electronic media, urbanization and access to new markets. Unlike singers before her, Mariam Bagayogo does not belong to a family with an established privilege of praise-singing, but rather she has learned from her masters/teachers, whom she acknowledges in her songs. The generation of musicians that followed her, however, no longer learned songs during long years of apprenticeship, but rather from listening to tapes. This practice created resentment among the praise-singers, who felt they were being deprived of their rightful profit. Just as, in a similar way, Mudimbe-Boyi studied the transition from oral to written literature, Diawara explores the passage of songs from oral performance to recorded and mediated products.

Alexie Tcheuyap explores the activities of copying in the music sector in Cameroon and discusses the experiences of Cameroonian musicians with piracy. Tcheuyap's elaborations make clear that in Cameroon, too, it was not the introduction of copyright law in colonial times, but rather the ready availability of copying technology, that created entrepreneurial opportunities for pirating recorded music. As Diawara observed in Mali, and Röschenthaler in Cameroon, musicians borrowed local performances and transformed them into 'new' pieces of music, a technique which made them the individual copyright holders to cultural expressions that had been either communally owned, or the property of specific local owners.

Alessandro Jedlowski studies the emergence of piracy in the Nigerian video sector, known as 'Nollywood' (Krings 2010; Larkin 2008), which resulted from the introduction, beginning in the 1980s, of new electronic technologies. These enabled an ever-broader population to record and copy moving images (videos), exactly what happened in smaller measure in Cameroon (and not only there) with music, as Tcheuyap describes. This video industry is characterized by low budgets, inexpensive technological equipment and informal networks of production and distribution. Piracy made Nigerian videos international 'best-sellers', but only by depriving the original producers of the videos of revenues which would otherwise have resulted from their investment. The low level of copyright enforcement in Nigeria, together with Nollywood's own high degree of informality, has created a suitable environment for its popular success, but at the same time endangers the continuance of the industry itself.

The contributors illuminate the genealogy of cultural expressions, and demonstrate that it is transformed media and markets which create both an awareness of individual ownership and practices of copying and piracy. Artists not previously considered individual owners of products, and who took their inspiration from a pool of artistic knowledge (Musangi) are now reaping the full rewards of music that, from the local perspective, also belongs to other artists, who – attributing their creations to the predecessors who had been their teachers – feel devalued and cheated of their rightful profits by the activities of new artists legally protected by copyright (Diawara). Others had already in pre-colonial times made cultural expressions into a marketable resource and developed ways to prevent the illegitimate copying of them (Röschenthaler). Some chapters discuss piracy from the perspective of the new artists who need to recover their investments and survive with their music (Tcheuyap) or video production (Jedlowski). Most Kenyan rappers perceive copyright as an obstacle to their creativity (Mose), whereas for some Nigerian writers it is not copyright but rather the restrictive criteria of publishing houses that stand in the way of their becoming successful book authors (Oloko).

Thus, copyright provokes varying reactions and interpretations. It can be a thread of hope against global inequalities for local artists (Erlmann), or, in other cases, it obliges artists to pay royalties for whatever use they make of the music of other artists. This is the flip side of the scenario proposed by Alexie Tcheuyap, in which he insists that artists must be supported to ensure their survival and that copiers be persecuted more intensely.

Part 4, 'Marketing culture and the body: performance, competition and media impact', looks at how cultural practices and values, such as performance skills, aesthetic ideals and inventions, have been transformed and shaped by mediatized mass events in an urban context. Wane discusses male body contests, whereas Dorothea Schulz analyses female body contests. These contests impose completely different aesthetic standards on the body, but both rate the inner values and rhetorical skills of the contestants highly. These aspects are, however, of less importance in Gruber's investigation of the World Cup, perhaps the most popular and widely mediated mass event in Africa.

Dorothea Schulz`s contribution addresses beauty pageants in Mali. The aspirants to prizes are evaluated not only with respect to their physical beauty; the criteria extend to costumes, hairstyles, 'inner beauty' and rhetorical skills. These contests are accompanied and punctuated by various side programmes such as musical and comedy performances. The pageants, although they inspire a wide range of reactions among Malian spectators, also shape notions of beauty and womanhood. Initially, the contests served to forge national identity with a focus on the Bamana culture, largely represented by populations situated around the capital. This norm has shifted several times; presently women from the northern parts of the country correspond more closely to the beauty ideal of slim models, predominant in the Global West, a shift reinforced by the participation of Mali in trans-West Africa contests and the arrival of private sponsors, particularly those from the international beauty industry.

Ibrahima Wane examines the evolution of wrestling from a competitive sport that had formed an integral part of village festivities embedded in the annual cycle, to a mass media event of national importance in Senegal. At first, wrestling was a contest of not only physical strength and prowess, but also of rhetorical skills in the invention and performance of praise songs, and all sections of society actively participated in the celebration. With the growth of urban centres in the twentieth century, however, wrestling became increasingly seen purely as a sport, and attracted media presence and commercial advertising. Popular singers now perform what had been the wrestlers' songs, and these are broadcast in the media and considered the singers' property. The real owners of the songs, the wrestlers of the old days, earn nothing when copyright rules are applied. Here, Wane's observations coincide with those of Diawara, and also with Röschenthaler's example of the artist who performs 'traditional songs' whose owners he praises, but who receive nothing from his sales.

Matthias Gruber studies the accessories which were invented and developed in the course of the World Cup 2010 in Johannesburg, and evaluates the varying prospects for copyrighting the vuvuzela horns, the *makarapa* helmets and the jerseys in the colours of the local club or of the national team. They became subject to IP to differing degrees that reflect established political hierarchies. Neither the vuvuzela horns, competing claims to invention of which circulated during the World Cup, nor the *makarapa* helmets, which were invented by an identifiable soccer fan, could be registered as trademarks. In contrast, the jerseys of the national team, sponsored by Adidas, already were a registered trademark and, unsurprisingly, fake copies flooded the market, as originals were beyond the means of ordinary citizens. All three items gained considerable economic value during the event, and Gruber traces the reasons why coloured jerseys were legally protected whereas the horns and helmets were not.

Among the examples of cultural transformation studied in this volume, beauty pageants have the fewest legal implications. Although the contests are an arena in which the body is commercialized and mediatized, each participant retains the rights to her representation in the media. Especially volatile are such major events as the wrestling contests in Senegal and the beauty pageants in Mali, where large sums change hands and which rivet the attention of the entire country or, in the case of the World Cup in South Africa, kept the entire world pinned to its screens. The interest groups which compete for profit from such major events are many, so regulations are indispensable, and yet not everything marketable calls ownership regulations into play. As Gruber's examples show, such readily commodifiable wares as the vuvuzela and the *makarapa* helmet excited great interest and became the objects of debates as to how they could be protected. But finally it was the restrictive application of copyright which gained the upper hand, as Africans could not lay legal claim to their own inventions, whereas Western firms were able to protect their wares; protection which was, ironically, of complete indifference to the pirates. Erlmann also noted these same inequalities in the application of copyright in the music sector, which perpetuates the historical exclusion of African artists and inventors from the global market (Peukert).

The contributions to this volume demonstrate that norms which regulate cultural expressions build upon existing practices. Some of them focus on the traceability of individual cultural elements (Diawara, Mudimbe-Boyi, Röschenthaler, Musangi), others on their amalgamation (Barber, Mose, Erlmann). They emphasize that the genealogies of their creation are implicitly or explicitly acknowledged in written texts (Mudimbe-Boyi, Oloko), in the performance of musical pieces (Diawara, Mose, Erlmann) and dance (Musangi, Röschenthaler). They pursue their social lives as commodities, as being subject to copyright law and also to piracy (Tcheuyap, Jedlowski). Piracy and plagiarism most often become subject of discussion when opinions differ as to whom profits belong to, and when loyalty conflicts arise between law and family- and friendship-based obligations to share what one owns. The mass-media events, studied by Schulz, Wane and Gruber are partly embedded in this legal framework and partly remain subject to other norms of marketing. The contributions describe how these new practices challenge established concepts of ownership and aesthetics, and situate them somewhere along the continuum that ranges from individual to family, performer-audience and collective ownership.

The question, then, is not whether introduced norms such as copyright or new media formats 'fit' African culture, but rather what local people do with them, and to what extent they find them useful. Consequently, this book looks into how local actors – not the global standards in themselves – transform their cultural expressions. When the authors note a wide gap between African practices and global regulations, this does not necessarily mean that the global laws are inherently wrong or superfluous, but rather simply indicates their inadequacy to deal with the complexity of human creativity and regulate the practices connected with it.

References

Altbach, Philip. 1986. 'Knowledge enigma: copyright in the Third World'. *Economic and Political Weekly* 21(37):1643–50.

Anon. 2005. 'Jazz has got copyright law and that ain't good'. *Harvard Law Review* 118(6):1940–61.

Appadurai, Arjun. 1986. 'Introduction: commodities and the politics of value'. In: Arjun Appadurai (ed.). *The Social Life of Things: Commodities in Cultural Perspective*. Cambridge: Cambridge University Press, 3–63.

——— 1996. 'Introduction'. In: Arjun Appadurai (ed.). *Modernity at Large: Cultural Dimensions of Globalization*. Minneapolis: University of Minnesota Press.

Aragon, Lorraine and James Leach. 2008. 'Arts and owners: intellectual property law and the politics of scale in Indonesian art'. *American Ethnologist* 35(4):607–31.

Arnoldi, Mary Jo. 1995. *Playing With Time: Art and Performance in Central Mali*. Bloomington: Indiana University Press.

Arnoldi, Mary Jo, Christraud Geary and Kris Hardin (eds). 1996. *African Material Culture*. Bloomington: Indiana University Press.

Asmah, Josephine. 2008. 'Historical threads: intellectual property protection of traditional textile designs: the Ghanaian experience and African perspectives'. *International Journal of Cultural Property* 15:271–96.

Barber, Karin. 1997. 'Preliminary notes on audiences in Africa'. *Africa* 67(3):347–62.

——— 1999. 'Quotation in the constitution of Yorùbá oral texts'. *Research in African Literatures* 30(2):17–41.

——— 2003. 'Text and performance in Africa'. *Bulletin of the School of Oriental and African Studies* 66(3):324–33.

———— 2007. *The Anthropology of Texts, Persons and Publics: Oral and Written Culture in Africa and Beyond.* Cambridge: Cambridge University Press.

Barthes, Roland. 1977 [1967]. The Death of the author. In his: *Image – Music – Text* (translated from French by Stephen Heath). London: Fontana, 142–8.

Benda-Beckmann, Franz von. 2000. 'Relative publics and property rights: a cross-cultural perspective'. In: Charles Geisler and Gail Daneker (eds). *Property and Values: Alternatives to Public and Private Ownership,* 151–74.

Benjamin, Walter. 1970. 'The work of art at the age of mechanical reproduction'. In his: *Illuminations.* London: Conathan Cape, 219–53.

Benthall, Jonathan. 1999. 'The critique of intellectual property'. *Anthropology Today* 15, 6:1–3.

Bigham, Elizabeth. 1999. 'Issues of authorship in the portrait photographs of Seydou Keïta'. *African Arts* 32(1) (Special Issue: Authorship in African Art, Part 2):56–67, 94–6.

Boateng, Boatema. 2004. 'African textiles and the politics of diasporic identity-making'. In: Jean Allman (ed.). *Fashioning Africa: Power and the Politics of Dress.* Bloomington: Indiana University Press, 212–26.

———— 2011. *The Copyright Thing Doesn't Work Here: Adinkra and Kente Cloth and Intellectual Property in Ghana.* Minneapolis and London: University of Minnesota Press.

Boone, Sylvia. 1986. *Radiance from the Waters: Ideals of Feminine Beauty in Mende Art.* New York and London: Yale University Press.

Bourgault, Louise. 1995. *Mass-Media in sub-Saharan Africa.* Bloomington: Indiana University Press.

Briggs, Asa and Peter Burke. 2001. *A Social History of the Media.* Cambridge: Polity.

Brown, Michael. 1998. 'Can culture be copyrighted?' *Current Anthropology* 39(2):193–222.

———— 2003. *Who Owns Native Culture?* Cambridge: Harvard University Press.

———— 2004. 'Heritage as property'. In: Caroline Humphrey and Katherine Verdery (eds). *Property in Question: Value Transformation in the Global Economy.* Oxford: Berg, 49–68.

———— 2005. 'Heritage trouble: recent work on the protection of intangible cultural property'. *International Journal of Cultural Property* 12:40–61.

Bruner, Edward. 1993. 'Epilogue: creative persona and the problem of authenticity'. In: Smadar Lavie, Kirin Narayan and Renato Rosaldo (eds). *Creativity/ Anthropology.* Ithaka, NY: Cornell University Press, 321–34.

Brush, Stephen and Doreen Stabisky (eds). 1996. *Valuing Local Knowledge: Indigenous People and Intellectual Property Rights.* Washington: Island Press.

Chang, Hsiao-Hung. 2004. 'Fake logos, fake theory, fake globalisation'. *Inter-Asia Cultural Studies* 5(2):222–36.

Chanock, Martin. 1985. *Law, Custom and Social Order: The Colonial Experience in Malawi and Zambia*. Cambridge: Cambridge University Press.

Charry, Eric. 2000. *Mande Music: Traditional and Modern Music of the Maninka and Mandinka of Western Africa*. Chicago: University of Chicago Press.

Comaroff, Jean and John Comaroff. 2000. *Millenial Capitalism and the Culture of Noeliberalism*. Durham: Duke University Press.

Comaroff, John and Jean Comaroff. 2009. *Ethnicity, Inc.* Chicago: Chicago University Press.

Coombe, Rosemary. 1998. *The Cultural Life of Intellectual Properties: Authorship, Appropriation, and the Law*. Durham and London: Duke University Press.

——— 2003. 'Fear, hope and longing for the future of authorship and a revitalized public domain in global regimes of intellectual property'. *DePaul Law Review* 52:1–15.

Cowan, Jane. 2006. 'Culture and rights after *Culture and Rights*'. *American Anthropologist* 108(1):9–24.

Cowan, Jane, Marie-Bénédict Dembour and Richard Wilson (eds). 2001. *Culture and Rights: Anthropological Perspectives*. Cambridge: Cambridge University Press.

De Jong, Ferdinand (ed.). 2009. *Hybrid Heritage. African Arts* 42(4) (Special Issue).

De Jong, Ferdinand and Michael Rowlands (eds). 2007. *Reclaiming Heritage*. Walnut Creek: Left Coast Press.

Diawara, Mamadou. 1990. *La graine de la parole*. Stuttgart: Franz Steiner Verlag.

——— 2003. *L'empire du verbe – L'éloquence du silence: Vers une anthropologie du discours dans les groupes dits dominés au Sahel*. Köln: Rüdiger Köppe.

——— 2011. 'Comment peut-on être auteur? De la création dans un contexte de tradition orale en Afrique subsaharienne'. In: Justin K. Bisanswa and Kasereka Kavwahirehi (eds). *Dire le social dans le roman francophone contemporain*. Paris: Honoré Champion, 33–52.

Diawara, Mamadou and Ute Röschenthaler. 2013. 'Normenwandel und die Macht der Medien im subsaharischen Afrika'. In: Andreas Fahrmeir and Anette Imhausen (eds). *Die Vielfalt normativer Ordnungen: Konflikte und Dynamik in historischer und ethnologischer Perspektive*. Frankfurt: Campus Verlag, 129–64.

Dorsch, Hauke. 2006. *Globale Griots: Performanz in der afrikanischen Diaspora*. Berlin: Lit.

Dutfield, Graham. 1999. 'The public and private domains: intellectual property rights in traditional ecological knowledge'. *Oxford Electronic Journal of Intellectual Property Rights*. Available online at: www.oiprc.ox.ac.uk/EJWP0399.html.

Edelman, Bernard. 2004. *Le sacre de l'auteur*. Paris: Seuil.

Eisenlohr, Patrick. 2011. Introduction: *What Is a Medium? Theologies, Technologies and Aspirations. Social Anthropology* (special issue) 19 (1):1–5.

Eriksen, Thomas (ed.). 2003. *Globalisation: Studies in Anthropology*. London: Pluto Press.

Erlmann, Veit (ed.). 1991. *Populäre Musik in Afrika*. Berlin: Staatliche Museen Preußischer Kulturbesitz.

Fabian, Johannes. 1990. *Power and Performance: Ethnographic Explorations through Proverbial Wisdom and Theater in Shaba, Zaire*. Madison: University of Wisconsin Press.

Fardon, Richard. 2007. *Fusions: Masquerades and Thought Style East of the Niger-Benue Confluence, West Africa*. London: Saffron Books.

Featherstone, Mike (ed.). 1990. *Global Culture: Nationalism, Globalization and Modernity*. London: Sage.

Featherstone, Mike, Scott Lash and Roland Robertson (eds). 1995. *Global Modernities*. London: Sage.

Finnegan, Ruth. 2007. *The Oral and Beyond: Doing Things with Words in Africa*. Oxford and Chicago: James Currey and Chicago University Press.

Fischer, Eberhard. 1984. 'Self-portraits, portraits, and copies among the Dan: the creative process of traditional African mask carvers' (trans. Christraud Geary). *Iowa Studies in African Art* 1:5–28.

Forst, Rainer and Klaus Günther. 2011. 'Die Herausbildung normativer Ordnungen. Zur Idee eines interdisziplinären Forschungsprogramms'. In: Rainer Forst and Klaus Günther (eds). *Die Herausbildung normativer Ordnungen*. Frankfurt: Campus, 11–32.

Foucault, Michel. 1984 [1969]. 'What is an author'. In: Paul Rabinow (ed.). *The Foucault Reader*. New York: Pantheon, 101–20.

Frith, Simon. 1988. 'Copyright and the music business'. *Popular Music* 7(1):57–75.

——— 1993. *Music and Copyright*. Edinburgh: Edinburgh University Press.

Furniss, Graham (ed.). 2004. *Orality: The Power of the Spoken Word*. Basingstoke: Palgrave Macmillan.

Geisler, Charles and Gail Daneker (eds). 2000. *Property and Values: Alternatives to Public and Private Ownership*. Washington: Island Press.

Geschiere, Peter. 2009. *The Perils of Belonging: Autochthony, Citizenship, and Exclusion in Africa & Europe*. Chicago and London: The University of Chicago Press.

Geschiere, Peter and Francis Nyamnjoh. 2002. 'Capitalism and autochthony: the seesaw of mobility and belonging'. *Public Culture* 12(2):423–52.

Geyer, Sunelle. 2010. 'Towards a clearer definition and understanding if "indigenous community" for the purposes of the intellectual property laws amendment bill, 2010: an exploration of the concepts "indigenous" and "traditional"'. *PER/PELJ* 13(4):127–43.

Globerman, Steven. 1988. 'Addressing international product piracy'. *Journal of International Business Studies* 19(3):497–504.

Goehr, Lydia. 1989. 'Being true to the work'. *Journal of Aesthetics and Art Criticism* 47(1):55–67.

Goldhaber, Michael. 2000. 'Language as a public good under threat: the private ownership of brand names'. In: Anatole Anton, Milton Fisk and Nancy Holmstrom (eds). *Not for Sale: In Defense of the Public Goood*. Boulder: Westview Press, 323–44.

Goodale, Mark. 2009. 'Introduction: Human Rights and anthropology'. In: Mark Goodale (ed.). Human Rights: An Anthropological Reader. Oxford: Blackwell, 1–19.

Goodman, Jane. 2002. '"Stealing our heritage?" Women's folksongs, copyright law, and the public domain in Algeria'. *Africa Today* 49, 1:85–97.

——— 2005. *Berber Culture on the World Stage: From Village to Video*. Bloomington: Indiana University Press.

Guillebaud, Christine, Victor Stoichita and Julien Mallet. 2010. 'La musique n'a pas d'auteur: ethnographies du copyright'. *Gradhiva* 12:5–19.

Hallam, Elizabeth and Tim Ingold. 2007. *Creativity and Cultural Improvisation*. Oxford: Berg.

Hann, Chris (ed.). 1998. *Property Relations: Renewing the Anthropological Tradition*. Cambridge: Cambridge University Press.

Hewitt, Barbara. 2007. 'Heritage as a commodity: are we devaluing our heritage by making it available to the highest bidder via the internet?' In: Ullrich Kockel and Máiréad Nic Craith (eds). *Cultural Heritages as Reflexive Traditions*. London: Palgrave, 194–208.

Hirsch, Eric and Marilyn Strathern (eds). 2004. *Transactions and Creations: Property Debates and the Stimulus in Melanesia*. New York: Berghahn.

Hoffman, Barbara. 2000. *Griots at War: Conflict, Conciliation, and the Caste in Mande*. Bloomington: Indiana University Press.

Hydén, Göran and Michael Leslie. 2002. 'Communications and democratization in Africa'. In: Göran Hydén, Michael Leslie and Folu Ogundima (eds). *Media and Democracy in Africa*. New Brunswick and New Jersey: Transaction Publishers, 1–27.

Ingarden, Roman. 1986. *The Work of Music and the Problem of Its Identity* (trans. Adam Czerniawski, ed. Jean Harrell). Berkeley: University of California Press.

Jackson, Michael. 1996. *Things As They Are: New Directions in Phenomenological Anthropology*. Bloomington: Indiana University Press.

Johns, Adrian. 1998. *Nature of the Book: Print and Knowledge in the Making*. Chicago: University of Chicago Press.

Joireman, Sandra. 2001. Inherited legal systems and effective rule of law: Africa and the colonial legacy. *Journal of Modern African Studies* 39:571–96.

Jones, Mark. 1994. 'Why fakes?' In: Susan Pearce (ed.). *Interpreting Objects and Collections*. London: Routledge, 92–7.

Kockel, Ullrich and Máiréad Nic Craith (eds). 2007. *Cultural Heritages as Reflexive Traditions*. London: Palgrave.

Kopytoff, Igor. 1986. 'The cultural biography of things: commoditization as process'. In: Arjun Appadurai (ed.). *The Social Life of Things*. Cambridge: Cambridge University Press, 64–91.

Kramer, Fritz. 1993. *The Red Fez: Art and Spirit Possession in Africa* (translated from German by Malcolm Freen). New York: Verso.

Krings, Matthias. 2010. 'Nollywood goes east: the localization of Nigerian video films in Tanzania'. In: Mahir Saul and Ralph Austen (eds). *Viewing African Cinema in the Twenty-First Century: Art Films and the Nollywood Video Revolution*. Athens OH: Ohio University Press, 74–91.

Larkin, Brian. 2004. 'Degraded images, distorted sounds: Nigerian video and the infrastructure of piracy'. *Public Culture* 16(2):289–314.

––– 2008. *Signal and Noise: Media, Infrastructure, and Urban Culture in Nigeria*. Durham: Duke University Press.

Lazar, Alan. 1971. 'Developing countries and authors' rights in international copyright'. *Copyright Law Symposium* 19:1–42.

Lehmann, John. 2006. 'Intellectual property rights and Chinese tradition section: philosophical foundations'. *Journal of Business Ethics* 69(1):1–9.

Lentz, Carola. 2006. 'Land rights and the politics of belonging in Africa: an introduction'. In: Richard Kuba and Carola Lentz (eds). *Land and the Politics of Belonging in West Africa*. Leiden and Boston: Brill, 1–34.

Lévi-Strauss, Claude. 1962. *La pensée sauvage*. Paris: Librairie Plon

Liep, John (ed.). 2001. *Locating Cultural Creativity*. London: Pluto Press.

Löhr, Isabella. 2010. *Die Globalisierung geistiger Eigentumsrechte: Neue Strukturen internationaler Zusammenarbeit 1886–1952*. Göttingen: Vandenhoeck & Ruprecht.

Long, Pamela. 1991. 'Invention, authorship, "intellectual property", and the origin of patents: notes toward a conceptual history'. *Technology and Culture* 32(4) (Special Issue: Patents and Invention 1991):846–84.

Lunsford, Andrea and Susan West. 1996. 'Intellectual property and composition studies'. *College Composition and Communication* 47(3):383–411.

May, Christopher. 2000. *A Global Political Economy of Intellectual Property Rights*. London and New York: Routledge.

Mazarella, William. 2004. 'Culture, globalization, mediation'. *Annual Review of Anthropology* 33:345–67.

Mazonde, Isaac and Pradip Thomas (eds). 2007. *Indigenous Knowledge Systems and Intellectual Property in the Twenty-First Century: Perspectives from Southern Africa*. Dakar: CODESRIA

Mbembe, Achille and Janet Roitman. 1995. 'Figures of the subject in times of crisis'. *Public Culture* 7:323–52.

McLeod, Kembrew. 2005. *Freedom of Expression. Overzealous Copyright Bozos and Other Enemies of Creativity.* New York: Doubleday.

McLeod, Kembrew and Rudulf Kuenzli (eds). 2011. *Cutting Across Media: Appropriation Art, Interventionist Collage and Copyright Law.* Durham and London: Duke University Press.

Mills, Sherylle. 1996. 'Indigenous music and the law: an analysis of national and international legislation'. *Yearbook for Traditional Music* 28:57–86.

Murphy, William. 1980. 'Secret knowledge as property and power in Kpelle society: elders versus youth'. *Africa* 50(2):193–207.

Nic Craith, Máiréad. 2007. 'Cultural heritages: process, power, commodification'. In: Ullrich Kockel and Máiréad Nic Craith (eds). *Cultural Heritages as Reflexive Traditions.* London: Palgrave, 1–18.

Ntarangwi, Mwenda. 2009. *East African Hip Hop-Youth Culture and Globalization.* Urbana and Chicago: University of Illinois Press.

Ouma, Marisella. 2006. 'Optimal enforcement of music copyright in sub-Saharan Africa: reality or a myth?' *The Journal of World Intellectual Property* 9(5):592–627.

Panzacchi, Cornelia. 1994. 'The livelihoods of traditional griots in modern Senegal'. *Africa* 64(2):190–210.

Pennycook, Alastair. 1996. 'Borrowing others' words: text, ownership, memory, and plagiarism'. *TESOL Quarterly* 30(2):201–30.

Philip, Kavita. 2005. 'What is a technological author?: the pirate function and intellectual property'. *Postcolonial Studies* 8(2):199–218.

Picton, John. 1995. *The Art of African Textiles.* London: Barbican Art Gallery.

Probst, Peter. 2011. *Osogbo and the Art of Heritage: Monuments, Deities, and Money.* Bloomington: Indiana University Press.

Probst, Peter and Gerd Spittler (eds). 2001. *Between Resistance and Expansion: Explorations of Local Vitality in Africa.* Münster: Lit, 211–29.

Ranger, Terence. 1975. *Dance and Society in Eastern Africa, 1890–1970.* Berkeley and Los Angeles: University of California Press.

——— 1983. 'The invention of tradition in colonial Africa'. In: Eric Hobsbawn and Terence Ranger (eds). *The Invention of Tradition.* Cambridge: Cambridge University Press.

——— 1993. 'The invention of tradition revisited: the case of colonial Africa'. In: Terence Ranger and Olufemi Vaughan (eds). *Legitimacy and the State in Twentieth-Century Africa: Essays in Honour of A.H.M. Kirk-Greene.* London: MacMillan, 62–111.

Raustiala, Kal and Christopher Sprigman. 2006. 'The piracy paradox: innovation and intellectual property in fashion design'. *Virginia Law Review* 92(8):1687–777.

Roitman, Janet. 2005. *Fiscal Disobedience: An Anthropology of Economic Regulation in Central Africa*. Princeton: Princeton University Press.

Röschenthaler, Ute. 2004. 'Neuheit, *Bricolage* oder Plagiat? Zur Entstehung neuer Tanzbünde im Cross River-Gebiet (im Südwesten Kameruns und Südosten Nigerias)'. *Paideuma* 50:193–223.

——— 2011a. *Purchasing Culture: The Dissemination of Associations in the Cross River region of Cameroon and Nigeria*. Trenton: Africa World Press (The Harriet Tubmen Series of the African Diaspora).

——— 2011b. 'Geistiges Eigentum oder Kulturerbe? Lokale Strategien im Umgang mit kulturellen Ressourcen'. *Sociologus* 61(1):45–67.

Röschenthaler, Ute and Mamadou Diawara. 2011. 'Immaterielles Kulturgut und konkurrierende Normen: Lokale Strategien des Umgangs mit globalen Regelungen zum Kulturgüterschutz'. *Sociologus* 61(1):1–17.

Rose, Carol. 1994. *Property and Persuasion*. Boulder: Westview Press.

——— 2005. 'Property in all the wrong places?'. *The Yale Law Journal* 114(5):991–1019.

Rose, Mark. 1993. *Authors and Owners: The Invention of Copyright*. Cambridge, MA: Harvard University Press.

Rovine, Victoria. 2001. *Bogolan: Shaping Culture through Cloth*. Washington and London: Smithsonian Institution Press.

Rowlands, Michael. 2002. 'Heritage and cultural property'. In: Buchli, Victor (ed.). *The Material Culture Reader*. Oxford: Berg, 105–13.

——— 2004. 'Cultural rights and wrongs: uses of the concept of property'. In: Caroline Humphrey and Katherine Verdery (eds). *Property in Question: Value Transformation in the Global Economy*, Oxford: Berg, 207–25.

Sachikonye, Llyod. 2008. 'Crouching tiger, hidden agenda?'. In: Kweku Ampiah and Sanusha Naidu (eds). *Crouching Tiger, Hidden Dragon? Africa and China*. Scottsville: KwaZulu-Natal Press, 124–37.

Samuels, Lisa. 2002. 'Relinquish intellectual property'. *New Literary History* 33(2):357–74.

Saunders, David. 1988. 'Copyright and the legal relations of literature'. *New Formations* 4:125–43.

Schulz, Dorothea. 2001. *Perpetuating the Politics of Praise*. Köln: Rüdiger Köppe.

Scollon, Ron. 1995. 'Plagiarism and ideology: identity in intercultural discourse'. *Language in Society* 24(1):1–28.

Seeger, Anthony. 1992. 'Ethnomusicology and music law'. *Ethnomusicology* 36(3):345–59.

Sherman, Brad and Alain Strowel. 1994. *Of Authors and Origins: Essays on Copyright Law*. Oxford: Clarendon Press.

Shyllon, Folarin. 2003. *Intellectual Property Law in Nigeria*. München: C.H. Beck.

Singer, Joseph. 2000. 'Property and social relations: from title to entitlement'. In: Charles Geisler and Gail Daneker (eds). *Property and Values: Alternatives to Public and Private Ownership*. Washington: Island Press, 3–19.

Smiers, Joost. 1999. 'Copyrights: a choice of no choice for artists and Third World countries'. *Iwalewa Forum* 3:5–38.

Sodipo, Bankole. 1997. *Piracy and Counterfeiting: GATT, TRIPPS and Developing Countries*. London: Kluwer Law International.

Somers, Margaret. 1996. 'The "misteries" of property: relationality, rural industrialization, and community in Chartist narratives of political rights'. In: John Brewer and Susan Staves (eds). *Early Modern Conceptions of Property*. London: Routledge, 62–90.

Spittler, Gerd and Hans-Peter Hahn (eds). 2001. *Afrika und die Globalisierung*. Münster: Lit.

Stewart, Gary. 2000. *Rumba on the River: A History of the Popular Music of the Two Congos*. London and New York: Verso.

Stokes, Martin. 2004. 'Music and the global order'. *Annual Review of Anthropology* 33:47–72.

Strang, Veronica and Mark Busse. 2011. *Ownership and Appropriation*. Oxford: Berg.

Strathern, Marilyn. 2006. 'Intellectual property and rights: an anthropological perspective'. In: Chris Tilley. Webb Keane, Susanne Küchler, Mike Rowlands and Patricia Spyer (eds). *Handbook of Material Culture*. London: Sage, 447–62.

Strathern, Marilyn, Manuela Carneiro da Cunha, Philippe Descola, Carols Alberto Afonso and Harvey, Penelope. 1998. 'Exploitable knowledge belongs to the creators of it: a debate'. *Social Anthropology* 6(1):109–26.

Strother, Zoë. 1998. *Inventing Masks: Agency and History in the Art of the Central Pende*. Chicago and London: University of Chicago Press.

Sundaram, Ravi. 2010. *Pirate Modernity: Dehli's Media Urbanism*. London: Routledge.

Theisohn, Philipp. 2009. *Plagiat: Eine unoriginelle Literaturgeschichte*. Stuttgart: Alfred Kröner.

Thomas, Pradip and Francis Nyamnjoh. 2007. 'Intellectual property challenges in Africa: indigenous property systems and the fate of connected worlds'. In: Isaac Mazonde and Pradip Thomas (eds). *Indigenous Knowledge Systems and Intellectual Property in the Twenty-First Century: Perspectives from Southern Africa*. Dakar: CODESRIA, 12–25.

Tournier, Jean-Loup. 1967. '*Rykstag 67* ou la fin d'un mythe?' *Revue internationale du droit d'auteur* 54:632–736.

Toynbee, Jason. 2006. 'Copyright, the work and phonographic orality in music'. *Social Legal Studies* 15(1):77–99.

US Copyright Office. 2010. 'International copyright relations of the United States'. *Circular* 38:1–12. Online at: www.copyright.gov/circs/circ38a.pdf, accessed 17 September 2012.

Vaidhyanathan, Siva. 2001. *Copyrights and Copywrongs: The Rise of Intellectual Property and How It Threatens Creativity*. New York: New York University Press.

Van Binsbergen, Wim and Peter Geschiere (eds). 2005. *Commodification: Things, Agencies and Identities*. Münster: Lit.

Van Binsbergen, Wim, Rijk van Dijk and Jan-Bart Gewald. 2004. 'Situating globality: African agency in the appropriation of global culture: an introduction'. In: Wim van Binsbergen, Rijk van Dijk and Jan-Bart Gewald (eds). *Situating Globality*. Leiden and Boston: Brill, 3–54.

Weiner, Annette. 1992. *Inalienable Possessions: the Paradox of Keeping-while-giving*. Berkeley: University of California Press.

White, Bob. 2008. *Rumba Rules: The Politics of Dance Music in Mobutu's Zaire*. Durham: Duke University Press.

Yung, Betty. 2009. 'Reflecting on the common discourse on piracy and intellectual property rights: a divergent perspective'. *Journal of Business Ethics* 87:45–57.

Ziff, Bruce and Patima Rao (eds). 1997. *Borrowed Power: Essays in Cultural Appropriation*. New Brunswick: Rutgers University Press.

I

PROTECTING IMMATERIAL CULTURAL GOODS:

AUTHORS, ARTISTS AND THE LAW

CHAPTER 1

The colonial legacy of the international copyright system[1]

©©©©©©©©©©

ALEXANDER PEUKERT

Introduction

Much writings about the current international intellectual property (IP) system suggest that patents, copyrights and other IP rights became a global phenomenon effectively only with the 1994 Agreement on Trade-Related Aspects of Intellectual Property Rights (TRIPS). TRIPS is considered a 'dramatic change' in the IP regulatory landscape (Levin 2011:12). And indeed, the Agreement establishes an unprecedented, comprehensive set of IP rules for 153 World Trade Organization (WTO) members. It incorporates the Paris Convention for the Protection of Industrial Property (PC),[2] the Berne Convention (BC) for the Protection of Literary and Artistic Works,[3] and the Treaty on Intellectual Property in Respect of Integrated Circuits.[4] To this pre-existing minimum level of protection, TRIPS adds many further requirements, for example with regard to the subject matter and scope of patents (Art. 27–34 TRIPS) and the enforcement of IP rights (Art. 41–61 TRIPS; see Deere 2009:46–56). Last but not least, the WTO dispute settlement system gives

---

1   Work on this article was completed on 31 January 2012. I thank Karolina Zawada for excellent research assistance.

2   www.wipo.int/treaties/en/ip/paris/trtdocs_wo020.html; in the following: PC; see Art. 2(1) TRIPS, accessed 31 January 2012.

3   www.wipo.int/treaties/en/ip/berne/trtdocs_wo001.html; in the following: BC; see Art. 9(1) TRIPS, accessed 31 January 2012.

4   www.wipo.int/treaties/en/ip/washington/trtdocs_wo011.html; see Art. 35 TRIPS, accessed 31 January 2012.

teeth to these substantive obligations, helping to enforce the implementation of TRIPS in the WTO member states (Art. 64 TRIPS, see Correa 2007:472–90).

However, it was not the TRIPS Agreement that introduced IP rights to the world. There was a global IP system in place already in 1994. Only twenty developing countries (DCs) lacked patent protection for pharmaceuticals or chemical products when TRIPS came into effect (Deere 2009:73). Only five out of the thirty least developed country (LDC) members of the WTO had not already signed international or regional treaties on various kinds of IP rights before TRIPS.[5] Nowadays, all LDCs being members of the WTO provide for copyright and industrial property rights in national and/or regional legislation,[6] although they are under no formal obligation to do so under TRIPS. The transitional period provided for in Art. 66(1) TRIPS, which discharges LDCs from *all* substantive IP protection requirements under the Agreement, has been extended until 1 July 2013 and will probably be further prolonged.[7] Until 1 January 2016, LDCs are furthermore not obliged to implement patent protection for pharmaceutical products.[8] In spite of this formal leeway, only Rwanda officially informed the WTO that it would make use of the latter option and not enforce patents on imported medicines.[9] All other LDCs that answered a request of the WTO to express their individual priority needs regarding TRIPS only addressed difficulties with the full implementation of TRIPS. No country claimed that it required a longer transition period to introduce IP protection in the first place.[10]

---

5   See annex. The five countries are: Angola, Mozambique, Djibouti, Burma and Solomon Islands.

6   See www.wipo.int/wipolex/en/ and copyright-watch.org, accessed 31 January 2012.

7   No. 1 Decision of the Council for TRIPS of 29 November 2005, Extension of the Transition Period Under Article 66.1 for Least-Developed Country Members, WTO Document IP/C/40; Ministerial Conference, Decision of 17 December 2011, WTO Document WT/L/845 ('We invite the TRIPS Council to give full consideration to a duly motivated request from Least-Developed Country Members for an extension of their transition period under Article 66.1 of the TRIPS Agreement, and report thereon to the WTO Ninth Ministerial Conference.').

8   Declaration on the TRIPS agreement and public health, 14 November 2001, WTO Document WT/MIN(01)/DEC/2.

9   WTO Document IP/C/W/548, para. 29.

10   Nr. 3 Decision of the Council for TRIPS of 29 November 2005, Extension of the Transition Period Under Article 66.1 for Least-Developed Country Members, WTO Document IP/C/40. Until December 2011, Senegal, Tanzania, Bangladesh, Uganda and Sierra Leone submitted documents; see www.wto.org/english/tratop_e/trips_e/ldc_e.htm, accessed 31 January 2012.

This long-lasting, overly compliant attitude of LDCs in particular calls for an explanation that goes beyond contemporary economic and political circumstances. With a focus on copyright, which was earlier and more systematically dispersed via empire rather than patents and other industrial property rights,[11] I argue in this chapter that the firm incorporation of the Third World into the global IP system can be attributed to the colonial roots and neo-colonial structures of this body of law. With colonization came IP rights (Deere 2009:34; Okediji 2003). Various legal and political efforts were undertaken to stabilize the colonial IP regime during decolonization in the second half of the twentieth century. These manoeuvres obscured the fact that imperial IP laws had only covered the *territory* of the colonies. They were meant to protect *European* right-holders active in colonial markets. The *colonized*, instead, were formally or at least in practice excluded from copyright protection. Nevertheless, many former colonies accepted the narrative that 'they' already formed part of the global IP system at the time of independence.

The following section describes how copyright was technically extended to the colonies. The next section explains how and why these colonial transplants continued to be effective after independence. The chapter concludes with alternative perspectives on TRIPS and the current global IP system when viewed in light of its colonial legacy.

Colonial copyright

Modern copyright legislation dates back to the eighteenth century. The 1709 English Statute of Anne is considered the world's first copyright act. The revolutionary French Literary and Artistic Property Act was enacted in 1793. During the nineteenth century, the concept of an 'author' owning his or her 'original work' of literature and art prevailed throughout Europe. By the end of the nineteenth century, creative products of the mind had become tradable commodities. All important colonial powers had enacted copyright and patent laws (Hesse 2002).

The problem was, though, that these national IP rights were limited to the territory of the state granting them: French authors' rights were valid only on French territory, not in Britain, Germany or elsewhere. Publishers, producers of technology and not least colonial powers, however, wanted to also control and regulate non-European markets. As a consequence, copyright

---

11   For example, there was no clear British patent policy for the colonies. Nevertheless, by 1864, already seventeen British colonies had adopted patent and other industrial property laws, among them India and New Zealand; see Bently 2011:163–71; Umahi 2011; on French colonial industrial property policy see Camara 1987.

was extended to the colonies. Two technical ways to implement IP protection in the colonies can be distinguished. Either the internal imperial legislation was amended to cover these territories. Or states declared that their accession to international copyright conventions also applied to their colonies.

EXTENSION OF NATIONAL COPYRIGHT ACTS

The first approach to extend national copyright acts to the colonies was adopted in the British Empire already in the early nineteenth century (see Bently 2011:171–81). At that time, copyright was not even established all over Europe. International exploitation of works was gradually regulated by bilateral treaties among European states. The multilateral copyright system came into being only at the end of the nineteenth century. Accordingly, cultural production within the Empire had to be regulated as an internal matter (Okediji 2003:323).

Following the Union of the two kingdoms of Great Britain and Ireland, the Copyright Act of 1801 extended the Statute of Anne so that it applied throughout the United Kingdom 'and any Part of the British Dominions from Europe'. 'Any other', i.e. all non-European, dominions were covered by the UK Copyright Act of 1814. On the basis of this act, civil actions for infringements of copyright could also be filed in 'any Court of Record' in the dominions.[12] The UK Copyright and Customs Acts of 1842 applied to 'all parts of the United Kingdom of Great Britain and Ireland, the Islands of Jersey and Guernsey, all Parts of the East and West Indies, and all the Colonies, Settlements and Possessions of the Crown which now are or hereafter may be acquired'.[13] Imperial copyright legislation reached its peak with the 1911 Copyright Act. This legislation differentiated between dominions, possessions and protectorates. Self governing dominions[14] were free to adopt the Act, which is what most of them actually did.[15] In other British possessions, a proclamation by the local governor was necessary to bring a potentially modified version of the Act into force.[16] In light of this diversity and flexibility, British 'colonial lawmaking' is assessed as having been 'much messier and more unpredictable than modern commentators assume' (Bently 2011:200).

---

12   UK Copyright Act 1814 (54 Geo. III, chapter 156); also available at Bently and Kretschmer 2008.
13   Low v Routledge (1868) L.R. 3 H.L. 100, 110.
14   Defined in the act as the Dominion of Canada, the Commonwealth of Australia, the Dominion of New Zealand, the Union of South Africa and Newfoundland; Section 35(1) Copyright Act 1911 (1 & 2 Geo. V chapter 46).
15   Section 25, 26 Copyright Act 1911 (1 & 2 Geo. V chapter 46).
16   Section 27, 37(2)(d) Copyright Act 1911 (1 & 2 Geo. V chapter 46).

All other colonial powers equally extended their copyright acts to their colonies. In 1857, the French revolutionary act on authors' rights of 1793 was formally applied to the French possessions, Spain followed suit in the 1880s (Moreira da Silva 1965:10), Germany in 1901 (Fischer 2001:115; Lüders 1914; Zimmerstädt 1911) and Belgium with regard to the Belgian Congo not until 1948, when independence was already on the horizon (Moreira da Silva 1965:50). These differences in time are due to divergent internal copyright policies of the metropoles and the limited significance of copyright in colonial markets where literacy was very low and basic technologies like the printing press were lacking or available only to few people within the colonial administration (for Canada see Moyse 2010:150). In any event, the common aim of imperial copyright law was to safeguard the business interests of metropolitan rights-holders, in particular London and Paris book publishers who wanted to control the colonial markets and were in fear of the global diffusion of communication technologies (Bently 2011:198; Drahos and Braithwaite 2002:74). Moreover, the regulation of commercial activities was supposed to be uniform throughout the territories under colonial rule (Birnhack 2011:215–6; Seville 2006:139).

Not uniform, however, was the personal scope of application of imperial copyright law. It was meant to benefit *European* right-holders and users having authorized access to printing presses and other technologies in the colonies (Adewopo 2002:755; Okediji 2003:324–5; Oloko in this volume). Local inhabitants of the colonies and their creativity were not taken into account, let alone the purpose of protection. This distinction between *territorial* and *personal* reach of colonial copyright was expressly provided for in the German legislation, which allocated IP rights solely to German citizens, not to '*Eingeborene*' ('natives') (Lüders 1914:37–40; Fischer 2001:166–7).

British and French laws did not directly discriminate as to the nationality of the author. However, the respective laws established additional requirements that effectively limited access to copyright protection to Europeans and potentially certain local elites. Until the UK International Copyright Act of 1886, a work had to be published first *in the United Kingdom* in order to acquire copyright throughout the British Empire; a publication in the colonies was insufficient. This prerequisite was specifically intended to induce first publication and thus encourage learning *in the UK*, not in the colonies.[17] In addition, copies of every book had to be delivered to several public libraries in the UK within one month after demand in writing, 'an enactment which

---

17   Low v Routledge (1868) L.R. 3 H.L. 100, 109; see also Jefferys v Boosey (1854) 10 E.R. 681 Privy Council.

in the case of a publication at the Antipodes could not be complied with.[18] Thus, until 1886, a work first published outside the UK by an inhabitant of the colonies was not eligible for British copyright protection throughout the Empire (Scrutton 1903:211). French copyright law entailed similar restrictions, presupposing a European setting. The Literary and Artistic Property Act of 1793 provided that copies of the work had to be deposited at certain institutions in France in order to have standing to sue for copyright infringement. Until 1852, the work had to be published first in France.[19]

Even if one supposes that colonized authors were formally entitled to copyright protection in the British or French Empire, the actual enforcement of such a title required that the indigenous resident of the colony had standing to sue in a court competent to adjudicate a claim for copyright infringement. Without going into the details of colonial court systems, such a scenario seems highly unrealistic. For example, French and Portuguese law provided for distinct legal systems for citizens exercising French and Portuguese legal rights on the one hand and African and other colonized persons on the other. Also, under the system of indirect rule native administration and courts applied what was considered 'customary law', not imperial statutes like the copyright act, to the benefit of Europeans (Roberts and Mann 1991:12–23; for German colonies Lüders 1914:37–40).

In any event, no successful copyright infringement claim filed by a resident of a colony based on imperial copyright acts is documented.[20] The scarce literature on the practical effects of colonial copyright only mentions European beneficiaries.[21] For example, the French Society of Authors, Composers and Music Publishers (SACEM) collected royalties for the public performance of works by African radio broadcasters well into the 1970s (Goodman 2002:88–89;

---

18   Low v Routledge (1868) L.R. 3 H.L. 100, 109.
19   See Bently and Kretschmer (2008) for the French International Copyright Act of 1852.
20   Low v Routledge (1868) L.R. 3 H.L. 100 concerned the US American author Maria Cummins who was temporarily resident in a British colony (Canada) when her book was published in the United Kingdom by a UK publisher. On the wealth of written African literature during colonial times see Hunt 1969; *Encyclopædia Britannica Online Academic Edition* 2012, www.britannica.com/EBchecked/topic/8275/African-literature, accessed 31 January 2012.
21   As regards industrial property rights, very few applications for patents and other rights requiring registration were filed with the metropole patent offices by European applicants active in the colonies; for German colonies see Lüders (1914:42; between 1896 and 1913 fifteen patents, forty-six utility models and ten trademarks); for the British Empire see Umahi (2011:9; between 1884 and 1899 seven patents filed from applicants from British West African colonies).

N'Diaye 1975:66). Book markets were also completely controlled by European publishers during colonial times. Long after independence, these companies and their local branches dominated book production in developing countries, mostly by importing Western books (Altbach 1986:1646; Kumar 1983; Okediji 2004:241). It is thus true that publishers in and from the colonies relied on copyright (on Mandate Palestine see Birnhack 2011:219–40). However, this body of law solely concerned Western modes of cultural production. It did not take into account nor did it have a basis in, for example, African cultures (Adewopo 2002:750). Indigenous oral literature and creativity only appeared in international copyright discourse after the end of formal empire under the topic of 'folklore'.

In sum, the aim of imperial copyright policy was to protect and incentivize European book and other cultural production (for Germany, Lüders 1914:40–41). The only remarkable exception proves this rule, namely the UK Foreign Reprints Act of 1847.[22] It allowed all colonial territories to import unauthorized foreign reprints of works under UK copyright subject to the payment of an import duty compensation to be collected for the benefit of British (sic) publishers. By this limitation of exclusivity, the Act indeed aimed at improving the availability and dissemination of books among readers outside the UK. Nineteen colonies implemented the option, with Canada as the most important one. Its neighbour, the US, did not protect foreign authors at that time. Thus, US publishers were able to offer reprints of British books in Canada at a much lower price than their British competitors. After severe Canadian complaints about a strict prohibition of imports of US reprints, the imperial legislator lifted the ban (see Bently 2011:174–6; Moyse 2010:159–63; Seville 2006:78–90). On the one hand, the UK Foreign Reprints Act highlights the flexibility of British imperial policy. On the other hand, it primarily concerned a settler colony with a large population of European origin over which the US exhibited a strong political and economic influence. Thus, general imperial considerations informed this exceptional deviation from mainstream colonial copyright policy. The UK Foreign Reprints Act does not signal a fundamental shift towards integrating and protecting all inhabitants of the Empire on a non-discriminatory basis.

EXTENSION OF INTERNATIONAL COPYRIGHT CONVENTIONS

At the end of the nineteenth century, copyright had widely won recognition in Europe. It had become apparent, however, that transnational commercial activities required more than mere national IP protection. As a consequence,

---

22 An Act to Amend the Law Relating to Protection in the Colonies of Works Entitled to Copyright in the United Kingdom, 1847 10 & 11 Vict. 95 (UK).

the Paris Convention for the Protection of Industrial Property and the Berne Convention for the Protection of Literary and Artistic Works were signed in 1883 and 1886, respectively. The two fundamental principles of these conventions have been to provide for certain minimum rights and to guarantee that all authors protected under the treaties enjoy in all countries of the two Unions the rights which national laws grant to the respective natives (national treatment). The purpose was to establish at least similar conditions for the exclusive exploitation of works in as many markets as possible (Seville 2006:41–77).

All major colonial powers were either original signatories of the Berne Convention 1886 (France, UK, Germany, Spain, Italy, Belgium) or adhered soon after (the Netherlands and Portugal; see Ricketson and Ginsburg 2006: vol. II, para. 17.45). Since the British and French colonial territories were at that time already covered by imperial copyright legislation, it was only logical to also incorporate them in the new IP unions. Thereby, right-holders from the European metropoles were guaranteed copyright protection not only in their respective national empire, but in all colonial territories throughout the world (Lazar 1971:6 on the Berne Convention, created during the 'heyday of colonialism').

Several techniques were applied to achieve this aim. First, colonies that formed part of the imperial state were considered to be automatically covered by the accession of the metropole (for Algeria/France, see Ricketson and Ginsburg 2006:vol. II, para. 17.53; for German colonies, Lüders 1914:37–40).[23] Second, formally independent protectorates became early members of the Berne Union. Tunisia is among the first signatories of the Berne Convention, and Morocco acceded already in 1917. Today, WIPO refers to these accessions as effectuated 'through France'.[24] Indeed, Tunisia was represented in Berne by a Paris law professor.[25] Dependencies on (former) colonial powers also account

---

23   For the Paris Convention see Swiss Federal Court, 18 July 1890, *Zeitschrift für Internationales Privat- und Strafrecht* (1, 1891:247–8).

24   See www.wipo.int/treaties/en/Remarks.jsp?cnty_id=1040C and www.wipo.int/treaties/en/Remarks.jsp?cnty_id=998C, accessed 31 January 2012.

25   During the third International Conference for the preparation of the Berne Convention, Tunisia was represented by L. Renault, Professor at the Law Faculty of Paris and at the Free School of Political Science; see Records of the Third International Conference for the Protection of Literary and Artistic Works Convened in Berne September 6 to 9, 1886, p. 150, www.oup.com/uk/booksites/content/9780198259466/15550024, accessed 31 January 2012.

for the fact that Haiti[26] and Liberia signed the original Berne Convention in 1886 (Hemmungs Wirtén 2011:40; N'Diaye 1975:62).

Third and most important, Art. 19 BC 1886 set out that 'Countries acceding to the present Convention shall also have the right to accede thereto at any time for their Colonies or foreign possessions.'

The provision had been proposed by the British delegation and was adopted without 'any comment'.[27] Until this very day, it forms part of the Berne Convention and other international copyright treaties. Only the wording changed over the years, depending on the prevailing terminology to describe colonialism. Art. 26 BC 1928 referred to 'colonies, protectorates, territories under mandate or any other territories subject to its sovereignty or to its authority, or any territories under suzerainty'. In 1948, the article was again amended to read 'overseas territories, colonies, protectorates, territories under its trusteeship, or to any other territory for the international relations of which it is responsible' (Ricketson and Ginsburg 2006:vol. II, para. 17.46–7). This plain language was replaced at the 1967 Stockholm revision conference by Art. 31, which under the opaque title 'Certain Territories' provides that

> any country may declare ... that this Convention shall be applicable to all or part of those territories ... for the external relations of which it is responsible.

Paragraph four of Art. 31 BC 1967/1971 goes on to stress that

> this Article shall in no way be understood as implying the recognition or tacit acceptance by a country of the Union of the factual situation concerning a territory to which this Convention is made applicable by another country of the Union by virtue of a declaration under paragraph (1).

Thus, the wording of colonial times is gone, but in substance, the 1885 British suggestion is still in force: territories under foreign rule may be put under the umbrella of the Berne Union by a simple, unilateral declaration

---

26 Haiti was represented by L.J. Janvier, Doctor of Medicine of the Paris Faculty, diplomat of the Paris Medical Faculty, diplomat of the School of Political Science of Paris (administrative section and diplomatic section); see *Records of the Third International Conference for the Protection of Literary and Artistic Works Convened in Berne September 6 to 9, 1886*, p. 150, www.oup.com/uk/booksites/content/9780198259466/15550024, accessed 31 January 2012.

27 See *Records of the Second International Conference for the Protection of Literary and Artistic Works, September 7 to 18, 1885*, p. 122, www.oup.com/uk/booksites/content/9780198259466/15550023, accessed 31 January 2012.

of the reigning power. The solution of the Berne Convention served as a blueprint for the Paris Convention in the field of industrial property.[28] It has furthermore been adopted in Art. XIII of the 1952 UNESCO Universal Copyright Convention (UCC)[29] – which signifies the entrance of the US into the multilateral copyright system (Lazar 1971:13) – and in Art. 27 of the 1961 International Convention for the Protection of Performers, Producers of Phonograms and Broadcasting Organizations.[30]

All colonial powers made extensive use of this strategy: first and foremost France and the United Kingdom, but also Spain, Germany, the Netherlands, Japan, Belgium, Denmark, Australia and New Zealand declared that their accession also covers their respective colonies (Moreira da Silva 1965; Ricketson and Ginsburg 2006:vol. II, para. 17.46–55). The declarations were usually filed at every accession to a new Berne Act so that the most recent and protectionist version of the Convention applied to the colonial territory. Never did a colonial power exclude colonies from its accession to a new Berne Act with the aim of keeping the obligatory minimum protection – for example with regard to the duration of translation rights – for this territory on a lower level so that residents of the colony would have easier access to existing works. Such consideration of specific needs of knowledge-importing colonies was way beyond Eurocentric colonial thinking.

Upon a declaration that a Berne Act applies to colonies, these *territories* became 'countries of the Union' without being regarded members thereof (Moreira da Silva 1965:30; Ricketson and Ginsburg 2006:vol. II, para. 17.46). Again, this *territorial* expansion of the international copyright regime has to be distinguished from the question of *who* benefitted. Art. 2(6) s. 2 BC proclaims that Berne's protection 'shall operate for the benefit of the author and his successors in title'. But who qualifies as 'author'? Only nationals of the colonial powers or also the colonized?

The original Berne Convention only protected 'authors who are subjects or citizens of any of the countries of the Union, or their lawful representatives' (Art. 2 BC 1886). Whereas 'citizen' clearly excludes residents of the colonies, the term 'subject' of a country seems to allow their inclusion irrespective of nationality. However, authors to which the Convention applied were guaranteed equal treatment with the 'natives' of other Union countries, pointing towards a more limited understanding of the personal scope of protection because the colonized were not considered 'natives' of the metropoles. The records of

---

28   See Art. 24 PC 1971 and Bodenhausen 1968:206.
29   portal.unesco.org/en/ev.php-URL_ID=15241&URL_DO=DO_TOPIC&URL_SECTION=201.html, accessed 31 January 2012.
30   www.wipo.int/treaties/en/ip/rome/trtdocs_wo024.html, accessed 31 January 2012.

the conferences preparing the 1886 convention also show that the delegates considered and thought of nationals of (European) contracting states only. The wording was meant to accommodate different legal techniques to define nationality.[31] It was amended in the 1928 revision. Since then, the Berne Convention has protected the 'nationals' of a country of the Union (Art. 3(1) (a) BC 1971). As revisions of the Berne Convention never reduced the scope and level of protection, this change in wording confirms that the prior term 'subject of a country' also meant 'nationals' of a contracting country, thus excluding the colonized. The same conclusion can be drawn from the fact that mere *habitual residence* of an author in one of the countries of the Union was only declared sufficient to trigger Berne protection at the post-colonial Stockholm revision conference in 1967 (see Art. 3(2) BC 1967/1971; von Lewinski 2008:103).

Therefore, works of inhabitants of a colony were eligible for Berne protection only under the condition that the work be *first published in one of the countries of the Union*. Under the original 1886 Act, first publication within the Union led to the acquisition of copyrights by the *publisher* of the non-Union author (Art. 3 BC 1886). Only since 1896 has protection been enjoyed by

> authors not being subjects or citizens of one of the countries of the Union, who first publish, or cause to be first published, their literary or artistic works in one of those countries.
>
> (Art. 3 BC 1896, 3(1)(b) BC 1971)

The question arising in this regard is whether *first publication in a colony* qualifies as a publication in a 'country' of the Union. The wording of the Berne Convention militates against this assumption. Colonies are called 'territories' and as such distinguished from an acceding 'country' (cf. Art. 31(1) BC 1971). Accordingly, British copyright law until 1911 required publication *in the UK* to award copyright throughout the Empire. The British imperial legislature apparently considered this requirement to be in line with its obligations under Berne. Against this, it is pointed out that colonies became 'Unionist countries.' Thus, it is argued, a publication in a colony occurred in a 'country of the Union', albeit not in a 'contracting country' (Masouyé 1962:110; Ricketson and Ginsburg 2006:vol. II, para. 17.46; Ronga 1956:21).

---

31 See Records of the Second International Conference for the Protection of Literary and Artistic Works Convened in Berne September 7 to 18, 1885, p. 127, www.oup.com/uk/booksites/content/9780198259466/15550023, accessed 31 January 2012.

Even if one accepts this highly sophisticated view as a correct interpretation of the Berne Acts before 1967 – when the status of inhabitants of colonies was never discussed – it still requires a 'publication' of the respective work. Published works, however, are only those works of which 'copies' have been issued to the public, 'whatever may be the means of manufacture of the copies' (Art. 3(3) s. 1 BC 1971; Ricketson and Ginsburg 2006:vol. I, para. 6.29). Art. 3(3) s. 2 BC 1971 expressly provides that

> the performance of a dramatic, dramatico-musical, cinematographic or
> musical work, the public recitation of a literary work … the exhibition
> of a work of art and the construction of a work of architecture shall not
> constitute publication.

As a result, *oral* literature and other creativity not fixed in tangible media have never qualified as 'publication' and therefore did not suffice to trigger Berne copyright protection. Exactly this mode of creativity, however, was prevalent in many, particularly African, colonies. It only entered the global copyright stage in the 1960s under the topic of 'folklore'. During formal empire, oral creativity from the colonies did not form part of the international copyright regime.

In sum, the Berne Convention operated not less Eurocentrically than the imperial copyright laws of the metropoles. It is based on the same specifically Western notions of 'author', 'work', 'ownership' etc. (for music see Mills 1996). '*Contracting States*', i.e. fully sovereign states, constituted the original Union of 1886. Colonial territories were quietly added as annexes to the metropoles. The significance of this extension was only made explicit in 1928 when Article 1 was amended to read that the Union consists of '*countries* to which this Convention applies' (Masouyé 1962:110; Ricketson and Ginsburg 2006:vol. I, para. 5.76–8; Ronga 1956:21).[32] This change in wording again confirms the *territorial* expansion of the copyright empire, which started among few 'contracting states' to finally cover unspecified 'countries' around the globe. In contrast, the *subjective/personal* reach of the Berne system remained limited to nationals of colonial powers and the few colonized who had access to Western modes of cultural production. Oral creativity and thus the great majority of indigenous residents of the colonies were deliberately excluded from the international copyright system. In spite of this discrimination, former colonies quickly adhered to this system in the second half of the twentieth century. Their smooth metamorphosis from 'certain territories' to 'countries of the Union' is directly linked to the colonial legacy of the global copyright regime.

---

32   The same change was effectuated in Art. 1(1) PC 1883 in 1934; see Bodenhausen
     1968:17.

Copyright at the end of formal empire

As explained, colonial copyright was of limited significance during colonialism. It regulated imperial exchange among European nations and citizens. Its long-term effects, however, have been all the more important.

CONSEQUENCES OF COLONIAL COPYRIGHT

First, colonial copyright spread a specifically Western model of creativity and its regulation: every 'original work' is to be exclusively owned by an 'author' to reward the genius and encourage further innovation and investment. This IP paradigm tends to neglect fundamentally different cultural and socio-economic circumstances in industrialized and colonized, later developing countries (for patent law see Umahi 2011). Its homogenous crystallization in international IP treaties facilitated the successful claim of the Washington Consensus that IP is just another type of property deserving universal recognition (Williamson 1990). The anomalies following from this approach are nowadays hotly debated under the rubric of 'IP and development' (Netanel 2009).

What I want to focus on, instead, is a second effect of the colonial copyright system. It concerns the stability and further growth of the international copyright regime after the end of formal empire. At first glance, this continuity comes as a surprise, because it would seem to stands to reason that the reception of a transplanted foreign law ends when the power of the imposed legal system ceases. In the early 1960s, the United International Bureaux for the Protection of Intellectual Property (French acronym BIRPI) in charge of administering the Berne and Paris Unions indeed feared that the international IP system might implode. As the 'guardian' of the Berne Union, BIRPI was concerned about 'a constant and big geographical shrinking, to the prejudice of the interests of authors'.[33] The head of the copyright division of BIRPI, Claude Masouyé, identified an 'exotic time' and wondered 'whether politically, economically, socially, it is good or evil' that one 'must record the contemporary phenomenon of the decolonization' (Masouyé 1962:84, 144).

These fears turned out to be unfounded. In the end, only four newly independent countries[34] denounced membership in the Berne Union, namely Indonesia in 1960, Syria in 1962, Upper Volta in 1969 and Mauritius in 1971 (Ricketson and Ginsburg 2006:vol. II, para. 17.59). Whereas Central and South

---

33   Truchon 1996:386; Masouyé 1962:86; critical Lazar 1971:17—28 ('neo-colonialism'); Drahos and Braithwaite 2002:75—84; Okediji 2003:323—34.

34   On this terminology see Art. 2 litera f Vienna Convention on Succession of States ('"newly independent State" means a successor State the territory of which immediately before the date of the succession of States was a dependent territory for the international relations of which the predecessor State was responsible').

American countries, as well as a number of former British colonies, opted for the US dominated UCC, former French, Belgium and British African colonies stayed in the more protectionist Berne system (Moreira da Silva 1965; Ricketson and Ginsburg 2006:vol. II, para. 14.06). Most African LDCs formally acceded to the Berne Convention as new members (e.g. Senegal 1962, Rwanda 1984, Kenya 1993; Ricketson and Ginsburg 2006:vol. II, para. 17.60). Others simply declared their '*continued adherence*', i.e. they confirmed the uninterrupted applicability of the Convention to their territories. National copyright legislation was either directly based on colonial acts and ordinances, or new laws closely resembling British or French models.[35] In addition, two regional IP organizations were established for West African, francophone countries and East African, anglophone countries. Assisted by the French National Patent Rights Institute (INPI) and BIRPI, twelve former French colonies created the African and Malagasy Patent Rights Authority (OAMPI) in 1962, establishing a unified IP system with a central patent office (Deere 2009:35). After several revisions, the Organisation Africaine de la Propriété Intellectuelle (OAPI, established 1977) today comprises sixteen members and provides for a comprehensive, completely unified level of IP protection clearly beyond the TRIPS minimum standards for LDCs (see Adewopo 2002:767–8; Deere 2009:35, 240–78). English-speaking African countries, i.e. former British colonies, gathered in the African Regional Intellectual Property Organization (ARIPO) in 1976, which grants patents, trademarks and industrial designs in an equally centralized procedure for seventeen countries (Adewopo 2002:765–7; Deere 2009:38). According to the self-portrayal of ARIPO, its establishment was a reaction to the fact that its members had 'dependent industrial property legislations', lacking the infrastructure to grant patents and other industrial property rights.[36] Thus, the purpose of OAPI and ARIPO has been to replace the French and British IP institutions with as little effect on the availability of IP protection as possible. 'Colonial control' was substituted 'by similar or identical juridical institutions, laws and statutes', ruling out alternative approaches on the national level (Deere 2009:242, 249).

INTEGRATION OF NEWLY INDEPENDENT STATES
These developments prove the significance of colonialism for the firm integration of the newly independent countries into the international IP system. But how was this 'success' accomplished?

---

35   Adewopo 2002: 749–50; Deere 2009:38; Kunz-Hallstein 1982:690; Moreira da Silva 1965:18; Okediji 2003:335–6.
36   www.aripo.org/index, accessed 31 January 2012.

The first question which arose after independence was whether the new states had to formally accede to the IP Unions or whether they were already members of the club. BIRPI formulated its position in that regard already in March 1960. In letters to colonies soon to become independent, BIRPI explained that 'continuity must normally be assured'. It also suggested an easy way to achieve this aim. For reasons of legal security, future states should clarify by declaration that the Berne Convention would remain in force without interruption (Masouyé 1962:122; Ricketson and Ginsburg 2006:vol. II, para. 17.61). Such declarations had been accepted by BIRPI in 1928, when Australia, Canada, New Zealand and India had announced that they would continuously adhere to respective 1887 British extensions of the Berne Convention (Ricketson and Ginsburg 2006:vol. II, para. 17.57).[37] The idea underlying this procedure was that the colonies had already been countries of the Union and that in absence of a formal denouncement this status did not automatically end at independence. It was argued that the Berne Convention was not a political treaty, but was intended to safeguard private rights with universal legitimacy. Moreover, the Berne Union was conceived of as establishing a transnational territory of copyright protection comprising 'countries of the Union' as well as 'Unionist countries', i.e. colonies (Masouyé 1962:122; Ricketson and Ginsburg 2006:vol. II, para. 17.64–6). One commentator went as far as proclaiming that 'colonial regime [is] only a step … towards independence' (Ronga 1956:22).

Benin, Mali, Cameroon, Congo, Zaire, Niger and Madagascar declared the uninterrupted continuity of Berne obligations between 1961 and 1966 (Ricketson and Ginsburg 2006:vol. II, para. 17.58). Early critics deemed the automatism and formalism of continued adherence to Berne a form of neo-colonialism (Lazar 1971:17–28; see also Moreira da Silva 1965: 34–40). Today, it is generally accepted that this procedure 'skilfully obscured the substantive retention of the indices of colonial rule' (Deere 2009:41; Hemmungs Wirtén 2011:50; Okediji 2003:330). From a legal point of view, BIRPI's position was indeed highly questionable. An informal declaration of continuity is not provided for in the Berne Convention. With regard to the Paris Convention for the Protection of Industrial Property, BIRPI did not assume that newly independent states were still bound by colonial obligations (Bodenhausen 1968:19). The principle of later state practice has also been a rule of 'clean slate' (International Law Commission 1970:12–25; Zimmermann 2000:146–66). According to Art. 16 of the 1978 Vienna Convention on Succession of States in Respect of Treaties,

---

37　See alsowww.wipo.int/treaties/en/ip/berne/ (details, contracting parties), accessed 31 January 2012.

a newly independent State is not bound to maintain in force, or to become
a party to, any treaty by reason only of the fact that at the date of the
succession of States the treaty was in force in respect of the territory to
which the succession of States relates.[38]

Interestingly enough, WIPO nowadays presents the date of a declaration
of continuity as the date of the entry into force of a Berne Act; the earlier
dates of colonial extensions are only mentioned in a 'note'.[39] If a former colony
remains silent, WIPO does not consider it a contracting party (Ricketson and
Ginsburg 2006:vol. II, para. 17.66).

The declaration of continuity was far from the only measure to secure
adherence of former colonies. A network of inter- and transnational
organizations promoted the idea of copyright during decolonization. Since
1958, BIRPI had coordinated its activities with the Intergovernmental
Committee administering the UCC, the second major and US-dominated
copyright circle of the time (Johnson 1970:98). UNESCO, having entered the
copyright arena in the early 1960s, was responsive to the specific needs of
developing countries, but also stressed the fundamental principle of exclusive
copyrights (Johnson 1970:94–8; Ricketson and Ginsburg 2006:vol. II, para.
14.07; UNESCO 1962:23–4). With the establishment of WIPO in 1967/1974,
the administration of the Paris and Berne Conventions and other IP treaties
was institutionalized within the United Nations (Olian 1974:102). Today,
the global IP network includes the WTO TRIPS Council and many other
organizations representing right-holders, e.g. copyright collecting societies,
and the IP system as such, e.g. patent offices (Deere 2009:278–82; Drahos
2010).

Ever since the early 1960s, this network has provided 'technical assistance'
to former colonies in IP matters, including model drafts for 'appropriate IP
legislation'.[40] With regard to Africa, the head of the copyright division of BIRPI
explained that

---

38   United Nations, *Treaty Series*, vol. 1946, p. 3. See preamble No. 1 ('Considering the
     profound transformation of the international community brought about by the
     decolonization process').

39   See, e.g. www.wipo.int/treaties/en/Remarks.jsp?cnty_id=991C (Mali), accessed 31
     January 2012.

40   Johnson 1970:94–103; Moreira da Silva 1965:22–6; Ricketson and Ginsburg
     2006:vol. II, para. 14.106 fn. 453; Sacks 1969:27–32; regarding the BIRPI patent
     model law of 1964 see Umahi 2011:5.

by this aid, a wider recognition of literary and artistic property should appear on a continent offering immense outlets to the dissemination of culture.

(Masouyé 1962:142)

The enterprise was put into action in August 1963, when fourteen high-level representatives of the Berne copyright community gathered with twenty-three representatives of the thirty at that time newly independent African countries for the first 'African Study Meeting on Copyright' in Brazzaville. After BIRPI's director Bodenhausen had praised the protection of 'the finest manifestations of the human mind', and copyright experts from Sweden and Germany had outlined copyright principles and its benefits, the African participants agreed that copyright protection was advisable, but that it should consider the special needs of newly independent countries (Kaminstein 1964; Ntahokaja 1963). During a five-day meeting at the premises of BIRPI in Geneva one year later, a Committee of seven African experts drafted – with the assistance of seven consultants of UNESCO, BIRPI and copyright societies – a comprehensive model copyright law for African countries, providing *inter alia* for a term of protection of the life of the author plus thirty years and exclusive translation rights (Committee of African Experts 1965; Johnson 1970:118–19).

Similar events were held in South America and Asia. In July 1966, UNESCO and the International Confederation of Societies of Authors and Composers (CISAC) convened an 'Inter-American Meeting of Copyright Experts' in Rio de Janeiro (Rojas y Benavides 1966). Two conferences took place in India. At a joint meeting of the UCC Intergovernmental Committee and the Berne Permanent Committee in 1963, the Indian Minister of Education observed that the Berne system resulted in 'a large expenditure of foreign exchange' on the part of India (Chagla 1967; Johnson 1970:116–18; Kaminstein 1964:233). Critical voices calling for a thorough consideration of the interest of developing countries to get access to translations and educational material were raised again during the BIRPI 'East Asian Seminar on Copyright' in New Delhi in January 1967 (Johnson 1970:158–63; Kirpal 1967; Krishnamurti 1967; Rao 1967).

It is therefore true that these seminars offered developing countries a platform to express their needs. For the first time, the copyright community was confronted with voices from the Global South (Ricketson and Ginsburg 2006:vol. II, para. 14.05). Silent 'territories' had become contracting parties. The negotiation about claims of developing countries dominated the Stockholm revision conference in the summer of 1967. The political dimension of this debate nearly blew up the hitherto small and homogeneous IP world. Commentators observed the first true 'crisis in international copyright'

(Johnson 1970; Sacks 1969). However, India and other critics did not require radical changes. They agreed to the fundamentals of the Berne system, in particular to the idea of exclusive copyrights. What they demanded and what they eventually got was a distinct 'Protocol Regarding Developing Countries', reiterating and reinforcing the distinction between the First (and Second) and the Third World. The Protocol allowed for a shorter term of protection in general (twenty-five instead of fifty years after the death of the author), the ceasing of the exclusive right to prepare a translation ten years after publication of the original work if no translation in the local language was available, and compulsory licences for reproducing works (Olian 1974:104; Ricketson and Ginsburg 2006:vol. II, para. 14.11–33).[41]

This result did not meet the approval of European right-holders and governments. The UK had already abstained from voting on the Stockholm Protocol. After the conference, a storm of protest broke out. Right-holders bemoaned 'confiscation' and 'theft'. Industrialized countries did not ratify the Protocol.[42] An exit of the Third World was again conceivable. In a combined effort of the dominant Berne (European) and UCC (US) countries and the international IP network, a 'package deal' was negotiated, leading to a simultaneous revision of both major copyright conventions, bringing them into line with each other, in 1971. Since then, essentially the same 'special provisions regarding developing countries' are provided for in an Appendix to the Berne Convention (Art. 21 BC 1971) and in Art. V[bis] to V[quater] UCC. Developing countries are allowed to issue compulsory licences for translations and reproductions, mostly for the purpose of teaching, scholarship or research. Compared to the 1967 Stockholm Protocol, however, the provisions are more restrictive and the procedures to grant such a compulsory licence are extremely complicated (Kunz-Hallstein 1982:694–5; Olian 1974:107). Only sixteen countries, most of them only after 2004, declared that they would avail themselves of the faculties provided for in the annex to the BC 1971. Even fewer implemented the annex in national law in order to actually put their choice into practice.[43] Not a single compulsory licence is documented under the parallel UCC system (Olian 1974:96).

One could assume that these experiences frustrated the newly independent countries. If at all, they found their demands reflected in separate and extremely

---

41 The Stockholm Act is available at www.oup.com/uk/booksites/content/9780198259466/15550021, accessed 31 January 2012.

42 Johnson 1970; Olian 1974; Ringer 1969:223; Ricketson and Ginsburg 2006:vol. II, para. 14.33–4; Sacks 1969:128.

43 Ricketson and Ginsburg 2006:vol. II, para. 14.106 only refer to Thailand; Kunz-Hallstein 1982:696 mentions seven countries.

limited licensing schemes requiring a very high level of legal and economic capacity to be implemented. Nevertheless, even after the full failure of the Stockholm and the effective failure of the Paris revision conferences, only Upper Volta (Burkina Faso) and Mauritius denounced the Berne Convention in 1969 and 1971 respectively, whereas many former colonies acceded. This puzzle calls for additional explanations (see also Okediji 2003:373–84).

First, the international copyright system exhibits a powerful network effect. If the newly independent countries wanted protection for their nationals in the former metropolitan markets, they had to become part of the Union and grant reciprocal protection to Western right-holders on their territory (Ntahokaja 1963:171). Switching to the less protectionist UCC was prevented by a rule euphemistically called 'safeguard clause'. An appendix declaration to Art. XVII UCC 1952 provided that works which have as their country of origin a country which has withdrawn from the Berne Union to be only a member of the UCC shall not be protected by the latter Convention in the countries of the Berne Union. In other words, the penalty for denouncing Berne but remaining in or acceding to the UCC was that the respective developing country would be obliged to protect foreign Berne authors under that scheme, but would lose for its nationals any copyright protection in other countries of Berne, including all former European metropoles. Former colonies having declared their continued adherence or accession to Berne were thus locked into the high level of protection of that system (Lazar 1971:14, 25). This ban was only lifted in 1971, when the Berne Convention and the UCC had been adjusted with respect to the treatment of developing countries (Kunz-Hallstein 1982:696).[44]

Second, the African, South American and Asian copyright seminars organized by the transnational IP network in the 1960s were anything but mere 'technical' assistance. These occasions created a local copyright elite having a strong individual interest in promoting a pro-IP agenda irrespective of the general effects of this policy for a developing country.[45] The self-referential concern of the global copyright elite was a positive development of the *international copyright system*, but not a positive development for the former colonies (N'Diaye 1975:84). According to Okediji,

> even at the decisive moment of independence, intellectual property laws
> were not directed at the domestic innovation environment, but were rather

---

44 Lit. b appendix declaration to Art. XVII U.C.C. 1971.

45 see e.g. N'Diaye 1975; Kunz-Hallstein 1982:697 (a 'whole new generation of Third World copyright experts' shares the view that copyright is favourable to development); on fellowship programmes, see Johnson 1970:134.

projected outwards to foreign nationals who would benefit from protection.
Developing countries, in essence, serviced the international system and not
vice-versa.

(Okediji 2003:331)

Third, copyright and IP in general were not high on the political agenda
of the newly independent states. These issues did not justify international
turmoil. Moreover, both the Western and the Soviet Bloc formed part of one
IP community (Lazar 1971:7). The USSR acceded to the Paris Convention in
1965 (Truchon 1996:353–70) and the UCC in 1973 (Olian 1974:92). It therefore
did not matter with which party of the Cold War one sided. What the new
states were striving for was visibility and recognition in the international
arena (Deere 2009:248; Moreira da Silva 1965:72; Rao 1967; Truchon 1996:385–
8). BIRPI seminars and particularly the 1967 Stockholm Conference lent
themselves to this end (Johnson 1970:109). The cost of this policy was, though,
that developing countries had to accept the fundamentals of the Berne system
(Okediji 2003:327).

Fourth, IP narratives of originality, the incentivizing effect of exclusive
rights and their positive correlation to development were prevalent in
contemporary discourse. In the 1960s and 1970s, copyright did not receive
the public attention it enjoys today. Debates were mostly taking place within
the limited circle of 'copyright experts'. These, however, were concerned
about the future of this area of law, not about decolonization. The idea
that under certain conditions, access to knowledge may be more conducive
to innovation and development than a high level of IP protection was not
systematically pursued (see Kumar 1983). Such critical thinking was blurred
by the claim that the rich creativity in former colonies deserves the same legal
protection as works originating in the Global North (N'Diaye 1975:84), a claim
which neglects the fundamentally different modes of creativity operating in
Western cultural markets and, for example, sub-Saharan oral literature and
music (Gana 1995:125–37). No one actively promoted the idea of exiting the
system and abolishing copyright altogether, or of following the example of
the eighteenth- and nineteenth-century US, i.e. deny copyright protection to
foreigners (Olian 1974:91–2; but see Strnad 1967:85). Even the fiercest critics
remained within the paradigm of exclusivity and suggested development aid
for educational purposes or an international copyright clearing house to ease
licensing (Lazar 1971:37–8).

Finally, the formal inclusion of the Third World was facilitated by
the promise to protect 'folklore', nowadays termed 'traditional cultural
expressions' or more broadly 'traditional knowledge'. At the 1960 session of
the General Conference of UNESCO, African countries had emphasized the

need to rediscover and preserve African heritage and culture, which had to be recorded before it disappeared. A new kind of legal protection for African culture was, however, not part of this claim (Johnson 1970:96). This idea was only brought up at the Brazzaville African Study Meeting on Copyright in 1963, not by an African participant, but by the German law professor Eugen Ulmer (see Ntahokaja 1963:251; Sherkin 2001:43). He succeeded in linking the desire to preserve African culture with notions of protection and copyright. On the one hand, Ulmer advertised Western authors' rights as a tool to foster progress. On the other hand, he extended the concept of copyright to 'folklore'. He thereby exemplified the responsiveness of the international copyright system. In addition, he set the framework for further discussions, which could only be concerned with 'protection', be it of 'original works' or 'folklore'. In essence, Ulmer offered a deal: if you, developing countries, join the global copyright club and protect our cultural products, we will protect your 'folklore'.

The prospect of this benefit has been very attractive. African delegates considered the protection of 'folklore' a matter of great urgency and importance (Johnson 1970:106; Kaminstein 1964:226; Kunz-Hallstein 1982:701–3). Developing countries in South America and Asia joined this view (Folklore Committee 1967; Rojas y Benavides 1966:52). The mere discussion of 'traditional knowledge' has had integrative effects. It kept the former colonies – or better to say their expert representatives – at the negotiation table. At home, they could argue that the Western IP community cares about concerns of indigenous communities in developing countries.

Unfortunately, fifty years of discussion about the protection of traditional knowledge spawned many model laws and national laws in the Global South, but not an international treaty requiring protection also in the former metropoles, where unauthorized exploitation of traditional knowledge occurs (Sherkin 2001:43). Art. 15(4)(a) BC 1967/71 was presented as if it addressed the issue. It provides that

> in the case of unpublished works where the identity of the author is
> unknown, but where there is every ground to presume that he is a national
> of a country of the Union, it shall be a matter for legislation in that country
> to designate the competent authority which shall represent the author and
> shall be entitled to protect and enforce his rights in the countries of the
> Union.

Like special compulsory licences for the benefit of developing countries, this provision too proved completely ineffective. It does not speak of 'folklore' or 'traditional knowledge' but operates with the Western concept of a 'work'.

Most importantly, it only applies to *unpublished* works. If, however, traditional cultural expressions become the object of commercial exploitation, they will be put on the market in tangible media such as books, rendering Art. 15(4) (a) inapplicable. In that case, the *publisher* whose name appears on the copy is deemed to represent the unknown author and in this capacity is entitled to protect and enforce exclusive rights (Art. 15(3) s. 1 BC 1971; Ricketson and Ginsburg 2006:vol. I, para. 8.119). Thus, the provision does not *in*clude traditional cultural expressions, but effectively continues their *ex*clusion from the international copyright regime. During colonialism, oral creativity occurring in the colonies did not qualify for copyright protection due to a *lack of* fixation and publication. After the end of formal empire, oral creative tradition remained outside the international copyright realm exactly *because of* commodification, a bitter irony indeed.

Ulmer's promise to finally acknowledge that 'folklore' is no less worthy of protection than 'original works' has remained unfulfilled (Dommann 2008; Mills 1996:76). What is worse, the discourse of protecting traditional knowledge as part of IP constructs otherness under terms of Western legal concepts, reiterating colonial distinctions (Rahmatian 2009:60–3). It functioned perfectly, however, as a political manoeuvre to prevent a significant shrinking of the Berne Union.

In sum, asymmetric power relations facilitated a neo-colonial stabilization of colonial copyright structures. Private parties with vested interests, such as publishers, their home governments and transnational IP organizations, dominated the copyright discourse (Drahos and Braithwaite 2002:75–84; Hemmungs Wirtén 2011: 62–3). On the other hand, many newly independent countries lacked expertise in copyright matters and remained heavily dependent on former colonial powers and international organizations. The lower the IP capacity of a country, the more vulnerable it is to a pro-IP agenda running against its interests as a knowledge importer (Deere 2009:241, 311; Okediji 2003:384). Whereas most of the so-called least developed countries (LDCs) rank among this group, states that achieved independence in IP matters before the Second World War and that had significant local book production and demand, have proven more active in pursuing an agenda of access to knowledge in order to foster literacy, education and scholarship. In this regard, one can refer to Canada, India and South American countries such as Brazil and Argentina (Deere 2009:35, 39).

Conclusion

The international copyright system came into existence in the heyday of colonialism. The Berne and Paris IP Unions enabled the reproduction of imperial colonialism on the level of international law (Bently 2011:200; Okediji

2004:220; Vec 2008:126). The Unions and national copyright legislation covered the *territory* of the colonies, but did not address and protect the *colonized*. The expansion of European copyright law was meant to integrate markets, not people.

This important limitation of colonial copyright was not debated during decolonization. A transnational IP elite successfully argued that newly independent states had already been 'Unionist countries' and that their colonial obligations should continue. Oral literature and creativity as practised in many colonies appeared in international copyright discourse only at the end of formal empire under the heading of 'folklore', thereby reiterating colonial stereotypes. The yet unfulfilled promise to recognize this kind of creativity within the global copyright system contributed to the smooth metamorphosis of 'certain territories' (i.e. colonies) to member states.

The colonial legacy of the international copyright system provides an explanation for its virtually universal reach already *before* TRIPS. Indeed, TRIPS 'may not have been possible but for the framework of existing national laws on the books in most developing countries' (Okediji 2003:339–40). As the annexed table illustrates, there appears to be a general correlation between colonial history and IP protection (Table 1.1). British and French colonies were early and firmly incorporated. The longer colonial domination and exclusion lasted, the stronger was the neo-colonial IP grip (cf. sub-Sahara Africa on the one hand and Canada on the other). Countries with changing colonial rulers entered the system later or not at all. For example, two of the three African LDCs that had not acceded to international or regional IP regimes before TRIPS had been Portuguese colonies (Angola, Mozambique). Portugal does not rank among the IP champions. It joined the Berne Convention only in 1911, extending its accession to its colonies on that occasion, but not again, with respect to later Berne Acts (Ricketson and Ginsburg 2006:vol. II, para. 17.51, 17.55). Its national copyright law was declared applicable to the colonies as late as 1940 (Moreira da Silva 1965:10). Depending on their geographical location, African countries with a Portuguese colonial history have thus only lately become members of the West African regional IP organization OAPI (Guinea Bissau) or its East African counterpart ARIPO (Mozambique). The third African IP-outsider before TRIPS was Djibouti, an East African French colony, which apparently could not be integrated into the West African francophone block.

The colonial perspective on the current global IP system also helps to understand why no LDC has taken full advantage of the extension periods still available under Art. 66(1) TRIPS. All LDC members of the WTO provide for copyright, patent and trademark protection.[46] Against this background, the extension of transition periods proves meaningless, because they must not be used to arrive at a 'lesser degree of consistency with the provisions of the TRIPS Agreement'.[47] Once again, the international IP system offers some kind of special benefit to former colonies, which at closer scrutiny turns out to be ineffective if not inapplicable to the concern at stake. In sum, the TRIPS Agreement is only an episode in a whole series of steps to incorporating developing countries into the global IP system without effectively addressing their needs (Deere 2009:34–45; Okediji 2003:334; 2004:240; Rahmatian 2009). Even the ongoing debate about the protection of traditional knowledge can be blamed for obscuring the colonial and neo-colonial spread of IP laws to the 'rest' of the world.

46 Supra note 5.
47 No. 5 Decision of the Council for TRIPS of 29 November 2005, Extension of the Transition Period Under Article 66.1 for Least-Developed Country Members, WTO Document IP/C/40.

Table 1.1: Least developed countries and the global IP system[48]

Country	BC	PC	U.C.C.	Rome Conv.	WCT	WPPT	WTO/ TRIPS	Regional IP system	Colonial power	Independence
Afghanistan	—	—	—	—	—	—	—	—	GB	1919
Angola	—	2007	—	—	—	—	1996	—	Portugal	1975
Bangladesh	1999	1991	—	—	—	—	1995	—	GB	1947
Benin	1961	1966	—	—	2006	2006	1996	OAMPI 1962 OAPI 1977	France	1960
Bhutan	2004	2000	2000	—	—	—	—	—	GB	1949
Burkina Faso	1963–70 1976	1963	—	1987	1996	1996	1995	OAMPI 1962 OAPI 1977	France	1960
Burma	—	—	—	—	—	—	1995	—	GB Japan GB	1948
Burundi	—	1977	—	—	—	—	1995	—	Germany Belgium	1962
Cambodia	—	1998	—	—	—	—	2004	—	France	1953
Central African Republic	1977	1963	—	—	—	—	1995	OAMPI 1962 OAPI 1977	France	1960
Chad	1971	1963	—	—	—	—	1996	OAMPI 1962 OAPI 1977	France	1960

48 As of 30 November 2011. Sources: www.wipo.int/portal/index.html.en and www.wto.org. Only declarations after independence are listed.

Country	BC	PC	U.C.C.	Rome Conv.	WCT	WPPT	WTO/ TRIPS	Regional IP system	Colonial power	Independence
Comoros	2005	2005	—	—	—	—	—	—	France GB France	1975
Dem. Republic of the Congo	1963	1974	—	—	—	—	1997	—	Belgium	1960
Dem. Republic of Timor-Leste	—	—	—	—	—	—	—	—	Portugal Netherlands Indonesia	2002
Djibouti	2002	2002	—	—	—	—	1995	—	France	1977
Ellice Island / Tuvalu	—	—	—	—	—	—	—	—	GB	1978
Equatorial Guinea	1997	1997	—	—	—	—	—	—	Spain	1968
Ethiopia	—	—	—	—	—	—	—	—	Italy	1941
Gambia	1992	1991	—	—	—	—	1996	ARIPO 1978	GB	1965
Guinea	1980	1981	1981	—	2002	2002	1995	OAPI 1990	France	1958
Guinea-Bissau	1991	1988	—	—	—	—	1995	OAPI 1998	Portugal	1973
Haiti	1887–1943 1996–	1958	—	—	—	—	1996	—	France & Spain USA	1934

Country	BC	PC	U.C.C.	Rome Conv.	WCT	WPPT	WTO/ TRIPS	Regional IP system	Colonial power	Independence
Kiribati	—	—	—	—	—	—	—	—	GB Japan GB	1979
Laos	—	1998	—	—	—	—	—	—	France Japan	1945
Lesotho	1989	1989	—	1989	—	—	1995	ARIPO 1987	GB	1966
Liberia	1886–1929 1988–	1994	—	2005	—	—	—	ARIPO 2010	USA	1862
Madagascar	1966	1963	—	—	—	—	1995	OAMPI 1962 OAPI 1977	France	1960
Malawi	1991	1957/1965	—	—	—	—	1995	ARIPO 1978	GB	1963
Mali	1962	1982	—	—	—	2001	1995	OAPI 1984	France	1960
Mauritania	1972	1965	—	—	—	—	1995	OAMPI 1962 OAPI 1977	France	1960
Mozambique	—	1998	—	—	—	—	1995	ARIPO 2000	Portugal	1975
Nepal	2006	2001	—	—	—	—	2004	—	—	—
Niger	1962	1963	1989	1963	—	—	1996	OAMPI 1962 OAPI 1977	France	1960
Republic of Vanuatu	—	—	—	—	—	—	—	—	France & GB	1980
Rwanda	1983	1983	1989	—	—	—	1996	—	Germany Belgium	1961

Country	BC	PC	U.C.C.	Rome Conv.	WCT	WPPT	WTO/ TRIPS	Regional IP system	Colonial power	Independence
Samoa	2006	—	—	—	—	—	—		Germany & USA New Zealand	1962
São Tomé and Príncipe	—	1998	—	—	—	—	—	—	Netherlands France Portugal	1975
Sierra Leone	—	1997	—	—	—	—	1995	ARIPO 1980	GB	1961
Solomon Islands	—	—	—	—	—	—	1996		GB	1978
Sudan	2000	1984	—	—	—	—	—	ARIPO 1978	GB Egypt	1956
Togo	1975	1967	2003	2003	1996	1996	1995	OAPI 1977	Germany France & GB	1960
Uganda	—	1965	—	—	—	—	1995	ARIPO 1978	GB	1962
United Republic of Tanzania	1994	1963	—	—	—	—	—	ARIPO 1983	Germany GB	1962
Yemen	2008	2007	—	—	—	—	—		GB & Turkey	1918
Zambia	1991	1964	—	—	—	—	1995		GB	1964

References

Adewopo, Adebambo. 2002. 'The global intellectual property system and sub-Saharan Africa'. *University of Toledo Law Review* 33:749–71.

Altbach, Philip. 1986. 'Knowledge enigma: copyright in the Third World'. *Economic and Political Weekly* 21(37):1643–50.

Bently, Lionel. 2011. 'The "extraordinary multiplicity" of intellectual property laws in the British colonies in the nineteenth century'. *Theoretical Inquiries in Law* 12:161–200.

Bently, Lionel and Martin Kretschmer. 2008. 'Primary sources on copyright (1450–1900)'. Found at: www.copyrighthistory.org, accessed 31 January 2012.

Birnhack, Michael. 2011. 'Hebrew authors and English copyright law in Mandate Palestine'. *Theoretical Inquiries in Law* 12:201–40.

Bodenhausen, Georg. 1968. Guide to the Application of the Paris Convention for the Protection of Industrial Property. Geneva: United International Bureaux for the Protection of Intellectual Property (BIRPI).

Camara, Ibrahima. 1987. 'Les droits de la propriété industrielle en Afrique francophone avant et après l'indépendance'. *Revue Editions Juridiques Africaines*:2–8.

Chagla, Shri. 1967. 'Address'. In: Indian Copyright Office (ed.). *International Copyright: Needs of Developing Countries.* New Delhi: Copyright Office.

Committee of African Experts. 1965. 'Draft model copyright law'. *UNESCO Copyright Bulletin* XVIII:9–47.

Correa, Carlos. 2007. *Trade Related Aspects of Intellectual Property Rights.* Oxford: Oxford University Press.

Deere, Carolyn. 2009. *The Implementation Game.* Oxford: Oxford University Press.

Dommann, Monika. 2008. 'Lost in tradition?: reconsidering the history of folklore and its legal protection since 1800'. In: Chrisoph Graber and Mira Burri-Nenova (eds). *Intellectual Property and Traditional Cultural Expressions in a Digital Environment.* Cheltenham and Northampton: Edward Elgar, 3–16.

Drahos, Peter and John Braithwaite. 2002. *Information Feudalism.* New York: The New Press.

Drahos, Peter. 2010. *The Global Governance of Knowledge.* Cambridge: Cambridge University Press.

Fischer, Hans-Jörg. 2001. *Die deutschen Kolonien.* Berlin: Duncker & Humblot.

Folklore Committee. 1967. 'Report'. *Copyright* 1:52

Gana, Ruth. 1995. 'Has creativity died in the Third World?: some implications of the internationalization of intellectual property'. *Denver Journal of International Law and Policy* 24(1):109–44.

Goodman, Jane. 2002. '"Stealing our heritage?": women's folksongs, copyright law, and the public domain in Algeria'. *Africa Today* 49:85–97.

Hemmungs Wirtén, Eva. 2011. *Cosmopolitan Copyright.* Uppsala: Uppsala Universitet.

Hesse, Carla. 2002. 'The rise of intellectual property, 700 B.C.–A.D. 2000: an idea in the balance'. *Daedalus* (Spring):6–45.

Hunt, Harriett. 1969. 'African folklore: the role of copyright'. *African Law Studies* 1:87–98.

International Law Commission. 1970. 'Documents of the twentieth session including the report of the commission to the general assembly'. In: *United Nations: Yearbook of the International Law Commission, 1968*. Vol. II. New York: United Nations.

Johnson, Charles. 1970. 'The origins of the Stockholm protocol'. *Bulletin of the Copyright Society of the U.S.A.* 18:91–181.

Kaminstein, Abraham. 1964. 'Global copyright: recent international copyright conferences in Africa, Europe, and Asia'. *Bulletin of the Copyright Society of the USA* 11:225–33.

Kirpal, Shri Prem. 1967. 'Inaugural address'. *Copyright* 1:50–1.

Krishnamurti, Shri. 1967. 'Needs of developing countries in the field of international copyright'. In: Indian Copyright Office (ed.). *International Copyright: Needs of Developing Countries*. New Delhi: Copyright Office.

Kumar, Narendra. 1983. 'Cultural imperialism and Third World publishing'. *Copyright* 17:17–21.

Kunz-Hallstein, Hans-Peter. 1982. 'Recent trends in copyright legislation of developing countries'. *International Review of Industrial Property and Copyright Law* 13:689–703.

Lazar, Alan. 1971. 'Developing countries and authors' rights in international copyright'. *Copyright Law Symposium* 19:1–42.

Levin, Marianne. 2011. 'The pendulum keeps swinging: present discussions on and around the TRIPS Agreement'. In: Anette Kur and Marianne Levin (eds). *Intellectual Property Rights in a Fair World Trade System*. Cheltenham and Northampton: Edward Elgar, 3–60.

Lewinski, Silke von. 2008. *International Copyright Law and Policy*. Oxford: Oxford University Press.

Lüders, Ewald. 1914. *Die Anwendung des deutschen Urheber- und Erfinderrechts in den Schutzgebieten*. Hamburg: Gräfe & Sillem.

Masouyé, Claude. 1962. 'Decolonization, independence and copyright'. *Revue International du Droit d'Auteur* 36:84–145.

Mills, Sherylle. 1996. 'Indigenous music and the law: an analysis of national and international legislation. *Yearbook for Traditional Music* 28:57–86.

Moreira da Silva, Mario. 1965. 'Le droit d'auteur et l'Afrique'. *Revue International du Droit d'Auteur* 39:5–77.

Moyse, Pierre-Emmanuel. 2010. 'Colonial copyright redux: 1709 v. 1832'. In Lionel Bently, Uma Suthersanen and Paul Torremans (eds). *Global Copyright*. Cheltenham and Northampton: Edward Elgar, 144–65.

N'Diaye, N'Déné. 1975. 'The influence of copyright on cultural development in the developing countries'. *Revue International du Droit d'Auteur* 86:59–89.

Netanel, Neil (ed.). 2009. *The Development Agenda.* Oxford: Oxford University Press.

Ntahokaja, J.-B. 1963. 'Réunion africaine d'étude sur le droit d'auteur'. *Le Droit d'Auteur* 76, 10:250–9.

Okediji, Ruth. 2003. 'The international relations of intellectual property: narratives of developing country participation in the global intellectual property system'. *Singapore Journal of International & Comparative Law* 7:315–85.

Okediji, Ruth. 2004. 'Africa and the global intellectual property system: beyond the agency model'. *African Yearbook of International Law* 12:207–51.

Olian Jr., Irwin. 1974. 'International copyright and the needs of developing countries: the awakening at Stockholm and Paris'. *Cornell International Law Journal* 7:81–112.

Rahmatian, Andreas. 2009. 'Neo-colonial aspects of global intellectual property protection'. *Journal of World Intellectual Property* 12:40–74.

Rao, Krishna. 1967. 'Statement'. *Copyright* 1:51–2.

Ricketson, Sam and Jane Ginsburg. 2006. *International Copyright and Neighbouring Rights.* Vols. I and II. Oxford: Oxford University Press.

Ringer, Barbara. 1969. 'Recent developments in international copyright'. *Bulletin of the Copyright Society of the USA* 16:223–48.

Roberts, Richard and Kristin Mann. 1991. 'Law in colonial Africa'. In: Richard Roberts and Kristin Mann (eds). *Law in Colonial Africa.* Portsmouth and London: Heinemann, 3–58.

Rojas y Benavides, Ernesto. 1966. 'Report, Inter-American meeting of copyright experts'. *UNESCO Copyright Bulletin* XIX:43–60.

Ronga, Giulio. 1956. 'Les colonies et l'Union de Berne'. *Le Droit D'Auteur* 69:21–6.

Sacks, Howard. 1969. 'Crisis in international copyright'. *Journal of Business Law* 13: 26–32, 128–34.

Scrutton, Thomas. 1903. *The Law of Copyright.* London: William Clowes and Sons.

Seville, Catherine. 2006. *The Internationalisation of Copyright Law.* Cambridge: Cambridge University Press.

Sherkin, Samantha. 2001. 'A historical study on the preparation of the 1989 Recommendation on the Safeguarding of Traditional Culture and Folklore' In: Peter Seitel (ed.). *Safeguarding Traditional Cultures: A Global Assessment.* Washington D.C.: Center for Folklife and Cultural Heritage, 42–56.

Strnad, Vojtech. 1967. 'Developing countries and international copyright protection'. In: Indian Copyright Office (ed.). *International Copyright: Needs of Developing Countries.* New Delhi: Copyright Office, 81–6.

Truchon, Isabelle. 1996. *La Convention de Paris pour la protection de la propriété intellectuelle.* Paris: Université Panthéon-Assas.

Umahi, Okechukwu. 2011. 'Access to medicines: the colonial impacts on patent law of
    Nigeria', found at: ssrn.com/abstract=1975928, accessed 31 January 2012.

UNESCO. 1962. Die Beschlüsse der 11. Generalkonferenz über das Programm der
    UNESCO in den Jahren 1961 und 1962. Bonn: Sekretariat der deutschen
    UNESCO-Kommission.

Vec, Miloš. 2008. 'Weltverträge für Weltliteratur'. In: Louis Pahlow and Jens Eisfeld
    (eds). *Grundlagen und Grundfragen des Geistigen Eigentums.* Tübingen:
    Mohr Siebeck, 107–30.

Williamson, John. 1990. 'What Washington means by policy reform', found at: www.
    iie.com/publications/papers/paper.cfm?ResearchID=486Speeches and
    Papers, accessed 31 January 2012.

Zimmermann, Andreas. 2000. *Staatennachfolge in völkerrechtliche Verträge.* Berlin:
    Springer.

Zimmerstädt, W. 1911. 'Die Stellung der Kolonien bzw. Schutzgebiete im
    Industrierecht'. *Zeitschrift für Kolonialpolitik, Kolonialrecht und
    Kolonialwirtschaft* XIII:605–7.

CHAPTER 2

Whose text is it?

Writing the oral [1]

ⒸⒸⒸⒸⒸⒸⒸⒸⒸⒸ

Elisabeth Mudimbe-Boyi

The question of intellectual property when applied to literature involves several related issues: the production of the property, its appropriation and dissemination, the rights of the owner or author, the rights of the publisher and the rights regarding specific uses, such as quotations from and the translation of the texts. In Africa, among many other consequences, modernity marks the transition from an oral to a written literature. How to consider the producers of these oral and written texts: owners, mediators, translators or authors? Several years ago, Roland Barthes declared 'The death of the author' and years later Michel Foucault raised the question of 'What is an author'.[2] Foucault's and Barthes' statements allow us to interrogate the meaning and the function of 'author' and ownership with respect to a written text which has originated in an oral text,[3] as is often the case with literary productions in modern Africa. This topic has been discussed by only few literary scholars.[4]

---

1   I would like to thank Ute Röschenthaler, Mamadou Diawara and Elliot Klein for their comments, suggestions and English-language editing.
2   See Barthes 1977:142–9; Michel Foucault's text 'Qu'est-ce qu'un auteur?' was first published in 1969. Here the reprint in *Dits et écrits I, 1954–1975* of 2001 is used.
3   I use the term 'text' in a very broad sense to indicate diverse forms of artistic expression that include the written, oral, aural, visual and pictorial. I consider oral text as virtual; it is actualized, that it becomes text, only through performance, while written text is already text before its performance through the act of reading. For text and performance, see Karin Barber's article 'Text and performance in Africa' (2003).
4   In the 2006 special issue of *Research in African Literatures* 37(1), see for example the articles by Abiola Irele 'In search of Camara Laye' and Roger Little, 'Reflections

My focus is on the genealogy of the written text. In most cases, traditional oral texts were anonymous and did not require the acknowledgment of one performer or the other as their creator or sole author. Each performer could appropriate the text according to personal or circumstantial criteria. I argue that even if the traditional performer of an oral text is not the one who first created it, he becomes, at the moment of performance, its owner, who has the liberty to modify it, improvise, add or retrieve 'lost' passages, use devices of his own as strategies to keep his audience attentive and responsive, and display the full range of his qualities and skills as performer. An oral text, whose first creator is generally unknown, can be – and almost always is – performed in constantly varying versions by a single or by different performers. The concepts 'performer', 'owner' and 'creator' have been discussed by anthropologists with respect to a number of African societies.[5]

As to the modern writer of African literature in colonial languages, he often reworks traditional texts within the context of contemporary rules and regulations, copyrights and IP claims that emphasize the exclusive and individual character of artistic production, and which make him the owner and the author of the text he has fixed in writing. The difference between the past and present of textual production immediately raises several questions: To what extent can an African oral text be translated into a written European language? How can we evaluate, determine and define the ownership and authorship of a text transplanted from one medium to another, from one language to another, made public and disseminated through the new commercial circuits of a market economy? I address these questions first with reference to some canonical oral texts outside Africa, and then take a closer look at examples drawn from African literature in French.[6]

In the beginning was orality

As academic curricula are organized today, the study of oral literatures rarely takes place in Language and Literature Departments, whose focus is national written literatures.[7]Although the relevance of oral literatures would be very

on a triangular trade in borrowing and stealing: textual exploitation in a selection of African, Caribbean, and European writers in French'. See also, Goodman 2002; Kane 1968; Milz 2008; Moura 2006; Quayson 1997.

5   See, for example, Barber 2003; Boateng 2011; Diawara 2011; Röschenthaler 2011.
6   One could, of course, study in the same way African literature written in other colonial languages, such as Portuguese and English, or even oral Arabic literature presented in French.
7   In the USA, when taught, it is in departments or programmes of African Studies, or of Medieval Studies, but is for the most part the proper domain of Folklore Departments (which are either independent or parts of Anthropology Departments).

difficult to deny, its formal study has been mostly left to anthropologists, socio-linguists and folklorists.[8] Some scholars of African literature even want to consider traditional oral literature and modern literature written in colonial languages in terms of a rigid dichotomy, while others do examine the intertextual relationships between the two genres. Although such literary scholars pay attention to orality, their focus is not orality per se, but rather the assertion of continuity between traditional oral literature and the modern African novel, a claim strongly supported by the Senegalese critic Mohamadou Kane, for example. According to Kane, it is only by recognizing this link that we can fully understand the problems raised in the African novel.[9]

While in some parts of Africa the transcription and the translation of oral literature do reflect the continent's transition to modernity inaugurated by the contact with the West, this process is by no means specific to the so-called 'societies without writing'. Ancient Greece, the Arab world and medieval Europe, for example, had coexisting oral and written traditions, and many texts long existed in oral form that would only much later be transformed into writing. Who were the authors of these texts? Scholars have endlessly debated the question with respect to such well-known originally oral epics as the Greek *Odyssey* and *Iliad*, the French medieval *Chanson de Roland*, and the Spanish medieval *Cantar del mío Cid*. The two Greek epics, today commonly attributed to Homer, generated discussions among seventeenth- and eighteenth-century classicists generically referred to as 'the Homeric question', some scholars attributing to Homer the authorship of both epics, and others denying it. If Homer, one among many *aoidoi* – the bards of ancient Greece who used to travel and recite poetry and epics – is not the true author of the two epics, he has since been recognized by most as the one who pulled together and gave a new status and a definitive, fixed written form to pre-existing anonymous oral versions (although perhaps also written, according to some scholars).[10] The authorship of the European epic or *chanson de geste* has also long been the subject of debate among medievalists.[11] Like other epics and oral texts of the time, *La Chanson de Roland* circulated in many different versions, as each *jongleur* (minstrel) was free to change the text according to the circumstances of the performance or

---

8   See, for example, Barber 2007; Belcher 1999; Finnegan 1970; Ong 1982; Paulme 1976; Propp 1958; Scheub 1984.

9   Kane 1982; see also Julien 1992; Kazi-Tani and Nora-Alexandra 1995; Kone 1993.

10 There is an abundant literature of both older and more recent studies regarding 'the Homeric Question', see, for example: Bréal 1906; Parry 1971; de Romilly 1983; van Gennep 1909; West 2001.

11 The best-known scholars engaged in the debate were Bédier (1907–8) and Menéndez Pidal (1924, trans. 1960); on authorship in the Middle Age, see Minnis 1984.

the reaction of the audience. The version contained in the Oxford manuscript (c.1140–70), the earliest known, has been adopted as the official one transmitted to literary posterity. The copying of manuscripts, carried out by monks in monasteries, was also subject to variation. Copyists often took the initiative to intervene in a text by adding, suppressing, correcting words and passages, or writing comments (glosses) in the margins, and subsequent copyists often integrated such alterations or comments into the text. Such common practices once again beg the question of 'who is the author?' With regard to *La Chanson de Roland,* virtually the entire debate about its author was based on the meaning of the verb *declinet* in the last verses of the epic:

> *Ci falt la geste que Turoldus declinet.*
> [Here ends the story that Turoldus *declinet.*]

The verb *declinare* is characterized, however, by its semantic indeterminacy. For some scholars, it means 'to write', in which case Turoldus would be the creator and author of the epic. It also means, however, 'to transcribe' or 'to inflect', which would reduce Turoldus' role to that of an intermediary in its transmission. Despite the fact that Turoldus, like Homer, is the one who fixed the written text of an oral epic as we know it today, while the *Odyssey* and the *Iliad* are universally attributed to Homer, no one ever cites Turoldus as the author of *La Chanson de Roland.* Homer holds authorship and Turoldus an indeterminate status.

Writing orality

The transition from the oral to the written in Africa is generally accomplished by two distinct undertakings. One is represented by scholars (linguists, folklorists or anthropologists) transcribing and translating indigenous oral texts into French (or another colonial language), with commentaries pertaining to the social and cultural contexts of the time and the place of production and performance. The researcher here signs as the author of a scholarly work, considered a *study in oral literature.*[12] The series *Classiques Africains* published by Julliard offers several exemplary publications of this

---

12   See, for example, Mufuta 1968. In his review of the book, Pierre Van Den Berghe (1972) raises a telling observation: 'One only wonders why he [Mufuta] did not take the ultimate step of raising his "informants" to the dignity of co-authorship. If oral tradition is literature, then surely its specialized practitioners are authors. Was Socrates Plato's informant, for example? No, because, happily, anthropologists had not been invented yet.'; see also, Amadou Hampate Bâ and Lilyan Kesteloot 1969; Biebuyck and Mateene 1969, Kagame 1952.

nature. The second approach is that of professional writers, whose names appear as authors of a *literary work*. While scientific linguistic translation seeks to adhere closely – sometimes all too closely – to the original indigenous text, the professional writer's project is marked by an aesthetic intentionality which makes use of literary conventions, such as tropes and other devices that enhance the text, in order to reflect his or her own artistic mission and talent.

Unlike Greek or medieval French epics and other originally oral texts that have reached us via various mediations, the new African novel or short story based on an oral version passes through deliberate interventions of a far more complex nature. From the time of recording to the time of the publication, texts in both categories face the challenge of what I call a 'chain of translations':[13] of medium (from oral to written, or from spoken words to recordings and their transcriptions), of language (in particular from an African language into French or another fundamentally distinct European idiom) and of the use of rhetorical devices. The performer (the *griot* or the storyteller) tells, recites or dictates the story to a researcher (anthropologist, linguist, folklorist, writer), who records it, transcribes the recording, translates or has it translated into French or another language, following which it is published, disseminated and possibly translated into yet other languages. These translations function as mediations between the oral and the written texts and raise fundamental questions concerning authorship and ownership.

Even without framing these questions in a theoretical debate, African writers have been concerned by their status with respect to the oral texts at the base of their literary creations. In *Koumen*, the writer Hampate Bâ states that Ardo Dembo Soh transmitted this narrative to him (Hampate Bâ 1961). Djibril Tamsir Niane, in his rendering of *Soundjata, épopée mandingue* in written form, acknowledges the *griot* Mamadou Kouyaté as the oral source for the epic, and laments the 'warmth of voice' lacking in its written form (Niane 2000). I will focus on three canonical works of the African Francophone literary tradition: Birago Diop's *Les contes-d'Amadou Koumba*, Laye Camara's *Le maître de la parole* and Tchicaya U Tam'si's *Légendes africaines*.

---

13   I intend translation in a sense going well beyond a simple linguistic translation to include other objects of translation: media, culture, artistic conventions etc. Any linguistic translation is a challenge, see Walter Benjamin 'The task of the translator: an introduction to the translation of Baudelaire's *Tableaux parisiens*' (1968). By using the expression 'chain of translations', I want to emphasize the complexity of these translations and how, more than in other contexts, the transition is a major question in regard to 'ownership' and 'authorship'. For the translation of an oral text into writing, see for example Anthère Nzabatsinda '"Tradutore Traditore"?: Alexis Kagame's transposition of Kinyaruanda poetry into French' (1999).

BIRAGO DIOP: LES CONTES D'AMADOU KOUMBA[14]

The ultimate source of these narratives, as acknowledged by Diop, is his own recall of the tales his grandmother told him when he was a child. A more recent, additional source was the family *griot*, Amadou Koumba, mentioned prominently and unambiguously in the title of Diop's book:

> On my return to my own country, having forgotten little of what I had learnt as a child, I had the great good fortune to meet by chance old Amadou Koumba, our family *griot*.... He taught me others, too, studded with maxims and morals, in which can be found the wisdom of our ancestors.... These same tales and legends – with slight variations – I also heard in the course of my travels along the banks of the Niger and across the plains of the Sudan, far from Senegal.... Other children like myself and other grown-ups, like my elders, listened to these tales with the same avidity, their faces illumined by the flames leaping high from the fagots.
>
> (Blair 1966:xxii–xxiii)

This quotation informs us about the sources of Diop's texts, but also implies that there might be alternative versions of the same tales he heard in his wanderings. More interesting is the way Diop defines his role in the production of the written text, and how losses occur in the transition from oral to written form:

> If I have not succeeded in transmitting to the tales the same atmosphere in which I, as the listener, and those whom I watched, were plunged, attentive, shuddering, or rapt in reverie, it is because I have become a man, that is to say an incomplete child, and so incapable of re-creating the miraculous. More especially it is because I lack the voice, the verve, and the powers of mimicry of my old *griot*.... Into the solid web of his tales and his maxims, making use of his clear-drawn warp, I have tried, unskilled weaver that I am, to turn out with my hesitant shuttle some strips of cloth to sew together into a *pagne*, in which Grandma, if she were to return, would discover the thread that she was the first to spin; and in which *Amadou Koumba will recognize*, though doubtless much faded, the colours of the fine stuffs that *he wove for me* of old.
>
> (Blair 1966:xxiii, my emphases)

---

14   Birago Diop, *Les contes d'Amadou Koumba* (3rd edition, 1961) was translated into English by Dorothy Blair as *Tales of Amadou Koumba* (1966).

In this statement the writer explicitly acknowledges his grandmother's and the griot Amadou Koumba's legacy, presenting himself as only a depository, an imperfect beneficiary and transmitter of their craft and knowledge. In the foreword to her English translation of his book Dorothy Blair states, with respect to Diop:

> Moreover, in spite of his instinctive and poetic literary gifts, he refuses to claim for himself any credit for the originality of these *Tales of Amadou Koumba*, which are presented in English. Instead he modestly offers himself as the *disciple, scribe, and translator* into French (which is the literary language of the country) of his household *griot* Amadou, son of Koumba.
>
> (Blair 1966:x, my emphases)

Blair, in her turn, admits the complexity of her own task as the translator into English of Birago Diop's French text:

> I have tried to find equivalent effects in English.... In this English version I have tried to be faithful both to the author, Birago Diop and to the *griot*, Amadou Koumba.... If any shreds of exoticism cling to the style, I hope that they will be accepted, not as negligence, but a deliberate faithfulness to the Wolof *griot* who inspired these tales.
>
> (Blair 1966:xvii)

LAYE CAMARA: LE MAÎTRE DE LA PAROLE (1978)

On 15 March 1963 Laye Camara went to visit Babu Conde, whom he describes as 'the most competent *griot*', and spent three days in his company, listening to him. Camara, like Diop, places himself in a secondary position, giving credit to the *griot* he considers the author of the book:

> Our major preoccupation in this study is the version of history made by the *griot*, the Belen-Tigi, or masters of the word. Babu Conde is the *author* of the legend that follows – we *are but the modest transcriber and translator* – [and he] was to traditional African society what the primitive cathedral sculptors and painters were in the European Middle Ages; the idea that he should sign his work – for he is a fine Arabic scholar – never entered his head. He was a man who considered himself a simple story-teller, not an artist, a man who had no desire to serve his own ends, but only the needs of society – to serve the word and the word beyond the word.
>
> (Camara 1980:24, 27, my emphases)

TCHICAYA U TAM'SI: LÉGENDES AFRICAINES (1968)

In this book, Tchicaya gives his own versions of tales he 'borrowed'. Tchicaya chooses not to mention any name as the source of his book, stating only that he has rendered legends as he 'had heard them', as 'told to him', which he has 'borrowed' from other authors, or 'recreated' through his own memory. Although he recognizes a pre-existing oral text, Tchicaya does not give credit to anyone in particular, and relegates his sources to an anonymity he expresses through the use of the French indefinite pronoun '*on*'.

Unlike Laye Camara and Birago Diop, who take great care to acknowledge the sources of their own written works, and humbly express their indebtedness to them, Tchicaya exhibits skepticism toward individual authorship in the transmission of such oral texts as legends, which he clearly considers collective creations:

> Qui peut se vanter d'être l'auteur de telle ou telle légende? Il faut *toutes les mémoires du monde pour que les légendes naissent et vivent!* Leurs variantes ne naissent pas seulement des pertes de mémoire qui comblent les trous comme elles peuvent; les variantes peuvent naître par l'inversion du sexe des protagonistes, par le changement des rôles dévolus aux comparses. On multiplie ainsi les cycles.
>
> (Tchicaya 1968:20, 22; my emphasis)

> [Who can boast of being the author of such or such a legend? It takes all the memories of the world for legends to be born and live. Their different versions originate not only in the losses of memory which fill in the holes as best they can; variants may also arise in reversals of the protagonists' gender or in the devolution of their roles to minor characters. In this way the cycles are multiplied. – My translation.]

Whose text is it?

In the transition of a text from oral to written form, the modern writer is indeed a mediator, a role attributed by Barthes and Foucault to all authors, but here with specified distances, in time and other dimensions, between them and what they mediate, but also – and this is key – what they openly acknowledge as *mediated*. Diop's, Camara's or Tchicaya's written texts have genealogies that may go back centuries, and have certainly already passed through several mediations and a 'chain of translations'. In questioning the role of the author and proclaiming his death, both thinkers, Barthes and Foucault, seek to de-emphasize his importance in the interpretation of texts and the meaning given to them. To stress the author's function somehow jeopardizes and limits the hermeneutic process, as Barthes states in 'The death of the author':

> To give a text an author is to impose a limit on that text, to furnish it with a final significance, to close the writing.
>
> (Barthes 1977:147)

The argument central to this chapter does not concern meaning, as such, but rather the source of a written text and the indeterminacy of authorship: 'whose text is it?' In orality, the appropriation by a performer of a pre-existing text is not contested or criticized by any individual, community or institution. On the other hand, the status of 'owner' may be conferred – whether justly or unjustly – on a modern writer of African literature in a colonial language such as French.

What, then, is an author?

The results of the different mediations and translations bring both losses and gains to the text. In oral performance the voice plays a major role. It is embedded in sounds, accents, intonations and their alterations. Of importance are gestures, mimicry, body language, pauses, acceleration or slowing of the recitation, onomatopoeias, repetitions and what Roman Jakobson (1963) calls the phatic function: that is, dialogic devices establishing a direct interaction between performer and audience. Unlike the oral text, whose actualization is limited to the time and the space of its performance, the written text remains the same and can be multiplied *ad infinitum*, performed or read simultaneously in different geographic spaces and times, by different individuals and transformed only by its translation into different languages. While the oral text is not fixed, and its performance engages a community of people, the written text, on the contrary, is fixed, and the act of reading evolves as an individual act and in solitude, or even loneliness.

African Francophone writers whose literary works originated in an oral text find themselves engaged simultaneously as individual producers and as participants in a collective production in which they represent the final stage. The semantic cluster around such terms as 'mediation' or 'transition' brings into proximity Barthes, Foucault, Blair, Diop, Camara and Tchicaya, all of whom designate the enunciator as 'mediator', 'scribe', 'disciple', 'transcriber' or 'translator', who proceeds by means of 'transition', 'transposition' or 'transplantation'. The proliferation of this lexicon and the examples of Greek and medieval epic suggest how difficult it is to define the term 'author', which is particularly elusive when applied to oral texts appropriated by writers. Further, given the complexity of a literary definition of the term, we can appreciate the

challenge of establishing a strict legal definition determined and regulated in a
modern context that considers individual authorship exclusive and protected,
and links creation, invention and commodification.

I would like to briefly revisit what Philippe Lejeune and Foucault propose.
Writing about autobiography, Philippe Lejeune cites the French law of 1957:

> The qualification 'author', unless there is proof to the contrary, belongs to
> the person or persons under whose name the work is made public.
>
> (1989:265, note 15)

Lejeune supports this legal definition but also seems to relativize it when he
writes:

> The author of a text is most often the one who wrote it, but the fact of
> writing is not sufficient to be declared an author. One is not an author in
> the absolute. It is a relative and conventional thing: one becomes an author
> only when one takes, or finds oneself attributed [with], the responsibility for
> the emission of a message (message that implies its production) in a given
> circuit of communication.
>
> (Lejeune 1989:192–3)

Foucault attempts to define the term concisely as follows:

> Auteur d'un texte, d'un livre ou d'une oeuvre dont on peut légitimement lui
> attribuer la production. [The author of a text, book or work is the person to
> whom one might legitimately attribute its production].
>
> (Foucault 2001:832, my translation).

Foucault is more interested in what he calls the *'fonction-auteur'*, and
suggests that this function establishes a *'rapport d'appropriation'* between
the author and his work, which entails ownership, but also responsibility
vis-à-vis the work. For Foucault, the author function is not limited to the
production of a book: it can be extended to the production of ideas and
theories, as epitomized by those he calls *'fondateurs de discursivité* [founders
of discursivity]', such Marx and Freud, whose works, Foucault asserts, lay the
foundations of other works or make them possible, generating new traditions
and disciplines, thus a *'possibilité indéfinie de discours* [never-ending possibility

of discourse]'.[15] On the other hand, Foucault admits the contingent dimension of the concept 'author' when he writes:

> *La fonction-auteur ne s'exerce pas d'une façon universelle et constante sur*
> *tous les discours.* [The author function does not work in a universal and
> constant way with respect to all discourse.]
>
>   (Foucault 2001:827, my translation).

With reference to Lejeune or Foucault, one could argue that the concept of authorship is fluid and polysemic: 'author' can apply to both the 'producer of the final text' and its 'original creator' (unknown in the case of most oral texts). It may also refer to the enunciator of a text, such as the traditional performer of oral texts. 'Author' can designate the one to whom is given, or who takes, the responsibility for the text. Semantics also suggests a close relationship between 'to author' and 'to authorize', which if one follows then positions the author of a text as the one who validates it in its final and definitive form, granting permission for its publication, circulation and dissemination according to defined regulations and rules of law. By submitting a text to a publisher under their names,[16] Camara, Diop and Tchicaya enter into a contractual agreement, officially attesting to their status as the work's exclusive owners and authors. From my perspective, however, these writers locate themselves in a perpetually ambiguous space,[17] one of 'having their cake and eating it too'. On the one hand, they expressly minimize their own roles in the production of a text, and position themselves, humbly, as 'disciples', 'scribes', 'translators', but not 'authors'. On the other hand, they assume a legal status as the individual authors and sole owners of a new text. I discuss elsewhere the

---

15 Foucault's *'fondateur de discursivité'* perhaps also exercises a prophetic function, as does Bourdieu's *auctor* (Bourdieu and Passeron 1970).

16 For Foucault, the author's name has a *'fonction classificatoire'* that enables the assemblage of a body of texts under a single umbrella which marks their distinctiveness from other bodies of texts.

17 One might think here of Pierre Bourdieu's dichotomy *'aucto-lector'*. The *auctor* creates the work, is therefore responsible for it and exercises authority over it. The *lector* occupies a lower, more 'humble' position. He or she does not create, but rather only reproduces, for instructive purposes, material originating with the *auctor*. See Bourdieu and Passeron (1970). One may note that Diop, Camara and, to some extent, Tchicaya, consider themselves as 'disciples' or 'transcribers' who acknowledge that their text derives from a pre-existing one, making them similar to Bourdieu's *lector*, without the professorial responsibility of teaching. At the same time, these writers, as authors, 'authorize' the text, exercise authority over it and take responsibility for it. My intention, in drawing an analogy between these writers and Bourdieu's *lector*, is to underscore their liminal position.

transformation of a fictitious oral text into the written text that constitutes Maryse Condé's novel *Moi, Tituba, sorcière noire de Salem*. I argue that Condé, as the legal author of the book, takes responsibility for it. At the same time, her book is entirely based on the oral narrative recited to her by Tituba, her character. Condé adopts the literary strategy of 'translating' Tituba's story, and, in so doing, identifies herself as a mediator (see Mudimbe-Boyi 2006:178–82). Her assumed function, although a literary device embedded in an invented oral narrative, is similar to Diop's, Camara's and Niane's translations from the genuinely oral, or Dorothy Blair's linguistic translation of Birago Diop's text from French into English (a translation of the translation). One should refer here to the intertextual process described by Julia Kristeva (1969), Michel Rifaterre (1979) and Gérard Genette (1982). Though there are nuances in their understanding of this process, they all refer to the adaptation of a pre-existing text. In the case of the African texts considered in this chapter, the final written text originates in a pre-existing oral text (or a fictitious pre-existing text) without which the published text could not have been conceived. What the different mediations have in common is that the process of transformation (of medium, language, rhetorical devices etc.) culminates in the production of a new text, in which the binary opposition between oral and written disappears in the fusion of both, realized as that which Genette terms a 'hypertext'. As a result, the written text and the writer reveal themselves to be the Same and the Other. They occupy a liminal space situated in both the past and the present, fixed in the local and at the same time participating in today's global market economy and worldwide intellectual property rights.

My contention is that even if a writer is heir to a collective oral creation transmitted through time, he is no less the author of his own written work. If a *griot* or a storyteller indeed provides the initial oral text, the published text is the product of literary labour that requires imagination and the invention of linguistic and rhetorical devices of translation, technical procedures and diacritical signs which all differ from the mnemonics of the oral. The writer has to devise new textual strategies to convey what is lost in the transition from the oral to the written, and it is these that allow him to suggest an atmosphere, create an ambiance, evoke gestures, facial expressions, emotions, smells, sounds. The final and written text owes its existence to the work of the writer. It is a reflection of his mind, heart, literary and cultural sensitivity and his skills; in other words, his creativity. Since there is no legal concept of '*auteur au second degré* [writer of the second degree]'[18], viewed from

---

18   I use this term to echo Genette's *littérature au second degré* ('literature in the second degree', which characterizes the hypertext. 'Second' here does not imply a hierarchization, but rather simply serves as a chronology marker.

today's perspective, one must cede to the claims of Laye Camara, Birago Diop or Tchicaya U Tam'si that they are the authors and owners of their texts, participants in a new market economy and commodification. Writers contribute a product, a book, to be published and disseminated. In exchange, they receive protection and control of the circulation of their product, via legal regulations. What might separate the legal definition from the literary one is, perhaps, the fluidity and the polysemy of the latter. In the field of literature, the exclusivity of ownership can indeed be relativized, contested, challenged or downplayed[19] by the use of literary procedures and techniques such as intertextuality, pastiche, collage or irony.[20] From a legal standpoint, the consumer is legally bound to the 'fair use' and respect of the author's text as it is: fixed forever, unless modified by the author him or herself, in, for example, a revised edition (or a translation). The existence nowadays of strict legal regulations to protect the authorship and ownership of literary and other texts, as well as legal actions taken against those who allegedly violate the laws and regulations by the misappropriation of others' works without their consent or an acknowledgment of their ownership, attest to the presence of the 'author'.

The (mis-)appropriation of local knowledge by colonials and missionaries in Africa without any reference to their sources or informants still haunts us today. '*Nègres littéraires*' continue to disappear, more often than not, in the books of the famous people for whom they write. From an ethical standpoint, then, the writers-authors discussed in this chapter all had the moral obligation to acknowledge the genealogy of texts derived from the pre-existing one of the *griot* or storyteller who transmitted it to them. Camara and Diop fully meet that ethical requirement by acknowledging explicitly, by name, the sources of their own written text, while Tchicaya, on the other hand, refers only in general terms to anonymous predecessors. As for the legal significance of ownership and authorship in Africa today, it is a sign of new times and of the new order of things that comes with modernity. Still, in the case of the transition from the oral to the written, the definition of authorship has to be confronted with cultural practices (collective versus individual production),

---

19 See for example Hennig (1997) and Peterson Haviland and Mullin (2009).
20 The *griot* also retains the right or privilege of continuing to sing his texts; see Diawara (1996), and see Diawara in this volume for a discussion of the transformation of oral texts and their fixation in CDs and other media. With respect to African writers, one may recall the *cause célèbre* of the Malian writer Yambo Ouologuem, author of the novel *Le devoir de violence,* who was unfairly accused of plagiarism, several decades ago, for what he himself considered a purely narrative device intended to parody the act of writing novels.

particularly in a context where the authors write and translate, in today's space, a text whose origins lay in the oral world of yesterday. The positioning of the African writers discussed between two media (oral and written), two languages (African and European) and two statuses (anonymity and identification) reflects the aftermath of Africa's contact with the West and with modernity, and how the construction of new African identities can only be dual and hybrid.

References

Barber, Karin. 1999. 'Quotation in the constitution of Yorùbá oral texts'. *Research in African Literatures* 30(2):17–41.

――― 2003. 'Text and performance in Africa'. *Bulletin of the School of Oriental and African Studies* 66(3):324–33.

――― 2007. *The Anthropology of Texts, Persons and Publics: Oral and Written Culture in Africa and Beyond.* Cambridge: Cambridge University Press.

Barthes, Roland. 1977. *The Death of the Author.* In his: *Image-Music-Text* (ed. and trans. Stephen Heath). London: Fontana, 142–9.

Bédier, Joseph. 1907-1908. *Les légendes épiques: recherches sur la formation des chansons de geste.* Paris: Champion, 2 vols.

Belcher, Stephen. 1999. *Epic Traditions of Africa.* Bloomington: Indiana University Press.

Benjamin, Walter. 1968. 'The task of the translator: an introduction to the translation of Baudelaire's *Tableaux parisiens*'. In his: *Illuminations* (ed. by Hannah Arendt, trans. by Harry Zohn). New York: Schocken Books, 69–82.

Biebuyck, Daniel and Kahombo Mateene (eds). 1969. *The Mwindo Epic from the Banyanga (Zaire Republic).* Berkeley: University of California Press.

Blair, Dorothy. 1966. 'Foreword'. In her: *Tales of Amadou Koumba.* London: Oxford University Press.

Boateng, Boatema. 2011. *The Copyright Thing Doesn't Work Here: Adinkra and Kente Cloth and Intellectual Property in Ghana.* Minneapolis and London: University of Minnesota Press.

Bourdieu, Pierre and Claude Passeron. 1970. *La réproduction: éléments pour une théorie du système d'enseignement.* Paris: Editions de Minuit.

Bréal, Michel. 1906. *Pour mieux connaître Homère.* Paris: Hachette.

Camara, Laye. 1978. *Le maître de la parole.* Paris: Plon. (Trans. James Kirkup 1980. *The Guardian of the Word.* Glasgow: Collins.)

De Romilly, Jacqueline. 1983. *Les perspectives actuelles de l'épopée homérique.* Paris: PUF.

Condé, Maryse. 1988. *Moi, Tituba, sorcière noire de Salem.* Paris: Gallimard.

Diawara, Mamadou. 1996. 'Le griot mande à l'heure de la globalisation'. *Cahiers d'Études Africaines* 144(XXXVI)4:591–612.

———— 2011. 'Comment peut-on être auteur? De la création dans un contexte de tradition orale en Afrique subsaharienne'. In: Justin K. Bisanswa and Kasereka Kavwahirehi (eds). *Dire le social dans le roman francophone contemporain*. Paris: Honoré Champion, 33–52.

Diop, Birago. 1961. *Les contes d'Amadou Koumba*. Paris: Présence Africaine (3rd edn). (Trans. Dorothy Blair 1966. *Tales of Amadou Koumba*. London: Oxford University Press.)

Finnegan, Ruth. 1970. *Oral Literature in Africa*. London: Clarendon.

Foucault, Michel. 2001. 'Qu'est-ce qu'un auteur?' In his: *Dits et écrits I, 1954–1975*. Paris: Gallimard (first published 1969 in *Bulletin de la société française de philosophie* 62).

Genette, Gérard. 1982. *Palimpsestes: la littérature au second degré*. Paris: Seuil.

Goodman, Jane. 2002. '"Stealing our heritage?": women's folksongs, copyright law, and the public domain in Algeria'. *Africa Today* 49(1):85–97.

Hampate Bâ, Amadou. 1961. *Koumen: texte initiatique des pasteurs peul*. Paris: Mouton.

Hampate Bâ, Amadou and Lilyan Kesteloot. 1969. *Kaïdara, récit initiatique peul*. Paris: Julliard (Classiques Africains no. 7).

Hennig, Jean-Luc. 1997. *Apologie du plagiat*. Paris: Gallimard.

Irele, Abiola. 2006. 'In search of Camara Laye'. *Research in African Literatures* 37(1):110–27.

Jakobson, Roman. 1963. *Essais de linguistique générale*. Paris: Editions de Minuit.

Julien, Eileen. 1992. *African Novels and the Question of Orality*. Bloomington: Indiana University Press.

Kagame, Alexis. 1952. *La divine pastorale: la naissance de l'univers*. Brussels: Editions du Marais, 2 vols.

Kane, Mohamadou. 1968. 'Les contes d'Amadou Coumba: du conte traditionnel au conte moderne d'expression française'. *Publications de la faculté des lettres et sciences humaines: langues et littératures* (Dakar) 16:229–40.

Kane, Mohamadou. 1982. *Roman africain et traditions*. Dakar: Nouvelles Editions Africaines.

Kazi-Tani and Nora-Alexandra. 1995. *Roman africain de langue française au carrefour de l'écrit et de l'oral (Afrique noire et Maghreb)*. Paris: L'Harmattan.

Kone, Amadou. 1993. *Des textes oraux au roman moderne: étude sur les avatars de la tradition orale dans le roman ouest-africain*. Frankfurt: Verlag für Interkulturelle Kommunikation.

Kristeva, Julia. 1969. *Sèmiôtikè*. Paris: Seuil.

Lejeune, Philippe. 1989. *On Autobiography* (trans. Katherine Leary). Minneapolis: University of Minnesota Press.

Little, Roger. 2006. 'Reflections on a triangular trade in borrowing and stealing: textual exploitation in a selection of African, Caribbean, and European Writers in French'. *Research in African Literatures* 37(1):18–27.

Menéndez Pidal, Ramón. 1960. *La Chanson de Roland et la tradition épique des Francs*. Paris: Picard (2nd edn, trans. Irénée-Marcel Cluzel 1924. *Poesía juglaresca y juglares: aspectos de la historia literaria y cultural de España*. Madrid: Tipografía de la Revista de archivos.).

Milz, Sabine. 2008. 'Inside and outside the hyena's belly: Nega Mezlekia and the politics of time and authorship'. *Journal of Canadian Studies* 42(3):152–71.

Minnis, Alastair. 1984. *Medieval Theory of Authorship: Scholastic Literary Attitudes in the Later Middle Ages*. London: Scholar Press.

Moura, Jean-Marc. 2006. 'Textual ownership in L'Étrange destin de Wangrin d'Amadou Hampâté Bâ'. *Research in African Literatures* 37(1):91–9.

Mudimbe-Boyi, Elisabeth. 2006. *Essais sur les cultures en contact: Afrique, Amériques, Europe*. Paris: Karthala.

Mufuta, Patrice. 1968. *Le chant kasàlà des Luba: textes édités et commentés par Patrice Mufuta*. Paris: Julliard (Classiques Africains 8).

Niane, Djibril Tamsir. 2000. *Soundiata ou l'épopée mandingue*. Paris: Présence Africaine.

Nzabatsinda, Anthère. 1999. '"Tradutore traditore"? Alexis Kagame's transposition of Kinyaruanda poetry into French'. *Journal of African Cultural Studies* 12(2) (Literature and History): 203–10.

Ong, Walter. 1982. *Orality and Literacy: The Technologizing of the Word*. London and New York: Methuen.

Parry, Adam. 1971. 'Introduction'. In: Adam Parry (ed.). *The Making of Homeric Verse: The Collected Papers of Milman Parry*. Oxford: Oxford University Press, ix–lxii.

Paulme, Denise. 1976. *La mère dévorante: essai sur la morphologie des contes africains*. Paris: Gallimard.

Peterson Haviland, Carol and Joan Mullin (eds). 2009. *Who Owns this Text? Plagiarism, Authorship, and Disciplinary Cultures*. Logan: Utah State University Press.

Propp, Vladimir. 1958. *Morphology of the Folktale* (trans. Laurence Scott). Bloomington: Indiana Research Center.

Quayson, Ato. 1997. *Strategic Transformations in Nigerian Writing: Orality and History in the Work of Rev. Samuel Johnson, Amos Tutuola, Wole Soyinka and Ben Okri*. Bloomington: Indiana University Press.

Rifaterre, Michael. 1979. *La production du texte*. Paris: Seuil.

Röschenthaler, Ute. 2011. *Purchasing Culture: The Dissemination of Associations in the Cross River Region of Cameroon and Nigeria*. Trenton: Africa World Press (The Harriet Tubman Series of the African Diaspora).

Scheub, Harold. 1984. *A Review of African Oral Traditions and Literature.* New York: Joint Committee on African Studies of the American Council of Learned Societies and Social Science Research Council.

Tchicaya U Tam'si. 1968. *Légendes africaines.* Paris: Seghers.

Van Den Berghe, Pierre. 1972. Review of *Le chant* kasàlà *des Luba : textes édités et commentés par Patrice Mufuta* (1968). *American Anthropologist* 74:25–6.

Van Gennep, Arnold. 1909. *La question d'Homère: les poèmes homériques, l'archéologie et la poésie populaire.* Paris: Mercure de France.

West, Martin. 2001. *Studies in the Text and Transmission of the Iliad.* Munich: K.G. Saur.

CHAPTER 3

Lion's share

Intellectual property rights and the
South African music industry

©©©©©©©©©©©

VEIT ERLMANN

On 22 March 2006, the world woke up to some unusual news. One of the world's media giants, the *New York Times* reported, had paid an estimated $1.5 million (about £933,000) to a South African family in settlement of a claim of copyright infringement with respect to 'The lion sleeps tonight', a song featured in the Broadway smash hit production *The Lion King*. It was not the first time that the song had been misappropriated: there had been more than 200 adaptations or covers prior to the *The Lion King*. Yet, under the provisions of the British Imperial Copyright Act of 1911 (in force at the time when the original version of 'The lion sleeps tonight' was written), the copyright to a work reverts to the author's estate twenty-five years after his or her death, a provision sometimes called the 'Dickens clause' or simply 'reversionary interest'. And as the composer of 'The lion sleeps tonight' had died in 1962, all uses subsequent to 1987 of the song 'The lion sleeps tonight' were required to be authorized by his estate and should have accrued reversionary interest (Dean 2006a).

Copyright violations are, of course, not uncommon in the music industry. Musicians sue other musicians for allegedly stealing parts of their material; huge amounts of bootlegged CDs and cassettes change hands in the developing countries every day; and peer-to-peer file-sharing continues unabated even if, after years of legal battle, it has been ruled illegal in numerous jurisdictions. So what is so unusual about the settlement of 2006? After all, such settlements are not out of the ordinary either, often saving defendants much larger payments, not to mention a lot of negative publicity. What is unusual is the direction of the charges and the broader context in which the case was brought, for the media giant is none other than Disney Enterprises, Inc., and *The Lion King* one of the most successful musicals ever, playing to packed houses around the world. The South African plaintiffs, for their part, were the three surviving daughters of Solomon Linda, a migrant labourer and the composer of the song 'Mbube'. Substantial parts of 'The lion sleeps tonight' are said to be based on that song. First released in 1939 on the Gallotone label, 'Mbube' is considered to be foundational of a new genre of migrant performance called *mbube* or *isicathamiya*. Unlike Disney shareholders, the Linda daughters lived in abject poverty, the third daughter Adelaide having died of HIV/AIDS because she could not afford the medication that would have prolonged her life.

So what, then, are we dealing with here? The triumph of justice at long last? The victory of reason, markets, property, artists' rights and creativity? For the first time in the history of the global music industry, a major suit was filed by a group of plaintiffs living on the periphery of the global economy against one of the industry's giants headquartered in the West, thus reversing a trend that Malawian-American musician Masauko Chipembere, reacting to the settlement, describes in these words: 'America's contributions are always recognized in Africa, but Africa's contributions are never recognized in America' (Hammonds 2004).

Yet the implications of the settlement go far beyond the fact that it focused attention on one of the most blatant examples of copyright infringement in the history of recorded music. The settlement has a significant impact on the future of intellectual property (IP) protection in the African cultural industries and on cultural practice in developing countries more broadly. It is a lesson in how IP law can perpetuate power imbalances in post-apartheid South Africa (and elsewhere), both in terms of judicial practice and, more especially, in light of the persistence of race in public discourse pertaining to the appropriation of the country's cultural heritage. Through an awkward conflation of race/nation and individual proprietary rights, the Disney lawsuit failed to address the broader moral issues at stake in contemporary cultural practice that transcend proprietary rights. Among these issues is the tendency among proponents of IP expansion and liberal stalwarts of 'free' cross-cultural creativity to reduce appropriation to the appropriation of artistic content, disconnected from the 'social networks and/or cosmological ecologies in which many of the world's peoples' "stories" locate their commitments and obligations' (Coleman and Coombe 2009:176). Another political issue concerns the struggles of artists, fans and activists in the developing world to redefine the relationship between proprietary rights, culture and citizenship in novel ways by counterposing their own *pirate modernity* to Western monolithic definitions of modernity (Sundaram 2009).

The chapter that follows is in three parts. I will begin by examining two seminal 'texts' that stand at the centre of the dispute over Disney's misappropriation of 'Mbube'. The first is 'In the jungle: who owns "The lion sleeps tonight"?', an article by South African journalist Rian Malan that appeared in *Rolling Stone* magazine and in which he charts the trajectory of 'The lion sleeps tonight' from, in his words, a South African 'ditty' to one of the most profitable songs in the history of recorded sound (Malan 2001b). Malan's text formed the backbone of the 'propaganda campaign' mounted by Owen Dean, litigating lawyer and former CEO of the renowned law firm Spoor & Fisher, as well as author of the widely used *Handbook of South African Copyright Law* (Dean 2006b). In Malan's essay, Linda figures as a doubly racialized subject, that is, as an artist who has been subject to exploitation in a system of racial oppression *and* as an individual whose authorship is, if not legally, rhetorically reclaimed in predominantly racial, ethnic and/or national categories, rather than in terms of the growing structural imbalances between private ownership and public access shaping South African cultural production.

The racialization of Linda stands in marked contrast to the findings of a close reading of the second text, Linda's 1939 recording of 'Mbube'. What emerges from this analysis is a form of creative practice that, while it may well fulfil the legal criteria of an original work and thus corroborate Linda's right to authorship, operates outside the racial categories frequently imputed to the work of South African artists. By shifting the focus from the alleged 'African' roots of twentieth-century migrant creative practice to the mechanisms, templates and norms of an industry governed by corporate interests, the analysis thus highlights the racial mythology underpinning liberal concepts of justice in colonial/post-colonial settings, as it casts considerable doubt on the ability of past and current legislation to adequately deal with the complexity of both historical and contemporary black musical practices.

In the second part of the chapter I offer a brief assessment of IP global expansionism and its impact on African cultural industries. The significance of the Disney settlement, I suggest, lies in the fact that it provided ideological support to the effort to establish South Africa as a serious player in the global copyright industries. Spearheaded by the South African government and the private sector, this effort involves and, at the same time, legitimizes the massive expansion of proprietary rights to cultural practices and artefacts that have historically been subject to legal regimes in which proprietary rights are but one of many ways of regulating control over such practices and artefacts. Increasingly, this IP expansionism is supplemented by the thinly veiled claim that the individual rewards to be reaped from a new spirit of musical entrepreneurship by far outweigh the broader social goods realized in communal, 'traditional' forms of cultural practice as a source of innovation and economic growth.

The third and final part of this chapter examines the production of 'original' works through what I call 'practices of the secondary'. In the case of 'Mbube' and 'The lion sleeps tonight', these practices involve a specific form of racial counterfeit in which a text that has become subject to various forms of interpretation and manipulation is not so stripped of its authentic African 'core' as one would assume. The term 'practices of the secondary' is useful, I argue, because unlike potentially derogatory terms such as 'copy', and in contrast to the positive connotations of practices of ambiguous legal status such as 'mash-up', in which two songs are 'stacked' on top of each other (as, for example, Bon Jovi's 'Livin' on a Prayer' has been with The Rolling Stones's 'Start Me Up'), it allows us to examine cultural production beyond the either/ or dichotomies underpinning much of the debate about IP.

'Outpost of civilization' – authorship and the politics of race

Rian Malan is one of the most controversial figures in South African journalism. In the dying days of the apartheid regime, Malan had caused a stir with *My Traitor's Heart*, an award-winning, gut-wrenching account of the hardships of ordinary and some not-so-ordinary people living under apartheid (Malan 1989). The enthusiastic reception of *My Traitor's Heart* (the book has been translated into more than ten languages) was only surpassed by the stir created by an essay entitled 'In the jungle: who owns "The lion sleeps tonight"?' (Malan 2001a). First published in 2001 in *Rolling Stone Magazine* and since anthologized numerous times, 'In the jungle' caused a minor tsunami in the music industry and inspired Cape Town-based film director François Verster to make the documentary *The Lion's Trail*. While all this helped to establish Malan's image as a champion of righteous causes, a slightly different kind of response greeted a series of articles written between 2001 and 2003 in which Malan distanced himself from the community of HIV/AIDS activists, by suggesting that the leading cause of death in South Africa was not the disease, and that health professionals were exaggerating the statistics in order to obtain more funding (Malan 2001b, 2003).

Here, then, is an excerpt from 'In the jungle':

> This is an African yarn, which begins ... in the loneliest outposts of
> civilization. One such place is Gordon Memorial School, perched on the rim
> of a wild valley called Msinga, which lies in the Zulu heartland, about 300
> miles southeast of Johannesburg. Among the half-naked herd boys who drift
> through the mission is a rangy kid called Solomon Linda, born 1909.... He
> and his friends sing at weddings and feasts.

In the mid-Thirties they shake off the dust and cow shit and take the train to Johannesburg, city of gold, where they move into the slums and become kitchen boys and factory hands. Life is initially very perplexing. Solly keeps his eyes open and transmutes what he sees into songs that he and his home boys perform a cappella on weekends. He has songs about work, songs about crime, songs about how banks rob you by giving you paper in exchange for real money, songs about how rudely the whites treat you when you go to get your pass stamped. People like the music. Solly and his friends develop a following. Within two years they turn themselves into a very cool urban act that wears pinstriped suits, bowler hats and dandy two-tone shoes. They become Solomon Linda and the Evening Birds, inventors of a music that will later become known as isicathamiya, arising from the warning cry, 'Cothoza, bafana' – tread carefully, boys.

Careful treaders were an embarrassment, widely decried for their 'primitive' bawling and backward lyrics, which dwelled on such things as witchcraft, crime and using love potions to get girls. The groups had names like the Naughty Boys or the Boiling Waters, and when World War II broke out, some started calling themselves 'mbombers after the dive-bombing Stukas they'd seen on newsreels. 'Mbombers were by far the coolest and most dangerous black thing of their time.

The Evening Birds were spotted by a talent scout in 1938 and taken to the top of an office building in downtown Jo'burg.... Solomon Linda and the Evening Birds cut several songs, but the one we're interested in was called 'Mbube'.... It was a simple three-chord ditty with lyrics something along the lines of, 'Lion! Ha! You're a lion!' inspired by an incident in the Birds' collective Zulu boyhood when they chased lions that were stalking their father's cattle. The first take was a dud, as was the second.... The third take almost collapsed at the outset as the unrehearsed musicians dithered and fished for the key, but once they started cooking, the song was glory bound. 'Mbube' wasn't the most remarkable tune, but there was something terribly compelling about the underlying chant, a dense meshing of low male voices above which Solomon yodeled and howled for two exhilarating minutes, occasionally making it up as he went along. The third take was the great one, but it achieved immortality only in its dying seconds, when Solly took a deep breath, opened his mouth and improvised the melody that the world now associates with these words: In the jungle, the lion sleeps tonight.

(Malan 2001a:65)

Malan here deploys a whole arsenal of stereotypes about migrant labourers, Zululand and African music. For instance, the Msinga area is described as 'wild' and a lonely 'outpost of civilization', and not as a dumping ground for migrant labour; a product, that is, of a 'wild' system of capitalist exploitation and as such integral to its operation. By the time Linda moves to Johannesburg, Solomon becomes Solly – echoing the white missus imposing an unwelcome sense of inter-racial intimacy on the garden 'boy'. Meanwhile the music retains all of its 'glorious rawness'. With its 'rocking' sound, 'simple' and 'improvised', made-up melody, it is the work of perplexed, 'unrehearsed' musicians.

Elsewhere in his piece, Malan attributes to Linda's composition a 'subversively rhythmic intensity', a feature he claims to have been introduced to South Africa by African-American performers such as Orpheus McAdoo and his Virginia Vaudeville Company, which toured South Africa for many years in the late nineteenth century. Of course, the notion of African-American music as 'subversive' and as being of 'rhythmic intensity' is a well-worn racial stereotype – so well-worn, in fact, that Malan, an accomplished rock guitarist, cannot help referring to his own 'truly astonishing sense of rhythm' without the qualifier 'for a white man' (Whyle 2011). But to hear the 'Orpheus-inspired syncopation thing', as Malan calls it (Malan 2001a:65), in Linda's 'Mbube' is completely erroneous, as a quick look at the responsorial relationship between the chorus and the leader shows. What is striking here is the absence of the non-simultaneous entry of the vocal parts, one of the main principles of Zulu vocal polyphony and a key component of African temporality. The simultaneous entry of the solo and the chorus is so accurate that it is impossible to consider this synchronism as the complete overlapping of 'call' and 'response'. The reason for this lack of the 'Orpheus-inspired syncopation thing' is that the lead singer's part, in the terms of Western functional harmony, is contingent on the chord progression of the chorus. Throughout the seventeen cycles the beginning of Linda's solo phrases coincides with the first note of the choral response and in all cases it is the tonic that is being stated.

What about 'unrehearsed musicians' and 'made-up' melodies? The regularity exhibited by the responsorial structure moving in synchrony with the basic harmonic framework is enhanced by the pairing of basic phrases and their syntactic arrangement in an overall symmetry. For instance, each cycle consists of four bars, and each bar contains only one chord. Moreover, two of the three melodic patterns sung by the lead singer are grouped in strict binary fashion. Hardly the stuff of an impromptu performance.

This rigid temporal organization of 'Mbube', finally, is mirrored in the polyphonic texture, one of the many parameters of musical organization routinely neglected in legal disputes over authorship. There are four parts called soprano, *altha* (alto), *thena* (tenor) and *bhes* (bass). The soprano part is sung by the leader, while alto and tenor are sung by one singer each. The bass part is taken by the remaining singers and consists of a fairly busy ostinato pattern whose strong triadic structure suggests the harmonic framework of the song. What is remarkable here is that this set-up very neatly reflects the vocal style being taught by dour missionaries at Gordon Memorial School. 'Mbube' choirs, from the outset, have been modelled on Western mixed choirs, soprano and *altha* substituting the female voice parts that were lacking in the all-male environment of migrant life. But this act of mimesis was mediated by a complex set of connotations based on migrant performers' conception of Western music as an articulated whole of performance style, aesthetics and social practice. For instance, a synonym for *bhes*, the bass part, is *doshaba*, those who sing the Do. In calling themselves *doshaba* these singers explicitly link the organizational structure of a choir to the idea of Western tonality, and not to an authentic Zulu core.

Clearly, 'Mbube' is anything but raw, spontaneous, subversive or, for that matter, 'African'. Instead, it represents a carefully rehearsed and shrewdly designed attempt at mobilizing a range of Western techniques as a way of working through migrants' experience of moving in and out of multiple social contexts and identities. 'Mbube' engages the conflicting strands of the migrant experience not from a position of racial difference located outside the text, but rather from within its own syntax and, more importantly perhaps, in the performative chain of signifiers it brings to the fore. This is why Malan's well-intentioned portrait of Linda deprives the singer of his agency in shaping the terms of engagement with the global music industry from a distinct, albeit almost defenceless, position. 'Mbube' is not concerned with setting up a separate code or with ironically setting a local world of authentic truth in opposition to white culture. Nor does the song parody the rigidity of Western mass-produced musical forms. Rather, it subtly inflects the received structure, and uses it as a mask behind which to focus on the chain of signifiers. 'Mbube', even where it seems to be cast in a Western mould, draws attention to the process of signification, rather than to a specific meaning as such.

Scholars of African-American performance have long insisted that such strategies of signification, in which the black subject is simultaneously being denied and evading the fixity and stability of the Enlightenment's transcendental ego, are crucial for those performing in the shadow of modernity (Gates 1988). By highlighting the alternative forms of identity and cultural appropriation (Schur 2009) embedded in and enabled by many forms of black creativity, these scholars have underscored the power of these creative practices to transform the very conditions under which they are being produced. Hence, whether by casting Solomon Linda as unrecognized African hero and unrehearsed, improvising natural genius or, for that matter, by constructing Linda as property holder, the 'propaganda campaign' mounted by Spoor & Fisher imputes the unity of the enlightened liberal subject to more fluid, alternative ways of grounding subjectivity in non-possessive forms of creativity.

Going global – the South African music industry in the twenty-first century

Recent years have witnessed an unusual amount of attention being paid to a rather unlikely player in Africa's search for meaningful participation in global affairs: the music industry. This may come as a bit of a surprise, as the African recording industry, after humble beginnings in the early years of the twentieth century and a steady rise until the cassette era, appears to be teetering on the brink of collapse. For instance, in 1999 the retail value of sound carrier (cassettes, CDs etc.) sales in Africa hovered around a mere 0.5 per cent of the global value of sound carrier sales. In contrast, in the same year the core copyright industries in the US contributed well over $250 billion (about £155 billion) to the economy annually, while the South African music industry, with 95 per cent of the total of sound carrier sales in Africa, was worth only about one billion Rand, i.e. a mere 140 million dollars. This picture did not change much in the 2000s, even though the South African market has doubled in size: in 2007 the US market accounted for 31 per cent of global sales, while only 0.778 per cent of world sales were realized in South Africa (Shaw 2010:209).

The broader economic picture on the African continent is even gloomier. With the near meltdown of the global financial system in 2008 having made short shrift of the goal set forth in the United Nations Millennium Declaration to eradicate extreme poverty by 2015, sub-Saharan Africa is the world's region most affected by the downturn. Nearly half of its population now lives under the international poverty line of $1 (about £0.60) a day.

There appears to be agreement that among the long list of problems plaguing Africa, the continent's declining share in international trade – which dropped from 5 per cent in the 1980s to less than 3 per cent in the 1990s and early 2000s – is one of the most severe. Sub-Saharan Africa is facing enormous obstacles to accessing markets in the developed world in areas where it holds a clear advantage, such as agriculture. These difficulties are compounded by African countries' inability to effectively negotiate better terms for competing in the global economy.

Yet, despite all these sobering figures (which are mitigated somewhat by a slightly brighter outlook over the last three years or so), observers see signs that the African music industry is rebounding. According to a study commissioned by the South African Department of Arts, Culture, Science and Technology (DACST), the South African music industry is on a par with that of countries like Colombia, Bulgaria, the Czech Republic and Brazil (DACST

1998). And if one looks at growth rates, the South African music industry is the fifteenth fastest-growing industry in the world.

Since the transition to majority rule in 1994, South Africa has moved to revitalize its music industry, aggressively promoting international sales and enforcing copyright legislation. The key players in this process, much like the larger reform effort after the demise of apartheid, are the state and the private sector. Other sectors of civil society, although a major force in other areas pertaining to IP, such as the right to produce generic retro-viral drugs, play a marginal role. Small wonder, that the overarching goal guiding these initiatives is framed in nationalist rhetoric, by the idea, that is, of placing South Africa on the international map as what one government-sponsored enquiry into the music industry calls a 'musical nation' (DACST 1998:88). This not only means that the government is seeking to emulate the success of other countries in defining 'national' styles as vital components of their economy, such as reggae in Jamaica, but that this national significance requires the government to play a major role in promoting and, in particular, providing legal protection for music considered to be of local origin.

In terms of the first goal – the promotion of local music – little headway appears to have been made in significantly altering the percentages of local and international sound-carrier sales: in 2000 20 per cent of sold units were of local origin, down from 23 per cent in 1996 and only slightly up from 19.6 per cent in 1994. Ironically, by 2007 the share of local product had increased to an unparalleled 52 per cent. In considering these figures we have to bear in mind that 'local' is not the same as 'African'. In South Africa, especially, a significant portion of local sound carriers are recordings by cover bands playing any number of Western styles, from pop to jazz. By contrast, it is fair to say that 'trad' (industry jargon for non-copyrighted music) has all but disappeared from the country's musical landscape, and that what little is left of the music of the past is big business dressed up as folklore. Such is the case with Ladysmith Black Mambazo, often held up as the country's most successful and, with two Grammys under its belt, internationally visible and yet profoundly local group. Another example are the myriad gospel groups which, although not strictly speaking traditional groups, are steeped in religious tradition and at the same time function as major industry players that tour worldwide and net millions of dollars annually.

Under these circumstances, it is no wonder that much of the debate surrounding the fantasy of the 'musical nation' as the pre-eminent source and home of local product has been framed in terms of a rather basic dichotomy; that is, whether in order to increase the economic and trade benefits of intellectual property the African music industry should target international audiences with international content or whether, by contrast, it stands a greater chance of succeeding globally by emphasizing local content. Of course, the supposed contrast between international, i.e. Western-oriented content and local African 'ideas' has shaped much of the debate about African cultural policy even before the advent of digital technology. Yet, like all dichotomies, the international/local binary serves to position stakeholders in a power struggle over interpretational sovereignty and the material benefits arising from it, rather than describing any particular meaningful practice. Thus, while the male a cappella choir Ladysmith Black Mambazo may be perceived in the West as a distinctly South African act with cross-over appeal, South African *kwaito* is seen as a variant of US hip-hop mostly performed in African languages and thus of limited appeal to US consumers. South African fans, in turn, would reject the notion that *kwaito* is local, with much of the hip-hop culture surrounding *kwaito* perhaps better being understood, borrowing a phrase coined by Charles Piot (1999), as 'remotely global'.

This leaves us with a second strand of the argument, that the African music industry may serve as a capacity-building force and that better copyright protection for African musicians is a vital component of the industry's revival. One of the most frequently invoked concepts in this regard is that of musical entrepreneurship. Having evolved in the aftermath of the devastating effects on the music industry of bootlegging, mp3 and peer-to-peer file-sharing, musical entrepreneurship is being fetishized by a chorus of voices that includes the World Bank, WIPO and WTO officials, local governments, NGOs and other development agencies as a wonder pill curing the woes not just of the culture industries but of entire nations. Broadly speaking, the rhetoric of musical entrepreneurship combines classical components of entrepreneurship such as innovation, creativity and individual risk-taking, with the recognition that in the information age such creativity and innovation predominantly occur in those areas that are governed by copyright law or patent law, i.e. works of art, software and patents. The ideal musical entrepreneur, in this perspective, would be a person who single-handedly develops patrons, starts a performing venue, becomes his own marketing department, acquires all the social and business skills of personnel found in conventional A & R (Artist and Repertoire) departments and, ultimately, in this way creates a new business model.

One may agree or disagree with this image of the musical entrepreneur as a viable alternative to the business models espoused by a struggling industry in the West, but attempts to map this image on the African landscape often border on naivety at best, or, worse, downright Orientalism. For instance, according to a 2005 law thesis there are two factors that distinguish the music industry from other IP systems and 'make it more suitable for African nations as a tool for economic recovery'. The first is the 'fact that music is based mainly in the natural talent of the rights-owner, and very little if any research and development costs are involved in the initial process of composition or performance of music' (Baloyi 2005:32).

There can be no denying, of course, that in order to make good music a minimum of talent is required. What is problematic is the largely unspoken conflation of 'natural' talent, ownership and Africa. The notion that Africa is blessed with an abundance of musical talent which only awaits 'discovery' (presumably from the outside) merges with the author-owner trope that has been one of the pillars of IP law since its inception in the eighteenth century. It is simply a myth to assume that music – in Africa or elsewhere – originates from the creative wellspring of an individual author, without the intervention of tradition, convention and, most importantly, technology. The musical entrepreneur of the twenty-first century is surrounded by an array of technologies, from the home studio worth thousands of dollars, to access to the internet. Since the vast majority of African 'talent' does not have access to such R & D (Recording and Distribution) tools (and the World Bank is unlikely to equip each and every one of the 30,000 musicians said to be active in Senegal alone with a home studio or a broadband connection), the image of the naturally talented rights-owner immersed in low-cost composition flies in the face of complex social networks such as those driving Congolese rumba. As Bob White has shown in his wonderfully evocative study *Rumba Rules*, Congolese music for decades flourished, and sustained a sizeable portion of the Congolese local and expatriate economy in Europe and North America, on the basis of a highly stratified set of power relationships. And it did so even when these relationships contravened Western industry standards or IP law (White 2008).

The second factor that distinguishes the music industry from other IP systems and makes it more suitable for African nations as a tool for economic recovery, according to the author of the law thesis, is that

> virtually all people simply love and appreciate music of some kind.
> Consequently new employment markets and avenues do not necessarily
> have to be researched before starting a successful career in music.
>
> (Baloyi 2005:32)

The assumption here is not only that African audiences are an undifferentiated mass with little or no concern for aesthetic choices, but that the African music market operates in a hyper-autonomous sphere, devoid of any agency or interest on the part of either consumers or producers. Of course, the South African music industry is not an island where different standards and strategies apply. As part of the global cultural industries, it is volatile and extremely sensitive to fluctuations of the market and, hence, highly dependent on research. Similar assumptions govern the World Bank's 'Africa Music Project' and various other initiatives (Penna, Thormann and Finger 2004). What is striking, then, is not so much the fact that institutions such as the World Bank would devote (albeit limited) resources to developing new policy spaces such as the African music industry in order to build African capacity for international trade, but that they do so on the basis of notions and recommendations that may have worked, if at all, in the nineteenth century, but are likely to undermine the broader objective of levelling the playing field by cementing Western hegemonic notions of originality, creativity and so on.

Practices of the secondary – making music 'African'

Joel Baloyi does not stand alone in his blanket defence of IP expansionism. A growing number of websites such as afro-ip.org and other initiatives suggest that the majority of African artists, intellectuals and activists welcome the protection promised by the wholesale expansion of IP law. But like indigenous communities elsewhere, many African communities – painfully aware of the long history of misappropriation of their natural resources and traditional knowledge – are also keen to expand the protection afforded mainly to Western IP through international agreements such as TRIPS to areas of knowledge and information that have previously been governed by different notions of property and legal access.

In many ways, this ready adoption of international IP regimes seems to bypass the critique advanced by legal scholars working within the field of Critical Legal Studies of the aggressive role of IP law in shaping concepts of authorship, creativity and subjectivity in global cultural production (Austin and Simon 2003; Coombe 1998). Legal systems of IP, these critics argue, do not exist in an autonomous sphere of rights and obligations that is separate from an extra-legal, social world in which claims are being generated which then require legal resolutions. Rather, IP law often produces the very signs and symbols with which social differences are given meaning in the first place. IP law is, in fact, not just part of culture, it is culture.

As crucial as the 'law as culture' concept is for contesting the corporate hold on IP, it tends to revolve around largely unexamined Western notions of creativity as an autonomous sphere. In the African context such notions are counterproductive because they fail to recognize the cultural spaces in which creativity becomes meaningful on the basis of socially contingent forms and relations. Thus, I depart from both conventional 'instrumentalist' interpretations of law and the critical perspective of law as a coercive force imposing itself on an unruly cultural sphere. I propose that musical practice shares with the law a fundamental concern with normativity. The relationship between musicians, audiences and the music industry – and frequently the way these are encoded within music itself – often appear to be more rule-like, canonical and self-referential than the model of law underpinning legal scholarship, having a profound impact on – and in many ways even creating – some of law's taken-for-granted concepts of authorship, originality and appropriation. Consequently, such practices do not stand outside the law, as in the majority of studies on music and IP, which frame the relationship between the music industry and the law as that of two distinct realms, music *and* the law; rather they are to be seen *as* law.

The law-like normativity of musical practice becomes most apparent perhaps in what I call the genealogy of originals. This is obviously an oxymoron. How can something that is original be traced further back to another work preceding it? If the status of musical works as original creations (and individual property) is established through legal acts, 'original' works also result from the normative power of mass-mediated processes of duplication. They thus have a genealogy that cannot be reduced to an author or to the moment of fixing. Rather they are the product of a more dialectical process than the one described by the majority of studies on IP and music. Instead of considering musical works ('songs') as 'originals' whose (mostly melodic) core subsequently becomes subject, in whatever form, to manipulation through sampling, mash-ups and other such secondary practices made possible by digital technology (see also Mose in this volume), I am reluctant to reduce the status of these secondary practices to that of subversive acts or mere 'copies'. And in contrast to post-structuralist theories of authorship that see the author, following Foucault, as a mere 'function', I see such appropriations as key vehicles in the production of normative, albeit culturally and historically contingent, concepts of (musical) substance, authority and ownership.

Covers are a case in point. From a cultural perspective, such adaptations of a – contemporary or previously recorded – commercially released song are not usually defined by the relative degree of similarity to or difference from a primary text or the song covered. Rather, they can and often do bestow on works the status of originals precisely because they add something to such works that has been absent from them in the beginning. This may happen when musicians wish to pay homage to other musicians whom they admire, or, conversely, when they wish to distance themselves from established traditions by irony or satire. In either case, the 'something' that is being added is often richer, more authentic and meaningful than the original. In a logic akin to horticulture, one might argue with Jacques Derrida, covers are a form of grafting. And as the part grafted onto another plant is not a supplement of a lesser status, but is the plant itself, now improved, covers as a form of grafting might be said to erase the distinction between original and copy (Derrida 1988).

How then does this dialectic of original and copy play out in 'The lion sleeps tonight'? Recorded in 1960 by the Tokens, the song quickly gained worldwide popularity, topping the charts for three consecutive weeks in 1961, ahead of The Beatles. In terms of melodic material, the Tokens cover is clearly indebted to Linda's 1939 recording, even though the phrase that occurs only in the recording's 'dying seconds' becomes the central element. But there are also a number of additional elements that arranger George Weiss (who is now credited along with Linda as a co-author of the song) inserted into the cover, especially a number of shouts and drum triplets.

From a technical vantage point, these triplets and shouts might of course be easily dismissed as 'handicraft'. At the same time, however, they do substantial cultural work; they veil the deadly monotony of the cover through some kind of performed 'Africanness', suggesting emotional spontaneity and 'rhythmic intensity' as key markers of African performance practice and, hence, as the mark of an original, racial subject at work. They are, thus, false currency or, as Carol Clover puts it in a parallel discussion of white appropriations of black dance in film, they are 'the "memories" that surface in the process of "forgetting", as though in a perverse bargain, they must be admitted *in order* to be overridden' (Clover 1995:743). In the same breath as the triplets and shouts remember the 'African' origins of 'Mbube', they forget them. Put another way, drums and 'wild' cries restore to the original, in a token act of equal exchange, an authenticity they denied to it by 'theft' in the first place.

Much the same can of course be observed in the infringing version used in *The Lion King*. Based on the Tokens version and arranged by South African composer Lebo M., it features an amalgam of pennywhistle playing (a hallmark of *kwela*, a 1960s urban street music), xylophone sounds and thickly layered choral textures enveloped in heavy reverb; all markers of 'Africa'.

Arguably, then, in recognizing that reversionary interest was to fall to the Linda heirs, the settlement between the Linda estate and Disney does more than establish the ownership of 'Mbube'. It in fact returns something to Linda, the individual, that was not part of his identity from the beginning. In proscribing certain forms of appropriation as theft, IP law does not authenticate individuals as holders of rights over their works, so much as it creates additional layers of meaning in which key aspects of cultural production in many parts of the world outside of Western consumer society – such as concepts of authorship – are being fundamentally altered.

If my hypothesis has any merit, it becomes rather difficult to maintain the notion that expressions of the mind can ever exist as originals. Does this mean, however, that there should be no legal protection for artists? I think not. What is questionable, I believe, is the tendency to reduce conflicts over the legitimacy of copies and the resolution of such conflicts to the a priori

distinction between a primary and a derivative work. The debate in South
Africa about alternative forms of IP has only just begun, and much as in parts of
the developed North it is increasingly taking on an aggressive, polarized form.
The proponents of a more flexible IP regime allowing for more exceptions and
limitations, such as the South African members of the A2K projects, appear
to be a minority. Much the same can be said about arguments in favour of the
attempt to balance intellectual property rights and constitutional rights such
as the freedom of expression. While such a scenario is not widely discussed, a
2005 trademark case heard on appeal at South Africa's Constitutional Court,
while reserving judgment on the freedom of expression, did affirm that
freedom of expression and intellectual property rights are of equal status, and
have to be dealt with on a case-by-case basis.[1] While it is not inconceivable
that the verdict might at some future point be applied to a case involving
copyright law, a more likely development in the medium term will involve the
very same 'Dickens clause' under which the action against Disney Inc. was
brought initially. If reinstated, if only for a limited time, the provision would go
a long way not only in offering redress for injustices suffered by the country's
musicians in the past, but it might also help to make a more stringent case for
linking intellectual property rights with social justice.

---

1   Laugh It Off Promotions CC v South African Breweries International (Finance)
     BV t/a Sabmark International and Another (CCT42/04) [2005] ZACC 7; 2006 (1)
     SA 144 (CC); 2005 (8) BCLR 743 (CC) [27 May 2005].

References

Austin, Sarat and Jonathan Simon (eds). 2003. *Cultural Analysis, Cultural Studies, and the Law: Moving Beyond Legal Realism*. Durham: Duke University Press.

Baloyi, Jele Joel. 2005. Intellectual Property, Entrepreneurship and the Music Industry: A New Ray of Hope for enhancing African International Trade Capacity. A South African Case Study. LLM thesis, University of Western Cape.

Clover, Carol. 1995. 'Dancin' in the rain'. *Critical Inquiry* 24:722–47.

Coleman, Elizabeth and Rosemary Coombe. 2009. 'A broken record: subjecting "Music" to Cultural Rights'. In: James Young and Conrad Brunk (eds). *The Ethics of Cultural Appropriation*. Chichester: Blackwell, 173–210.

Coombe, Rosemary. 1998. *The Cultural Life of Intellectual Properties: Authorship, Appropriation and the Law*. Durham: Duke University Press.

Dean, Owen. 2006a. 'Case law: the return of the lion'. *WIPO Magazine* 2:8–10.

——— 2006b. *Handbook of South African Copyright Law*. Johannesburg: Juta & Co.

Department of Arts, Culture, Science and Technology (DACST). 1998. *Cultural Industries Growth Strategy (CIGS): The South African Music Industry*. Pretoria.

Derrida, Jacques. 1988. *Limited Inc*. Evanston: Northwestern University Press.

Gates, Henry Louis, Jr. 1988. *The Signifying Monkey: A Theory of Afro-American Literary Criticism*. New York: Oxford University Press.

Hammonds, Alyse B. 2004. 'Johannesburg vs. Mickey Mouse'. *Black College View* 1(1):1.

Malan, Rian. 1989. *My Traitor's Heart: A South African Exile Returns to Face his Country, his Tribe and his Conscience*. New York: Atlantic Monthly Press.

——— 2001a. 'In the Jungle'. In: Harold Evans (ed.). *The Best American Magazine Writing 2001*. New York: Public Affairs, 50–82.

——— 2001b. 'AIDS in Africa: in search of the truth'. *Rolling Stone Magazine*, 22 November 2001.

——— 2003. 'Africa isn't dying of Aids'. *Spectator*, 14 December 2003.

Penna, Frank, Monique Thormann and Michael Finger. 2004. 'The Africa Music Project'. In: Michael Finger and Philip Schuler (eds). *Poor People's Knowledge: Promoting Intellectual Property in Developing Countries*. Washington: World Bank Publications, 95–112.

Piot, Charles. 1999. *Remotely Global: Village Modernity in West Africa*. Chicago: University of Chicago Press.

Schur, Richard. 2009. *Parodies of Ownership: Hip-Hop Aesthetics and Intellectual Property Law*. Ann Arbor: University of Michigan Press.

Shaw, Jonathan. 2010. *The South African Music Business*. Johannesburg: ada enup cc.

Sundaram, Ravi. 2009. *Pirate Modernity: Delhi's Media Urbanism*. New York: Routledge.

White, Bob. 2008. *Rumba Rules: The Politics of Dance Music in Mobutu's Zaire*. Durham: Duke University Press.

Whyle, James. 2011. Rian Malan – The Information. Found at: www.icon.co.za/~whyle/MALAN.htm, accessed 15 December 2011.

II

CREATING NORMS AND GENRES:

MODELLING, QUOTING AND MIXING

CHAPTER 4

Authorship, copyright and quotation in oral and print spheres in early colonial Yorubaland

ⒸⒸⒸⒸⒸⒸⒸⒸⒸⒸ

Karin Barber

In this chapter, I will explore a zone of experimentation in which a local intelligentsia in Lagos, Nigeria, tried out the potentials of print alongside those of oral creativity in the Yoruba language. My suggestion is that in this case (as in many others in colonial West Africa) we need to jettison any simple model of a collective folk orality appropriated and transformed by the 'impact' of an alien system of intellectual property rights. What we see in early twentieth-century Lagos is a highly educated elite, well aware of the uses of copyright law, applying it selectively alongside other very different conceptions of text in order to constitute a new kind of print sphere. The Yoruba newspapers of the 1920s reveal how creatively these writers and readers brought into juxtaposition – within the same pages and often within the same text – ideas of anonymity and named authorship, of individual ownership and shared textual resources, and of a known coterie audience and an indefinitely wide public. In doing this they mobilized some of the aesthetic and creative dispositions already present in a tradition of complex Yoruba oral texts.

Print has transformative potential, and 'print revolutions' have occurred worldwide. But we cannot subsume all these histories into a single universal narrative moving from orality through scribal culture into print, with the same effects and outcomes at every stage. It is more interesting to try to pinpoint specificity: in this case, to identify what it was that made the 1920s print culture of Lagos singular – 'original' in Jane Guyer's sense of the term (Guyer 1996) – and thus expand our sense of the possible forms that cultural innovation can take in specific historical circumstances.

In a pioneering and influential study, Elizabeth Eisenstein showed how, in late fifteenth-century Europe, print began to transform a thousand-year-old scribal culture. With the increasing commodification of text and ascription of ownership to named individual authors, ideas of copyright began to emerge. The beginnings of mechanical mass production of a fixed, standardized product raised questions of property rights in a new way. In the pre-print era, 'makers of books' were more often than not people who copied or annotated existing texts, adding their own contributions in the process. The thirteenth-century St Bonaventura listed the *scriptor* (copyist), the *compilator* (someone who copied a text but also added others' material), the *commentator* (someone who copied a text and also added his or her own comments) and the *auctor* (someone who wrote his or her own text and added those of others for confirmation) (Eisenstein 1979:121–2). This shows that manuscript production was in some ways akin to many oral modes of textual production, where each transmitter of the text may make incremental changes – embedding commentary, expansion or elaboration in the act of performance, but without claiming credit for, let alone ownership of, the whole text. In print manufacture, because of the fixity and exact reproducibility of the printed text, it became easier to distinguish between authorial, editorial and mechanical roles – easier to distinguish between an individual's creation and the tradition within which he or she worked. Only the person able to position him/herself as the originator of the text became its owner, with rights controlling its sale, use and further reproduction during and beyond his or her lifetime.

Eisenstein suggests that with the advent of the idea of the text as a property, rights in which could be owned, there arose the idea that individual authorial originality was what gave the text its value. Plagiarism at worst, derivative writing at best, was the judgment on those whose generation of text hewed too closely to the shared resources of a tradition. But, I would emphasize, while the author became more distinctive and highly specified, the reader became less so: print culture fostered the conception of an anonymous reading public, in principle unknown and indefinitely extensive. Because print survived not through the careful transmission of precious handwritten copies through family generations, but rather through multiplication of instantiations of a given text – some of which survived even when many others perished – and because to make the investment in printing presses pay off, ever expanding markets had to be conquered, it became normal to conceptualize books and other printed texts as going out to unknown places and people, as well as potentially being read simultaneously by large numbers. This conception of the potential public (even when actual print runs were comparatively small) underpinned or was informed by new ideas of self and other. In Europe, this history of the commodification of text, the invention of the author and the conceptualization of the anonymous, extensive public unfolded over several hundred years.

In most of Anglophone West Africa, however, writing and print arrived simultaneously,[1] installed by missionaries from the mid-nineteenth century onwards, and adopted and utilized by colonial administration. Manuscript and print thus coexisted from their inception, and both interacted extensively with a vital and evolving repertoire of oral genres. Indeed, in the earliest days of missionary education in Western Nigeria, many adult pupils learnt to read but not to write, and were familiar only with printed characters, not with handwriting (Ajayi 1965:133). Thus print in a sense preceded manuscript culture. And though the Protestant missionaries' aim was to awaken converts' 'conscience' (Peel 2000:250–5) and foster inner edification through reading, what local intelligentsias seized upon was the inherently public nature of print. Unlike a handwritten letter, diary or recipe, print is always outward-turning, addressed to a plurality of others. The Lagos elite from the second half of the nineteenth century onwards focused on print as a means to constitute a quasi-secular urban public culture around civic, social and political concerns. Print was seen as a means to promote civic virtues, foster progress, benefit future generations, inspire the black race to self-affirmation, and to retrieve and preserve cultural heritage. The Church Missionary Society's news-sheet *Iwe Irohin,* published in Abẹokuta 1859–67, was soon dwarfed by a succession of Lagos weekly and fortnightly newspapers owned and edited by elite individuals interested in public, civic and social affairs.

But their imagined reading public, addressed as indefinitely large, extending to the 'four corners of the world' and into the future, was in actuality anchored in a very small educated stratum concentrated in Lagos and along the West African coast in the nineteenth century, with the addition in the early twentieth century of ribbons of enclaves up the railway line, where educated people were posted as civil servants and representatives of commercial firms. The real readership was made up of people many of whom were personally known to the newspapers' editor-proprietors and were often addressed by name. Address to the unknown, indefinitely extensive public could at any moment switch to a playful or intimate wink to a fellow-member of the clubby, oligarchic urban culture of Lagos. This sense of the public being simultaneously immensely extensive and abstract, and highly specific and localized, gave rise to a play with anonymity and disclosure that permeated the 1920s Yoruba press, as it did the English-language press brilliantly analysed

---

1   That is to say, writing in Roman script. Manuscripts written in Arabic script – in African languages as well as Arabic itself – pre-existed the missionary endeavour but were not widely used outside the context of Islamic scholarly circles.

by Stephanie Newell (2013). Pseudonyms were used all the time, sometimes concealing, sometimes advertising the identity of the writer. That these creative ploys were a conscious art is shown in their concentrated use in the text now known as the 'first Yoruba novel', *Itan Igbesi-Aiye Emi Ṣegilọla* ('the life-story of me, Ṣegilọla'), which was published in the weekly newspaper *Akede Eko* in the form of a series of letters purporting to be from an ageing and repentant prostitute writing under the nickname Ṣegilọla. The central narrative ploy is an artful and prolonged tease about who the 'real' Ṣegilọla was (see Barber 2012; Newell 2013).

Litigious Lagos

Print and the law were the twin engines of political action in 1920s Lagos. Electoral politics was making its tentative debut, with a severely limited franchise and a small number of elected positions on the Lagos Town Council and the newly constituted Nigerian Legislative Council. But the issues which galvanized the townspeople and gained popular followings for leading members of the elite throughout the 1920s were carried forward mainly through lawsuits and newspaper campaigns. The most prominent of these issues was the 'Eleko affair'. The Eleko or traditional ruler of Lagos was suspended, and then deposed and exiled in 1925, by the colonial government. The Eleko had little official power, but great symbolic significance for the majority of Lagos townspeople. Radical members of the elite, led by Herbert Macaulay, seized the opportunity to acquire a popular following by championing the cause of the Eleko and campaigning to get him reinstated.

The Eleko affair sparked off an explosion of activity in both the press and the law-courts. On the back of it, newspapers proliferated: in 1920 there were three English-language weekly newspapers and none in Yoruba; by 1931, when the Eleko was finally reinstated, eleven new English-language papers had been created, including six dailies, as well as no fewer than five Yoruba-language weeklies (Omu 1978:253–4). Some of the English-language papers and all of the Yoruba ones supported Macaulay and the Eleko, with a constant stream of editorials, poems, commentaries, polemics and historical arguments. In tandem with the press, the pro-Eleko party mobilized the law. The day after the Eleko's deposition was announced, in August 1925, Macaulay's lawyer friends went to court to contest the legality of the order. For the next six years they exerted pressure on the government through a series of court cases, which eventually reached the Privy Council and paved the way for the Eleko's reinstatement. The press and the law were intertwined and mutually reinforcing. The Eleko court cases were all exhaustively reported in the Lagos press, sometimes with verbatim transcripts, and every nuance of successive rulings was examined, explained and commented upon in detail. The

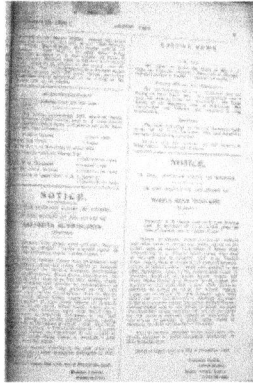

Figure 4.1   Akede Eko, 10 January 1929; legal notices were a staple of this paper (digital photograph by K. Barber in the Nigerian National Archive, Ibadan).

government's handling of the legal case was in turn affected by fear of further agitation stirred up, as they saw it, by the press.

But the twin centrality of the law and the press in Lagos civic and political life did not depend only on the Eleko issue, prominent as that was. Newspapers drew on legal news of all kinds as a staple source of material, ranging from announcements of the grand opening of a new session at the Supreme Court to details of humble people's entanglements with the law, as in the case of the petty clerk who was charged with stealing twenty-seven envelopes.[2] Government used the local press to post legal notices, and executors of private people's wills announced proceedings.

Lawyers and newspapermen were among the most visible and influential figures in the crowded, commercial urban environment of Lagos. Newspapermen of this period were almost all one-man bands, enterprising individuals who founded, edited and managed their papers, often writing large portions of the text themselves and recruiting friends and associates to write the rest, while also handling advertising and distribution. The papers were platforms from which they could project their views and their personalities. Papers of the period carried little in the way of hard news; the staple items were editorials, opinion pieces and commentaries, as well as snippets of social and personal news. They were epistolary in form, and rather than reporting events in the third person they tended to address the reader or the person under discussion. The editor-proprietor hosted a discursive space to which anyone seeking social visibility would seek access, soliciting the editors with donations, annual gifts and friendly visits in order to ensure their doings were

---

2   *Eko Akete*, 21 April 1923:3.

noticed. The editor was thus both an observer (often wry and sarcastic) and a social presence in the small world of the elite, both a dispenser and a recipient of public attention. And lawyers were among the figures the newspapermen hailed most often. Clergymen, teachers, doctors, surveyors, architects and engineers were also prominent in social and political life, but by the 1920s the law appeared to be the profession that people aspired to most. Around the inner circle of prominent and wealthy barristers and solicitors, there were many more men training, or aspiring to train, for the profession, and many were the lawyers' clerks who hoped eventually to convert themselves into lawyers. Some of the most prominent men of the time, ranging from the arch-conservative Sir Kitoyi Ajasa (who was also the editor-proprietor of the *Nigerian Pioneer*) to the fiery radical J. Egerton Shyngle, Herbert Macaulay's right-hand man in his proto-nationalist campaigns, were barristers at law.

The proliferation of lawyers was not regarded as an unmixed blessing. Adeoye Deniga, editor of *Eko Akete*, wrote:

> About thirty years ago, we could count the lawyers amongst us one by one: and they were as sharp as razors in their work: and the honour in which we held this profession at that time caused the drummers to salute them with this song:
>
> > Esu [the Yoruba god of transformations] has turned his brain
> > The lad who fools with a lawyer
>
> But a few years ago, so many of our people went to train as lawyers in London that it seemed there was no other profession as prestigious as this, although there are countless other lines of work such as medicine, surveying, architecture, agriculture and so on which one can go and study in England, and get degrees in just the same ... and in the end, very often, this kind of lawyer will live to regret it, when he gets no clients.... We all know that soup without salt is tasteless, but I ask you – who can eat an excess of salt in their soup?[3]

But this did not dilute Deniga's appreciation of the powerful, prominent and successful barristers of the present day. They were valued for their social and civic contributions as well as their professional abilities. In an open letter to J. Egerton Shyngle, just three weeks after the above polemic, Deniga addresses him as 'Dear Old Blackstone', and commends 'the exemplary part

3   *Eko Akete*, 18 November 1922:3.

played by you the other evening, whilst discharging the duty of Chairman for the Play got up at the G.M. Hall under the auspices of the Bethel Church Choir, nor do I overlook the act of some of your distinguished Supporters, to wit, the redoubtable 'H.M' [Herbert Macaulay], 'Ọmọtaku' Thompson [the barrister Montacute Thompson] and others.... Well Done, thou worthy scion of the Illustrious House of Laṣọrè'.

Copyright in Lagos

With so much legal and journalistic expertise concentrated in the city, it is not surprising that writers and publishers had long been familiar with the idea of copyright. The earliest mentions of copyright in the Lagos press concerned foreigners – firms or individuals based in Britain, Europe or Russia.[4] But the reports on these cases showed a local interest in the implications of copyright law.[5]

Within Lagos, it is clear that ideas about copyright were in circulation at least from the second decade of the century, and were being applied to local concerns. An advertisement placed in the *Lagos Weekly Record* and the *Lagos Standard* in April and May 1910 stated

> WANTED: Copyright of good Native Plays (Dramatic, Melo-dramatic, Comic or Serio-Comic) not hitherto produced on the Stage, for use by 'the Lagos Glee Singers'. Play to be submitted to the President, Dr O. Obasa (Breadfruit Street Lagos) or the secretary, not later than July 31, 1910, for examination by expert judges. A prize of 3 guineas will be awarded to the author of the best play submitted.

---

4   For example, in 1901 the *Lagos Weekly Record* reported a trademark and copyright case in the Supreme Court of the Colony of Lagos. Both plaintiff and defendant were British companies (*Lagos Weekly Record*, 6 July 1901). In 1910, the same paper reported that Count (Leo) Tolstoy had bequeathed all his literary property to his youngest daughter Alexandra, who intended to sell the rights, so that 'the copyright would then become public property' (*Lagos Weekly Record*, 31 December 1910).

5   Contributors to Lagos newspapers could also go out of their way to demonstrate their own awareness of the law and compliance with it: the *Nigerian Pioneer*'s column 'Our London Letter' noted that 'There some good pictures of the West African prisoners in the *Daily Mail* yesterday, but I couldn't get the copyright for the PIONEER. Anyhow, I hope to have some for the readers soon.' (*Nigerian Pioneer*, 26 March 1915). The *West Africa* magazine was more generous than the *Daily Mail*: reprinting a report from the *West Africa* magazine on the Oluwa land case, which had reached the Privy Council Court in 1921, the *Nigerian Pioneer* noted that it was a 'Verbatim report … – strictly copyright except to newspapers printed in West Africa.'

Copyright in the form of performing rights was clearly taken seriously: in one published statement of accounts for an entertainment staged at the Colonial Church, items included 'licence' (10/-) and 'copyright' (15/-) (*Lagos Standard*, 25 May 1910).

Awareness of the concept of copyright clearly extended to home-grown print publications.[6] But in this domain it was applied only selectively. In the newspapers, the articles that were singled out for assertion of copyright were almost always series rather than stand-alone pieces. An early example is the long sequence of articles headed 'Burial Customs of the Yoruba country', by someone writing under the name 'Adesola', in the *Nigerian Chronicle* (May–November 1909): each instalment carried the legend 'All Rights Reserved'. In the 1920s papers, this trend was confirmed. Herbert Macaulay's history of the nineteenth-century Lagos leaders Kọsọkọ and Dosunmu, published in Yoruba in instalments in *Eko Akete* in 1922, was labelled 'Copyright'. A series of pieces of advice and reflection on life, titled 'Kilopọ?' ('what's the use of worrying?') by '*EDITOR*, EKO AKETE', carried the warning 'A ko gbọdọ da Iwe yi tẹ lai gba'asẹ' ('this text must not be reprinted [as a stand-alone publication] without permission'). The common feature of the pieces over which copyright was asserted seems to have been that they were suitable for republication as a free-standing pamphlet or book. The possible motivations for this will look familiar to students of European print culture: on the one hand, books and pamphlets are nearer to being identified as a profitable commodity than a newspaper article (especially as most of the Yoruba newspapers struggled to break even and sometimes launched appeals for donations to keep them going); on the other hand a book was the best instantiation of a cultural monument, preserving the author's memory while at the same time providing a foundation for future civic progress. Authors of books therefore had good reasons for wanting publication not only to be under their own name but for this to be legally affirmed.

Materials could move in both directions – from newspaper serial format to pamphlets or books, and vice versa. I.B. Thomas's English-language *Life of Herbert Macaulay* was first published as a booklet in 1924, to coincide with the great man's sixtieth birthday;[7] three years later, a condensed version, in

---

6   Eagle-eyed Lagos lawyers scrutinized colonial legislation as it applied to Nigeria: when the Criminal Code Ordinance was promulgated in 1915, the *Times of Nigeria* published a supplement listing objections to several of its provisions: these included 'Offences in relation to copyright'.

7   A second edition was published in 1931, to celebrate the Eleko's reinstatement; and a third edition came out in 1946, after Macaulay's death, and with extensive additional materials about the great man's last days, his final illness, the funeral,

Yoruba, was published in *Eko Igbẹhin*[8] – accompanied by a fierce warning that Thomas would take legal action against anyone who dared to take the piece and publish it as a pamphlet. Several serials – including the first two works later recognized as early Yoruba novels[9] – were later gathered up and published as pamphlets or booklets, while books such as Samuel Smiles's self-help treatise were serialized. But despite the porous boundaries between these formats, it is clear that when text took on the status of a book or booklet (most books at the time were less than 100 pages) it became something more like a property, rights in which could be defended.

Assertions of authorial proprietorship, however, could be bafflingly unstable. The editor of *Eko Akete*, Adeoye Deniga, published in 1923 a series in English entitled 'Short Studies on Yoruba Warriors', marked as 'Copyright' and 'By the editor'. Five years later, the identical text (apart from a few typos that had now crept in) was reprinted in the same newspaper. Again it was marked 'Copyright', but it was now credited to a different author, one Agbaje! In light of this, one may speculate that the assertion of copyright was not necessarily intended to secure an individual's authorial proprietary rights. Its function may have been to affirm the distinctiveness, identity and value of the text *as* text – and as a constituent part of a distinctive newspaper, which as we have remarked represented the expanded aura of the owner-proprietor.

Newspaper discursivity

Most newspaper articles were not copyrighted and many were written under pseudonyms or not credited to any name at all. Assertions of copyright sat in the midst of a prevailing style that ran counter to the trend to claim identifiable individual ownership of a text. This prevailing style was characterized by two key features: extensive borrowing, recycling and culling from other publications on the one hand; and the prevalence of inventive nicknames, aliases and pseudonyms, often proverbial in form, and often laying claim to moral authority, on the other.

Quoting, excerpting and republishing materials from other newspapers were so pervasive as to constitute the West African press as a continuous

---

the funeral orations, and the letters of condolence. Like many books and booklets produced in Lagos in the first half of the twentieth century, it was clearly a work in progress for more than twenty years.

8   *Eko Igbẹhin*, 18 November 1927:9–14.

9   *Itan Emi Ọmọ-Orukan* (The story of me, an orphan), by E.A. Akintan, was serialized in fits and starts in Akintan's paper *Eleti Ọfẹ* in 1926, 1927 and 1930, and then published as a booklet in May 1931. The more famous *Itan Igbesi-Aiye Emi Sẹgilọla* (The life-story of me, Sẹgilọla), by I.B. Thomas, was serialized in Thomas's paper *Akede Eko* in 1929–30 and then published as a booklet in July 1930.

shared field of textual resources. The newspapers were set up as open webs
hosting materials from a variety of identifiable and unidentifiable sources. The
1920s Yoruba papers were particularly attached to their short-lived Lagosian
forerunner *Iwe Irohin Eko* (1888–92) and frequently republished entire articles
from it. The editors also read the Gold Coast and Sierra Leone papers and
republished pieces from them, as well as a variety of British publications. In
an eighteen-month period in 1922–3, *Eko Akete* carried extracts or reprinted
articles from *West Africa* magazine, published in London, more than a dozen
times, and drew on a number of other British-published papers: the *Daily
Mail*, *John Bull* magazine, *Reynold's Newspaper*, *The Times* (Weekly Edition),
the *Sunday Times* and the *News of the World*. It used the *Gold Coast Leader,* the
Gold Coast Independent, the *Sierra Leone Weekly News* and Marcus Garvey's
paper, *Negro World*. In an eighteen-month period in 1929–30, *Akede Eko* was
equally lavish in its excerpting and cross-referencing, though the focus had
now shifted towards other Nigerian papers: it was in constant dialogue with
the *Nigerian Daily Times* (more than twenty references, usually hostile, most
savagely so when that paper trashed Thomas's pioneering serialized work of
fiction, *Itan Igbesi-Aiye Emi Segilola*) and also drew from Herbert Macaulay's
paper the *Lagos Daily News*, the *Nigerian Pioneer*, the *Lagos Weekly Record*,
the *Nigerian Daily Telegraph* and *Eleti Ofe*. Though *Akede Eko* showed a shift
in orientation from the West African coastal culture zone to the Nigerian
national entity, the connections out to England and the British press were
retained. Thomas drew on *West Africa* magazine for information or for whole
articles; he also read and made use of *The Overseas Daily Mail*, the *Journal
of the West African Students' Union*, *News of the World* and *Pearson's Weekly*.
Sometimes he addressed himself directly to the paper in question, as when
he published an open letter to Charles Pilley, the editor of *John Bull*, taking
exception to his racist vocabulary.

When articles were reprinted, the Lagos papers usually acknowledged the
title of the source publication, but not the date or the name of the author. Not
acknowledging a source at all was sometimes seen as cheating: as in the case of
a contributor who submitted a story in Yoruba to *Eko Akete*, only to provoke a
sarcastic letter from a reader pointing out that it was in fact a translation of a
piece published in George Newnes's popular British paper *Tit-Bits*. However,
there is no suggestion that editors sought permission, let alone paid royalties
for these borrowed materials. There would not have been time: editors often
announced that their papers were carrying items extracted from publications
that had just arrived on the mail steamer. This suggests that what was important
was demonstrating that they were in touch, had access to a wide spectrum of
publications, and could bring important information and choice items (in fact,
tit-bits) from different sources far and wide to interest their readers.

Figure 4.2   I.B. Thomas, editor-proprietor of Akede Eko, advertises his paper by means of his briefcase (from I.B. Thomas's book The Life History of Herbert Macaulay CE, Lagos: Tika-Tore Press, 1946, 3rd edition, p. 14).

The textual network constituted through excerpting and cross-referencing, that linked all the Lagos papers and stretched to Freetown and the Gold Coast and on to London and beyond, fostered a kind of triangular or polygonal correspondence. Editors not only constantly responded – sometimes obliquely, sometimes directly – to statements made in other publications, but correspondents who objected to something in one paper would write to another paper to complain. This suggests that there was a presumption that the papers constituted a single field.

The use of nicknames and pseudonyms compounded the pervasive sense of the newspaper as a web of shifting intertextuality, where authorship was at times acknowledged and at times half-acknowledged or concealed. Very famous people, like Herbert Macaulay and A.K. Ajiṣafẹ, the Ẹgba historian, and very humble people, like readers who wrote in on particular issues, seem to have preferred to use their own names. And to at least one editor, this was seen as a proof of *bona fides*. E.M. Awobiyi, the unlucky editor-proprietor of the short-lived *Eko Igbẹhin* ('Latter-day Lagos'), started his career as editor with a violent altercation with the rival paper *Eko Akete*, which accused him of poaching its pseudonymous contributors 'Atari Ajanaku' ('Elephant Cranium') and 'Akirimanu' ('One who wanders without getting lost'), and hinted that 'Atari Ajanaku' was actually a pen-name for Herbert Macaulay himself. Awobiyi replied in the following terms: 'Ye tan ilu jẹ pe Kiniun Onibudo ti wa lo nkọ Atari Ajanaku. Ta ni ko mọ pe Kiniun Onibudo ti wa ko jẹ kọ iwe kan ko ma fi orukọ ati ibugbe rẹ si.' ('Stop trying to deceive the town into thinking that our Lion of the War Camp is the person writing [under the name] Elephant Cranium. Who does not know that our Lion of the War Camp wouldn't dream of writing anything without appending his own name and address.')[10] In other words, Herbert Macaulay, nicknamed 'Lion of the War Camp', was so famous and so bold that he did not need to disguise his authorship of the stream of essays, polemics and disquisitions that flowed from his fluent pen. By implication, 'Atari Ajanaku' was a mere disguise for a less prominent, less honest writer. It is not at all clear from this exchange of diatribes whether the grievance relates to the stealing of names, or the purloining of contributors. Such is the blurred discourse around name, authorship and identity.

Apart from the very famous and the very humble, however, most contributors to the newspapers did use pseudonyms, without normally attracting the kind of criticism implicit in Awobiyi's comments. In some cases an alias was a playful and easily penetrated disguise or even just a popular honorific nickname. For example in a report in *Eko Igbẹhin* on the twenty-first birthday celebrations of one R.G.A. Smith, the author says 'Agidi-Adaba was the first invited guest to be there in his gorgeous blue coat amusing himself with Grammophone before the majority came'.[11] Here, both the author and his readers are presumed to know the identity of 'Agidi-Adaba' ('Headstrong Turtle Dove') – who was himself a frequent contributor to the weekly papers under that pseudonym. But very often, aliases served to disguise identity and claim an authority deriving from that very anonymity. Contributors asserted their impartiality, honesty and fearlessness in the face of malevolence by calling themselves things like 'Ẹni-a-fẹ-lamọ' ('We know whom we love [but we don't know who loves us]'), 'Ojumito' ('I'm an eye-witness'), 'Kosẹhin-Ọlọrun' ('Nothings happens without God's knowledge'), 'A-fi-otitọ-inu-tu-ẹru-ika-palẹ' ('One who uses honesty/truthfulness to unpack the luggage of the wicked') and 'Inawọleokunkunpada' ('Light enters, darkness disappears').

Sometimes a pseudonym might have been used for protection – not only from a Government which had been known to imprison newspaper writers for sedition, but also from irate victims of satire and exposure. If that was the case, it did not always work: witness the libel case brought by Lawyer Adeyẹmọ Alakija against Herbert Macaulay, Johnny Akilade Caulcrick and Frank Macaulay (Herbert Macaulay's son) for defamatory remarks about him published in Macaulay's paper the *Lagos Daily News* under the pseudonym

---

10   *Eko Igbẹhin*, 5 February 1926:4.
11   *Eko Igbẹhin*, 17 June 1927:6.

'Joker'. Alakija asserted in court that Frank Macaulay was 'Joker', that everyone knew this, and that Frank had told him so himself. According to Alakija, the nickname was an accurate depiction of character: Frank 'is never serious and is irresponsible' and the only thing he really cares about is getting enough beer to drink.[12] Whether or not it protected the bearer from retaliation, pseudonymity certainly seemed to embolden the satirist, as with Otitọ Inu (Inner Truth) who threatens to 'unpack the luggage of the wicked': and who states 'if I see anyone packing wickedness into his load in this city, I will unpack it without hesitation, even if it's the Ọba, a chief, a rich person, a distinguished person'.[13]

The pervasive use of pseudonyms meant that asserting authorial rights over specific published items could not have been a priority – for even when a pseudonym was quite famous, it was hard to prove beyond doubt to whom it belonged. In the quarrel between Awobiyi and Deniga mentioned above, another contributor to *Eko Igbẹhin* backed Awobiyi up with the observation that no one can claim sole ownership of a name – there are more than a thousand people with the nickname Atari Ajanaku in Lagos alone![14] Similarly, it is impossible to establish just how many people were involved in writing any newspaper, for it was always on the cards that the editor-proprietor, lacking contributors, might write the whole thing himself under multiple pseudonyms.

Thus, rather than laying claim to identifiable authorial rights, the names attached to newspaper articles often laid claim to truth and credibility in the very act of playing games of subterfuge and concealment.

In her groundbreaking study of pseudonymity in English-language newspapers in West Africa, Stephanie Newell suggests that 'writers' practices of self-naming and re-naming can be regarded in large part as strategies to thwart imperialist modes of labelling and containing Africans' (2013:8), but also represented an aspiration to set aside individual status and personal entanglements in order to articulate public opinion to the colonial authorities. Habermas speaks of the 'bracketing' of personal status and interests that accompanied entry into the public sphere of late eighteenth-century Europe. In the coffee house debates, the bourgeoisie were not obliged to defer to the nobility: status differences were suspended, in a fiction which was nonetheless consequential (Habermas 1992 [1962]). Newell shows that newspapermen in the English-language West African press similarly insisted that the press was 'the fourth and only estate', the only space where public-spirited political debate by the colonized could be conducted, and asserted that in this public sphere of print they set aside 'personalities' (scandal, personal grievances and self-

---

12   *Akede Eko*, 19 September 1929:9.
13   *Eko Igbẹhin*, 8 January 1926:7.
14   *Eko Igbẹhin*, 5 February 1926:8.

interested goals) in order to serve the public good. In this context, Newell argues, pseudonymity could function as a form of 'bracketing'. Thus it was not only the readers that could be conceptualized as an anonymous and unidentifiable public, but also the writers; and in the intimate atmosphere of the educated West African elites, writers and readers frequently changed places. And this new public space was a site of experiment and innovation. It was in the newspapers, above all, that new genres took shape and many new conjunctions and reformulations of existing genres were tried out – and sometimes abandoned (Barber 2012). Pseudonymity and anonymity, as Newell shows, sustained this culture of innovation, creating a space in which writers could 'experiment with voices, genders, genres, and opinions' (Newell 2013:5).

The use of pseudonyms was a widespread feature of nineteenth- and early twentieth-century newspapers around the world, as was the practice of reprinting miscellaneous pieces culled from other publications. This does not mean, however, that in specific locations these characteristics cannot be linked to specific local conditions, projects and antecedents. The Yoruba-language papers participated in the Anglophone West African press's project of constituting a new public sphere defined and articulated through print. In doing so, I wish to suggest, they generated a form of textuality that had much in common with Yoruba oral textual modes, even though the newspaper editor-proprietors were highly conscious at the same time of the new possibilities of print.

In 1920s Lagos, culling and the use of pseudonyms were in keeping with a specific aesthetic, that of Yoruba oral genres such as *oríkì* (praise poetry) and *ẹsẹ Ifá* (divination poetry). This is not to claim that print culture was a continuation of an oral world. But neither was there a definitive break, with one mode superseding the other, 'modernity' displacing 'tradition'. Rather, what we see in the Yoruba newspapers is the creation of a space that accommodated several modes simultaneously. It evoked new ideas of public space while basking in the existing aesthetic satisfaction with oral text as a polyvocal, continually emergent practice of quotation. New possibilities were added without jettisoning older ones.

Naming and authorship in *oríkì* and in the newspapers

Yoruba oral genres do not share to any great extent the practice, documented for Somali and Rwandan oral poetry, of preserving the names of individual composers believed to be the sole creators of discrete, carefully transmitted texts (Andrzejewski 1964; Kagame 1969). Yoruba *oríkì* (praise poetry) are, on the contrary, assemblages of name-like formulations, each of which may have been composed by a different person, at a different time, and in response to a different event or observation. An individual accumulates *oríkì* over a lifetime, a town or deity possibly over a much longer time span. A performer of *oríkì* brings together a profusion of such textual chunks and links them, partly through temporary associations of sound and sense, but partly simply by intensely addressing them to the subject of the praise, who functions as the centre of gravity of this centripetal outpouring. Not only this, but though the core of the formulations are highly prized and regarded as unchanging, 'truer than history', the style and phrasing are varied by the performer, who thus incrementally changes the elements of the text with each performance. Skill at linking, deviating, approaching a well-known formulation from an unexpected angle, and adding unexpected flourishes are esteemed as the mark of a gifted performer. Untraceable multitudes have thus had a hand in the composition of any corpus of *oríkì*.[15] But while the names of authors are not a concern, the names of the addressee are profusely cited: the whole text of the *oríkì* is nominal in form, every segment of text functioning as an appellation or attribution.

The Yoruba newspapers were like *oríkì* in that they brought together a multiplicity of pieces from different sources without (usually) identifying their authors. Clearly, however, the frequent absence of authorial attribution in the Yoruba newspapers was of a different order from the incremental multiple composition of *oríkì*. A pseudonym, like the attribution 'Anon', 'denotes the insistence of the authorship question; though it does not identify, it marks a space for identity, a need to know "who is speaking"' (Masten 1994:361). One could go further. In the context of Yoruba naming, pseudonyms function essentially like real names. Traditionally, personal names were not labels but evocations of potential. Some names were 'brought from heaven' (*àmútrunwá*): these recognized intrinsic characteristics of the child, indicated by their appearance at birth, the manner of their birth or their birth order. But *àbíso* names – those given to a child in response to something in the family circumstances at the time – may express parents' aspirations (Bámikólé – 'Build a house for me'), their joy (Moróhuntódùn – 'I see something sweet'), their gratitude (Olúwaṣèyí – 'God did this'), their satisfaction in the status of the family (Ọmóṣaléwá – 'The child chose which house to come to') or their warning to the child not to die prematurely (Kòsókó – 'There is no hoe [with which to dig a grave for you]'). Such names are complete sentences. The child, then, bears utterances that are not his or her own, but which express others'

---

15   It is true that spectacularly creative performers can be remembered by name, and distinctive formulations in their performances may be remembered as their own creation for many years. But the bulk of any *oríkì* chant is always made up of a multiplicity of formulations generated at different times and by different people whose identities are not preserved.

sentiments and wishes. A child grows into a name by living up to it; he or she may also grow out of a name, in the sense that some of the many names he or she is given at birth may fall out of use. A name is not a unique identifier but a living statement and a work in progress. In addition, pleasure and interest in naming stimulate the generation of all kinds of aliases, nicknames, abbreviations and honorific or joking sobriquets. Pseudonyms fit into this field of alternative and multiple names. Like *àbísọ* names, they make statements of desire or intent (in this case the bearer's desire or intent rather than that of his or her parents); they are often sentences proclaiming the qualities he or she intends to live up to. Thus a pseudonym in the newspaper is more like a name than an absence of name: the pseudonym is one of a number of alternative appellations, on-page and off-page. But none of them has as its prime function the fixing of a unique, permanent, legal identity.

By the 1920s, especially in the capital, this culture of naming had been reshaped by colonial legal, religious and administrative requirements and by changing social orientations among the elite. By then, all the elite had distinct surnames and a limited number of forenames. Name changes were announced in the press and legally processed. It is interesting to note, however, that surnames – which among the elite were often derived from missionary or other European patrons (there were large numbers of Johnsons, Williamses and Thomases) – were referred to by the elite themselves as 'foreign names'.[16] Local names were still the meaningful ones, still took the form of statements, and still participated in a creative mode of profusion and elaboration.

The Yoruba newspapers' naming practices resembled *oríkì* less in their style of anonymity than in their profuse addressivity (Bakhtin 1986) to their readers. The Yoruba newspapers continually hail their subjects with nicknames, epithets, salutations and actual *oríkì* – strongly echoing the vocative mode of praise poetry. The prominent photographer Akin Adeṣigbin, who took pictures free of charge at a meeting chaired by Dr Oguntọla Sapara at Breadfruit School, is thanked by the editor of *Eko Akete* with the epithet '*A-fowo-ṣe-ẹni-lore*' ('One who spends his money doing good

---

16   The lawyer Adeyẹmọ Alakija testified in court that '*mo yi orukọ ajoji mi gẹgẹbi Placido Assumpcao pada si Adeyẹmọ Alakija emi ṣe eyi, ko nṣe fun nkan meji lẹhin pe emi ko fẹ lati tun ma jẹ orukọ ajoji mọ*' ('I changed my foreign name Placido Assumpcao back to Adeyẹmọ Alakija and I did this for no other reason than that I did not want to bear a foreign name any longer'), *Akede Eko*, 19 September 1929:9. Likewise, the original translation of *Itan Igbesi-Aiye Emi Ṣegilọla*, serialized in *Akede Eko* in 1931–2, translates '*orukọ "Misita" alagbaja ti orukọ ọkọ mi na njẹ*' (literally, 'the "Mister" so-and-so name that was my husband's name') as 'his foreign name' (Barber 2012:392–3).

turns to others'),[17] while Dr Sapara himself is saluted with '*ẹbọra-ninu-iṣẹ-gbigba-ẹbi-ọmọ*' ('magician in the art of midwifery').[18] Yakubu Lawani Kekereogun is nicknamed 'Akuru-yẹ-jo' ('One who is short but graces the dance').[19] When Ẹbun da Rocha holds a needlework exhibition at the Race Course ground, she receives a compliment from the editor of *Akede Eko*: '*Iṣẹ ọwọ rẹ wu wa, iwọ abepo-rẹ Ẹbun da Rocha: ọwọ a ma ya siṣẹ o, Ẹbun tiwa ọwọn!*' – 'Your handiwork pleases us, you, friend of palm-oil [i.e. light skinned] Ẹbun da Rocha: more power to your elbow, oh our dear Ẹbun!'[20] More generally, much of the text of the Yoruba newspapers is in the first and second persons – an 'I' speaking to a 'you', in the form of letters, editorials, advice and comment.

Quotedness in *oríkì* and in the newspapers

Oríkì are constituted out of materials recognized as coming from existing textual repertoires. Phrases, passages, fragments of other genres – chunks of Ifá divination verses, proverbs, riddles, songs, chain-narrative poems and much else – are continually incorporated into *oríkì* chants. Because the utterance of *oríkì* is evocative and empowering, profusion is valued. There is a positive incentive to the performer to demonstrate that she has vast reservoirs of text at her disposal, in numerous genres, to swell her chant and expand the addressee's reputation. Such incorporated materials can be converted into attributions by various techniques: by grammatical nominalization, by the use of introductory expressions such as *ọmọ* ... ('child of'), by explicit 'bestowal' of the material on the subject, and so on. Yet they often still retain recognizable features of the genre from which they were drawn. They are not fully assimilated to their host environment, but neither do they remain fully distinct. They are co-opted but retain, as it were, the aura of otherness and the possibility of reverting or opening out into a different text (Barber 1999).

The effect of this mode of textual constitution is one of pervasive quotedness. Words, in being uttered, are highlighted as having pre-existed the moment of utterance, and as possessing a recognizable identity of their own. This has two effects. First, it demonstrates the composer-performer's skill in assembling and adapting a profusion of textual materials. Far from being considered derivative or lacking in originality, this ability to 'quote' is the height of artistic achievement. Second, presenting words as a citation draws attention to their existence as text, as distinct from the quotidian flow of unremarked discourse. If they pre-existed the present moment of utterance, they can be

---

17   *Eko Akete*, 21 April 1923:3.
18   *Eko Akete*, 27 January 1923:3.
19   *Akede Eko*, 17 January 1929:4.
20   *Akede Eko*, 5–12 December 1929:4.

experienced as durable formulations that have the capacity to transcend time. They can be regarded, in Akinnaṣọ's words, as 'intrinsically valuable objects, objects whose value is thought to transcend that of conversation or other everyday use of language' (Akinnaṣọ 1985:346).[21]

The 'quotedness' of Yoruba oral genres goes well beyond the normal intertextuality which is the condition of possibility of all literature. It is an aesthetic feature which is deliberately highlighted and elaborated. Performers draw attention to their own practice of citation. For example, rather than simply hailing a subject as 'One who rises at dawn to eat the heads of fish', the performer may say '"One who rises at dawn to eat the heads of fish" is what you are worthy to be called, Lágbájá'. Rather than merely uttering the subject's appellations, she is citing them, thus implicitly evaluating their appropriateness to the subject and drawing attention to her own act of praising.

The cellular structure characteristic of *oríkì* is not one in which one element x grows out of a preceding element y, within the text, so that one is defined or produced by the other, as described by Riffaterre;[22] rather, the text makes a space which facilitates bringing x and y together. Each retains its potential to open up and expand into something more complex. The expansion of x may have nothing to do with y. Potentiality, rather than truncation or impairment, is the aesthetic effect. The virtual presence of these potential expansions is the mode of existence of *oríkì*, whose function is to enhance and expand reputation. *Oríkì* are invented in order to transcend flux and the passage of time: not by imitating monuments, but by their perpetual potentiality. Each performance calls attention, through its allusive and quotative practices, to the richness and diversity of the shared field of textual resources from which it was drawn. And in showing themselves to be at home in this field, able to roam freely amongst its constituents, the performers also consolidate their own reputation and presence.

The editor-proprietors of the Yoruba newspapers of 1920s Lagos, like successful performers of *oríkì*, showed their mastery and enhanced their own reputation by bringing together a diversity of elements from different sources and constituting themselves as the hub of a network of textual traffic. Self-advertisement went hand in hand with publicity for their papers and was their stock in trade.

---

21 Akinnaso is speaking only of relatively rigid, rote-learned 'ritual' texts, that is, Ifá and Ẹrìndínlógún verses. But the perception of texts as 'intrinsically valuable objects' extends to more fluid and fragmented forms such as *oríkì*, and is not dependent on the fixity of the tradition as such.

22 'The text as locus of significance is generated by conversion and expansion' (Riffaterre 1978:47). Riffaterre was referring to the way a sign is multiplied and extended until an entire unified poetic text has been produced from a single 'matrix'.

Eisenstein remarks on the likelihood that print, by identifying authors and distinguishing their original creations from the tradition they inhabited, fostered a new emphasis on individual identity, linked to new forms of celebrity. Again, though, what is striking in the Yoruba case is the continuity between oral and print modes of constituting reputation. The Lagos newspapers revolved around personalia. They not only magnified and publicized the editor-proprietors' personalities and opinions; they also commented continually on the doings and sayings, comings and goings of the more prominent members of the elite. The three most popular Yoruba papers of the 1920s – *Eko Akete*, *Eleti Ọfẹ* and *Akede Eko* – all had pages devoted to snippets of social news and odd anecdotes about known individuals. Dr Oguntọla Sapara's go-cart horn was stolen from right inside the grounds of the law-court;[23] Mr Claudius A. Williams, '*ọpẹlẹngẹ ọkunrin jẹjẹ kiki-anu*' ('the slender peaceable man full of kindness'), an important senior clerk at Nigerian Railways, is about to take a three-month holiday during which he will travel to Kaduna and other northern cities;[24] the driver of vehicle no. 610, please drive more carefully! – last Friday, as he passed the P.W.D. building where it abuts on Ajẹlẹ Street, he knocked an old lady down and almost killed her.[25] This minute observation and commentary are like a prose version of the material out of which *oríkì* also grew. *Oríkì* were dedicated to hailing the remarkable and idiosyncratic in every subject. They are believed to encapsulate the essential, irreducible individuality of persons, lineages, animals, gods, material objects and ideas, while still affirming their alignment with strongly normative shared measures of value. The individuality of subjects is evoked through allusion (often oblique and hard to decipher) to peculiar incidents, characteristics or utterances associated with them: allusions which could only have been formulated in a face-to-face community where everyone's actions and sayings were scrutinized, discussed and remembered. Personal distinctiveness was highly valued. Competition raged between 'big men' who employed a diversity of means to increase their wealth and influence at each others' expense. Bold assertions of autonomy, immunity and idiosyncrasy were their stock in trade, and reputation – fame – was an integral element in an individual's success, for power depended on the ability to attract adherents ('having people').

In the newspapers, however, this *oríkì*-like mode of hailing idiosyncrasy lay cheek by jowl with other, newer ways of representing personhood. Several of the Yoruba newspapers featured informative, third-person biographical summaries giving facts and dates in the terse style of entries in *Who's Who*.

---

23 *Eko Akete*, 22 July 1922:1.
24 *Akede Eko*, 19 September 1929:4.
25 *Eleti Ọfẹ*, 30 April 1925:3.

Adeoye Deniga pioneered this style of biographical narrative in *Eko Akete*, particularly during electoral campaigns, when he profiled the candidates of the NNDP, Herbert Macaulay's party. He even published a compilation of such profiles in an annual *Who's Who in Nigeria* volume. Later, *Akede Eko* followed suit, with a long series of biographies of prominent Lagosian men and women. One mode did not drive out the other: 'trade does not strangle trade', as the proverb goes.

The multiplication of modes of conceptualizing persons in the press meant that the idea of the 'public' was never unitary. On the one hand, the editor-proprietors of the Yoruba papers, like their English-language counterparts discussed by Newell, envisaged an anonymous extensive public of a new kind. They saw themselves as representatives of civic interests, occupying a new discursive space, a public sphere in which personal identities and individual goals were bracketed in the interest of the common good. On the other hand, the newspaper writers gossiped, addressed named subjects personally, and lavished praise upon prominent individuals. Print was a medium in which they could magnify their own individual presence and that of their chosen addressees, in a continual stream of salutations and notices of individual projects and actions (journeys, engagements, utterances). It provided a new means for the constitution of individual celebrity and an expanded sense of the public before whom individual distinctiveness could be paraded.

We see here the paradoxical character of the pseudonym – the authorial name which evades copyright. On the one hand, it can indicate a withdrawal from individual identification, and an espousal of a generic, neutral position from which authoritative truths can be told ('one who unpacks the luggage of the wicked'). It can even function as a comment on or key to the text itself, supplementing the text's content, so that the identity of the 'author' becomes subsumed into the identity of the text (Newell 2013). But on the other hand – and at the same time – pseudonyms were epithets, often taking the form of *oríkì*, which hail the subject's idiosyncrasy and affirm his or her singularity and superiority.

The print sphere thus hosted diverse modes of representing and evoking persons. The reasons for not asserting copyright were correspondingly complex. I would suggest that though all the newspaper editors were aware of copyright law, other projects generally held greater attractions – creative, imaginative and in some ways mutually incompatible visions of the potential of print as a new medium.

What we do not see here is an individualistic print culture superseding some imaginary pre-print, oral world in which the individual was submerged in a collective communal identity. As we have noted, the 'oral world' of the Yoruba focused intensely on individuality: difference was the principle of identity. Similarly, a model built around a contrast between evanescent orality and permanent print would be misleading. Both *oríkì* and the Yoruba newspapers assembled texts by quoting and recycling materials already in circulation; both constituted open webs hosting multiple, often anonymous contributions; both were fluid and heterogeneous assemblages of diverse fragments; and both were nonetheless strongly oriented towards permanence, to the constitution of a text out of discourse – a form that would endure. Neither newspapers nor *oríkì* were regarded as evanescent. *Oríkì* were regarded as being supremely able to capture and preserve core nuggets of the past, making the powers of ancestors available for reactivation in the present. Newspapers were preserved and re-read, sometimes decades later, and were valued for their capacity to pin down the events of the present for quotation by future historians. These habits of preservation showed that quoting was neither laziness nor larceny: it was a form of respect for text, and a way of giving the text a further lease of life, projecting it further into the future, where it could benefit coming generations.

Conclusion

This comparison is not intended to suggest that the texts of early Yoruba print culture were constituted in the same way as the flourishing oral traditions that surrounded them. The Lagosian elite were well aware of the different potential of print, and were excited by it. It was the perceived capacity of print to reach out to the 'four corners of the world' that stimulated experiments with addressivity and sustained the newspapermen's games with anonymity and identity. In print, both writer and reader could be evoked as immediate, known, idiosyncratic presences on the one hand and as a faceless, disinterested author addressing a vast unknown public on the other – often in the same text and even at the same moment, and with many intermediate scales of magnitude and inclusiveness. Both the possibility of asserting a legal claim to individual textual ownership and its obverse, the possibility of masking or vacating a determinate authorial identity, took shape with the establishment of a print sphere. But it is equally clear that there was no break with orality. The writers and editors of the early Yoruba print sphere mobilized available ideas and procedures that were highly developed in the complex field of oral genres. Ideas about the relationship between naming and being; about the essential idiosyncrasy of individual persons and entities; and about the generation of textual value through processes of quotation and incorporation are strongly present in the Yoruba-language newspapers of the 1920s. The fluid, inventive and varied ways in which the authors and editors of these papers combined and juxtaposed different models of authorship, different relations between writer and public, and different ideas about the identity and properties of the

printed text show that this was a site of experimentation – and a formative
stage in the history of Yoruba print culture. Despite its staid appearance,
the Lagos press of the 1920s was a hotbed of innovation. This makes it an
interesting point at which to slice into this particular example of the history of
local media in Africa.

References

Ajayi, J.F.A. 1965. *Christian Missions in Nigeria 1841–1891: The Making of a New Elite.*
    London: Longmans.
Akinnaso, F. Niyi. 1985. 'On the similarities between spoken and written language'.
    Language and Speech 28(4):324–59.
Andrzejewski, B.W. 1964. *Somali Poetry: An Introduction.* Oxford: Clarendon Press.
Bakhtin, M.M. 1986 *Speech Genres and Other Late Essays* (trans. V.W. McGee). Austin,
    Texas: University of Texas Press.
Barber, Karin. 1991. *I Could Speak Until Tomorrow:* Oríkì*, Women and the Past in a
    Yoruba Town.* Edinburgh: Edinburgh University Press.
——— 1999. 'Quotation in the constitution of Yorùbá oral texts'. *Research in African
    Literatures* 30(2):17–41.
——— 2012. *Print Culture and the First Yoruba Novel: I.B. Thomas's 'Life Story of Me,
    Ṣẹgilọla' and Other Texts* (ed., trans., intro. Karin Barber). Leiden: Brill.
Eisenstein, Elizabeth. 1979. *The Printing Press as an Agent of Change:
    Communications and Cultural Transformations in Early-modern Europe.*
    Vol. 1. Cambridge: Cambridge University Press.
Guyer, Jane. 1996. 'Traditions of invention in equatorial Africa'. *African Studies Review*
    39(3):1–28.
Habermas, Jürgen. 1992 [1962]. *The Structural Transformation of the Public Sphere*
    (trans. Thomas Burger with Frederick Lawrence). Cambridge, Mass: MIT
    Press.
Kagame, Alexis. 1969. *Introduction aux grands genres lyriques de l'Ancien Rwanda.*
    Butare, Rwanda: Editions universitaires du Rwanda.
Masten, Jeffrey. 1994. 'Beaumont and/or Fletcher: collaboration and the interpretation
    of Renaissance drama'. In: Martha Woodmansee and Peter Jaszi (eds). *The
    Construction of Authorship: Textual Appropriation in Law and Literature.*
    Durham NC: Duke University Press, 361–81.
Miller, Hillis. 1979. 'The critic as host'. In: Harold Bloom *et al.* (eds). *Deconstruction
    and Criticism.* New York: Seabury Press.
Newell, Stephanie. 2013. *The Power to Name: A History of Anonymity in Colonial
    West African Newspapers.* Athens, OH: Ohio University Press.
Omu, Fred. 1978. *Press and Politics in Nigeria, 1880–1937.* Atlantic Highlands, NJ:
    Humanities Press.

Peel, J.D.Y. 2000. *Religious Encounter and the Making of the Yoruba*. Bloomington: Indiana University Press.

Riffaterre, Michael. 1978. *Semiotics of Poetry.* Bloomington: Indiana University Press.

Thomas, Isaac Babalola. 1930. *Itan Emi Ṣẹgilọla, Ẹlẹyinju Ẹgẹ Ẹlẹgbẹrun Ọkọ l'aiye.* [The Life-story of Me, Ṣẹgilọla of the fascinating eyes, she who had a thousand lovers in her life]. Lagos.

CHAPTER 5

In whose image or likeness?

Publishing and the literary order in

early post-colonial Nigeria

ⒸⒸⒸⒸⒸⒸⒸⒸⒸⒸ

PATRICK OLOKO

In the promotion of literary works one is basically giving to hitherto unknown writers a certain amount of symbolic power and in the canonization of their work this power is transformed into an enormous amount of symbolic capital which confers the power to set agendas and give authority to a hierarchy of literary values.
(Becky Clarke 2003:166)

We are niche publishers with a specialist product. We have lost many of our links with our core academic market chasing pipe dreams that each and every book that we publish, often by an unknown author, should be treated by the international literary world as if it were a new Chinua Achebe.
(Heinemann Management Memo 1992, quoted in Barnett 2006:28)

The canon is chosen, not born.
(Sarah M. Corse 1997:9)

Introduction

When Keith Sambrook of Heinemann and Chinua Achebe, the publisher's Nigerian flagship author, started to work together on the African Writers Series (AWS)[1] imprint in 1963, both 'shared two ambitions', in the words of James Currey (2008:xv): 'they wanted students in African schools and universities to be able to read imaginative work by Africans; and they were determined

---

1   Henceforth AWS.

to introduce African writers to an international literary audience'. Their joint pursuit of these ambitions has undoubtedly led to what Achebe has described as 'the efflorescence of modern African literature' (1996:xiii), making Heinemann the most visible player in the literary economy of the continent. Currey's memoir, aptly titled *Africa Writes Back: The African Writers Series & The Launch of African Literature* (2008), gives insight into how the business strategy of Heinemann was experimental, goal-oriented and need-specific, thereby leading to results that gave the publisher considerable edge over its competitors. That positioning enabled the company to set standards, agendas and frameworks for publishing in Nigeria and Africa as a whole for a long period.

A close scrutiny of the canons in many national or regional literatures often reveals the specifiable tastes and values of identifiable interests or groups running through them. Writers and publishers, as agents of value construction and codification, may find themselves empowered at certain historical moments to decide the shape and character of literary values that the national chain could assume or should accommodate (Bourdieu 1984). This has led to the view that, in general, 'canon formation and maintenance are meaning-making processes shaped by the tastes and social locations of those who create and maintain canons' (Corse 1997:11). In regions with relatively short histories of statehood (such as post-colonial Nigeria), where value creation and sustenance necessarily demanded the collaboration of all citizens and institutions, close partnerships between publishers and authors as specified above have been crucial in the evolution of a modern national literature. More importantly, the very recentness of such a literature, and the general essence of the Nigerian example as a counter narrative, would tend to make such a pattern of entrenched privileged values more likely and traceable. Thus, following the view of Corse that canons are subject to manipulation – 'some texts and some social conditions will be ignored, while others are emphasized, and still others are mis-specified or only partially acknowledged' (1997:11) – the authors, titles and types of literature that the ambitions of Sambrook and Achebe led them to privilege and support with Heinemann's vast publishing infrastructure, and what authors and text-types they were constrained to leave out, ignore or censor in their effort to constitute a publisher's canon of modern African literature, has come under consistent review. To fully understand Heinemann's success story in the inauguration of modern African literature, questions relating to the order of publishing that it introduced, the criteria of value that informed its editors' selection of manuscripts for publication, and how that process became an important filtration mechanism for constituting the African literature that we know today, need to be fully explored.

This chapter draws attention to unpublished manuscripts as a neglected but fresh source for those seeking to understand such issues and the politics of publishing and literary canon formation involved in them. The manuscripts themselves, and factors surrounding their status as 'unpublished' and therefore unapproved or silenced entertainment items, when carefully assessed and interpreted, can greatly enrich our understanding of the social orders and economies in which cultural leisure goods are produced. Various complex and backstage activities influence the production of literary materials. A malleable cultural good such as the novel can be shaped by a variety of tastes and preferences aimed at hewing and consolidating a particular social order or ideology. The forms it assumes and the meanings it eventually produces are subject to a number of factors including the norm or order of writing with which writers consciously or unconsciously align themselves. For this reason, a manuscript can transform into a novel or can be prevented from making that critical transformation for various reasons ranging from considerations of its commercial viability and ideological appropriateness to more technical matters of quality. Studying the strategies of novel production and the processes that lead to the categorization of a manuscript as 'publishable' or otherwise in a given society or culture can enrich our understanding of how leisure goods tend to embody strategies for normalizing and perpetuating social orders.

To make these issues clear and manageable I examine, as a case study, an unpublished manuscript written by Nigerian writer, Akachi Adimora-Ezeigbo, and subject the phrase summarizing the editors' rationale for its rejection to semantic scrutiny. My main argument is that the literary values normalized at the inception of modern Nigeria, the production of which were dominated by Heinemann publishing, and in which Chinua Achebe and his outputs functioned as crucial determinants of what constituted 'publishable' materials, do not seem to have given much room for the emergence of alternative styles, themes and traditions of the Nigerian novel. I conclude that the career of a young or aspiring writer can gain significantly from that of an older writer in terms of inspiration, influence, discipline and talent-honing. But when it is leashed to the career of a pioneer writer by a dominant publisher working in close association with that writer, the strategic partnership can lead to interesting questions and answers about power and its relationship to literary and social agendas.

Adimora-Ezeigbo is today one of contemporary Nigeria's most prolific writers. She has to her credit a wide range of fictions, plays, poetry and children's literature that has won most of the numerous prizes for literature in the country. Her initial publishing experience, given this standing in the annals of the nation's literature, can be instantly brought into sharp focus and gives contextual and comparative perspectives to the on-going debate reappraising what Heinemann has meant to the development and growth of Nigerian post-colonial literature.

Figure 5.1   Adimora-Ezeigbo when she was about eighteen years old and had just completed writing the story during the civil war (1967–70), waiting to be able to deliver the manuscript to Heinemann. The picture was taken in a photo studio (by kind permission of Adimora-Ezeigbo).

Figure 5.2   Adimora-Ezeigbo, during the civil war; note the hairstyle, fashionable at the time. The picture was taken in a photo studio (by kind permission of Adimora-Ezeigbo).

*Figure 5.3   Theodora Akachi Adimora (as she was then called) in military
fatigues during the one-year national assignment which is
compulsory for all university graduates in Nigeria. This picture
was taken in 1975, about five years after the manuscript rejection
episode (by kind permission of Adimora-Ezeigbo).*

Cult-slavery in Igbo social life: between 'Tainted Custom' and *No Longer At Ease*

In 1971, Akachi Adimora-Ezeigbo, then known as Theodora Adimora, presented (through her literary agent, Nkem Nwankwo)[2] a manuscript entitled 'Tainted Custom', which she had written at the age of twenty, to the publishing company Heinemann. Her story is the response of a young writer to the *osu* social segregation practised in Igboland in south-eastern Nigeria. The *'osu'* is a cult-slave group ostracized from the active communal and cultural life of Igbo communities on account of their being dedicated to a deity for ritual functions (Bersselaar 2005; Nwosu 1999). They are distinguished from the *ohu* or regular slaves owned by entrepreneurs, and who could obtain freedom either by buying it or after a period of service. Financial success, in particular, could enable an *ohu* slave to integrate easily into the community and become a free participating citizen. For the *osu*, integration was virtually impossible.[3] In Igbo culture and social life, the children of *osu* are condemned to sharing the fate of their parents: excluded from the rights and privileges of the community, they can relate only with members of their group.

As a largely segmentary society, the Igbo are a closely knit ethnic group with a strong inclination for social segregation according to criteria of common

---

2   The author of *Danda* (AWS 67) and *My Mercedes is Bigger than Yours* (AWS 173).
3   Bersselaar points out that from around the 1900 many *osu* became economically independent, though their stigmatization persisted, manifesting mostly in the fact that they could not marry freeborns (2005:56).

Figure 5.4   Adimora-Ezeigbo in the 2000s (by kind permission of Adimora-Ezeigbo).

descent. Despite their avid tendency to migrate and settle in other lands, they often maintain a strong sense of community wherever they live, leading to the formation of a cluster of diasporic cultural associations and hometown unions through which they are able to maintain regular contact both among themselves abroad and with the home community. Scholars of Nigerian history and society have aptly documented this, and have also shown how the unions and associations have over time grown to become important development conduits that provide, among other things, educational scholarships to indigent members of the community, infrastructure and social amenities (Amadiume 1987; Bersselaar 2005). The protagonist of Chinua Achebe's novel, *No Longer at Ease* (1960) (to which we shall return later) is the beneficiary of one such scholarship to study in the United Kingdom. One result of this close-knit relationship is that disadvantaged groups like the *osu* continue to be stigmatized, even in the Igbo diaspora. Their vulnerability occurs more in marriage than in other social institutions. Final decisions as to whom a family member may marry are taken only after scrupulous investigations of lineage histories in order to avoid the consequences of a freeborn family being tainted with *osu* heritage. Bersselaar, quoting a government official, observed that 'however high an *osu* might rise, he could not marry a freeborn girl, and he tended to be shunned socially by the freeborn members of the community' (2005:64). Education, the Christian religion, urbanization and a rising consciousness of human rights and social justice in Nigeria has, in reality, significantly reduced the pervasiveness and stigma of *osu* social segregation. However, writers and filmmakers still find the conflict and politics of social integration associated with Igbo society's stance on marital relations with an *osu* a fertile creative territory. In this respect, they are following the literary archetype whereby, from Shakespeare through Shaw to Soyinka, marriage has permeated the literary imagination as an appropriate and revealing site for testing tolerance and its limits in interpersonal relationships across race, class and other social barriers. For the writers being examined, it is an arena for imagining and representing the struggle of the *osu* for social acceptance in a modernizing society.

The manuscript we are discussing engages the predicament of this social group by permitting the marriage of freeborn male to an *osu* female. Adimora-Ezeigbo's sense of social justice, shaped largely by the Christian-mission education she had received and also by the general presumptions of freedom, equality and human rights embodied in the post-colonial ideal of an emerging multicultural world, was awakened to the condition of the group. According to her, seeing

> how unhappy and silenced they and their children were in the community,
> I felt keenly the injustice of their oppression, even as a child, and my heart
> went out to the victims. So I decided to write about it in 'Tainted Custom'
> when I had the urge to start writing creatively.[4]

So she sets her story in the context of social fluxes and rural/urban interface and within these frameworks subverts Igbo customs by resolving her plot, against the grain, in a progressive manner. The manuscript, it must be stated, is not entirely free of the stylistic blots which we must grant the limited skill of a twenty-year-old.[5] It is, however, readable and could have benefitted from editorial intervention to become a better story, stylistically.

Adimora-Ezeigbo was not the first Nigerian writer to be intrigued by the osu phenomenon of Igboland. The issue had received tangential treatment

---

4   Email correspondence with Akachi Adimora-Ezeigbo, 16 May 2011.
5   Prior to presenting 'Tainted Custom', Adimora-Ezeigbo had published a short story entitled 'The Call of Death' in *Drum* magazine, of which Nkem Nwankwo had been an editor. As she informed me, the joy of not just being published, but being paid handsomely, made her consider writing as a career and motivated her to study English at university. Conversation with Akachi Adimora Ezeigbo, 14 November 2010.

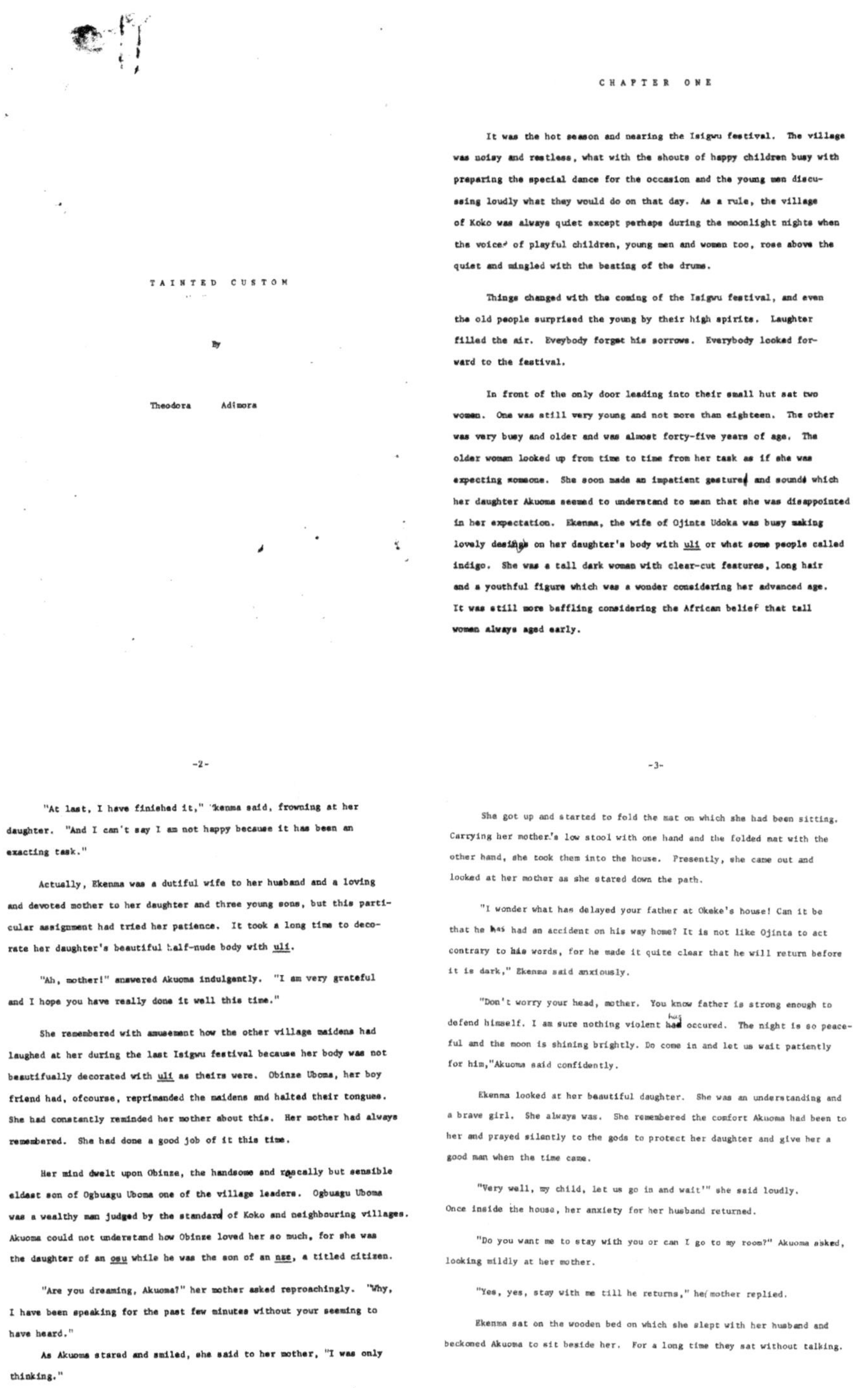

TAINTED CUSTOM

By

Theodora   Adimora

CHAPTER ONE

It was the hot season and nearing the Isigwu festival. The village was noisy and restless, what with the shouts of happy children busy with preparing the special dance for the occasion and the young men discussing loudly what they would do on that day. As a rule, the village of Koko was always quiet except perhaps during the moonlight nights when the voices of playful children, young men and women too, rose above the quiet and mingled with the beating of the drums.

Things changed with the coming of the Isigwu festival, and even the old people surprised the young by their high spirits. Laughter filled the air. Eveybody forgot his sorrows. Everybody looked forward to the festival.

In front of the only door leading into their small hut sat two women. One was still very young and not more than eighteen. The other was very busy and older and was almost forty-five years of age. The older woman looked up from time to time from her task as if she was expecting someone. She soon made an impatient gesture and sounds which her daughter Akuoma seemed to understand to mean that she was disappointed in her expectation. Ekenma, the wife of Ojinta Udoka was busy making lovely designs on her daughter's body with uli or what some people called indigo. She was a tall dark woman with clear-cut features, long hair and a youthful figure which was a wonder considering her advanced age. It was still more baffling considering the African belief that tall women always aged early.

-2-

"At last, I have finished it," 'kenma said, frowning at her daughter. "And I can't say I am not happy because it has been an exacting task."

Actually, Ekenma was a dutiful wife to her husband and a loving and devoted mother to her daughter and three young sons, but this particular assignment had tried her patience. It took a long time to decorate her daughter's beautiful half-nude body with uli.

"Ah, mother!" answered Akuoma indulgently. "I am very grateful and I hope you have really done it well this time."

She remembered with amusement how the other village maidens had laughed at her during the last Isigwu festival because her body was not beautifually decorated with uli as theirs were. Obinze Uboma, her boy friend had, ofcourse, reprimanded the maidens and halted their tongues. She had constantly reminded her mother about this. Her mother had always remembered. She had done a good job of it this time.

Her mind dwelt upon Obinze, the handsome and radically but sensible eldest son of Ogbuagu Uboma one of the village leaders. Ogbuagu Uboma was a wealthy man judged by the standard of Koko and neighbouring villages. Akuoma could not understand how Obinze loved her so much, for she was the daughter of an osu while he was the son of an nze, a titled citizen.

"Are you dreaming, Akuoma?" her mother asked reproachfully. "Why, I have been speaking for the past few minutes without your seeming to have heard."

As Akuoma stared and smiled, she said to her mother, "I was only thinking."

-3-

She got up and started to fold the mat on which she had been sitting. Carrying her mother's low stool with one hand and the folded mat with the other hand, she took them into the house. Presently, she came out and looked at her mother as she stared down the path.

"I wonder what has delayed your father at Okeke's house! Can it be that he has had an accident on his way home? It is not like Ojinta to act contrary to his words, for he made it quite clear that he will return before it is dark," Ekenma said anxiously.

"Don't worry your head, mother. You know father is strong enough to defend himself. I am sure nothing violent has occured. The night is so peaceful and the moon is shining brightly. Do come in and let us wait patiently for him," Akuoma said confidently.

Ekenma looked at her beautiful daughter. She was an understanding and a brave girl. She always was. She remembered the comfort Akuoma had been to her and prayed silently to the gods to protect her daughter and give her a good man when the time came.

"Very well, my child, let us go in and wait'" she said loudly. Once inside the house, her anxiety for her husband returned.

"Do you want me to stay with you or can I go to my room?" Akuoma asked, looking mildly at her mother.

"Yes, yes, stay with me till he returns," her/mother replied.

Ekenma sat on the wooden bed on which she slept with her husband and beckoned Akuoma to sit beside her. For a long time they sat without talking.

Figure 5.5   The first four pages of the manuscript 'Tainted Custom' (by kind permission of Adimora-Ezeigbo).

in two works of Nigeria's most acclaimed novelist, Chinua Achebe. In *Things Fall Apart* (1958), Achebe points to the social insignificance of the group by highlighting general communal indifference to its mass conversion to Christianity.[6] In *No Longer at Ease* (1960), where there is an extended treatment of the issue, Obi Okonkwo, the Western-educated protagonist of the novel, is in love with a nurse, Clara, who is an *osu*, but Achebe makes him bow to the wishes of his parents and community (in effect, the forces of Igbo culture) by not marrying her. This plot resolution enables the writer to probe into, and assess, the readiness of a people recently liberated from political oppression to permit a liberal social order shorn of discrimination and prejudice.

Both texts (that is, *No Longer at Ease* and 'Tainted Custom') assume a deep entrenchment of the issue in Igbo social relations, describe the angst surrounding it at a period of rapid social change and communicate each writer's perspectives on the change. While fervid cultural nationalism in a recently decolonized state could, in 1960, lead Achebe to justifiably represent resistance to its abolition, in 1971, when Adimora-Ezeigbo wrote, one could say that the Igbo society had undergone significant enough shifts in its orientations on issues of social justice to imagine the possibility of some degree of intolerance of the practice and assume that it can be represented in revolutionary terms as Adimora-Ezeigbo did in the manuscript.[7] In this respect, 'Tainted Custom' can be read as the intervention of its author in the effort to adjust social behaviour in a post-colonial Nigeria in urgent need of social and ethnic integration.[8] Heinemann editors considered the manuscript and returned a verdict of 'not publishable', pointing out in the accompanying rejection letter that the writer of 'Tainted Custom' was attempting to do

---

6   The community rationalized the conversion this way: 'If a gang of *efulefu* [useless people] decided to live in the Evil Forest it was their own affair. When one came to think of it, the Evil Forest was a fit home for such undesirable people.' (Achebe 1958:110).

7   The scholar, Emmanuel Obiechina, observes in this regard: 'The Igbo ... have an open, egalitarian, achievement-oriented native culture which permitted them to slide with the minimum of adjustment into modern situations and to adapt readily to the requirements of new, unusual situations.' (1973:7–8). With specific regard to slavery, Bersselaar notes that in the 1920s *ohu* who had migrated to the cities and acquired money used their financial power and 'eventually succeeded in renegotiating their social position.' He notes, however, that social discrimination against the *osu* slaves continued despite their social advancement in the professions and the civil service (2005:58).

8   The civil war which broke out in 1967, barely six years after independence from Britain, has often been attributed to improper integration of the various ethnic groups in the nation (Nwaezeigwe 1998:5).

'what Chinua Achebe could do better.'[9] This rationalization makes no explicit accusation of copyright violation. Rather, it suggests that a specific sphere of social experience had been allotted, contracted or copyrighted to a specific author.[10]

In 1978, seven years after Heinemann editors rejected Adimora-Ezeigbo's manuscript, Elechi Amadi's *The Slave* which, like 'Tainted Custom', is entirely devoted to the cult-slavery theme, was published as AWS 210, despite objections by some members of the editorial team.[11] Amadi's theme overlapped with Achebe's, but goes further back in temporal setting. Its spatial setting is among the Ikwerre of the Niger Delta. So, the decision to publish him could well have been based on the 'interesting comparison' which his temporal and spatial perspectives brought to the understanding of Achebe's novel (Currey 2008:48). An interesting point of such comparison would be the alignment of their views. Amadi's 1978 novel validates Achebe's 1960 view that cult-slavery was deeply entrenched in Igbo life. Adimora-Ezeigbo's unpublished manuscript is, on the other hand, set in a more contemporary society. But while it may fulfil the vision of a revolutionary young writer for her society in a period of rapid social change, it lacked that crucial alignment of perspective deemed necessary for publication, not to talk of canonization.

As far as the theme of cult-slavery is concerned, publishing *The Slave* and rejecting 'Tainted Custom' reveal that at Heinemann, decisions on manuscripts which explored themes of earlier publications were not arbitrary. Factors such as the market viability of an author, thematic concerns and Heinemann's definition of a comparative perspective were crucial. The possibility of establishing a genre or canon of cult-slavery fiction was essentially dependent on the agreement of perspectives within a local or in-house framework of plot resolution. Not even in imaginative literature were the slaves permitted to enjoy a measure of freedom.

Considering the market performance of *The Slave*, it is conjecturable that a published author could have a waiver and be published irrespective of

---

9   Conversation with Akachi Adimora-Ezeigbo, 14 November 2010.

10 Gbolagunte Ayedun, the publishing manager at Longman Nigeria in charge of the *Drumbeat Series*, told me that while it was quite unprofessional to phrase the rejection in such terms, the professional explanation would be that there might have been a contract between 'the publishing house and Achebe at the time that things like that [meaning exploration of such themes] would be done by Achebe. So they wouldn't want that contract breached.' (Interview, 22 May 2011).

11 Currey notes that two editors, Henry Chakava and Laban Erapu, commented thus on *The Slave* manuscript: ' the East African reader will feel quite disappointed that after 200 titles in the AWS, we are taking him back to the period before *Things Fall Apart*. But strictly as a novel it reads well.' (Currey 2008:48).

sales forecast, provided there is the crucial alignment with acceptable views on certain subjects and the possibility of previous publications making up for loss in revenue.[12] So, for a young author with no record of previous bestselling publications, the chances of getting published were minimal: authors such as Adimora-Ezeigbo had a double disadvantage if their perspectives did not pass what seemed to be the litmus test of denouement alignment. As far as this theme is concerned, the initial statement made by Achebe about the *osu* condition being insurmountable closed the canon to alternative explorations, opinions or conclusions.

These considerations implicitly touch on the issue of ownership and use(s) of immaterial cultural goods by raising questions about what is individual property, what belongs to the common pool and, most importantly, what conclusions the publisher reaches about originality. Under the law, the individual achievement of the author as the creator of a story is recognized and protected.[13] But some literary principles assume, without necessarily undermining the recognition and protection, that the story, having become a poem, a novel or a play, is now part of a collective, a pool to which no individual may lay sole claim. Intertextuality, for example, could be seen to an extent as a kind of antitrust mechanism to prevent the cartelization of literary spaces through promoting a variety of perspectives within genres. When writers appropriate subjects or materials from the existing pool of stories and rephrase them in an attempt to offer competing perspectives on the human condition, they are engaged in a creative process that Turk (2011:295) calls 'the collaborative construction of narrative'. Yet, as the foregoing analysis suggests, this creativity can account for the refusal to publish the resulting manuscript. So what seems to be the principal factor in text production is the publisher's definition of originality, a definition which can be informed by several considerations.

Achebe and Heinemann: ancestor worship as 'norm' in manuscript selection and text protection

How does a manuscript constitute and describe the relationship between a new writer seeking to be heard and an older or published writer authorized to give voice? In early post-colonial Nigeria, various commercial, ideological and political interests litter the space between the completion of a manuscript and its publication. These interests must be engaged and negotiated with,

---

12   The combined sales for Amadi's titles, *The Concubine*, *The Great Ponds* and *Sunset in Biafra* in 1982 stood at 400,000 (Currey 2008:49).

13   Nigerian copyright law supports the moral rights of the author and protects unpublished manuscripts (Shyllon 2003:63–6).

despite what seems to be a virgin space for both writing and publishing. As founding editor of AWS, Achebe chose the series' first hundred titles (Clarke 2003). In spite of his performance of this job 'shockingly without pay' (Clarke 2003:164), there are misgivings about what he might have done wittingly or otherwise towards fostering a canon of his tastes. Mpe (1999) has pointed to a 'uniformity of approach to writing and politics within the AWS' and how 'it led to a concentration of titles from West Africa' (112).[14] Stec (1997) and Umeh (2010) write of other strategies of inclusion and exclusion that have given the canon of African literature its character, with Stec concluding that Heinemann exemplifies how '[t]he publishing industry has a significant impact on the production, maintenance and destruction of "literary value"' (1997:146). In the following view, Griffiths (1997) also observes that Heinemann and Achebe might have collaborated in the framing of themes and setting of agendas for the Nigerian novel.

> Heinemann Educational proceeded by appointing Achebe as General Editor of the series with a roving commission to seek out young writers, and the early volumes of the series contain clear evidence of Achebe's novels serving not only as examples to would-be young writers but also as literary templates of what a modern Nigerian novel in English might be. So much so, in fact, that each of Achebe's novels can be said not only to have established a text but also a genre. Thus, *Things Fall Apart* and his third novel *Arrow of God* established what we might call the novel of colonial impact crisis; whilst his second novel, *No Longer at Ease,* and the fourth, *A Man of the People*, established the novel of identity crisis and political corruption in post-independence Nigeria.
>
> (Griffiths 1997:133)

Following this view, Charles Nnolim observed implicitly in his essay titled 'The Sons of Achebe: example of John Munonye' (2010), that a procedure for manuscript selection and publication included allegiance to persons and

---

14 Even though Currey (2003) and Clarke (2003) have suggested that this accusation is untenable, new and forceful evidence continues to emerge to reinforce its validity. The author of a recent biography of Flora Nwapa, a Nigerian female writer and the first woman to be published in the AWS, tends to validate the opinion of Mpe. According to her, while Western education taught Nwapa 'how to transform the African oral narrative traditions into the written traditions of Europe ... [h]er association with Chinua Achebe, Chukwuemeka Ike, Mabel Imoukhuede Segun, J.P. Clark and Wole Soyinka, to name only five writers, guided her into the arena of Nigerian elites and their challenges to create indigenous literature' (Umeh 2010:109).

adherence to ideological positions. According to him, John Munonye, Elechi Amadi, Onuora Nzekwu, T.M. Aluko and Flora Nwapa are Nigerian novelists whose works show explicit traces of Achebe's influence. In his opinion, these "'sons" of Achebe follow his tradition of cultural nationalism by trying, like him, to rehabilitate the dignity of the black man bruised and denigrated by the colonial master' (2010:186).

To make sense of the angst expressed here and to understand how the scenario came about, one needs to note that early post-colonial Nigeria lacked crucial canonization structures such as higher educational institutions with relevant literature curricula to 'regulate' tastes, as Corse (1997:65) has shown to be the case of the United States and Canada. Nigerian literature of the early post-colonial period did not enjoy the benefits of such intervention for two reasons. The first is that universities were just being established, and the literature curricula largely reflected foreign tastes and excluded local writings because of the nature of staff recruitment in the English Departments (Okunoye 1999). The second, as already pointed out, has to do with the counter-discursive nature of what was turning out to be 'acceptable' local writing: it lacked the necessary variety and scope to attract the needed intervention and mediation which higher educational institutions would normally provide, even if there was a willingness to offer such support. So it is possible to point out in one respect that what we now see as Achebe and Heinemann's hegemony was, in fact, necessary to hoisting the literature into place. However, the issue being contested is the shape which the literature assumed, and the fact that it could have been better without the identified blemishes in its provenance.

Let us discount the possibility that the success of Chinua Achebe might have spawned a generation of writers who 'set out consciously or unconsciously to imitate' him (Nnolim 2010:184). Let us also take for granted the fact that '[t]he importance of [his] texts in establishing what kinds of things a young Nigerian writer using English might do was clearly in part the result of the power and force of the texts in and for themselves' (Griffiths 1997:133). It is a curious fact, however, that the clan of writers identified by Nnolim constituted the core of those who got published in the early days (between 1962 and 1972) of AWS, when Achebe was 'the establishing author and general editor of the only publishing series devoted to and actively seeking out African authors' (Griffiths 1997:133). Were manuscripts selected for publication on the basis of their thematic congruence with Achebe's oeuvre? How would a young female writer exercising the quintessential right of a writer to change things by transgressing the existing order fare in this clannish publishing environment? The position of Chinua Achebe as the inaugurator, gravitational force and pillar of African post-colonial literature is beyond controversy. But the question of how much the canon he inaugurated reflects his preferred social experience needs to be answered. And, in this connection, the conclusions of the editors on 'Tainted Custom' gives added force and significance to views of the canon (whether of modern African literature or the Nigerian novel) as less than multi-focal, having been founded on frameworks and premises suitable to the commercial interests of Heinemann,[15] and the ideological objectives which Achebe expected the post-colonial novel to achieve.

Achebe was indeed the writer who brought representational distinction to Igbo caste discrimination in his second novel, *No Longer at Ease*. The novelty of subject in his first novel, its accessible language and style as well as its challenge of the imperial literary tradition which had erected Conrad, Cary and others as producers of 'African' literature of high value (Stec 1997:142) soon seized the imagination of readers in Nigeria, Africa and elsewhere. This accorded the author a cult following in literary circles that continues to this day. Editors in publishing houses, critics and scholars at the universities and allied institutions, reviewers in newspapers and journals and others who are professionally engaged with literature, turned to *Things Fall Apart* to justify their endorsement of, or objection to, new writing by others.[16] *No Longer at Ease* enabled the author to consolidate his position as the writer of the first Nigerian novels of literary merit and the inaugurator of what might be called the Nigerian tradition in the novel.

As the discussion in the next section will show, having produced the first *written* Nigerian novel with global appeal, Achebe and his writings became the clearing house for standards and literary value. This is understandable in a society just beginning to frame codes for the evaluation of its cultural products. The most visible narrative product naturally became the framework on which strategic decisions about publishing were based or explained. Both writer and publisher became the fulcrum of a nascent literary culture. And, for good or otherwise, they seem to have constituted a symbiotic, tag-team relationship

---

15 Clarke notes that those who tend to praise the publisher are the writers published and given a voice by the firm, while criticism has often come from 'field practitioners whose job it is to enquire into literature and the coding of literary value' (2003:166). Although this construction oversimplifies the configurations of the debate, there is however, some truth to the view that discussions of Heinemann's role in the growth and development of African literature often takes passionate and dispassionate dimensions.

16 Early reviews of *Efuru* and *Idu*, two novels written by the first Nigerian female writer, Flora Nwapa, seem to betray the hostility and resistance to portraits of issues outside the typology being made popular by Achebe. Adeola James, who was to later recant her view, described Nwapa as driven by basic impulses in her novels. See Adeola 1971 and 1990.

to further the frontiers of writing and the publishing of African 'stories of reconstitution and reclamation' (Clarke 2003:168) to 'an international market both within Africa and across the world' (Currey 2008:583).

Publishing in colonial and early post-colonial Nigeria

British multinational publishing firms such as Nelson, Longman, Evans and Heinemann have long been a part of the history of Nigerian literary publishing. In colonial times, doing business in the virgin Nigerian publishing space enabled them to conduct the trade in a more professional manner than their local counterparts. Their existence and business activities in the region gave force to what has been described as the 'special closeness between colonization and literature, between the reality of colonial subjugation and its many stories' (Achebe 1996:xiii). Not only were they setting standards in the trade, but they also performed the important role of weaning writers from the oral to the written medium, from writing in local languages to writing in English; and from using rudimentary English to the sophistication that we find later in Achebe and his contemporaries. Even though their activities in the pre-independence knowledge economy have been assailed as tending to render invisible local perspectives in order to further the interests of empire (Achebe 1996:xiii; Hill 1998, quoted in Clarke 2003:163), it is also true that at the early stages, these publishers played important roles in the development of not only writing, but also of publishing in general by setting and promoting acceptable industry standards.

For example, as early as 1938, Nelson began publishing literature in local Nigerian languages with a novel in Yoruba, written by Daniel Fagunwa. Later, in 1952, Faber and Faber published Amos Tutuola's *The Palm Wine Drinkard*, written in quaint English and described by Currey as leading the way for a genre of 'Englished novels' (Currey 2008:42). In 1954, Andrew Dakers published *People of the City*, a novel by Cyprian Ekwensi, who had started to hone his literary career by writing in English and publishing with local or indigenous publishers at Lagos and the commercial city of Onitsha.[17]

A close examination of the language(s), style and early careers of these pioneer writers reveals that the overseas publishers adopted a gradualist, purpose-driven approach to publishing literary materials in a region where Western literacy as well as the mastery of the English language required for the reading and writing of literature were still in their infancy. British multinational publishers and their local counterparts existed side by side in the early stages of the publishing trade, but played different roles with regard

---

17 Ekwensi's earliest works, *Ikolo the Wrestler* and *When Love Whispers*, were published in 1947 by Tabansi Bookshop at Onitsha. See Obiechina (1973:3).

to the quality of writing their weaning of writers from an oral to a writing culture produced, and the types of audience or markets to which such writings were made available.

In 1958, however, Heinemann hewed written Nigerian English-language literature of merit into shape by publishing *Things Fall Apart*. In 1962, it inaugurated the AWS and opened modern publishing facilities to 'serious' writers in the country. Pioneering a new genre of literature that highlighted the nationalist temperaments of the time made Heinemann a powerful medium and gave it a significant head start in the preferences of Nigerian authors and would-be authors, even after other publishers introduced rival series to the AWS.[18] Heinemann was the norm in literary publishing. Any writer seeking authority, authenticity, acclaim and access to local and international readership went there. As might be expected in such a situation, 'the number of writers submitting manuscripts was high and this put much pressure on Heinemann (Clarke 2003:170; Currey 2008:580), making it inevitable that some of its decisions would be injurious to new writers.[19] In the recently decolonized Nigeria, more people seemed to have had stories to tell than were willing to pay to read them.[20] Publishers in such an 'abnormal' business environment need to take tough decisions and rationalize them in appropriate, professional ways. In this regard, one can imagine how expectations of educational reforms and the restructuring of the literature curriculum might be instrumental to the marketing designs of Heinemann, enabling it to dictate, 'literally ... the forms and in many cases the styles of successful writers in the 1960s and even early 1970s' (Griffiths 1997:135).

The second excerpt at the beginning of this chapter, which seems to express anxiety about the business fortunes of Heinemann, underscores the value and brand status of Chinua Achebe for the organization. Theo Vincent, a notable Nigerian critic and first reviewer of Ben Okri's early novels, views the partnership in cynical terms:

---

18 The earliest of them was Three Crown Series, established in 1963 by Oxford University Press. Others are Fontana Paperback, promoted by Collins and which published Buchi Emecheta; the Modern African Library promoted by Andre Deutsch, and the Drumbeat Series, published by Longman. For how these competed with the AWS, see Currey (2008:14–6).

19 Currey puts the ratio of unpublished/published manuscripts at 'forty or fifty to one' (2003:580).

20 Ku-Mesu (1998) argues that in Nigeria those who have mastered the English language well enough to understand its intricate literary usage often read materials other than literature 'to get about the business of everyday life'.

When you are publishing in a strange environment, you need advice. But there is the danger of stereotyping if you rely too much on a particular source of advice. While the dangers of replication are obvious, a good publisher would be able to see the extra dimensions which other writers bring to a theme. However, publishers sometimes become hostages. To prevent this, you can use the assessment of someone who doesn't have an interest..., someone who is not competing with anybody.[21]

Between authority and dissent

The struggle of a writer or novelist to be published in early post-colonial Nigeria was part of a larger struggle to negotiate a new frame in the novel for old subjects suited to the oral medium. Modern methods of publishing seemed to have made the struggle a competition of sorts, in which advantages accrued to writers depending on their temporal locations. So while a pioneer writer had all the early-bird advantages, a young writer shaped by the same socio-cultural environment was saddled with a latecomer's disadvantages in a game where the rules of play had been framed by a party to the competition. This is one way to look at the issue under review. The immediate fallout of the novelty and spirit which Achebe brought to the Nigerian novel was the conferment on him of what amounted to a copyright to the subjects he treated, notwithstanding their appropriation from the communal repertory, the public domain of Igbo cultural practices.

Although the relationship between the writer and the publisher as enunciated by Clarke in the excerpt at the top of this chapter is couched in symbiotic terms, it translates, under closer scrutiny, as akin to that between a horse and its rider. The power of the writer is dependent on the willingness of a publisher to publish and promote the work. The writer may have a voice but it still needs to be activated by the publisher. The writer might have a subject, but it must fit into the agenda and tone of the publisher. Essentially then, the power which writing confers is attained largely at the behest of the publisher.

Essentially also, to return to the manuscript, the issue at stake is the conflict in ideas of how to relate to cultural goods introduced by new methods of tale production, dissemination and consumption associated with printing technology. The freedom permitted to the oral narrator to add, delete or extend the oral tale is appropriated by Adimora-Ezeigbo in a modern setting and used to reveal her personal vision of society and to propose change. Although her proposition tallies with ideas of how existence *should* be transacted in a modern, post-colonial nation, its ends or purposes are subversive to established

---

21   Interview with Professor Theo Vincent, 10 May 2011.

institutions.[22] In representing a social anomaly, she adduces an interesting dimension, but one that goes against the grain. Achebe, on his part, narrates tradition and interrogates it cautiously and tactfully to show his modern post-colonial awakening to an uncertain future where new ideas such as human rights, social justice and other ideals need to be fully tested and understood before being used. This approach tallies with a theme that runs through his oeuvre, namely, that society will always find a way to recreate itself.

The complex requirements of modern literary communications in particular, and writing culture in general, have brought the interpretations of materials taken from the same cultural environment into competition for acceptance and canonization. This is not to suggest that societies with oral cultures did not encourage competition among their artists. But that competition took a different form by enabling narratives to come alive or to be 'published' before the audience. In other words, competition was crucial to the transmission and flourishing of narratives as evident in festivals and other occasions of that ilk. Modern competition in the literary context entails, however, that unsuitable tales or narratives are silenced before they get to the audience, at the stage of manuscript selection, a process often lacking clearly defined procedures and subject to the tastes and fortunes of publishers. In the competition, the conflict is not really between tradition and modernity. Nor is it necessarily between art and trash, which would be the easy conclusion of any uncritical examiner of the issues. Rather what is on show is more or less an aspect of the eternal struggle for supremacy between authority and dissent in which the anti-normative, seeking recognition and legitimacy, engages the normative order. It is also an aspect of the archetypal struggle between innocence and experience, which has nothing to do with the age, achievements or status of the writers in question, but much to do with activism and a desire to deploy art for practical and functional purposes in a society in dire need of reform.

Let us return once again to the phraseology of the rejection. The decision as to whether to publish a manuscript may be taken after consideration of several explicit and implicit factors.[23] While the explicit factors may relate in general

---

22 Significantly, Adimora-Ezeigbo's career as a writer has been largely defined by this tendency to appropriate materials from oral tradition for subversive use in fighting discrimination. See Arndt (2008) for how the technique is used in the interrogation of sex discrimination.

23 With regard to the publisher in review, Barnett (2006:21) has put the scenario succinctly in the following terms: 'The process of canonization, in which Heinemann played a critical role through the construction of the AWS list, is not best thought of as a process of inclusion and exclusion, but more in terms of a process of selection by reference to explicit and implicit criteria.'

to the environment in which the business of publishing is conducted as well as the quality of the document being considered, the 'implicit' factors, as the term implies, lie outside the domain of transparency. But the marginalization of a minor writer becomes an important political issue when it cannot be convincingly justified. At a nascent period in national literary history, when what got published was significant in framing the direction of the canon, an attempt at such a justification through relating the minor writer to a major one in an ambiguous phrase can lead to questions and doubts which may, in turn, also lead to major discoveries. For example, considering the uses to which a pioneer publisher can put its wide discretionary power, would Heinemann be willing to undertake the business risk of instituting the process of canonizing a young writer who is intertextually subversive to Chinua Achebe, its pioneer and best-selling author? Can one imagine, as part of the implicit criteria for manuscript selection, 'sacred' spheres of representation allotted to specific authors at this time in Nigerian literary history?[24] Answers to these questions are likely to be couched in conjectural terms that can only further increase the semantic jigsaw puzzle of the rejection terminology. However, certain conclusions from the speculations can become food for thought in view of the peculiarity of the situation we are discussing.

Publishing decisions, when rationalized in terms such as the editors of Heinemann had used, easily acquire implications, understandings and interpretations (probably never intended) that put the integrity of the publisher in focus, even if they are consistent with the realities and procedures of the trade.[25] When the rejection of a manuscript is phrased in terms that centralize a publisher's best-selling author as background and litmus test for the selection of manuscripts, grounds abound for speculations about politics, power plays and the role that positions and privileges evoke in reaching strategic decisions on publishing and canon formation. In consequence, an unpublished manuscript, which ordinarily is a negligible and neglected source because it is never allowed the chance to make the transition from an immaterial cultural item, is invested with narratives and significant material data on backstage activities that can enrich understanding of underlying issues shaping the institution and composition of literary canons and cultures.

---

24   'There could have been an existing arrangement [or internal policy of Heinemann unknown to Achebe] that if it is in this or that area, we continue to deal with Achebe and no one else.' Gbolagunte Ayedun, Interview, 22 May 2011.

25   The view of Clarke (2003:171) is particularly illuminating in this regard: 'Often, publishers who are not culturally grounded or choose to ignore the importance of such a background are the managers and decision-makers who control the final selection processes.'

Studying it would therefore perform two vital functions. The first is that it can highlight a story hitherto consigned to eternal silence and reveal another world outside the visible, copyrighted and therefore protected story of the published document. The other is that it can deepen our understanding of literary issues and history, in particular the roles that 'invisible' forces play as part of their organizing principles. A lot of writing goes on, and many more works are generally condemned than are published. Unpublished manuscripts tend to indicate what preoccupies people who attempted to write, their ideas, themes, the kind of social order they desired and the statements they try to make. Sometimes their themes may be relevant, but the execution might not be good enough, or vice versa. But what is quite clear is that they are part of the intellectual fund of particular periods in literary histories. For this reason, they deserve some examination by researchers, and publishers should be encouraged to keep copies for that purpose.[26]

Conclusion

The foregoing discussion has shown that if Heinemann had a policy of grooming young writers in the early days of its operations in Nigeria, 'it erected Chinua Achebe as the model to follow. Young writers who had struck progressive, prophetic and socially relevant themes were largely obliged to align themselves with his craft and ideology. Works like 'Tainted Custom' fitted within a schema of 'experimental techniques that do not comply or conform to … standards of authority [and were therefore less] suitable for didactic engagement' (Clarke 2003:165), a manuscript selection criterion crucial to the market success of Heinemann as an educational publisher. Part of the long term effect of this is the fear that Nigerian literature is in danger of stagnation because contemporary writers have largely been unable to sustain the tradition of Achebe and his generation.[27]

These issues are intricately connected with the late emergence of *written* literature in Nigeria and the fact that writers suddenly found themselves in a competitive literary environment where, among other things, 'publishers publish what they decide to publish for a variety of reasons, not least among the

---

26 In the course of research for this chapter, I asked publishers to let me into the archives to look at unpublished works. I was informed that publishers maintain archives of published, not unpublished, manuscripts. 'Once a manuscript is considered not publishable, it is returned', says Gbola Ayedun, who told me he receives, on the average, ten manuscripts monthly for consideration for the *Drumbeat Series* of Longman (Interview, 22 May 2011).

27 Charles Nnolim, 'Contemporary Nigerian Fiction'. A keynote address presented at the Annual Convention of the Association of Nigerian Authors (ANA), Imo State Branch, 6–7 July 2005.

reason [being] that they are in business to make money.'[28] The codification of
the tale or local literary materials in new and retrievable forms made possible
by the introduction of print technology may portray the advance of a literature
and the keen efforts of its producers to key into the modernization processes
of the time. The advancement came, in early post-colonial Nigeria, however,
with significant modifications of the underlying structures and principles of
narrative production, transmission and consumption, and generated tension
and controversies about ownership and originality.[29] Much of the controversy
and tension had to do with the emergence of a literary web in which the
publisher is located between the writer and the reader as the superintending
partner with powers to dictate tastes, canons and entertainment options.

The new structure differs from the old, pre-writing literary order in
which the oral tale had existed in the communal repertory largely as a fluid,
immaterial cultural item which the oral artist may render or reorder to suit
defined local purposes, audiences and exigencies (see also the contributions of
Barber and Diawara in this volume). Though he has retained the prerogative
to extract tales and redesign plots for certain purposes, the writer lacks the
latitude of the oral artist in such matters largely because he must take into
account a variety of interests and issues such as contexts, influences and
versions as defined by the publisher. That is, he must deal with the publisher
by operating within the ambit of the tale as a *material*, concrete or printed
structure, with a fixed or identifiable owner.

In such a circumstance, the understanding between readers and writers
that multiple perspectives on a subject both enrich the medium and also map
social transformation, though still at the core of tale designs and redesigns
such as that done by Adimora-Ezeigbo in 'Tainted Custom', must now be
redefined or qualified to accommodate publishers' interest. In the past century
or so, plot redesign in oral narratives would have been fully explanatory and
accessible to the tale consumers. Now they require a more elaborated form
to better reflect changing social realities, and, in their written form, to reach
a larger public. As direct transfer of narratives began to decline with the
rise of print literature, the publisher, with his facilities and ideologies, could

28 See the editorial in the inaugural volume of *African Literature Today*, cited in
    Jones (1979:5).
29 In one such controversy, Achebe was accused of having plagiarized a pamphlet
    titled *The History of Umuchu*, written by Simon Nnolim, in his novel, *Arrow
    of God* (see Nolim 1977). A counter-argument, however, was that 'both Simon
    Nnolim and Chinua Achebe tapped from the same oral source' (Bodunde 1998:56).
    The conclusion of Nnolim overlooked influence as a valid creative technique,
    and this oversight seemed to be symptomatic of the tension characterizing the
    transition from an oral to a written medium.

significantly shape what the tale should be and be about, its proprietary structure and consumption patterns. Tale ownership in early post-colonial Nigeria, as a result of this development, became tied to its *written* provenance, with new rights and privileges vested in the *writer*. Even though he may have appropriated it from the communal repertory, he had the foresight to secure ownership through early registration of copyrights and/or signing of contract terms, with the publisher.[30]

References

Achebe, Chinua. 1958. *Things Fall Apart*. London, Ibadan and Nairobi: Heinemann.

——— 1963. *No Longer at Ease*. London, Ibadan and Nairobi: Heinemann.

——— 1996. 'Foreword'. *n:* Henry Chakava. *Publishing in Africa: One Man's Perspective*. Boston and Nairobi: Bellagio and EAEP (Bellagio Studies in Publishing 6), xiii–xiv.

Adimora, Theodora. Tainted Custom. Manuscript.

Amadiume, Ifi. 1987. *Male Daughters, Female Husbands: Gender and Sex in an African Society*. London and New Jersey: Zed Books.

Arndt, Susan. 2008. 'Paradigms of intertextuality: orature and writing back in the fiction of Akachi Adimora-Ezeigbo'. In: Patrick Oloko (ed.). *The Fiction of Akachi Adimora-Ezeigbo: Issues and Perspectives*. Lagos: ACI, 15–65.

Barnett, Clive. 2006. 'Disseminating Africa: burdens of representation and the African Writers Series'. *New Formations* 57:74–94.

Bersselaar, Dmitri Van Den. 2005. 'Imagining home: migration and the Igbo village in colonial Nigeria'. *Journal of African History* 46:51–73.

Bourdieu, Pierre. 1984. *Distinction: A social Critique of the Judgement of Taste* (trans. Richard Nice). Cambridge, MA: Harvard University Press.

Bodunde, Charles. 1998. 'Sources, influences and originality: issues in critical controversies'. *Kola* 10(31):3–12.

Chakava, Henry. 1996. *Publishing in Africa: One Man's Perspective* (Bellagio Studies in Publishing 6). Boston and Nairobi: Bellagio and EAEP.

Clarke, Becky. 2003. 'The African Writers Series – celebrating forty years of publishing distinction'. *Research in African Literature* 34(2):163–74.

---

30   Part of the throes of this transition was evident in the fact that local publishers were either unaware of or deliberately ignored paying royalties to writers. As a result, they were losing business to British publishers. For example, in 1959, Nigerian Printing and Publishing Company 'published' T.M. Aluko's *One Man One Wife* without signing a contract and paying royalties to the author. Not until 1967, when Heinemann expressed interest in taking over the title via reprinting rights was the author paid royalties (see Currey 2008:43).

Corse, Sarah. 1997. *Nationalism and Literature: The Politics of Culture in Canada and the United States*. Cambridge: Cambridge University Press.

Currey, James. 2003. 'Chinua Achebe, the African Writers Series and the establishment of African Literature'. *African Affairs* 102:575–85.

——— 2008. *Africa Writes Back: The African Writers Series and the Launch of African Literature*. London: James Currey.

Griffiths, Gareth. 1997. 'Documentation and communication in postcolonial societies: the politics of control'. *The Year Book of English Studies* 27 (*The Politics of Postcolonial Criticism*): 130–6.

James, Adeola. 1971. 'Idu'. A review of Flora Nwapa's novel. *African literature Today* 5:150–3.

——— 1990. *In Their Own Voices: African Women Writers Talk*. London: James Currey.

Jones, Eldred. 1979. 'Editorial: ten years of African literature today'. *ALT 10 (Retrospect & Prospect)*:1–5.

Ku-Mesu, Katalin Egri. 1998. 'African literature survival outside the realm of large world publishers: illusion or reality?' *Mots Pluriels* 5 (www.arts.uwa.edu.au/ Mots Puriels/MP5984.html).

Heinemann Management Memo. 1992. 'The African and Caribbean Writers Series Performance Analysis, 21st August, 1996'. University of Reading, Department of Archives and Manuscripts, HEB File No 56/6.

Mpe, Phaswane. 1999. 'The role of the Heinemann African Writers Series in the development and promotion of African Literature'. *African Affairs* 58(1):105–22.

Nnolim, Charles. 1977. 'A source for *Arrow of God*'. *Research in African Literature* 8:1–26.

——— 2005. 'Contemporary Nigerian Fiction'. A keynote address presented at the Annual Convention of the Association of Nigerian Authors (ANA), Imo State Branch 6-7 July 2005.

——— 2010. 'The Sons of Achebe: Example of John Munonye'. In: *Issues in African Literature*. Lagos: Malthouse Press Limited, 181–94.

Nwaezeigwe, Nwankwo. 1988. 'Ethnicity and the politics of Igbo Yoruba relations: a case of celebration of defeat?' Special Lecture Series II, Department of Political Science, University of Lagos, October 1998.

Nwosu, Okenwa. 1999. 'Osu caste system: a Cultural Albatross for the Igbo Society'. www.nigeriaworld.com (19 June 1999).

Obiechina, Emmanuel. 1973. *An African Popular Literature: A Study of Onitsha Market Pamphlets*. Cambridge: Cambridge University Press.

Okunoye, Oyeniyi. 1999. 'Captives of Empire: early Ibadan poetry and poets'. *Journal of Commonwealth Literature* 34, 2:109–16.

Shyllon, Folarin. 2003. *Intellectual Property Law in Nigeria*. Munich: Verlag C.H. Beck.

Stec, Loretta. 1997. 'Publishing and canonicity: the case of Heinemann's "African Writers Series"'. *Pacific Coast Philology* 32(2):140–9.

Turk, Tisha. 2011. 'Intertextuality and the collaborative construction of narratives: J.M. Coetzee's *Foe*'. *Narrative* 19, 3:295–310.

Umeh, Marie Linton. 2010. *Flora Nwapa: A Pen and a Press*. New York: Triatlantic.

CHAPTER 6

Covers, remixes and mash-ups

Locating African hip-hop in intellectual property rights discourse[1]

©©©©©©©©©©

Caroline Mose

Introduction[1]

Hip-hop is a popular urban cultural and musical form that has its modern origins in late 1960s and early 1970s New York City (Chang 2005; KRS One 2003; Toop 2000). Riddled by poverty and a seeming lack of attention by federal and state government, the predominantly immigrant and African-American population of New York's less glamorous neighbourhood of the Bronx began to coalesce around a new form of musical and cultural expression that included disc jockeys (DJs) producing live music and oratory masters (MCs) reciting simple rhymes over the music in what were termed 'block parties' (Chang 2005). The DJ would, in coming years, evolve into the producer, while the MC would evolve into the rapper, adept at creating complex and thought-provoking rhymes (Forman and Neal 2004). The two would form a special partnership that exists to this day and is responsible for the creation and production of rap music.

---

1   This chapter is based on research conducted in Nairobi, Kenya, between September 2009 and April 2011 for both a doctoral thesis and two workshops of the Cluster of Excellence, Goethe University, Frankfurt, held in Bad Homburg, Germany in December 2010 and June 2011. Special thanks are due to the Felix Trust, School of Oriental and African Studies (University of London), and convenors of the Bad Homburg workshops, Mamadou Diawara and Ute Röschenthaler. A more detailed version of this chapter appears in a broader doctoral thesis on Kenyan hip-hop, submitted in 2012.

In later decades, specifically from the late 1980s to the early 1990s, African hip-hop (re)-emerged across African cities in similar settings that required budding artists to perform live in front of eager audiences, with no accompaniment save a microphone and a 'beat' originated by dance hall DJs playing around with keyboards and rudimentary machines (Keyes 1991). Most of these 'beats' were bits and pieces of the foreign rap music that had gained a devoted following among listeners in countries that were undergoing a liberation of their airwaves after the political changes in Africa in the early 1990s (Kirschke 2000) that saw a proliferation of independent radio and television stations playing this music. Since then, hip-hop music – rap – has come a long way. Created, at its inception, through a variety of fascinating processes that included borrowing and appropriating sounds from different sources, it has currently re-invented these processes. Together with globalization and the current market system in which consumer goods are exchanged for income, these processes provoke interesting debates surrounding intellectual property (IP) ownership, norms and practices. In this chapter, I examine Kenyan hip-hop and the norms and the legal framework that determine its creation, ownership and dissemination. I question who can own music that ends up being remixed and co-opted into hip-hop, and who ultimately owns the finished product. Finally, I examine the issues around piracy and the 'cannibalism' of texts that hip-hop intrinsically integrates, examining the decontextualization of existing sounds that are appropriated by hip-hop, and thereafter re-contextualized as new (legitimate or illegitimate) music.[2]

African hip-hop and intellectual property norms – why now?

In the highly globalized world that has been spurred on by capitalism, hip-hop culture and its music finds itself interacting and negotiating with the market through the production of commodities that get exchanged for capital. The commodity I am referring here is rap music, and by capital I am making direct reference to Bourdieu's arguments that distinguish between symbolic and cultural capital, both of which translate into monetary and other forms of value (Bourdieu 1991, 1993).

In Africa generally, especially within the last decade, music shows have spread far and wide, with cable television services like South Africa's DSTV

---

2   I have used research data collected in Nairobi, Kenya, but apply it in a more general sense to analyse broader African hip-hop as well, specifically mentioning examples from Tanzania and South Africa. My focus remains Nairobi except where I make generalizations based on available literature and sources on African hip-hop.

having subscribers across the continent. Music programmes such as those made by South Africa's Channel 'O' and Nigeria's MTV Africa are also being broadcast across borders, with the bulk of their content being from southern, eastern and western Africa. This means that artists from these regions are challenged to produce music for continent-wide broadcast. Popular music is also being celebrated in Africa through music awards such as MTV Africa Music Awards (MAMAs), held annually at an African capital and shown worldwide.[3] The MAMAs have been held since 2008, and the 2009 awards were hosted in Nairobi. Together with the Channel 'O' music video awards (MVAs), the MAMAs have developed different categories for music from sub-Saharan Africa, covering genres with Anglophone, Francophone and Lusophone origins. These developments have had, and continue to have, a profound effect on the production of popular music across the continent, showing that there is both the market and aesthetic demand for African artists to embrace the production and marketing of their music, far beyond their immediate locales. African music is also generally becoming more globalized as more international stars collaborate musically with African artists. American rapper Snoop Dogg in 2011 produced a collaborative album with Nigerian popular musician D-Banj,[4] while R. Kelly, another renowned American artist, has produced a collaborative single with African artists, including Kenya's Amani, Congolese Fally Ipupa and Nigeria's 2Face Idibia.[5] Emily Wither and Teo Kermeliotis of CNN report that the R. Kelly project is ongoing towards a full album production.[6] In the case of the MAMAs, international popular personalities like English producer Trevor Nelson and American rappers Eve and Wyclef Jean have come, since its inception, to act as hosts and MCs, giving the award ceremony an international aura and in a sense legitimizing African popular music and its production on the global arena, further thrusting it onto an international stage.

In Nairobi, hip-hop artists produce music videos and compact discs that are broadcast on local television and on the internet via interactive websites such as YouTube. Locally, this music is sold to individual consumers by being marketed at live concerts or by being aired on local radio and television

---

3   The MAMAs are increasingly being attended by international musicians like Kanye West, Jay Z, Wycleff Jean, just to name three. The MC of the MAMAs held in Nairobi in August 2010 was Wycleff Jean.

4   See odili.net/news/source/2011/jul/10/809.html, accessed 10 September 2011.

5   See theglobalafrican.com/?p=218, accessed 10 September 2011.

6   See E. Wither and T. Kermeliotis, 22 Feb 2011 report at articles.cnn.com/2011-02-22/entertainment/one8.africa.rkelly_1_african-countries-pan-african-sony-music?_s=PM:SHOWBIZ, accessed 1 February 2012.

stations, especially the ones that feature local or hip-hop music. Hip-hop radio stations are a recent occurrence in Nairobi, arising from the phenomenon of community radio stations, many of which are the initiatives of hip-hop artists. An example is Koch FM, broadcasting within the Korokocho slum in Nairobi's Eastlands, and Ghetto Radio, the leading Sheng station in the country, whose broadcasting concept was the brainchild of rapper Mwafrika. Starting in the mid-1990s, the proliferation of FM stations, especially in Nairobi, served to win over an audience that had previously only the government-sponsored and controlled Kenyan Broadcasting Corporation (KBC) radio to listen to. There are now dozens of FM stations in Nairobi, necessitating the specialization of radio content, so that stations play specific types of music that other stations do not. Kiss FM, for instance plays, 'Fresh Hits', Metro FM specializes in Reggae music, Easy FM is the official Rhythm and Blues station.[7] Many other FM stations exist, including ones broadcasting in each of Kenya's forty-strong vernacular languages. On the television front there are about ten free-to-air stations broadcasting in Nairobi alone, and further cable television that subscribers pay for privately. I am belabouring the development of the radio and television sector because, according to Kenyan law, radio and television stations must broadcast at least 40 per cent local content if their licences are to be maintained and renewed.[8] Since the Kenyan film industry is not as robust as, for instance, Nigeria's Nollywood (see Jedlowski in this volume), local television stations have filled in the local content requirement with music videos by local musicians that are cheap to make, while radio stations, regardless of specialization, have been forced to broadcast local music, most of it popular urban music such as hip-hop. This has spurred the growth of local music industries, from live performance to compact discs and video.

The growth of social media and internet use in Africa is also slowly influencing the production (and subsequent distribution) of popular music, including hip-hop. From the MySpace, which provided social and virtual spaces for interaction, to Facebook and Twitter, the internet is providing a new medium for distribution of music to a potentially global audience. These recent developments are throwing the hitherto made-for-locals African popular music onto a cross-border and international stage that is governed by norms that include the quality of production, the type of language employed, and of course, the copyright standards that govern the distribution and

---

7   'R&B' specifically refers to the genre of music that developed after the demise of Disco in the early 1980s, but is now used generally to describe contemporary urban music encapsulated by artists like Michael Jackson.

8   See Jevans Nyabiage, 'Kenya: new content requirements to hit local broadcast stations', allafrica.com/stories/201107070156.html, accessed 6 July 2011.

marketing of these commodities. It is therefore an inevitable fact that IP rights, especially copyright, are soon going to become a reality for these artists, and the debate on this point must of necessity be started with regard to African popular music, and especially hip-hop.

Hip-hop as commodity and property

The process of turning hip-hop music into a commodity, also referred to as 'producing', has resulted in transformations that have direct implications for the end product, i.e. the music and the subsequent identity an artist bears.[9] It also has implications for the type of content that ends up being consumed by audiences. When militant and politically themed music is produced, a decidedly political reaction will be elicited from these audiences. Most producers, especially those that do not double up as artists themselves, only get recognized through the artists they produce; conversely, hip-hop artists become famous because producers take their live performance and transform it into a marketable product. This fact by itself points to a special symbiotic relationship between artists and producers, and by extension, audiences. Hip-hop music (rap) has become both famous and infamous[10] because it has been made, produced and put on the market as a consumer good. There are two distinct features that are considered during the process of production of the music video or the compact disc (or any other medium for the audio recording) – that is, the beat and the lyric or text. Hip-hop music is interesting in the way that these two elements can be separated from each other, and analysed independently, though contextually, as they are intertwined. Adam Sexton points out that the basic components are:

> 1. The crucial backing tracks (including but not always limited to, samples);
> 2. Lyrics; 3. A rapper's delivery or 'flow' – articulation, phrasing – and the like; 4. Everything else, more or less: 'look', originality, aura of legitimacy, charisma. The hard-to-quantify stuff.
>
> (Sexton 1995:8)

---

9   I have argued elsewhere (Mose 2011) that hip-hop artists in Africa need not be necessarily identified by the brand of music they produce, because artists often cross genres, performing political music at one point and party-themed music at another, due to differing demands.

10 While rap music has been lauded as politically conscious and responsible for paradigm shifts in many communities across the world, it has also gained infamy for being misogynistic and promoting violence. See Armstrong 2001, Haupt 2003 and hooks 1994, among others.

Sexton's fourth point alludes to what Bourdieu means by 'capital', which for a hip-hop artist stems from this aura, and which Shipley (2009) refers to as 'swagger'. Swagger (or what is sometimes referred to as 'swag') is the overall identity marker an artist acquires. This swag is important to note, as it is the symbolic form that gives both the lyric and the beat its market value. For this chapter, I focus less on this symbolic form and more on the two components, backing track and lyric, distinct from each other, which together comprise the defining characteristic of hip-hop music. The question as to whether lyrical texts are original creations or compilations from material that never fell under copyright in the public sphere[11] is of secondary importance. My discussion in this chapter therefore concentrates mainly on the IP rights debates surrounding the beat, and to a lesser extent on those concerning the lyrical content of hip-hop.

With regard to both the beat and the lyrics, a core element of hip-hop culture and music is that of production, which in turn introduces other factors, especially sampling, that have a direct bearing on normative orders such as copyright and IP rights.

THE HIP-HOP BEAT

Producing the hip-hop beat is simply creating background music, and usually refers to the non-lyrical and instrumental aspects of hip-hop. Hip-hop producers, the makers of this music, mainly use samplers, synthesizers, turntables and sequencers (plus other standard music-making studio equipment that I will not delve into here) to create the background tracks that accompany hip-hop lyrics. These background tracks are referred to as 'beats' or 'the beat'. From its inception, hip-hop DJs popularized the genre using collections of bits and pieces of chants, beats, speeches and sounds found from many different sources and mixed into what Houston Baker refers to as a 'hybrid sound' (1993a), what Michael Dyson calls a 'creative symbiosis' (2004) and what Richard Shusterman describes more elaborately as

---

11   I use the term 'public sphere' to indicate the public space in which musical commodities in question (music beat and lyrics in this case) already exist. In other words, works that are already in circulation. I make no distinction at this point whether these works are held within IP or are in the public domain, as that is not the crux of my argument. The debates arising from this non-distinction, especially in the way Kenyan hip-hop artists borrow material from different sources, is the focus of my discussion, and I argue that there is an increasing need for this trend to change in the face of globalization and legitimization of African popular music in general on the global stage.

(the) devices of cutting, mixing, and scratching [which] give rap a variety of
forms of appropriation, which seem as versatilely applicable and imaginative
as those of high art – as those, say, exemplified by Duchamp's moustache
on the Mona Lisa, Rauschenberg's erasure of a De Koonig canvas, and Andy
Warhol's multiple re-representations of pre-packaged commercial images....
Not only does it sample from a wide range of popular songs, it feeds on
classical music, TV theme songs, advertising jingles, and the electronic
music of arcade games. It even appropriates non-musical content, such as
media news reports and fragments of speeches by Malcolm X and Martin
Luther King.

(Shusterman 1991:617)

Shusterman here opens up a discussion into the production of hip-
hop, and the idea of 're-representation' as part of packaging hip-hop music.
One must start by understanding that hip-hop music is, first and foremost,
a compilation and sampling of different sounds and beats from a variety
of sources. The lyric and the beat are two composite parts of a whole that
evokes different meanings and contexts according to the specific connection
of the one to the other. They can be both mutually exclusive and inclusive.
For instance, a particular hip-hop rhyme, accompanied by a beat that has
the background sounds of a cooing baby (American producer Timbaland's
trademark)[12] will conjure up interpretations and contexts that are different
from those of the same rhyme accompanied by a beat with alternative sounds.
The rhyme may remain the same, but the accompanying beat gives it a certain
interpretative meaning. Therefore, the beat is taken very seriously by artists,
and finding the right beat can make or break a hip-hop song. Finding the right
lyric is also important, as textual rhymes accompany a specific beat to produce
contextual meanings.

A SHORT HISTORY OF PRODUCING: FROM NEW YORK TO NAIROBI
New York DJs in the 1970s, sampling music and sounds from different sources
during block parties, perfected their scratching and mixing skills at live
performances. Due to the racial segregation of the time, these South Bronx
block parties were attended mainly by African-American and immigrant

---

12   Timbaland was the first hip-hop/R n B producer to ignore samples and create
     tracks from original beats, inserting whimsical sounds like cooing babies or
     neighing horses. See www.answers.com/topic/timbaland-magoo (no author),
     accessed 20 February 2012.

communities,[13] and it would be obvious to conclude that these DJs had no fear of lawsuits over copyright infringement. However, while creativity in mixing music for a party may have been difficult to legislate, when hip-hop music began to be marketed and sold, these mixes became problematic, with issues of copyright creeping up to question where the DJs and record producers working in the studios acquired the background beats that accompanied rap rhymes (Considine 1995; Chang 2005).

The predominant American literature suggests that hip-hop producing was first done by Afrika Bambaata, one of the forefathers[14] of hip-hop culture and music, who produced the Furious Five in the 1980s using samples from different songs.[15] In the mid-1980s, hip-hop group Run DMC produced the songs 'It's like that' and 'Sucker MCs', opting exclusively to use digital beats and ignoring samples altogether. Since then, hip-hop producers have adopted either of these two techniques; that is, creatively using samples and remixing them, or simply producing digital beats (Schur 2009). In the 1990s and into the 2000s, producers became more and more creative with sampling and digital production, including all manner of sounds in their mixes.

In Kenya, as elsewhere in the world of hip-hop (and even from the inception of hip-hop in the South Bronx), it is the producer who looks for a beat. The producer, who also functioned as the DJ in the early days of hip-hop, samples different sounds and finds an appropriate combination that suits the artist. In the late 1990s and early 2000s in Nairobi, as hip-hop artists began to emerge, and with them a market demand for their music, most musicians opted to feature on compilation albums that featured a variety of artists performing different genres of songs. A compilation album is one in which budding artists or groups each contribute a song in the making of

---

13 Chang (2005:80–115) recounts how the inner city was racially divided, and how the system of apartheid in South Africa in the 1960s fired the African-American imagination into describing the inner city of New York as being an apartheid city. He further recounts how dangerous, if not deadly, crossing these racial boundaries was. It is therefore safe to conclude from these discussions that in all likelihood, white record executives might not have been aware of, and therefore did not legislate for, the mixing and scratching of records for early hip-hop music.

14 The tag 'forefathers of hip-hop' was given to the three 1970s New York DJs who revolutionized the hip-hop scene via the block party. They are DJ Kool Herc, Afrika Bambaata and Grandmaster Flash (Forman and Neal 2004).

15 While Bambaata is credited as the first-ever DJ, there have been claims that Jimmy Savile from North Yorkshire, England, was the first radio DJ to use the turntable, in 1947. See www.guardian.co.uk/culture/2004/apr/20/guesteditors2, accessed 10 January 2012.

an album. These artists are usually young men,[16] inexperienced, and with
few resources for creating artist-branded albums. The artist pays nothing
to have his song included in the album, and expects little in return also, but
reaps real rewards from publicizing his presence and his brand of music.
For instance, Kalamashaka's first production was in a compilation tape that
included other artists of different genres. This was a typical occurrence,
as there were few studios to choose from; in 1996, one of the few available
studios was Tedd Josiah's Audio Vault Studios (now named Blue Zebra), which
produced the compilation albums *Kenyan: The First Chapter* and *Kenyan: The
Second Chapter*, in 1998 and 1999 respectively.[17] These two albums featured
Hardstone and Kalamashaka, both credited as Kenya's pioneer rappers and
hip-hop maestros (Nyairo and Ogude 2005; Mose 2011).

Producing albums has come a long way since then. The compilation album
format has been abandoned as artists aspire to be known on their own merit.
Studios have proliferated in Nairobi, with production hardware and software
becoming more available, especially as the internet becomes more and more
accessible in the country, although first- and second-generation software
and equipment that may well be obsolete in the West is still in use.[18] Music
producer Nik Punk notes that since producers usually charge artists per song,
and as renowned producers can be costly, many artists prefer to have different
producers construct beats for the different songs in an album. An artist's final
album could easily have songs produced by Clemo of Calif Records, Mandugu
Digital and Nik Punk. On the other hand, some producers, like Clemo and the
Ogopa DJs sometimes sign on artists for exclusive album contracts and then
produce all the songs on an album (production houses double-up as music
labels in Nairobi). It all depends on the level of symbolic capital or *swag* an
artist has acquired. Artists with larger auras or *swag* get these exclusive record

---

16   The Kenyan hip-hop scene is predominantly male-oriented, from its rappers to
      its producers, and female rappers in the country are very few. Many of these are
      between the ages of 20 and 40, self-taught and medium to low income earners. In
      this chapter, the word 'artists' refers mainly to rappers, but also includes producers
      in certain contexts.
17   See Douglas Patterson, 'The evolving music scene in Kenya', www.eastafricanmusic.
      com/trends2.htm, accessed 3 February 2012.
18   The internet is rife with countless versions digitizing software such as
      Multitrackstudio, Freestudio and Studiohelper. These have free-trial versions and/
      or bootleg copies that producers download for free and proceed to use to produce
      tracks. The availability of these kinds of software on the internet has given rise to
      a new brand of freelance producer. However, it must be noted that these are basic
      software versions. More sophisticated brands are quite costly and require some
      expertise to employ.

deals, while the unknown, upcoming artists hop from producer to producer, depending on the money they have. Ultimately, they may opt to go to smaller, less well-known and less experienced producers, who will charge them less for an album. Nik Punk calls these less well-known producers *'maproducer wa mtaani',* or street producers. They are usually armed with a laptop and free downloaded studio software, and operate where they are able to find some workspace, including in downtown Nairobi pubs, where I have interviewed some. Finally, some artists may opt to self-produce, armed with some digital mixers or software and, of course, some rhymes.[19]

SAMPLING

Sampling is the act of taking a portion of an existing sound recording and re-using it within another production. Samples usually consist of intros (the first few seconds of a song) and breaks (the spaces in-between chorus and verse in a song), and the selected portions may be embellishing using other sounds, or by changing playback speeds. Sampling also consists of creating sounds by virtually any means and then digitizing them with synthesizers and software (Rose 1994:73).[20]

Sampling can be a complex procedure that requires years of practice and increasingly sophisticated digitizing equipment and software. I am not interested in the complexities of sampling for the purposes of this chapter, but rather in laying the foundation for debates in IP within hip-hop. I have identified three general stages that the African hip-hop producer and artist, working with limited resources, basic software and second-hand hardware, utilize in producing music. This is what I call the 'hip-hop sampling curve'.

Typically, the producer or, less frequently, the self-producing artist, will create a beat by sampling sounds and tunes from virtually any source, depending on (generally) his tastes, exposure, creativity and exploratory skill. The end result of his endeavours can be classified as falling somewhere on the sampling curve. This sampling curve consists of three general outcomes which I discuss here in order of complexity, starting with the simplest.[21]

19　Personal interviews with artists Brayo and Swaleh, and producer Nik Punk, in Nairobi, November 2009. Producers in Nairobi currently are young men, mostly self-taught, with access to digitizing equipment and software. Some, like Kitu Sewer, also double up as rappers. Others, like Musyoka, also worked with DJ academies like The Homeboys.

20　See Rose (1994:73) for a more detailed history of sampling, including the idea that originally samples were used to 'flesh out' already existing musical pieces, or to mask the identity of one so as to make it sound like totally 'new' music.

21　Again, this is a very general summary of a more complex process, and in between these three general forms of sampling are other multi-layered results. However,

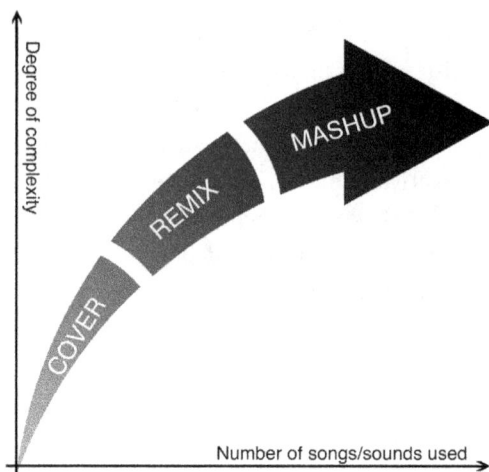

Figure 6.1   Hip-hop sampling curve (graph by T. Simmert):

> *Cover: The instrumental of the song is nearly unaltered. New rap lyrics are added, while playback speed and length may be slightly altered.*
>
> *Remix: Reworking of more than one existing song, using different parts of originals, as well as other sources and sounds.*
>
> *Mash-up: Variety of songs and sounds that form a new 'hybrid' beat. The individual parts are not easily recognizable anymore, if at all.*

First is the cover, which is a performance or recording where one original song is left virtually unchanged, save for re-writing the lyrics. The background beat is easily recognizable, with very little transformation in its form, though the speed at which it is played may vary (slowed down or quickened), and its length cut or increased through repeating the chorus or climax. The use of the cover is not new and Kenyan artists have used covers from songs done by other artists from all over the globe, as have other artists as well. The cover is the quickest and easiest form of sampling, as the artist just replaces existing lyrics with his own and perhaps slightly alters the tempo of the original. Its one advantage is that listeners immediately recognize the background music, and turn their attention to the rap lyric. If the background is from a famous artist, the one using it as a sample immediately gains the artistic aura of the original artist, especially if his lyrics are as rhythmic and thought-provoking

---

these three represent the main distinctions between these various other end results of sampling and are used here for the purposes of this discussion.

as the original. Mwafrika has successfully done this using American Snoop Dogg's 'Lay Low', as has VBO, who has sampled Young Jeezy's 'My President'.

Second is the remix, which consists of several songs picked from the public domain and mixed together in a series of loops and repetitions to form a new entity of beats. Brian Lamb calls the remix

> the reworking or adaptation of an existing work. The remix may be subtle, or it may completely redefine how the work comes across. It may add elements from other works, but generally efforts are focused on creating an alternate version of the original.
>
> (Lamb 2007:13)

In a remix, the original songs are also recognizable, though they are usually not sampled in their entirety as in the cover. A remix is usually more embellished, with the original songs creatively mixed, cut, looped and redesigned into a new entity. New sounds may also be used to embroider the beat, including speeches, musical instruments and even singing. Ukoo Flani Mau Mau, one of Kenya's most prolific hip-hop groups, have used this technique in their music, and even sang melodies in their songs like 'Mashairi (Poetry)', 'Dandora L.O.V.E' and 'Angalia Saa (Look at the time)'.

At the top of the curve is the mash-up, a term that may conjure up different meanings.[22] The mash-up consists of a variety of songs and sounds found in the public domain, all picked and cleverly re-designed into a completely new hybrid beat (Jackson 2009). Lamb (2007:12) envisions the mash-up as involving 'the reuse, or remixing, of works of art, of content, and/ or of data for purposes that usually were not intended or even imagined by the original creators', pointing out the vast array of sources from which a producer may derive sounds and music in creating the final beat. The original sounds and music may not be easily recognizable – if at all – as only a few seconds of each may have been borrowed in the first place. Mash-ups also include created sounds from all possible sources, including synthesized sounds, and are by far the most creatively made samples. In the United States, mash-ups are protected under fair-use laws due to the concept of transformation, which deems the created sound completely different from its original.

---

22 Brian Lamb (2007) recounts that Oliver Paradis, writing in *Wired* magazine, has complained that the word mash-up is a 'manufactured buzzword … drip(ping) with tacky artificiality, marketing innuendo, and vague implications … [that have been applied as a metaphor to] art, video, laptops, cell phones, movies, sneakers, cars, toothbrushes, and who knows what else'. Lamb counters these ambiguities by offering clear definitions of his own that I have appropriated in this work.

Questions have inevitably arisen with the use of these various forms of samples. J.D. Considine starts off the debate on sampling when he asks:

> Despite what they say about imitation – is sampling really flattery? How
> ethical is it to swipe a piece of another artist's recording – slicing off a sliver
> of sound as if it were just so much sausage – and drop it into your own?
> Is sampling something inventively postmodern, an appropriate, artistic
> response to expanding technology and the quick-cut pace of modern
> culture? Or is it simply theft? Such questions would be easier to answer
> if sampling were merely a matter of quotation. After all, there's a world of
> difference between echoing a famous phrase – say Shakespeare's 'Who steals
> my purse steals trash' – and claiming it as your own. But a sample doesn't
> simply reprise a melody the way a literary citation repeats someone else's
> words; it blurs the line between quotation and plagiarism by parroting bits
> of a recorded performance.
>
> (Considine 1995:58).

Considine points out the subtle differences between sampling (in any of its forms) and plagiarism of other texts when he argues that samples don't merely pick and mix, but exist in a complex and multilayered form consisting of variations of an original that may render it unrecognizable. However, the legality and legitimacy of these different forms of sampling cannot be judged using the same criteria, as they are different in form, increasing the complexity surrounding them.

Enter copyright as norm

Copyright is, essentially, a system of rules governing the distribution of knowledge and IP (Altbach 1986). It structures the relationship between an 'author' of knowledge in any form and the 'consumers' of that particular knowledge. Frith (1988) wrote that 'the whole point of copyright is to ensure that the author of a work, its "absolute owner", is duly rewarded for other people's enjoyment of that work – without such rewards there would be no economic incentive to make musical or literary works in the first place'. He further states that 'popular music genres are constructed – and must be understood – within a commercial/cultural process' (1996). Frith's argument cements the idea that artistic works are created within a market system in which artists of various kinds expect to gain financially from their endeavours. Obviously, in between the author and consumer are the producers, distributers and promoters of that particular piece of IP, and this presents a set of complex networks (Frith 1988).

Copyright has three aspects which date back centuries. First, is the European approach that stresses the moral right of the author to have control over his creation. Second, is the American approach that stresses the legal right of the author over the commercial exploitation of his work. This approach aims at stimulating creativity and invention and views copyright through a commercial lens, meaning that the incentive of financial remuneration for an author is intended to stimulate further creativity. Authors therefore enter into artistic production with the expectation of remuneration for their endeavours. Third, is the Soviet approach that accords greater importance to societal access to a given piece of intellectual creativity than to the rights or claims to it of any sole author (Altbach 1986).

Classically, all international and national (Kenyan) copyright laws are based in part or wholly on these three concepts of copyright. In many cases, especially in the Global South, copyright laws are based on adaptations of these approaches, and for post-colonial Africa, national IP laws depend on which colonial legacy a country has. For Kenya, therefore, copyright law leans heavily on the British interpretation.

However, scholars such as Altbach (1986) point out that the Third World[23] has been a recipient of second-hand interpretations of international copyright laws. Africa, for instance, adopted the three conceptual frameworks of copyright, and found itself saddled with laws that have been progressively shaped and re-written to suit the evolving interests of Western systems. African countries, including those which inherited copyright laws and norms from their former colonial governments, have been inducted into an international copyright system that incorporates the Berne Convention, which is administered by the World Intellectual Property Organization (WIPO). The Berne Convention was a result of the International Convention for the Protection of Literary and Artistic Works of 1886. It is the oldest copyright treaty in the world, with several amendments that have of necessity included the Global South (Altbach 1986). These international conventions, however, reflect few African interests, perhaps because the continent has long been perceived as a field for collecting rather than producing knowledge (Musila 2009, 2010), and copyright, after all, is geared towards protecting the production of knowledge. Even when an African country like Kenya ratifies these international conventions, its producers of knowledge and creative works are far removed from these laws, and do not necessarily relate

---

23 I use the term 'Third World' here in the way Altbach (1986) has used it in his argument. I am aware that current scholarship is less receptive of this dated term and the concept it represents, and therefore, I also use the term 'Global South' where Altbach has not directly used it.

to them. There is usually a gap between the global/international and the national-African popular art form, specifically Kenyan hip-hop. International copyright laws are not taken too seriously in Kenya, and even though there is a comprehensive Copyright Act in effect, it is still not really taken into account, especially by hip-hop artists, and by extension artists and musicians in other genres too. In the rare cases in which artists are aware of the existence of the Copyright Act of Kenya, its relevance seems quite remote to them.

The Music Copyright Society of Kenya (MCSK) frequently refer to the Act, especially when enforcing local laws covered by it. Recently, Nairobi music producer BuddhaBlaze engaged in an altercation with the MCSK, when it demanded he pay royalties for playing local music at a public event he had organized. He refused, arguing that the musicians whose music he was playing, the majority of them hip-hop artists, were not MSCK members. This refusal nearly got him arrested and fuelled a debate on Twitter on the 'corrupt nature' of the MSCK and its inutility for local artists.[24] This reaction is part of the ongoing uneasy relationship between artists and copyright norms (represented here by the MSCK), which is one of victimhood and fear, in which the local artist views the norm as a foreign force bent on depriving him of the chance to make a song and a reasonable living by curtailing creativity and enterprise (for a different view on the same problematic in Cameroon, see Alexie Tcheuyap in this volume).

The MCSK is the Kenyan copyright collective body[25] that pays royalties to those musicians registered in it, at a fee, by charging money to anyone who plays their music at any public event, including in public transport vehicles and in business establishments such as malls and stores. However, hip-hop has traditionally not been seen as 'real music' in Kenya, and therefore hip-hop musicians, especially those from Eastlands,[26] where a majority of rappers come from, are not registered members. This huge gap between law and practice alienates the artist from both national and international norms. Such alienation is detrimental to an art form that is inevitably expanding its fan base across real and virtual borders, because it cements ignorance and sets the Kenyan (read 'African') artist on a collision course with these norms by exposing them to exploitation. It is not surprising to hear that some artists have had their songs registered by other more renowned artists because they

---

24   See Buddha Blaze twitter account at twitter.com/#!/ItsBuddhaBlaze, accessed 20 December 2011.
25   See www.mcsk.or.ke, accessed 20 December 2011.
26   Eastlands is the collective term for the low-income housing estates to the east of Nairobi's central business district. Hip-hop music was first established in Eastlands in the early 1990s (Ntarangwi 2009).

were too ignorant about international norms to stake their claim to their own music. A good example is Kenyan Fadhili Williams' hit song 'Malaika', which is attributed to a number of artists, including South African songstress Miriam Makeba. Williams did not receive any royalties for 'Malaika'.[27]

Creator-owner as problematic concepts in African hip-hop and copyright norms

Interesting narratives of the 'author' and the 'owner' emerge in hip-hop music, where lyric and beat are two separate and independent entities. When a hip-hop artist says 'this song is mine', he means that he is the one who wrote the lyrics, even though the beat may be sampled either as a cover, remix or mash-up, and largely unacknowledged. For instance, one Kenyan artist has done a rap song with Brazilian singer Caetano Veloso's 'Burn it Blue' as the background track. 'Burn it Blue' was popularized by the Hollywood film *Frida*, the biography of the iconic female Mexican painter Frida Kahlo. The background track in the Kenyan rapper's song is a substantial sample of the Brazilian singer's song, and Veloso's voice singing the chorus can be heard in the background in a loop. On the sampling curve, the rap track would fall somewhere between a cover and a remix, though when talking to this rap artist he told me 'yes, I wrote that song, it is mine'. He admitted that he had no idea who had written the background track, or who the male singer on the loop was.[28] His claim to being the owner of the song presents us with questions of ownership, authorship and creativity. Rap tracks like this, using other songs in the public domain as covers, are common.

Rap artists in Nairobi have used as background tracks original songs popularized by other rappers such as Americans Nas, Nate Dogg and Sean 'P. Diddy' Combs, simply inserting their own lyrics in Sheng and other local languages. However, whether Nate Dogg or P. Diddy were the original writers of these songs is itself in question, as they too have been known to sample from other sources and continue to do so. This suggests that the sampling curve is more complex than it may at first appear to be, and stretches back in time, even to the nth degree, as there may be no way of knowing where the sampling started, and what was truly the 'original' form. But in between the different degrees of sampling are various artists who claim ownership of these songs, albeit having altered them by inserting their own lyrics or by further sampling them in one way or another. And as the terms 'owner' and 'author' may be used interchangeably, the distinction between them remains unclear.

---

27 See www.eastafricanmusic.com/fadhili.htm, accessed 22 December 2011.
28 Personal interviews, Nairobi, 2009.

Many artists have claimed a song as their own simply because they wrote the lyrics, though not the beat. To these artists, the 'song' is the lyrical content, which is entirely original in the sense of being newly written by the artist as 'author', 'owner' and 'creator'. The beat, in this sense, is a mere accompaniment that can be done away with, replaced or altered to suit different contexts. However, one background beat may provide a specific contextual aura that another beat would not. For instance, the rap song discussed above with Caetano Veloso's 'Burn it Blue' as a background has as a result a poignant, moody feel that it would not have had with a different beat. The background vocals by Veloso, which the producer of this song did not blank out, seem to have influenced the lyrics that this rap artist decided to write, as the song is about a woman that the rapper wishes to be with. Known previously for his gritty performances, this rapper admitted to having been affected by the mood of the song. In this case, the rap song seems to be a direct product of the background track. However, Schur problematizes the idea that hip-hop music is solely a product of its sampled music when he argues that

> hip hop does not simply draw inspiration from a range of samples, but it
> layers these fragments into an artistic object. If sampling is the first level of
> hip hop aesthetics, how the pieces or elements fit together constitute the
> second level. Hip hop emphasizes and calls attention to its layered nature.
> The aesthetic code of hip hop does not seek to render invisible the layers
> of samples, sounds, references, images, and metaphors. Rather, it aims to
> create a collage in which the sampled texts augment and deepen the song/
> book/art's meaning to those who can decode the layers of meaning.
>
> (Schur 2008:207)

Schur's argument liberates the rap, in the case of a sample, from being integrated into the song's main body, as he sees the hip-hop lyric as having its own set of meanings, which are only augmented by the samples. For the rap song with Veloso's background track, the producer's loops, together with the rapper's rhymes, result in a song that is almost a 'new' entity, or at least a different one. While the 'originator' of the background song has not been credited, raising questions here as to the difference between owner, author and creator, the result of the sampling is a new form with its own identity that challenges the concepts of author and creator.

Other similar examples exist in Kenya and elsewhere on the continent, where artists sample songs by other artists to varying degrees, as per the sampling curve. From the covers to the mash-ups, both sides of the copyright infringement argument have a large measure of validity.

Roland Barthes declared the 'death of the author', who is replaced by a *scriptor*. This *scriptor*, according to Barthes, cannot create anything 'new' because 'new' is a category which does not exist. Therefore, any piece of creativity (for Barthes, the novel) can only be scripted from material that already exists in the public imagination, based on 'a web of citations' and diverse acts and experiences. Barthes states that

> we know now that a text is not a line of words releasing a single 'theological' meaning (the 'message' of the Author-God) but a multi-dimensional space in which a variety of writings, none of them original, blend and clash.
>
> (Barthes 1977:146)

Barthes clearly argues that (creative) texts are essentially a conglomeration of many different texts in the public domain, insisting that none are original (see also Mudimbe-Boyi in this volume). Hip-hop texts, in this case both textual/lyrical and musical, seem to embody this concept. For instance, in the original Caetano Veloso song, Veloso is only the performer. The author of the melody is Elliot Goldenthal, who composed the music for the film *Frida*; the lyricist is Julie Seymour, the director of the film.[29] However, Veloso's vocals are what the song is most remembered for, giving him a sense of ownership, despite it not having been written by him. The multi-layered nature of the texts of music and sampling makes issues of copyright and ownership complicated. For example, South African rapper HHP reportedly paid American rapper Nas $10,000 (about £6,200) for permission to use one of his songs as a background beat, only to learn that Nas had gone ahead and produced the same song with another artist.[30] The new song was already produced and circulating, meaning that a release by the South African rapper would be seen as second-best, a mere 'remix' of the original song, and therefore, a waste of his money. HHP is left to question whether it would have been wiser to sample the song, either as cover, remix or mash-up, without paying the money. While the issue here may have been a simple contractual misunderstanding, the narrative that HHP feels he was 'cheated' while trying to follow IP rules is of much interest, as is the narrative of the knowledge, understanding and practice of IP by African artists on a global scale. It also illustrates the incapacity of legal concepts to control what people are actually doing with music in daily life.

---

29   See www.soundtrack.net/features/article/?id=99 on an interview with Elliot Goldenthal, accessed 27 August 2011.

30   See www.wonted.co.za/index.php?option=com_content&view=article&id=197: nas-does-hhp-foul&catid=925:tune-news, accessed 2 February 2012.

Similarly, Daddy Owen, a Kenyan gospel artist, has sung 'Tobina', also known as 'Kupé dé kallé', a gospel song that won an MTV Africa Music Award for best new act in December 2010. Daddy Owen has claimed 'Tobina' is entirely a product of his creative endeavours, although it does have Ivorian, French and Lingala lyrics directly lifted from other secular songs, albeit well remixed.[31] In the original '*coupé-décalé'/'allez tobina*' song, one of the performers raps in Lingala and still uses lyrics from another song. These languages are not spoken in Kenya. Again, owner and creator are not distinguishable, all the less so in this case because Daddy Owen's song was nominated to win its award by audiences across the continent, and no complaints of plagiarism were made. The song was therefore legitimized by the award as Owen's, despite it having been being 'borrowed' and therefore not being 'original'.

On the other hand, the term 'creator' can refer to the producer of a song, in essence, the originator of the beat. In the case of the Kenyan rapper who sampled Caetano Veloso's song, when pushed to tell me if he knew that his rap song had been done over a track by Veloso, he said 'my producer sent me the beat, and it sounded good, so I just composed the song over the beat and that was it'. During my research in Nairobi, interviewees periodically stated '*ah, mtu anaeza jua beat ya producer yeyote vile tu inasound*', meaning that every music producer has a specific style that distinguishes his from the rest, ascribing a certain identity to the producer as 'creator'.[32] In this case, the producer essentially becomes responsible for the beat, and therefore, the entire song. The catch is that the song only becomes recognizable because of its lyrics, and because of the vocals of the rapper, meaning that its identity and that of the rapper are entwined. This presents another layer of complexity, as the terms 'owner', 'creator' and 'author' are not distinguishable from each other, nor are they exclusive, as there are many players implicated within one piece of music. Many artists rely exclusively on their producers for the background tracks to which they formulate rap lyrics, without too much concern about their origins. As long as they are 'bare', in the sense that there is no other rap lyric in them, they are considered 'new', a tabula rasa to fill

31   Daddy Owen and the artist Dunco, his co-performer in this song, have come under a lot of criticism for lifting these secular phrases and directly implanting them uncritically into Tobina. For instance, the French/Lingala song from where they borrowed the phrases starting with 'allez Tobina' are said to make references to sexual intercourse, which obviously becomes very problematic in a (Kenyan) gospel track. Daddy Owen and Dunco have responded, saying it is God who inspired them when writing 'Tobina'. See www.the-star.co.ke/news/article-86323/daddy-owen-and-dunco-clear-air-tobina, accessed 17 October 2013.

32   Interviews with rappers Rawbar, Swaleh, Brayo and Jua Cali, Nairobi, November 2009.

with lyrics in order to create a new song.[33] When artists have knowledge regarding the source of the song, either by recognizing the beat from another rap song, for instance, or from another known source, creative licence along the sampling curve comes immediately into play. Joseph Schloss explains that this creative licence is part of hip-hop, where 'the more rules producers can take on without compromising the quality of the finished product, the greater their skill is considered to be' (2012:612). According to Schloss, the general rule of thumb for most producers is to refrain from borrowing beats and musical material from other hip-hop artists (ibid.:612–13). Other genres are fair game, he argues, and appropriating from them is acceptable as long as it is done creatively. Schloss points out that producers feel no need to justify sampling, as 'it is the foundation of the musical system' (ibid.:610).

This rings true for the Kenyan producer, who samples as creatively as possible, within his given capabilities and available resources, to ensure that the ensuing beat sounds as original as he can manage. Where covers are used, artists call these 'Kenyan versions', seeing them as completely different from the original in terms of content, and therefore, in their view, entirely new.[34] While problematic because of direct borrowing (for example, VBO's 'Orezzo Wangu [My President]' is obviously a cover version of Young Jeezy's 'My President', including the title), one can see the merit in the argument that it is completely new in its lyrical content and the contextual imagery it evokes: that of critiquing a corrupt political system in the Sheng language, which only local Kenyans can understand.

This argument with respect to claims to ownership can also be extended to the lyrics of a rap song. Veteran artist Rawbar of Kalamashaka once made the claim to me that another veteran Bongo artist, Professa Jay, had stolen the song 'Hapo Vipi' from him. According to Rawbar, a visiting Professa Jay had heard him freestyling verses during a rap-artist congress held in Nairobi, in which the chorus was a call and response chant in which the rapper asks '*hapo vipi?*' (how's that?) and the audience replies '*hapo sawa*' (that's cool). Rawbar then asserts that an impressed Professa Jay had dashed back to Dar es Salaam, where he had been in the midst of producing an album, and proceeded to add the song to his new CD as his own. The song ended

---

33 This is a heuristic conclusion on my part based on observation conducted while interacting with rappers and producers over the four-year course of my research. These conclusions suffice, as scholarly work on hip-hop and copyright in Kenya is scanty at best.

34 Personal interviews with artists Brayo and Rawbar, Nairobi, May-June 2010.

up being Professa Jay's hit single from his album.[35] The interesting thing for
me in this story was Rawbar's claim of ownership over a 'freestyle', which is
generally considered spontaneous and therefore unique to the moment of
composition or performance. The freestyle is typically used in hip-hop to
portray a rapper's skill in producing 'rhymes' at the drop of a hat. The true hip-
hop artist is seen as one whose spontaneous rhymes are meaningful, thought
provoking and even incendiary, all at once. However, I found that many times
the freestyle, cleverly orchestrated as a 'spontaneous event' and billed as an
outpouring of inspired delivery of poetic rhymes by hip-hop artists, is often
a misrepresentation aimed at perpetuating the myth of the inspired rapper
that is rife in hip-hop lore. In reality, artists spend hours writing, re-writing,
memorizing and practising the lyrics they use during a freestyle.

This is why Rawbar could confidently say that Professa Jay had stolen
his lyrics (or his song), as had the lyrics been spontaneous at the point of the
freestyle, they in most likelihood would not have been remembered in such
detail. Rawbar's claim to ownership of the lyrics, and therefore ownership of
the song, makes for an interesting case when considering the complexities of
ownership in a music field that distinguishes between beat and lyric, but also
considers each part a 'song'. When freestyling with Professa Jay in attendance,
Rawbar was not accompanied by any beat, but on recognizing his freestyle
lyrics on Professa Jay's completed CD, although accompanied by other beats,
he still claimed ownership of it based on the lyrics alone. In any case, Rawbar
felt powerless to do anything about Professa Jay's seeming duplicity, further
demonstrating the lack of practical knowledge concerning the application of
IP norms by hip-hop artists. However, one can also question the extent of
Professa Jay's 'borrowing' in this case, arguing that Professa Jay used Rawbar's
lyrics as inspiration to write a totally 'new' song, as, short of recording
Rawbar's freestyle, he could not possibly have remembered it word for
word and duplicated all of it. The dilemma is determining to what extent he
'borrowed' (without due acknowledgments and monetary payment) Rawbar's
lyrics, a continuing theme in hip-hop sampling.

Let us for a moment consider the reference by Shusterman (1991:617) to the
idea that hip-hop music is a distinct art form in itself, the finished product of
beats and music borrowed from a variety of sources, equating it to Duchamp's
Mona Lisa or Andy Warhol's artistic representations, all considered finished
products in their own right. This type of description adds a new dimension
to the idea of hip-hop as a stand-alone product with merit, and not as a genre
that pirates or plagiarizes music from other sources. Shusterman's argument

---

35   See hipipo.com/kenya/radio/389/Professor-Jay/Professor-Jay-Hapo-Vipi, accessed
     15 December 2011.

extends the questions posed with respect to sampled hip-hop music, or, more specifically, whether the borrowing of beats to form the intertextuality of hip-hop music can be legitimate.

There are arguments suggesting that sampling is not theft, but rather a clear case of re-contextualization that naturally follows decontextualization. Considine (1995), also referring to Shusterman, suggests that Andy Warhol's soup-can paintings work in the same way as hearing a James Brown scream outside a James Brown song, changing its meaning by 'reducing its emotional resonance to the level of mere recognition.' While a James Brown scream would be instantly recognizable, he argues, its meaning shifts and changes when used outside its original context, thereby creating a totally new context, meaning and product. Further, Considine asserts that sampling and re-contextualization are not unique to hip-hop, but are used regularly within other musical genres, including rock. He also argues that the amount of effort and creativity needed to compile several sounds into one hybrid sound is similar to the creative energy used to write a guitar solo, giving hip-hop producers a form of legitimacy and professionalism that is far removed from mere copying and dropping of 'slivers of sausage' (Considine 1995:58–61). This argument would suggest that a hip-hop song, remixed or sampled into a different entity, exists in a different context and is therefore unrelated to the original song. However, this view is problematic, as, like Barthes' argument, it opens up a debate on ownership. For literature, the author, or Barthes' scriptor, can still claim ownership over his book, and, indeed, one cannot normally access a book without making a purchase. For the hip-hop musician, this debate ends in a stalemate, but only in the technical production of hip-hop; Barthes' 'birth of the reader' (1977) can be applied to hip-hop, where different contexts created by different samples in one song can mean different things for different listeners.

Conclusion

There is need for more debate regarding sampling and copyright, and perhaps, a re-negotiation of the place the Global South, and especially Africa, occupies in the wider scheme of copyright and IP. Africa especially needs to be reconceptualized as a site of knowledge production, and not just as a second-hand consumer of knowledge and technology. This would perhaps bring the continent into the mainstream of copyright legislation and create a level playing field for the production and marketing of popular music. Such a development remains, for the moment, hypothetical, as American influence on hip-hop and other popular cultures and music is so prominent and even hegemonic.[36] Currently, African music is classified as 'World Music' (Brennan 2001) in forums such as online radio, in-flight music on flights and online music-purchasing platforms like iTunes. The category remains obscure, as it lumps together all forms of music that do not conform to certain Western paradigms. More problematic is the fact that many hip-hop artists do not produce music that can be played in these international forums due to lack of access to, and operating knowledge of, technological hardware and software that is in use in the West. It therefore remains to be seen if a genre like African hip-hop can compete fairly on the international market, firstly due to this technological challenge and secondly because 'African music' is a category that has long been associated in a stereotypical way with drumming. The idea of African hip-hop sounds strange and derivative on the global stage. Rawbar of Kalamashaka recounts a trip to Norway to entertain his fans, during which he was put on the spot with respect to the phrase 'Kenyan hip-hop' by some white businessmen, who asserted that it was an oxymoron because hip-hop was American.[37] Hip-hop in Africa, with its own unmistakable aura and identity that is quite distinct from its American influences, has yet to be acknowledged as such, in large part due to the comparative scholarly work that has defined African hip-hop as an extension of its American counterpart.

Some Kenyan artists started MySpace pages – the website offers musicians a platform for posting samples of their music for fans to hear, with links to other sites such as iTunes where the music can be bought. MySpace has since been overtaken by Facebook and Twitter as the social networking sites of choice for internet users. Further research is needed to examine the extent to which African (and Kenyan) artists are adopting internet technologies to market themselves. Only then can the impact of international copyright norms be realized and re-negotiated. For now, Kenyan artists will continue to target Kenyans living in the diaspora with live performances, while these fans visit YouTube for music videos posted by these artists. Producers also continue to get creative with samples, knowing that, in the words of the artist who sampled Caetano Veloso's song, the music executives at Sony BMG are not likely to take any action against him. In his words, he asked 'So what will Sony do? They can't come here to arrest me and take me to court, I mean, it's not

---

36 The recent 24-hour shut-down by sites like Wikipedia to protest the American imposition of its copyright infringement laws (the Stop Online Piracy Act [SOPA] and Protect Intellectual Property Act [PIPA]) on the entire planet is an indication that the discussion on IP rights and copyright is taking a new turn, as is the retaliatory hacking of American FBI and affiliated websites by internet experts calling themselves 'hacktivists' (see bit.ly/wtfZju, accessed 18 January 2012).

37 Personal interview with Rawbar, Nairobi, March 2010.

like if they tell me to pay damages I will be able to, right?'[38] Obviously, these artists are aware of the North-South inequalities and where these inequalities place them, as they see themselves as 'poor Africans' far removed from the global arena in terms of knowledge and cultural production.

The picture of the poor African artist is, however, being deconstructed by the advances made in locating African popular culture on the global map. African artists are increasingly placing themselves in positions where they have the potential to make as much wealth as anyone else. Indiscriminate sampling is no longer an option, especially if artists are keen on selling their music continent-wide and internationally. In the end, as African music gets a footing on the global front, it is clear that the language of copyright will become a necessity, and, therefore, sampling will become more closely scrutinized. It remains to be seen at what speed African artists will adapt to copyright laws, or if they will influence a shift in the application of these laws to suit their interests. It is no longer a case of if, but of when.

---

38   Personal interview, artist Garang, Nairobi, April 2009.

References

Altbach, Phillip. 1986. 'Knowledge enigma: copyright in the Third World'. *Economic Weekly* 21 (37):1643–50.

Armstrong, Edward. 2001, 'Gangsta misogyny: a content analysis of the portrayals of violence against women in rap music 1987–1993'. *Journal of Criminal Justice and Popular Culture* 8, 2:96–126.

Baker Jr., Houston. 1993. *Black Studies, Rap and the Academy.* Chicago: University of Chicago Press.

Barthes, Roland. 1977. *The Death of the Author.* In his: *Image-Music-Text* (Essays selected and translated by Stephen Heath). London: Fontana, 142–9.

Bourdieu, Pierre. 1991. *Language and Symbolic Power.* Oxford: Blackwell.

——— 1993. *The Field of Cultural Production.* Cambridge: Polity Press.

Brennan, Timothy. 2001. 'World Music does not exist'. *Discourse* 23(1):44–62.

Chang, Jeff. 2005. *Can't Stop, Won't Stop: A History of the Hip-Hop Generation*, New York: Ebury Publishing.

Considine, J. D. 1995. 'Larcenous art?' In: Adam Sexton (ed.). *Rap on Rap: Straight-up Talk on Hip-Hop Culture.* New York: Dell Publishing, 58–61.

Dyson, Michael Eric. 2004. 'The culture of hip-hop'. In: Murray Forman and Mark Anthony (eds). *That's the Joint! The Hip-Hop Studies Reader.* New York and London: Routledge, 68–76.

Forman, Murray and Mark Anthony Neal (eds). 2004. *That's the Joint! The Hip-Hop Studies Reader.* New York and London: Routledge.

Frith, Simon. 1988. 'Copyright and the music business'. *Popular Music* 7(1):57–75.

——— 1996. *Performing Rites: On the Value of Popular Music.* Cambridge: Harvard University Press.

Haupt, Adam. 2003. 'Hip-hop in the age of Empire: Cape Flats Style'. *Dark Roast Occasional Papers Series* 9 (Cape Town, Isandla Institute).

hooks, bell. 1994. 'Gangsta culture – sexism and misogyny: who will take the rap?' In her: *Outlaw Culture: Resisting Representations.* New York: Routledge, 115–23.

Jackson, Michele. 2009. 'The mash-up: a new archetype for communication'. *Journal of Computer-Mediated Communication* 14(3):730–4.

Keyes, Cheryl. 1991. Rapping to the Beat: Rap Music as Street Culture among African-Americans. Doctoral Thesis, Ann Arbor, Michigan.

Kirschke, Linda. 2000. 'Informal repression, zero-sum politics and late third wave transitions'. *Journal of Modern African Studies* 38(3):383–405.

KRS One. 2003. *Ruminations.* New York: Welcome Rain Publishers.

Lamb, Brian. 2007. 'Dr. Mashup; or, why educators should learn to stop worrying and love the remix'. *EDUCAUSE Review* 42(4):12–25.

Mose, Caroline. 2011, '*Jua Cali-Justice:* navigating the "mainstream-underground" dichotomy in Kenyan hip-hop culture'. In: P.K Saucier (ed.). *Native Tongues: The African Hip-Hop Reader.* Trenton, NJ: Africa World Press, 77–97.

Musila, Grace. 2009. 'Phallocracies and gynocratic transgressions: gender, state power and Kenyan public life'. *Africa Insight* 39(1):39–57.

——— 2010. 'The Redykyulass generation's intellectual interventions in Kenyan public life'. *Young: Nordic Journal of Youth* 18(3):279–99.

Ntarangwi, Mwenda. 2009. *East African Hip Hop- Youth Culture and Globalization.* Urbana and Chicago: University of Illinois Press

Nyairo, Joyce and James Ogude. 2005. 'Popular music, popular politics: Unbwogable and the idioms of freedom in Kenyan popular music'. *African Affairs* 104(415):225–49.

Rose, Tricia. 1994. *Black Noise: Rap Music and Black Culture.* Hanover: New England University Press.

Schloss, Joseph. 2012. 'Sampling ethics'. In: Murray Forman and Mark Anthony (eds). *That's the Joint! The Hip-Hop Studies Reader* (2. edn). New York and London: Routledge, 609–30.

Schur, Richard. 2008. 'Hip hop aesthetics and contemporary African American literature'. In: Lovalerie King and Linda Selzer (eds). *New Essays on the African American Novel: From Hurston and Ellison to Morrison and Whitehead.* New York: Palgrave Macmillan, 166–89.

——— 2009. *Parodies of Ownership: Hip-Hop Aesthetics and Intellectual Property Law.* Michigan: University of Michigan Press.

Sexton, Adam. 1995. 'Introduction'. In: Adam Sexton (ed.). *Rap on Rap: Straight-up Talk on Hip-Hop Culture.* New York: Dell Publishing, 1–13.

Shipley, Jesse. 2009. 'Aesthetic of the entrepreneur: Afro-cosmopolitan rap and moral circulation in Accra, Ghana'. *Anthropology Quarterly* 82(3):631–68.

Shusterman, Richard. 1991. 'The fine art of rap'. *New Literary History* 22:613–32.

Toop, David. 2000. *Rap Attack 3: African Rap to Global Hip Hop* (expanded 3. edn). London: Serpent's Tail.

III

Transformations of cultural goods:

imitation, appropriation and piracy

CHAPTER 7

'Be faster than the pirates'

Copyright and the revival of 'traditional dances' in south-west Cameroon[1]

ⒸⒸⒸⒸⒸⒸⒸⒸⒸⒸ

UTE RÖSCHENTHALER

During a trip to Cameroon in December 2010, I met Arrey Bate Nico (Figure 7.1), a popular singer and performance artist from Manyu Division in Southwest Region, the area in which I have carried out most of my field research since the late 1980s. At our meeting in the Seme Beach Hotel near Limbe, Bate Nico presented me with six DVDs he had produced together with his wife, Nkongho Regina, also from the Manyu Division. He explained that whenever a new DVD is out on the market, people instantly begin to copy it. So his strategy is to sell it as quickly as possible to as many people as he can 'in order to be faster than the pirates'. This entails frequent travelling between the coastal area in which he lives and the Manyu Division, further in the hinterland, his home area.[2] He had also registered his DVDs with the Cameroonian copyright office, but said that so far he had received hardly any royalties from them.[3]

---

1   This contribution has been developed from a larger project on history of the dissemination of associations and cult agencies in the Cross River area of south-west Cameroon and south-east Nigeria, which was supported between 1987 and 1988 by the German Academic Exchange Service and the Graduiertenförderung des Landes Berlin. Between 1998 and 2001 the project was hosted at the Institut für Ethnologie, Goethe University Frankfurt am Main and supported by the Deutsche Forschungsgemeinschaft (German Research Council). More research was carried out on the topic in the frame of the Cluster of Excellence 'The Formation of Normative Orders' at the Goethe University Frankfurt am Main in 2008 and 2010.
2   Conversation with Bate Nico at Seme Beach Hotel in December 2010.
3   These were SOCINADA, CMC and SOCAM, in order of existence. For more details see Alexie Tcheuyap in this volume.

Figure 7.1 Bate Nico, in special dance costume, ready for performance, at Mutengene, Southwest Region of Cameroon, 2010 (photographer unknown, by kind permission of Bate Nico).

When he publicly performs with his dance group and produces his videos, he has to cope not only with the effectiveness of the pirates but also with local regulations on immaterial cultural goods. Such regulations existed in this area long before the global introduction of individual authors and copyrights.[4] In the Cross River region in south-west Cameroon and south-east Nigeria, during the past centuries, clear ideas about rights in the ownership

---

4   Local rights in immaterial cultural goods, existing pre-colonially, have been documented by Röschenthaler (2011) and in a number of dispersed sources, including, for Nigeria, Bohannan and Bohannan 1968:228–9; for Central Africa,

of cults, performances and the display of insignia were developed in response to trade incentives and as the result of local creativity. These rights were subject to transaction, and their purchase was prerequisite for them to be lawfully disseminated across the region. This development also required the creation of effective means to protect these rights against illegitimate use (Röschenthaler 2011).

More generally, illegitimate copying and fakes prevail where particular goods are highly valued. Every culture and historical period has had its own valuable cultural goods that have been subject to piracy. In ancient Egypt, these were religious cults; in the European Middle Ages, the relics of Christian saints; and, in the present, music and branded products (Jones 1994). In south-west Cameroon, cult associations are among such valuables.

During colonial times, international copyright laws were introduced to African countries (see Peukert, this volume). They were first and foremost intended to secure the rights of white colonialists (Fischer 2001, for Cameroon). Over time these laws have been elaborated by national governments to coincide with international regulations and agreements, and they have become an institution of growing importance for Cameroonian artists, especially musicians, who are confronted with both local regulations and the international copyright regime when they engage in 'traditional dances' and produce music and videos for a wider audience in their endeavour to make a living from their performances.

In this chapter I will explore how the concurrent conceptions of local and international regulations relate to each other; define the contexts in which international copyright law becomes relevant; trace the development of local rights over the course of time, and analyse how staging performances in various environments and media, where different regimes of rights apply, affects their meanings. I will argue that both rights regimes in their attempt to protect immaterial cultural goods have become important at specific historical conjunctures and have appealed to differing interests as a basis to negotiate claims. Central to the growing importance of the goods protected were their market value, i.e. the possible gains to be made. The elusiveness and fragmentariness of immaterial goods when they are recombined, quoted or imitated make it extremely difficult to define what exactly can be protected and how this is achieved. I will begin with Bate Nico's video production, analyse his staging of established performances and his coming to terms with the two rights regimes, the local and the international.

Kubik 1993; for South America, Lowie 1928; and for Melanesia, Malinowksi 1922:185–6; for further sources see Harrison 1993 and Hirsch and Strathern 2004.

Bate Nico's music videos and the revival of 'traditional dances'

This section looks first at Bate Nico's family background, which inspired his career as a performing artist. It then explores the way in which he combines established performances with the urban imaginary populating the dreams of the young, and how, while reviving 'traditional culture', he transforms the meaning of performances.

A FAMILY OF DANCERS AND MUSICIANS

Bate Nico grew up in a family of dancers and musicians. In the village of Kembong, his late grandfather was a renowned singer. In the 1950s his late father Arrey Ebot, together with other hunters, founded the very successful dance group Ngunjo, with the objective of reviving dances that were on the verge of being forgotten. Some years after Ngunjo's foundation, the family moved to the coastal area around Mt. Cameroon, as many people from the Manyu Division had already, in search of work on the plantations (Ardener, Ardener and Warmington 1960) and opportunities for education. During my research in 1988 I met Arrey Ebot several times in his home near Mt. Cameroon, where he had formed a coastal branch of Ngunjo (Figure 7.2), while the main society continued on in Kembong village (Röschenthaler 2004a).

In the late 1990s Bate Nico visited me in Kembong in the compound of the family I stayed with during research periods. He told me about his experiences as a performer in his father's Ngunjo dance group, and that he wanted to make traditional performance still more attractive and widely known by using modern media. Since then, Bate Nico has married a talented singer and dancer, Nkongho Regina, from the same area. They began to work together, establishing a dance group. They produced the six DVDs and were increasingly invited to perform at festivities. He told me that they both compose the songs, she designs the dresses and he organizes the dancing and the filming. They are often invited – in addition to the local dance associations, men's and women's societies and church choirs –to come to the Manyu Division to embellish chiefs' installation festivities with their performance and songs.[5]

The couple quickly became popular in the Manyu Division, in the migrant community from Manyu on the coast and even in the diaspora. In his home village, Kembong, a Bate Nico Fan Club was founded by family members, friends and fans. Most of its members are dancers and musicians themselves,[6] but the club also functions as one of the many local savings and credit associations (cf. Niger-Thomas 2000). Bate Nico is not only asked to

5   Interview in December 2010 at Seme Beach Hotel.
6   My interpretation of a letter from my assistant, Richard Etchu Ayuk, in June 2011.

Figure 7.2   Bate Nico's late father with the Nkpe mask of Ngunjo, at their home near Mt. Cameroon, 1988 (photo by U. Röschenthaler).

perform far and wide in the Southwest Region and in cities such as Douala. In 2010, the MECA (Manyu Elements Cultural Association) of the United States invited him to their annual convention in Washington, and placed hundreds of photographs of his reception on the Facebook page of the Bate Nico Fan Club.[7] A number of his video clips can also be found on YouTube and other popular

---

7   en-gb.facebook.com/pages/Bate-Nico-Fan-Club/164019766944884, accessed 21 February 2012. He was again invited to MECA meetings in the USA in 2011 and 2012.

websites. Manyu people, above all in the European and American diaspora, place the clips there.

Bate Nico's objectives with his musical productions are 'to revive traditional culture and make it attractive again to the youths'. In contrast to his father, who performed with his dance group at festivities only, Bate Nico also intends to materialize the volatile and ephemeral performances[8] and the installation ceremonies of chiefs on modern sound carriers (DVDs). By means of such fixation, his performances can become more widely known and for a longer time, and also people can acquire them who did not have the opportunity to be present at the festivities.[9]

THE VIDEOS AS AN ARTISTIC COLLAGE

Bate Nico's DVDs are composed of video from several sites combined with sound recordings from the studio. His producer is also from Manyu Division. With increasing production experience, their DVDs became more and more professional. The videos combine scenes from a variety of performance sites in short sequences: scenes from the village, from town and from the global diaspora; traditional and modern dances; children performing with elderly Ekpe chiefs, and with the rich and the poor. He mixes ancient and new elements, rural and urban imagery, traditional and modern music, dresses and performance styles. Thus he produces the illusion of unity despite differences in place, time, degree of modernity and economic opportunity, and despite generational gaps.[10]

Most of the time, the DVDs show the group performing 'traditional dances' known from the village, such as the Nkim and Ekong dances performed by young girls called Moninkim (Figures 7.4–7.6).[11]. These are performed on the pavements of the big streets in towns, in front of bars and popular restaurants, or in front of imposing natural features such as trees, flowers or

---

8   Performances are not completely ephemeral, but build on previous contexts and
     experiences, and are remembered and actively interpreted by audiences (Barber
     2003).

9   Conversation with Bate Nico at Seme Beach Hotel in December 2010.

10   Bate Nico's creations are one further example of dissolving the division between
     'traditional' and 'popular' genres and cultures, a tendency stressed by Karin Barber
     (2003) and Ruth Finnegan (2007). The mediations with which these performances
     work make society 'imaginable and intelligible to itself in the form of external
     representations' (Mazarella 2004:346), though it must be added that these are not
     always uncontested.

11   Moninkim are the young women who have completed their one year seclusion
     ritual, after successful delivery of their first child (Röschenthaler 1998 and
     2011:238–41).

Figure 7.3   Covers of Bate Nico's DVDs, volume 1 and 5, signed by the artist and Nkongho Regina; note the Ekpe chiefs' insignia he wears on the cover of vol. 1.

earth mounds. Other scenes show Bate Nico performing in Ekpe insignia, with the walking stick and traditional cap with the white Ekpe feather (Figure 7.3, left), or together with masked dancers representing Obasinjom (a cult agency searching for thieves and witches), Angbu (a young men's association chasing ghosts with masked dancers) or Nchebe (a masked dancer, associated with judicial matters, whose village performance requires a blood sacrifice).[12] Then there are scenes in which dancers enact village activities (hunting, harvesting, performing sacrifices etc.) wearing dresses which combine fashionable with traditional elements (Figure 7.3, right). Next, modern dancers appear in disco or rappers' outfits, joined by urban youths in city streets, in front of trendy restaurants or in indoor performances.

Dramatic scenes which treat contemporary issues such as schooling of girls, cliterodectomy, HIV/AIDS, or the conditions of unsurfaced roads during the rainy season are also presented. These can be followed by popular dances in which both men and women participate, such as the Band Dance, also called Bellesumbo (monkey's belly), which has existed since the 1920s in imitation of European ballroom dancing.[13] Nkongho Regina often plays the major role in these as lead singer. There are also scenes in which he is seen dancing side by side with his wife. In the villages, couples do not normally dance together like this. On one video Bate Nico even kisses his wife in public.

---

12   For detailed descriptions of these cult associations and their performances see Röschenthaler (2011).

13   For a short description of Band dance, see Röschenthaler (2011:300).

Figure 7.4   Bate Nico (left) with his dance group, at a funeral celebration in
Mutengene, Southwest Region, Cameroon, to which his group has been
invited to perform, in 2011 (photographer unknown, by kind permission
of Bate Nico).

Furthermore, Bate Nico can be seen in the villages performing at official festivities to which he and his dancers have been invited. These are most often the chief's installation festivities, when the Ekpe (the men's leopard society) celebrates the enthronement of a new Seseku (chief of Ekpe), and Bate Nico is seen performing together with the Ekpe. There are also scenes from concert halls, migrant meetings in the urban centres, and from his invitation to the MECA convention in the United States. Other scenes show

Figure 7.5   Nkongho Regina performing the Ekong dance in her home village, Ossing, at a funeral celebration to which their dance group has been invited to embellish the festivities, 2011 (photographer unknown, by kind permission of Bate Nico).

Bate Nico recording in the studio. Bate Nico and Regina Nkongho's voices, and occasionally those of other chorus singers, recorded in the studio, can be heard throughout the entire video, accompanied by an electronically reproduced and relatively fast drum beat. Bate Nico produces the individual components of this beat with local musical instruments (drums, shakers) and subsequently mixes them in the studio.

Figure 7.6   Bate Nico (centre behind) with his dance group in Mutengene, Southwest
Region, Cameroon, at a funeral celebration at which his group has been
invited to perform in 2011 (photographer unknown, by kind permission
of Bate Nico).

Bate Nico demonstrates that the 'modern' and 'traditional' need not be
contradictory. Of course not everyone identifies with this fusion, as it upsets
established generational and political hierarchies. Indeed, his performance
are controversial. Some people told me he is adulterating Ejagham culture,
distorting it with 'white-man music' and mixing things together which have
nothing in common.[14] Most people, however, emphatically state that he is the
most popular and most often invited musician in the entire region.

The idea of reviving 'traditional culture' implicitly entails its transference
to a different temporal, spatial and/or media environment and a new
performance context. These revived performances are decontextualized and
rearranged in new combinations. So when staged in an urban environment
and fixed on video, the revived dances often function as a quotation or assume
an emblematic role representing a different time, space or context, and the
performances assume a different meaning.

For example, in Bate Nico's videos the Moninkim dancers appear partly
in 'traditional' and partly in fancy attire, not necessarily on the village square
but in the natural environment. Watching Moninkim dancers generally makes
people smile in admiration and pride. They represent the local ideal of beauty
and make people think of the Moninkim dance groups in the villages. Those

---

14   Conversations and interviews with elders and youths in the Southwest Region in
     December 2010.

who know more will be reminded of the 'real' Moninkim who, until a couple of decades ago, underwent a ritual seclusion with cliterodectomy, and were subsequently trained in artistic skills for about a year. This elaborate ritual began during the days of the slave trade, when the seclusion became a way to display the wealth of families in a position to adorn their daughters with money (beads, bracelets, brass spirals for legs) earned from trade. During her solo performance the Moninkim put on show part of her family's wealth on her body (Eyo 1986; Röschenthaler 1998, 2011). Thus, different memories are evoked, insofar as the spectators recall historical knowledge reaching back in time and space. For the urban youths, who have rarely seen the villages at all and do not have access to such memories, the dancers in the video simply represent 'tradition'.

The Nkim dance does not belong to a cult association, as many other performances with secret elements which fall under local regulations do. At an early point in his career – Bate Nico's first DVD was not yet out – the Ekpe society, the most important men's association in the villages, summoned him to decide whether to impose a fine on him. Some Ekpe chiefs had threatened prohibiting his dance group and its performance in Ekpe insignia, as Ekpe had the exclusive right to wear these. He was forced to travel to Kembong, his home village, to explain his project to the Ekpe there, asking them to support it. He negotiated with them the extent to which they would allow him to appropriate and display certain performances, masked dances and insignia which they regarded as theirs. The Ekpe in his village eventually accepted his endeavour to revive Manyu culture without being an Ekpe member himself, honoured him with the title of 'parrot' – someone who is a brilliant singer – and instead fined the Ekpe chiefs who had summoned him.[15] After this agreement had been reached, and the chiefs in the village had validated his performance group, he was regularly invited to enrich Ekpe festivities in the villages, and since then he sings and dances on his videos in Ekpe insignia, even together with authentic Ekpe performers with their impressive imagery and awe-inspiring processions, masked dancers and secret Ekpe voice.

Before discussing further the rights to performances and their modified meanings, I will outline the history of the associations' development in the Cross River region in order to further comprehend the position of the elders

---

15 This decision by Ekpe is certainly part of the rivalry of different sections of the Ekpe society in Kembong, which has produced a good number of conflicts, as a result of which people have been heavily fined (Röschenthaler 2011:314–22). Especially because they are not written down, rules are flexible and subject to interpretation according to the requirements of specific political situations (Lentz 2006).

of Ekpe, and show how notions of alienable rights of ownership of cult associations and masquerades emerged, and to whom they belong.

History of women's and men's associations in pre-colonial times

In the framework of a larger research project I have traced the histories of the men's and women's associations that became the owners of many of these performances or 'traditional dances'. Their history can be traced for about two hundred years, from their emergence during the times of the slave trade in the eighteenth and nineteenth centuries to the present. To be able to understand their provenance and diffusion, I visited more than a hundred villages in the sparsely populated Cross River region of south-west Cameroon and south-east Nigeria, and collected the histories of villages and their cult associations and dances. The comparison of all these research findings enabled me to reconstruct their dissemination and establish their associationscape(s).[16]

In the history of the cult associations, there are several important phases, in the course of which the owners elaborated some of their cults into cult associations, and the rules of what people were allowed to do with them were modified again and again. Fundamental to this history, was the development of the possibility to acquire rights in the ownership of cult associations and their performances.

THE EMERGENCE OF PURCHASABLE ASSOCIATIONS

There oldest cults were, and still are, exclusive and attached to one village or clan, and only members from that clan or village can participate in them. The owners of these early cults made them responsible for the well-being and protection of the community and for success in hunting and warring. Membership in these cults came from inside the clan and created no ties among villages not related to each other by blood.

With the growing transatlantic slave trade, more and more people began to engage as middlemen in this activity between the coast and the more

---

16   Appadurai (1995) coined the term 'scape' to describe processes of globalization and made out five such 'scapes' (ethnocscape, ideoscape, financescape, technoscape and mediascape). I have adapted Appadurai's usage of the term 'scape' or 'landscape' to describe the complex regional networks of cult and dance associations in the Cross River region that have emerged in the process of their dissemination across the region. Some of the associations even reached global dimensions when they arrived with the slaves in Cuba (Miller 2009) and again returned from there to different African countries (De Aranzadi 2012). The details of the history of the cult associations in the Cross River region, summarized in this section, have been described in some detail, and with many maps and illustrations, in Röschenthaler 2011.

densely populated Cameroon Grassfields north-east of the Cross River region. The increase of trade required new techniques of organization, in particular the formation of binding networks, and wealth acquired by trade also modified the status system. In this process, some of the localized cults were made mobile and purchasable: at first only membership was purchased, and then in a further step, the entire cult with its different positions and performers was re-established in other villages, not by imitation but by transfer of ownership rights and knowledge in exchange for money, goods and services.[17]

My research findings show that this development began at the coastal trading village of Isangele (Rio del Rey). In order to create binding networks with the hinterland, the people of Isangele began to expand their local cult organization Ogbe and initiate people from the adjacent villages in the back country, something which had earlier been thought of as impossible. This worked out only within a certain geographical perimeter, beyond which people could not regularly travel as far as the coast for meetings. So, to solve this problem, and to integrate more traders, the entire cult association was made transferable to other places. Along with the rights to own and perform the cult, the knowledge of how it functioned, the secrets of its performance, its secret sign language, and the right to sell all this to other interested parties under certain conditions were acquired. In this way, Ogbe was disseminated under the name of Ngbe (Ekpe or Niamkpe) (Figure 7.7) far into the hinterland and to Calabar to the west.

Common ownership of and membership in the same association provided the means to surmount obstacles to trade. Trade across several villages had previously been possible only by forming marriage and blood alliances. Traders who were association members could now trade freely as far as the cult was disseminated. This is how Ekpe emerged at the coast from a local cult to become the most important association in the region: in addition to facilitating trade, it was attractive and gave prestige, had appealing performances and offered many other advantages. Ekpe had a chief who managed the society and determined the internal rules; and the Ekpe society had several titled positions and branches, each with its own captivating play (Röschenthaler 2006, 2011).

The emergence of Ekpe as a transferable cult association inspired other communities to develop their own cults for sale, which were also de-localized and purchasable in exchange for goods, services and money. The cult

---

17 Different from the European trade guilds in the Middle Ages, which did not alienate their rights in the ownership of specialized knowledge (Firth 1997; Somers 1996), people in the Cross River region offered the acquisition of rights of ownership and performance to interested parties, although in a controlled way.

Figure 7.7   Ekpe dancing in front of the chiefs, Ekoneman Awa, 1999 (photo by U.
Röschenthaler).

associations themselves offered a variety of different services: some acted as
a court, divined theft or witchcraft as did Obasinjom (Figure 7.8), collected
debts, or were hired to perform at festivities. Success in trade provided
the means for initiation into the associations, or/and for inviting other
associations to perform at prestigious events. Trade brought wealth, and this
was partly re-invested in the acquisition of cult associations, and in costumes
and masks for stunning performances.

   The women developed similar associations, among them Njom Ekpa
(Figure 7.9), the female complement to Ekpe. During the same period, female

Figure 7.8   The cult agency Obasinjom performing at Ebam, 2000 (photo by U. Röschenthaler).

Figure 7.9   Njom Ekpa of Mbakang performing at Kembong, 2001 (photo by U. Röschenthaler).

initiation rites were developed at Calabar on the coast and diffused by marriage under the name of Nkim or Moninkim to the hinterland (Figure 7.10). Wealth coming from trade enabled families to keep some of their daughters in 'idle' seclusion, in which they were taught dancing and other arts. At the coast, the ritual was most elaborate, with three variations for girls at different ages. In the

Figure 7.10   Moninkim at Old Ndebiji, 1999 (photo by U. Röschenthaler).

hinterland it was only for firstborn daughters, and deeper in the countryside, around the village of Kembong, people practised the Nkim dance but did not adopt the seclusion ritual.

The Moninkim ritual seclusion was disseminated by marriage, but the Nkim dance itself was more widespread. Anyone could perform this dance, although all acknowledged that the Moninkim, as the young women were called, were the most perfect and beautiful dancers of Nkim, and more skilled than others by virtue of their long training period during seclusion.

LOCAL REGULATIONS TO PROTECT PERFORMANCES

The purchase of a cult association did not mean the rights to individual dances or songs were acquired, rather it gave the right to own the association and stage certain performances with secret voices etc. This implied a combination of having the right to do this, the knowledge of how it worked and the skills acquired by training.

Agreement between the association owners, who formed a network of members, was essential so as to restrict the knowledge and the rights amongst themselves, and to allow only certain parties from other villages to acquire them. The first-comer landowning families' heads owned Ekpe and other minor associations that they had acquired and given to the youths. Whoever performed Ekpe had to be able to indicate whence they had acquired it. If the performance was simply copied, then this became quickly clear because they could not perform the secret signs correctly. They would be fined for fraudulently pretending to own Ekpe. If they performed correctly but could not say where they had learned to do so, it was automatically assumed that someone had told them the secret. Then the members of all the Ekpe associations in the surrounding villages assembled and forced the performers to confess who had divulged secret knowledge to them. They then had to pay an enormous fine and buy the rights for a very high price. If they were unable to do so in pre-colonial times they would be sold into slavery.

These regulations comprised a bundle of rights that defined social relations between the parties involved: rights of ownership, of performance, of communicating in the sign language, of copying or reselling any or all parts of the cult, and of access to the society's management secrets.[18] It was possible, however, for people to found a different society with a similar performance but under a new name. This was not considered a problem, so long as they did not pretend that it was Ekpe or another established society. The invention or the acquisition of a new society, however, had first of all to be accepted by the village council, which usually placed it under the auspices of the law-making association of the village, such as Ekpe itself. In this way, all association performances were protected, because the genealogy of their purchases and sales were known and memorized, and villages who had Ekpe from the same source regularly met at festivities and exchanged news. So some of the performances were in the ownership of associations, and were disseminated by purchase; while others were disseminated by marriage relations (such as the Nkim dance) or by the imitation of a performance seen in another village (Röschenthaler 2011).

---

18 See Röschenthaler (2011:345–60) for details on the concept in the Cross River region; see also May (2000:18–21).

Figure 7.11   Ngunjo performing at a funeral in Kembong, 2001 (photo by U. Röschenthaler).

NEW DANCE ASSOCIATIONS IN THE 1950S

Colonial governments greatly discouraged cult associations and their performances: internationally imposed borders interrupted trade so that fewer means for initiations were available locally; people were requisitioned for colonial projects so that they had less time for cult activities; and above all, many associations were simply banned and prohibited. This was not their end, sometimes quite the contrary, but they did experience a difficult time. Independent governments, although not always more receptive to associations, at least encouraged the revival of 'traditional dances'.

The revival of local culture already began in the 1950s, with the prospect of independence. A number of new dance associations, specialized in dancing only, were founded by youths. Most of them combined ancient warrior dances with wondrous performances and new attractive accessories obtained in urban markets. Their objective was to be invited to festivities in return for payment and to win dance competitions. With Ngunjo in Kembong, Bate Nico's father was the founder of one of the earliest and most successful of these dance associations (Figure 7.11).[19] Ngunjo's greatest success was being selected in 2000 to perform at the National Festival of Arts and Culture

---

19   Other dance associations, founded at the same time, are the women's Monogbere of Mfuni and the mixed Egbobha of Inokun (Röschenthaler 2004a, 2011).

Figure 7.12   Oyim Ntim dance group performing in front of their Ekpe hall in Ekoneman Ojong Arrey, a very remote village north of Korup National Park, in 1998 (photo by U. Röschenthaler).

(FENAC), which was staged at Limbe in the Southwest Region.[20] Festivals such as FENAC encouraged youths to engage in further artistic activities and found more dance groups. Prerequisite for participation in such competitions, however, was the official registration of the association against a fee, also making it a subject to legal regulations.

The youths who founded these new dance associations struggled to keep them independent from their elders and from Ekpe. Formerly, the youths had been obliged to hand over to their elders all the revenues won with their performances, both because of the elders' authority and because it was they who had given the youths permission to perform in the first place. With time, however, the youths gained more and more liberty. They still had to ask the blessing of the elders for any acquisition or foundation, and had to inform them whenever they performed, but could keep most of the profits. The price was that the performances were no longer protected by the local rights regime sanctioned by the Ekpe society, and so imitation and copying of performances

---

20   Already in 1988, the first National Festival of the Arts and Culture had been held in Douala in the Littoral Region. Each Region holds the festival in turn. The selection of dance groups, choirs and artists is organized nationwide in the same way and according to administrative units. That Ngunjo won the competition was considered a great success because one Region could be represented by about four dance groups, and most Regions had more than four Divisions.

*Figure 7.13   Moninkim dance group at Mfuni village, 1998 (photo by U.
Röschenthaler).*

proliferated. Nevertheless, the youths preferred independence to security, and
tried to prevent copying by diffusing gossip and rumours about the authentic
knowledge that was necessary to perform their dances with perfection. Some
youths indeed bought performance rights from others and enjoyed the prestige
acquired with the ownership of a purchased association. Others just imitated
a performance and gave it a new name. This happened particularly to the
Oyim Ntim dance association, which was first observed among the Nigerian
Ejagham and within a few years spawned many variations under different
names also in Cameroon (Röschenthaler 2004a) (Figure 7.12). Moninkim
dance groups were also founded in many villages (Figure 7.13).

DEVELOPMENTS OF THE 1990S
Throughout the 1990s and 2000s youths continued to found more dance
associations. They can be considered a major driving force in cultural creativity,
but their elders, in an attempt to preserve their privileges and the power of
their institutions, have also contributed to new developments. The efforts of
democratization and decentralization inspired cultural activities that favoured
the perception of a common culture within the administrative boundaries of
Manyu Division, in the interest of adding weight to its voice in the nation-state.
By the end of the 1990s the Ekpe and the Obasinjom unions, which united all
the Ekpe and Obasinjom associations that existed in the Manyu Division, were
founded. Their objective was to strengthen their powers, fuse their knowledge
and, as a consolidated pressure group, exercise more influence in the affairs

of the Division. This implied that the interests of the associations were to be coordinated centrally, income pooled and that decisions would be made for all by the union. It also meant that individual associations could no longer be sold independently, outside of the union. Thus the associations became once again less mobile and more restricted than they had been since they had been made available for purchase (Röschenthaler 2011).

Alongside the development of the unions, the elites from Manyu Division, working in state institutions in town, encouraged people in the rural areas to reflect about their cultural heritage. In Manyu Division, chiefs and elites quickly proclaimed that Ekpe, Obasinjom and the Moninkim dances were their immaterial cultural heritage. They declared them as henceforth belonging to this administrative unit (and not to any other) as its cultural property. That some of the neighbouring administrative units also have these same institutions (Ekpe, Obasinjom and Moninkim), particularly in the south-west, from where they had been acquired, was of no concern to the Manyu elites. Thus, the objective of preserving culture also encouraged a politics of difference, and people began to imagine themselves as part of a larger community with a common culture, now defined in terms of a Division, and thus co-opting the notion of a cultural heritage owned together by the four ethnic groups of Manyu Division.

Ownership rights, shifting performance contexts and the value of culture

I have traced how, in the course of the past few centuries, people in the Cross River region created a network of owners that controlled the circulation of cult associations and the staging of their performances. Their politics of dissemination had an impact on the value accorded certain parts of culture and the perception of these as a resource. I will now examine some of the implications of ownership rights in cult associations and the shifting meaning of individual performance elements when they are imitated and appear in a different context or another medium, as well as legitimate and illegitimate forms of their appropriation.

VALUE CREATION, OWNERSHIP AND THE ASSOCIATIONS' RULES OF CONDUCT
Initially, clans owned cults, to which were connected certain performances which its members staged to celebrate important events together. With the emergence of purchasable associations, cults no longer exclusively belonged to a clan, but were made transferable. Individuals belonging to first-comer landowning families of other villages could acquire them and become founding members of the cult in their village. Their heirs inherited their title in the association, but they had to pay all the necessary fees and undergo initiation

before taking advantage of their entitlement. So the important positions and
the management of cults were organized by certain families. Non-members
in a village could identify with the associations and regard them as 'their own'
when these associations performed in another locality, but only in a figurative
sense. The collective ownership of performances by any single ethnic group
larger than a clan does not exist, and all the less so in that cult associations
and dances have been disseminated across the region irrespective of ethnic or
other boundaries. The idea of collective ethnic 'ownership' arose in this area
only with decentralization and the preservation of cultural heritage.

Notions of the value of immaterial cultural goods also find their expression
in the convention that only association members have the right to talk about
any matters of the association that go beyond the limits of purely entertaining
stories, and only when the other members are assembled. Men cannot talk
about women's institutions, nor can women speak about those of men, without
permission. The reason is that all cult members have paid initiation fees with
the objective that they alone should make and share any profits gained by the
association. Even an Ekpe chief cannot discuss the association without inviting
his members, as otherwise they would force him to pay a high fine for violating
the rules. Thus, information about the association and entertainment by its
performances are considered valuable goods that cannot be given away for
free. A problem arises when an individual acts against association laws. Ekpe
has internal rules guiding the conduct of its members, but it also has another
set of rules, issued for the local village government and concerning everyone.
All these rules can differ from one Ekpe society and one village to another.
Ekpe is always on the lookout for reasons to fine individuals and thus produce
additional money, food and drink for the members to enjoy.

This was the case when some Ekpe members accused Bate Nico of
performing in the insignia of an Ekpe chief, with the specifically tied loincloth,
the white eagle's feather in his cap, the towel over his shoulder and a decorated
staff. They insisted he had profited from wearing Ekpe insignia without
having paid initiation fees to the association. Once Bate Nico had explained
his intentions to them, however, the position taken by the Ekpe of his home
village Kembong was that only members can be fined by Ekpe, and since Bate
Nico was not a member, he could not be fined by it. They did not perceive
his activities as a loss for Ekpe, but as enrichment in the sense that he was an
excellent dancer and singer whose performance enhanced the reputation of
the village and the value of Ekpe among the urban youths from Manyu. This
case also shows that Ekpe is not always of uniform opinion, and factions often
dispute the management and leadership of the associations, also with respect
to what members (or non-members from Manyu) in towns and abroad (in
other African countries and continents) are allowed to do. The judgement fell

in favour of Bate Nico, but things could easily have turned out differently in another village or in former times, as there are known cases in which Ekpe has successfully obliged individuals and groups of people to pay for membership or even acquire the entire association. On the one hand, Ekpe rules have been modified and relaxed with respect to work and life in towns, the duration and severity of initiation rituals and the performance of insignia, secret voices and Ekpe masks in towns and abroad. On the other hand, the unions of Ekpe and Obasinjom were founded precisely in order to unify, coordinate and better control the conduct of all its members.

THE PERFORMANCE CONTEXT: RITUALIZED PERFORMANCES

In the Cross River region the person who managed to bring an association to a village enjoys great prestige and importance. This person provided the village with something valuable, an achievement for which he or she, acknowledged as the association's founder, will be venerated as its ancestor. The fame of this person, however, whether he or she is the association's creator or purchaser, will depend in the end on his or her capacity to develop it into a powerful institution with astounding performances that can arouse the desire of other parties to acquire it. These new owners will then spread the name of this person far and wide, so that it will live on in the memories of people.[21]

The performances organized by cult or dance associations (as opposed to dances for fun) are staged in a specific performance context, as Karin Barber (2003) has also noted, more generally, for Africa. An association mask or its main dancer is always accompanied by a group of assistants who produce the music and collect the money 'sprayed' on the dancers by important spectators. In the Cross River region a performance consists at the very least of a lead singer and chorus, musicians, a messenger and a person who collects gifts. Some associations have up to thirty or forty performers.

The performance context implies following a certain protocol. First, the village chief has to be asked for permission to stage a public performance, if he himself is not the one who has initiated the festivities. Before the performance begins, the event is opened by a libation to the ancestors. Then the performance is announced by the association's messenger, following which the performers march, singing, in a procession to all the entrances of the village.[22] When they

---

21 Purchase entails the rights to the immaterial elements of the association, the necessary material objects have to be commissioned by another specialist. This specialist, mostly a carver of masks or other insignia, has no further rights in the objects, however, once he has been paid for them (Röschenthaler 2011).

22 Migrants from the area also follow this procedure when they perform dances in cities: They march to both ends of the street before dancing in the hall. For more

arrive in the village square, their first song always stresses the name of the association, so that no one will remain unaware of which group is performing. The group faces the chiefs, seated in a shaded place, while the other spectators form a circle around the performers, and may also dance with them. Then follow several songs of about ten to twenty minutes each. The lead singer starts and the chorus answers. The other performers dance with or without masks. The audience sings along with them and also comments on the performance. After the dance, the members continue celebrating the event with a drinking ritual, which is closed by a libation to the association's ancestors.

Associations purposefully limit the frequency of their performances in order to increase their prestige and value. They only perform when the village chief or another personality has invited them to dance at a specific event or a funeral. Unless they are compensated and fed, they do not perform. They also insist on drinks before and after the performance. This demonstrates a high awareness of the value of performance, which reflects the way in which these associations emerged. Bate Nico largely follows these conventions when his dance group is invited to perform at festivities, but he also experiments with different environments and places (town halls, stages in the city and in other countries), and above all when producing DVDs, which inherently obliges him to abridge and fragment his performances.

THE MEDIATIZATION OF CULTURE IN THE MANYU DIVISION

The consciousness of the value of local culture in Manyu Division was further enhanced by the foundation of a rural radio station in 1997. Radio encouraged the mediatization of local culture and music, but also modified the audience's perception of a performance. As we have seen, association dances in the village square require a full performance context and the complete ritualized procedure. When presented on the radio, television or on video tapes, however, the media formats and programmes do not admit more than isolated parts of performances. The radio moderator – just like the messenger on the village square – will announce the name of the group and the song, but then only one song from the entire performance will usually be broadcast.

The dancers in the village carry out the complete ritualized performance, even when the technicians recording it only require a few good songs. Performers normally welcomed the technicians who had come to tape their songs, which they enjoyed listening to when they were broadcast in the radio (and occasionally also on national television). Initially, just as the associations had always insisted on being rewarded for a performance at festivities, they also asked the media to pay for the use of their music. When they had to

details about the performance protocol, see Röschenthaler (2011:414–40).

accept, however, that the rural radio station could not pay them, they came to perceive their – finally more than sufficient – reward in the broadcast of their songs for everyone to hear, which would enhance their fame, the reputation of the entire village and the association's value by the reproduction of selections of its repertoire in a highly appreciated medium, something that gave them a clear edge in their competition with the associations of other villages.

The videotaping of dances at festivities by local individuals was also accepted, if not explicitly encouraged, especially if made by the family whose occasion was being celebrated in an event they wished to record for posterity and the fame of which they desired to spread. Association owners stated that the essential knowledge of a cult association such as Ekpe, which comprises its value, could not be captured by the recording of a performance, as learning and reproducing secret sign languages or voices requires skills obtainable only through initiation, and not from watching a video.

The association members would, of course, have preferred to be paid, but came to appreciate the broadcast of their songs as free publicity for their association. It was clear to everyone that the radio had no money and that it was unable to pay its workers. At the time, nobody talked about the registering of songs the radio broadcasted. One could argue that the radio should have to pay the artists for the right to reproduce their songs, but no less convincingly argue that the association owners have to pay the radio for playing their songs to a wider audience than they could ever hope to reach otherwise. Neither was the case in the first decade of the 2000s. The radio, however, asked private individuals and commercial advertisers to pay for the broadcast of their announcements and publicity. Rural radios derived most of their income from making private announcements such as death celebrations and the communication of personal greetings.[23]

The advent of electronic media can thus be seen as an intersection where local and international concepts of commercializing immaterial goods and redistributing revenues are negotiated. Previously, the town crier and/or the cult associations themselves had acted as the media to announce important forthcoming events (Diawara and Röschenthaler 2013), and the associations had provided paid entertainment.

VALUE AND PIRACY

When talking about their associations, people expressed a clear sense of the value of their performance. Association owners unabashedly stated that they had acquired the institution with the aim of making money with it, procuring

---

23 For an account of rural radio working in a similar manner in Benin, see Grätz 2000.

additional food and drink, and providing themselves, in the process, with lasting prestige. An association was considered a service enterprise and its owners can therefore be termed cultural entrepreneurs. This is perfectly expressed in the metaphor 'an *okum* [association] is like a farm'. When well managed, the undertaking is worthwhile from a long-term perspective. Acquiring an association is generally expensive. It can easily cost 150,000 to 300,000 FCFA (about £180 to £360) in addition to requiring the investment of a similar amount in the confection of masks and costumes. Ekpe societies were always the most expensive to acquire. It is for this reason that some Ekpe members tried to accuse Bate Nico of illegitimately appropriating their performance, devaluing Ekpe and depriving it of privileges and profit. Bate Nico himself, however, at no point understood his project in these terms, but rather as an attempt to revive 'traditional culture', arguing that his performances created new value for Ekpe and other associations among both rural and urban youths.

To maintain its value, the associations developed a strategy of limiting performances (Appadurai 1986). People will welcome any opportunity to dance for fun, but as we have seen, the performance of an association is staged only when it is compensated for the entertainment provided. There is an unspoken agreement among associations to perform only when they have received an official invitation that guarantees an appropriate fee. The introduction of the FENAC has contributed to the multiplication of dance associations, but also contradicted this strategy. Many complain that the organizers do not pay them, and that there is no guarantee that they will profit from performing, let alone cover their travel expenses. If the wealthy elite with political ambitions, eager to enhance their reputation, had not stepped in to sponsor pre-selection events, the competition of dance groups to participate in FENAC would probably not have been so successful (Röschenthaler 2004a).

As mentioned earlier, highly valued goods are especially prone to being copied. Many youths told me that their performances were 'stolen' by other youths, but that there was nothing they could do about it except make their complaints public. This does not mean, however, that these very same youths would not copy songs and dances themselves, as in the towns the young systematically pirate electronically mediated musical and video productions of other artists (see also Tcheuyap in this volume).[24]

---

24   Piracy of musical performances on modern sound carriers makes sense only where people have the equipment and power supply to consume these products. In Manyu Division, wherever electricity is functioning, more and more people own the facilities to watch DVDs. Access to the internet and connecting to the migrant

Bate Nico's productions are prone to be copied on two different levels. First, his entire performance idea could be imitated, although this would require excellent performance skills on a par with his own. This is the situation dance associations in the villages also have to face. Second, his mediatized performances (DVDs) are extensively pirated, as he indicated in his statement quoted at the beginning of this chapter, mentioning his strategy of trying to be 'faster than the pirates'. Bate Nico's pirates most likely come from his large fan community, which recruits mainly but not exclusively among his own people from Manyu Division. By copying his products, they also make him more widely known. In addition to this, migrants in urban centres and abroad use the internet to upload videos of his performances – and their own tapes of installation festivities for chiefs and the celebrations of funerals – to YouTube and other websites, destined for migrants from Manyu Division all over the globe, with still further implications for the ownership of the performances. All these activities allude to the intricacies of the notion of value, especially of immaterial culture, which depends on the perspective from which it is regarded: this can diminish but also enhance the value of the performances, creating revenues, in the long run, for the artist.

Old and new local ideas about ownership and copyright

This section looks at the extent to which local claims to performances come into conflict with the idea of reviving culture, and to what degree association members perceive Bate Nico's attempts at cultural revival as a common and legitimate practice of quoting of performance elements. It is important to note that it is not particular dances, as such, that cult associations claim the exclusive right to perform. In the end, it is difficult to define, in any clear-cut way, what they insist belongs only to them, and it is precisely this openness to interpretation that enables people to articulate their own claims. What can be said is that there are central association songs and powerful performances with elements considered particularly secret, and connected, for the most part, with blood sacrifices which the association claims as its sole privilege to stage. But individual parts of a performance can be appropriated and staged by other associations.

As mentioned earlier, Bate Nico's father founded Ngunjo, one of the first dance societies in Kembong, with the objective of reviving Ejagham 'traditional' culture. He gathered into the repertoire the commonly practised Nkim dance, the Nki and Ndem dances that belonged to two once very influential women's associations; and the men's Nchebe and Nkpe, which were

communities has been possible in a few internet cafes since about the mid-2000s, but they are not fully reliable in this rural area due to the weak phone lines.

only rarely staged at that time. In Kembong, the rights to perform Nkpe and Nchebe, and a couple of cap masks, whose appearance at special festivities requires blood sacrifices and is rewarded by the gift of a goat, are held in family ownership. These families did not object, however, when the Ngunjo dance group began to perform masks with the same names, because they – as well as the Nkim, Ndem and Nki dances – were understood to be mere quotations from a larger performance context.

Bate Nico's father also borrowed performances of cult associations which were fully functioning, in particular Ekpe and Obasinjom.[25] He performed the Nkanda dance of Ekpe, with dancers in Moninkim dresses in the colours of Cameroon, one of them carrying a hoop. Ekpe also regarded this as an acceptable quotation at the time. Obasinjom represented, however, a different case, as the mask, at the centre of this cult agency's performance, was charged with powerful medicines. Bate Nico's father had been a member of Obasinjom, and so in the village, at the beginning, the empowered Obasinjom mask occasionally performed with Ngunjo. But when he moved to the coast in the 1980s, the Obasinjom association of Kembong prohibited Bate Nico's father from performing with this mask in town.[26]

Bate Nico took over most of these dances, but also added new masks. He also took up the Obasinjom again, ordering a mask from a carver, which he adorned only with feathers. When Bate Nico, who is not a member of either of the Ekpe or the Obasinjom associations, performed the 'powerless' mask with two assistants in town, the association in the village no longer objected. Performing such an 'empty mask' would have been ridiculous in the villages, but in the coastal area it served as the perfect advertisement of the powers of the real Obasinjom.[27] It was perceived as a legitimate quotation, just as when the British colonial officer Percy Amaury Talbot (1912) had observed children performing with a small (unloaded) Obasinjom mask in a village.

What aroused the attention of the Ekpe members in his home region, however, was Bate Nico's wearing status insignia for which he had not paid initiation fees. So some Ekpe members, while questioning his wearing these insignia as a non-member, suggested that as a freeborn of Kembong he was

---

25   See Röschenthaler for more detailed descriptions of Moninkim or Nkim (2011:238–41), Nki (2011:224–5), Ndem (2011:243–50), Nchebe and Nkpe (2011:65–84), Ekpe (2011:99–157), and Obasinjom (2011:194–202, and 2004b).

26   An empowered Obasinjom mask has medicines (herbs, roots, organic material) plastered on its wooden front by the association members after the head has been created by a carver (Röschenthaler 2004b and 2011:194–202).

27   Around the Mt. Cameroon a few villages also owned Obasinjom associations that they had acquired from the Manyu Division (Ardener 1970; Geschiere 2001; Röschenthaler 2004b).

entitled to acquire the rights to do so. But, as mentioned earlier, yet other Ekpe members, who had also joined the Manyu Ekpe union, banned his dance group, obliging him to travel to his home village of Kembong to negotiate the case with the Ekpe members who had insisted that it was their exclusive right to perform with Ekpe insignia and dresses in public, wherever they were. Bate Nico had not even attempted to perform with an Ekpe masked dancer, but Ekpe nevertheless made clear, for good measure, that any of its powerful performances with secret voices or masked dancers could be presented only with the authorization of its owners in the village, formally granted in the presence of all members and following a libation or sacrifice given by its chief. These were also the means to authenticate the Ekpe performance.

Bate Nico eloquently negotiated with Ekpe, explaining that he was performing Ekpe in town only to encourage the youths to maintain their interest in their traditional culture. He insisted that he wanted to keep the Ekpe songs and imagery alive in the minds of urban youths by preserving them as performance and on video, and that doing so would also advertise the power of Ekpe as cultural performance. Ekpe eventually accepted his arguments, and, instead, the Ekpe members who had threatened him were fined. The village council of Kembong even honoured Bate Nico with the title of 'parrot', as already mentioned.

Although Ekpe accepted his endeavours and the village council acknowledged his dance group, Bate Nico did not become an Ekpe member by initiation, nor did he acquire his own Ekpe association, despite his right to do either or both, as he was not interested in the many advantages offered by membership in the society, but rather only in performing. He simply wanted to be an artist and, with his performances, contribute to keeping the 'traditional' dances alive. The arguments with Ekpe were not primarily a generational conflict between youths and Ekpe elders, as occasionally occurred in the area (Röschenthaler 2011:314–16). Bate Nico, while keeping his distance from the association, has no intention of provoking further conflict with Ekpe members, not the least because they have become an important source of income for him when they invite him to perform at their festivities.

Following this incident, and its favourable solution, he has been ever more often invited by Ekpe chiefs in the villages, whom he praises with his songs in exchange for (paid) invitations to perform at their festivities. These events are multi-purpose for Bate Nico, who also documents them on video, later enhancing the recordings with his songs recorded in the studio, and combines them with other outdoor recordings to produce DVDs which he then pays to register with the Cameroonian organization for authors' rights, in the hope of receiving royalties from their sales and broadcast. In this context, Bate Nico's

Figure 7.14   Bate Nico at the US MECA convention in Washington with their Obasinjom mask (right), 2011 (photographer unknown, by kind permission of Bate Nico).

products are considered his own creations. Thus, Bate Nico moves between the two property regimes, having negotiated to participate in both.

Some of these same association performances are also reproduced by emigrants in different parts of the world. The migrants continue to modify the performance during their annual meetings in the diaspora. The owners of associations in the villages, and migrant association members in the urban centres and diaspora, have argued a great deal as to whether the Ekpe masked dancer should be allowed to appear there, with or without the voice. Ekpe in the villages finally decided that members were allowed to display their insignia in town, but neither the masked dancer can appear nor the secret voice be heard. In the diaspora meetings, however, the masked dancer is performed, albeit without the secret voice – as is Obasinjom, without its medicines (Figure 7.14) – but ancestral libation speeches can be delivered in front of the microphone. On their videos, some of which can be watched on YouTube, however, secret voices are electronically reproduced and visual effects can evoke the eerie feeling of the presence of nonhuman powers, and sacrifices and the entrance to the association's forest can be also shown, thus reinforcing respect for 'traditional culture'.

Ekpe's translocal power was based on the closely knit network of member villages. This has become more difficult to maintain with migration, but Ekpe manages to sustain a grip on its members living abroad. It collects information on them, and when they return home to assist at funerals or festivities they are fined for any violations the association has recorded.

The transformation of performances by their revival

In this section I will have a closer look at what happens to the meaning of performance elements when they are taken out of their established context. This takes place on several levels at once. A performance with a larger number of performers is reduced to one dancer representing the troupe, a kind of synecdoche emblematic of their combined power. One performer can also imitate a role from another performance as a quotation. For a public performance, each mask or central performer had a company of drummers, singers and dancers accompanying him or her. These roles are extracted from distinct times and contexts to be reintegrated into a new performance context or on new media as a kind of collage, assuming new meanings. This is what Bate Nico does when he revives 'traditional' dances in town or on a video. He combines them into a new context, presenting side by side dancers who would previously not have appeared together.

In the village performance context, performers and masked dancers are always accompanied by an ensemble of performers and the chief of the association.[28] Although comprised of a solo singer and dancer, the Moninkim also always performs together with a group of assistants (singers, drummers, guardians). Obasinjom is accompanied by his own orchestra and singers, the interpreters of his messages, a 'trumpeter', gun holders and a medicine man. In Bate Nico's videos, the assistants of the different masked dancers are most often no longer visible, replaced by his own dance group. If they are onstage at all, they no longer have a powerful function. Bate Nico's Obasinjom masked dancer runs around in fast steps with his long floating gown blowing up in the wind, as if he were searching for witches, thieves and sorcerers. But the number of his helpers has been reduced, to what extent depending on the site, and his performance, imitating the powerful Obasinjom, has become an art form. He no longer has the power to discover malevolent people. The mask's head is empty, devoid of the potent substances administered to his forehead. In meeting halls in the city, functioning guns, used in village performances as signs of power, cannot be carried.

This practice of condensing and quoting performance elements is not new in the region, but rather has a long tradition. The youths in their dance

---

28 When one of their laws has been broken, the peaceful and well-ordered public appearance of the associations ends, and they bring about a state of emergency, until the culprit has been judged and the owners of the masks regain control of the situation (Röschenthaler 2011).

Figure 7.15 Moninkim dance group in Limbe town hall, 1998 (photo by U. Röschenthaler).

associations are fond of reproducing performance elements from other, mostly earlier, associations, reviving memories of the times when headhunting was central to acquiring prestige. Children also imitate performances of associations in this way. Women quote, in their dance and cult associations, male roles such as the diviner, the hunter, the policeman, the cult-agency owner (Mfam, Efim), the association which disinters the corpses of people who had appeared as ghosts (Angbu) and also beautiful girl dancers (Moninkim). Male dancers also occasionally perform the Moninkim.[29] They are all free to do this, so long as they do not reproduce the cult elements or claim to represent the entire association.

The individual cultural elements are taken out of a previously established context when they are quoted from other performances and are reorganized in a new framework in which they gain new meaning through their combination with other performance elements also removed from their earlier contexts. When reviving dances in the 1950s, the youths were preoccupied with this kind of rearrangement of elements with different provenances and from different times (Röschenthaler 2004a). With his recordings on DVD, Bate Nico combines performance and music elements from a still wider variety of origins in a new way, and within a legal framework that recognizes him as the sole author of these creations. Karin Barber (1999) has observed the practice of quotation in the oral and written literary domain, and recognized that this de- and re-contextualization with altered meanings is the organizing principle of quotations. Similar practices of *bricolage* are known as sampling in recent

---

29   See Röschenthaler 2011 for descriptions of Angbu (285–91), the cult agency Mfam (191–4) and Efim (173).

music creations (see Caroline Mose and Veit Erlmann in this volume) and as collage (McLeod and Kuenzli 2011), a concept derived from the visual arts. All these practices challenge concepts of exclusive ownership of artistic work.

In addition to the rearrangement of material, the spatial displacement of performance also transforms its meaning. Spatial decontextualizations of performances already began with the dissemination of dances across a region, and whenever associations were invited to perform at festivities in another village. The important sacrifices, however, could only be carried out in the home village. Different spatial arrangements continued during the twentieth century in the Cross River region when associations performed for entertainment at official festivities and stadiums, when migrants performed in meeting halls (Figure 7.15) or on the stage, and when, with the introduction of new technical possibilities, performances were recorded and reproduced in the media and on the internet. Sacred forests, blood sacrifices, secret voices, the nature of insignia (functioning guns, for example), ritualized performance, the arrangement of the dancers and interaction with the audience were transformed or omitted to different degrees or replaced by more popular elements.

Conclusion

Through the example of the Cameroonian singer and performance artist Bate Nico, I have discussed the impact of two different rights regimes on performances and artistic products. One is international copyright, which in Cameroon is based on the French system and acknowledges an individual artist as the creator of a particular performance or product. The artist is supposed to be compensated for his creation and receive royalties from the profits made by others with his creation. The other is the local regime that protects the rights of the owners of a performance and their privilege of creating income with it by offering services and stage performances. These rights are about ownership and do not concern an entire village or ethnic group as such, but only the group of people who have acquired them. I have shown that this concept of transferable rights in immaterial cultural elements emerged during the times of the transatlantic slave trade, when exclusive clan cults were transformed and elaborated into transferable institutions as soon as their ownership promised profit. The rights in their ownership and performance, and of the knowledge of their functioning, became transferable against payment, and their use was sanctioned by the network of all the owners of the same institution.

The two regimes of rights have in common that they consider immaterial goods a valuable resource and that they attempt to control performance. On the local level, however, there is so far hardly any connection between these regimes. It even appears that the existence of the local rights concept does not in any way facilitate the establishment of the international copyright regime. On the local level the youths had to place their performances under the regime of their elders. In the 1950s, they began to loosen the grip of their elders' system of rights on their dance associations, accepting the lack of protection of their performance, although later they complained about the piracy of their dances. With the advent of the music industry, the international copyright regime protecting individual artworks became increasingly relevant. Then individual artists such as Bate Nico, who operate on a translocal level, registered their creations to protect the product but not their local performance as such. Bate Nico furthermore had to get along with both regimes in their attempts to reconcile the different interests in performances.

Most recently, discussions of cultural heritage have led to the promotion of the idea of the collective ownership of immaterial cultural goods. Of particular interest has been the creation of the unions of the two most important associations (Ekpe and Obasinjom) in the Manyu Division in the 1990s, with which their owners attempted to strengthen the powers of their associations. At the same time, these unions made culture more exclusive and immobile once more, and created a new sense of belonging by excluding the same associations in other Divisions and by promoting culture as an ethnic property. Such an organization could create the possibility of filing claims on behalf of all the member villages of the union, and even foster the idea of protecting immaterial cultural heritage in the name of the Manyu people as a whole (now trying to fuse several ethnic groups into one), something difficult to imagine previously. Manyu unions of associations would coincide quite well with the concepts used by NGOs and international institutions, who consider entire ethnic groups or collectives the owners of a specific cultural heritage.[30] This could have new consequences for both the individual artists and the individual association owners with regard to the use of local performances.

The ongoing dialectics between claims of controlling valuable immaterial goods and the endeavours to use them freely has a long history. Control has been circumvented by copying and by playfully quoting individual elements of performances, or by transforming and disguising them. Bate Nico continues these practices when he recombines established dances with often only apparently traditional accessories, and village festivities with street performances and diaspora meetings. Different audiences also permit new performance environments. In the village context, dancers interact with

---

30   A very similar problem with respect to collective and individual ownership of women's folk songs in Algeria is raised by Jane Goodman (2005). See also the contribution of Neo Musangi in this volume.

the audience and need assistants to collect the gifts. The mediatization of performances (on DVD, TV, YouTube) allows dancers to perform alone in a natural environment. This makes sense only when the performance is mediated (recorded) and the audience is differently imagined. In the end, what is acceptable in a certain local context is always a matter of negotiation between the different interest groups involved. Various local associations, as well as Bate Nico, have quoted elements of the Ekpe performance, and when dancing with the insignia of high Ekpe members Bate Nico tested how far he could go with this. To the local rights regime and the international copyright for individual artists has now been added a third conception of rights, that of collective rights in cultural heritage and local knowledge, promoted by international organizations. In the end, it will depend on the interpretation by the different interest groups involved whether Bate Nico's recombination of modern and ancient cultural elements will be considered an innovative, new and individual creation, or whether it will be considered part of the cultural heritage of Manyu Division.

As a counterpoint to this increasing international judicialization of the intellectual property debate, the global public demands the democratization of music production, and aims at resisting the control of the state or production companies, even though this also dispossesses the artists. In Bate Nico's case, piracy includes a similar paradox: His videos are pirated because music is highly valued, and at the same time the copiers – his fan community – do not pirate in order to deprive him of his profit but due to a desire, almost a duty, to share the subject of their admiration with friends and disseminate the artist's name widely in the region to enhance his fame and fulfil the highest aspirations of Big Men in the region.

References

Appadurai, Arjun. 1986. 'Introduction: commodities and the politics of value'. In: Arjun Appadurai (ed.). *The Social Life of Things: Commodities in Cultural Perspective*. Cambridge: Cambridge University Press, 3–63.

——— 1995. 'The production of locality'. In: Richard Fardon (ed.). *Counterworks: Managing the Diversity of Knowledge*. London and New York: Routledge, 204–25.

Ardener, Edwin. 1970. 'Witchcraft, economics, and the continuity of belief'. In: Mary Douglas (ed.). *Witchcraft: Confessions and Accussations*. London: Tavistock, 141–60.

Ardener, Edwin, Shirley Ardener and W.A. Warmington. 1960. *Plantation and Village in the Cameroons*. London: Oxford University Press.

Barber, Karin. 1999. 'Quotation in the constitution of Yorùbá oral texts'. In: *Research in African Literatures* 30(2):17–41.

———— 2003. 'Text and Performance in Africa'. *Bulletin of the School of Oriental and African Studies* 66(3):324–33.

Bohannan, Laura and Paul Bohannan. 1968. *Tiv Economy*. London: Longmans.

De Aranzadi, Isabela. 2012. 'El legado cubano en África: ñáñigos deportados a Fernando Poo: memoria viva y archivo escrito'. *Afro-Hispanic Review* 31(1):29–60.

Diawara, Mamadou and Ute Röschenthaler. 2013. 'Normenwandel und die Macht der Medien im subsaharischen Afrika'. In: Andreas Fahrmeir and Anette Imhausen (eds). *Die Vielfalt normativer Ordnungen: Konflikte und Dynamik in historischer und ethnologischer Perspektive*. Frankfurt: Campus Verlag, 129–64.

Eyo, Ekpo (ed.). 1986. *The Story of Old Calabar: A Guide to the National Museum at the Old Residency, Calabar*. Calabar: The National Commission for Museums and Monuments.

Finnegan, Ruth. 2007. *The Oral and Beyond: Doing Things with Words in Africa*. Oxford and Chicago: James Currey and Chicago University Press.

Firth, Alison. 1997. 'Distinctive signs and early markets: Europe, Africa and early Islam'. In: Alison Firth (ed.). *The Prehistory and Development of Intellectual Property Systems*. London: Sweet and Maxwell, 125–58.

Fischer, Hans-Jörg. 2001. *Die deutschen Kolonien: Die koloniale Rechtsordnung und ihre Entwicklung nach dem ersten Weltkrieg*. Berlin: Duncker & Humblot.

Geschiere, Peter. 2001. 'Witchcraft and new forms of wealth: regional variations in South and West Cameroon'. In: Paul Clough and Jon Mitchell (eds). *Powers of Good and Evil*. New York and Oxford: Berghahn Books, 43–76.

Goodman, Jane. 2005. *Berber Culture on the World Stage: From Village to Video*. Bloomington: Indiana University Press.

Grätz, Tilo. 2000. 'New local radio stations in African languages and the process of political transformation: the case of Radio Rurale Locale Tanguiéta'. In: Richard Fardon and Graham Furniss (eds). *African Broadcast Cultures*. Oxford: James Currey, 110–27.

Harrison, Simon. 1993. 'The commerce in cultures in Melanesia'. *Man* (ns) 28:139–58.

Hirsch, Eric and Marilyn Strathern (eds). 2004. *Transactions and Creations: Property Debates and the Stimulus in Melanesia*. New York: Berghahn.

Jones, Mark. 1994. 'Why fakes?' In: Susan Pearce (ed.). *Interpreting Objects and Collections*. London: Routledge, 92–7.

Kubik, Gerhard. 1993. *Makisi nyau mapiko. Maskentraditionen im bantu-sprachigen Afrika*. München: Trickster.

Lentz, Carola. 2006. 'Land and the politics of belonging in Africa: an introduction'. In: Richard Kuba and Carola Lentz (eds). *Land and the Politics of Belonging in West Africa*. Leiden and Boston: Brill, 1–34.

Lowie, Robert. 1928. 'Incorporeal property in primitive society'. *Yale Law Journal*
    37(5):551–63.

Malinowski, Bronislaw. 1922. *The Argonauts of the Western Pacific*. London:
    Routledge and Kegan Paul.

May, Christopher. 2000. *A Global Political Economy of Intellectual Property Rights*.
    London and New York: Routledge.

Mazzarella, William. 2004. 'Culture, globalization, mediation'. *Annual Review of
    Anthropology* 33:345–67.

McLeod, Kembrew and Rudolf Kuenzli (eds). *Cutting Across Media: Appropriation
    Art, Interventionist Collage, and Copyright Law*. Durham and London: Duke
    University Press.

Miller, Ivor. 2009. *Voice of the Leopard: African Secret Societies and Cuba*. Jackson:
    University Press of Mississippi.

Niger-Thomas, Margaret. 2000. *Buying Futures: The Upsurge of Female
    Entrepreneurship Crossing the Formal/Informal Divide in South West
    Cameroon*. Leiden: Research School CNWS.

Röschenthaler, Ute. 1998. 'Honoring Ejagham women'. *African Arts* 31(2):38–49, 92–3.

——— 2004a. 'Neuheit, *Bricolage* oder Plagiat? Zur Entstehung neuer Tanzbünde
    im Cross River-Gebiet (im Südwesten Kameruns und Südosten Nigerias)'.
    Paideuma 50:193–223.

——— 2004b. 'Transacting Obasinjom: the dissemination of a cult agency in the
    Cross River area'. *Africa* 74, 2:241–76.

——— 2006. 'Translocal cultures. the slave trade and cultural transfer in the Cross
    River Region'. *Social Anthropology* 14(1):71–91.

——— 2011. *Purchasing Culture: The Dissemination of Associations in the Cross River
    Region of Cameroon and Nigeria*. Trenton: Africa World Press.

Somers, Margaret. 1996. '"Misteries" of property: relationality, families, and
    community in the making of political right: urban roots of artisanal
    property in skill'. In: John Brewer and Susan Staves (eds). *Early Modern
    Conceptions of Property*. London: Routledge, 62–92.

Talbot, Percy Amaury. 1912. *In the Shadow of the Bush*. London: Heinemann.

CHAPTER 8

From communal practice to intellectual property

The Ngqoko Cultural Group, political

claim-making and the judicialization

of performance in South Africa

ⓒⓒⓒⓒⓒⓒⓒⓒⓒⓒ

NEO MUSANGI

Introduction

My interest in the music of the world-famous South African Ngqoko Cultural Group began with my encounter with the group in 2008 in a TRC[1]-based play. In the play, *Molora* – an adaptation of Greek mythology by producer and director Yael Farber – five women and one man from the group were cast as the chorus (Farber 2009).[2] The six performed a particular form of overtone singing known as *umngqokolo*, which is prevalent among the Thembu-Xhosa people of South Africa. Since then, I have begun taking great interest in the history of the group and in the processes of the mediation of their performance, in particular in the way parts of 'culture' are re-invented, contested and claimed by practitioners, individuals, corporations, government departments and sections of the media. In the course of my research project on the music of the Ngqoko Cultural Group, I became increasingly aware of how global systems of meaning can change the relationship that local actors have with cultural expression. Tourist and heritage performances, for instance, have an immense impact on the way culture is presented, interpreted and

---

1   The Truth and Reconciliation Commission (TRC) is a restorative justice body formed in 1995 after the fall of apartheid in South Africa. Formed under the Promotion of National Unity and Reconciliation Act, No. 34 of 1995, the mandate of the commission was to bear witness to, record and in some cases grant amnesty to the perpetrators of crimes relating to human rights violations, as well as reparation and rehabilitation. See www.justice.gov.za/trc, accessed 4 March 2011.

2   The play was only published after the theatrical production and performance.

understood by different publics. This packaging of aspects of culture as ethnic, primordial, timeless and unchanging is best exemplified in competing claims in intellectual property rights regimes, especially in the category of music often known as 'traditional' or in its commercialized global market form, World Music.

Edwin Wilmsen (1996) has argued that, '[p]rimordialist ethnic claims are nothing more than claims to ownership of the past and rights to its use for present purposes' (1996:3). That is indeed a plausible argument, given how ancestral past(s) have been re-imagined in the present in post-colonial Africa.[3] However, Wilmsen seems to underestimate the cultural value that some of these claims may hold. Beyond rights and claims to ownership, particular genres of cultural expression have serious significance for certain communities. Divination songs, for instance, are a medium through which people connect with ancestral and/or spiritual worlds. However, in a case such as that of the Ngqoko Cultural Group, certain forms of music seem to have acquired meanings that go beyond the sphere of ritual and the very specific contexts in which this music connects the worlds of the living and the living dead or ancestors. Whether the 'new' contexts of performance are national music competitions, presidential tours, festivals and concerts, or white-wedding receptions, what becomes evident are conflicting claims to the ownership of and performance rights to particular musical genres and styles.

In this chapter I seek to examine the correlation between these competing local articulations of *rights* in the *ownership* of cultural expressions and existing global and local normative orders. This study is primarily based on discourses of intangible cultural heritage, in particular with respect to the music of the Ngqoko Cultural Group in Lady Frère (Eastern Cape). The chapter entails two components: first, a theoretical examination of South African legislation on Cultural Heritage, Intellectual Property (IP) and Indigenous Knowledge Systems (IKS) in an international context. Second, a practical exploration of the various ways in which local actors lay claim to certain repertoires of knowledge and performance with respect to their mediation and mediatization. It also tracks the various co-existing, competing and shifting notions of *ownership, authorship* and *rights* as articulated both by members of the Ngqoko Cultural Group and by other local actors in Ngqoko and in other areas in which I have conducted ethnographic research.[4] The

---

3   In Tanzania, for example, Kelly Askew (2002) has demonstrated how musical/
     cultural troupes were integrated into a discourse of nation-building in the late
     1960s and 1970s.
4   Apart from Ngqoko, these other areas were specifically the Isipongweni and
     Maseleni areas of Idutywa. I am grateful to Volkswagen Stiftung, Germany, for

chapter investigates ways in which global forces – such as the politics of
IKS with its legislation and regulation of processes of cultural creation and
performance – complicate an already intricate relationship between a people
and their cultural practices. It specifically looks at the way in which communal
practices in parts of the Eastern Cape, through the Ngqoko Cultural Group
(and of course many other such groups and individuals),[5] become goods
that can be marketed and sold, not as embodied but as copyrighted goods,
especially in the contexts of cultural preservation, 'World Music' and heritage.

The looming questions are: if the policies on protection of IKS in South
Africa are geared towards protecting local communities against exploitation
by 'outsiders' (such as researchers, recording companies and commercial
industries), what happens when sections of the same population acquire legal
copyright to communal practices? Whom do these rights protect and against
whom, and as Michael Brown (1998) asks, can culture be copyrighted? Again,
what happens within the local communities as a response to the emerging
and constantly changing 'ownership rights', which basically cater to a no less
shifting market for cultural goods? And finally, what are the obstacles to fitting
IKS within existing regulations on IP and copyright if such legal provisions in
the end advocate the economic gain of the local communities involved?

The central argument in this chapter is that by adapting a stage format, the
Ngqoko Cultural Group already alters the context(s) of performance within
which Xhosa music is experienced amongst the Xhosa. These alterations
imply changes in ideas of ownership and rights in the cultural repertoire of a
community. The new contexts of performance, by a registered performance
group, in this case the Ngqoko Cultural Group, trouble the notion of *communal*
property as the materialization of these performances in mediatized formats
(CDs and DVDs) and more concretely introduce questions of copyright and IP
into *communal* practice. This last transformation, in which practices become
goods, is concisely summarized in Simon Frith's formulation that 'each piece

---

funding my Ph.D. fieldwork trips to the Eastern Cape in 2009 and 2010, and
to colleagues and advisors in the 'Passages of Culture: Media and Mediation in
African Societies' project under which this research was undertaken. A draft of
this chapter was discussed in two workshops at the Cluster of Excellence of the
Goethe University, Frankfurt. Many thanks to Ute Röschenthaler and Mamadou
Diawara for facilitating the workshops and the many suggestions made at and after
the workshops.

5   Some of the well-known 'traditional' Xhosa musicians who have gained entry into
the music industry through performances and recordings are Madosini Latoza
Manqini, who has recorded albums with the Cape Town-based AmaMpondo,
and popular South African songstress Thandiswa 'Red' Mazwai, who has travelled
widely performing on the *uhadi* and the *umrhube*.

of music represents a basket of rights' (1988:57). By recording their music the Ngqoko Cultural Group acquires such rights via existing regulations that submit such recordings to copyright law.

The chapter further argues that even in the absence, or inadequacy, of state legislation on cultural practices (legally articulated under Traditional Knowledge, IKS and Communal Knowledge), when heritage projects, media(tiza)tion and tourism become part of certain spheres of cultural production (and/or vice versa), especially in areas where certain repertoires of knowledge are construed as shared knowledge, the search for 'authenticity' becomes intensified. In this search segments of the 'local population' begin to view themselves as having a more 'natural' copyright to practices and knowledge than others within the same community.

The Ngqoko Cultural Group: a genealogy

The Ngqoko Cultural Group's repertoire of music extends along a continuum that moves back and forth between ritual and entertainment. For example, ceremonies such as diviner installation (*ukuthwasa*) require the singing of diviner songs (*iingoma zamagqirha*) in the same way that initiation ceremonies involve the singing of and dancing to initiation songs (*iingoma zomtshotsho*). For both occasions, the performances involve elements of ritual and entertainment, but within the specific context of 'traditional' ceremonies. The Ngqoko Cultural Group's repertoire is derived from this 'common pool' of cultural practices, and as NoFirst Lungisa tells me, individual members of the Ngqoko Cultural Group – prior to and after the formation of the group – separately, and together, sang the same songs, danced to the same rhythms and played the same instruments that they now do within the group.[6] As long as they were part of this larger cultural reality, these 'practices of the everyday' (to borrow from de Certeau 1984) were not yet performed on stages in South Africa and across the world, and were not a source of livelihood for this group of Thembu women and men. As individuals, they were not representative of any larger community and were not registered as a society of performers before the formation of the Ngqoko Cultural Group. Only after David Dargie's arrival in Ngqoko did the realization of a performance group became possible.

The critical role that the ethnomusicologist David Dargie played in the formation of the Ngqoko Cultural Group is evident not only in his own published work on the group (Dargie 1986, 1988, 1991, 2001, 2007) but also

---

6   Mrs NoFirst Lungisa is a member of the Ngqoko Cultural Group. Lungisa is one of the group's five *umngqokolo* singers and the only *ikitari* (a bow instrument with a tin resonator initially played only by men or boys) player since the death of Sponono Klas in 1998. Interview, 15 July 2010.

in various other works on the group and on so-called traditional music in South Africa in general (among others, Dlamini 2004; Dontsa 2008; Herbst, Nzewi and Agawu 2002; Levine 2005; Spencer 1991; Tracey 2008). The most striking account of Dargie's intervention is that by Andrew Tracey, under whom, coincidentally, Dargie had obtained his Ph.D. in Xhosa Christian hymnody at Rhodes University in 1986. In his speech – as the then director of the International Library of African Music – for the posthumous presentation of an award to NoFinish Dywili[7] at the 2002 Arts and Culture Trust Awards, Tracey asserted that 'NoFinish's music might have remained unknown forever ... if it had not been for *a chance meeting* in about 1979 between NoFinish and the Revd Dave Dargie, who was working on Africanizing the music in the Catholic liturgy' (my emphasis).[8] According to Tracey, once Dargie heard NoFinish playing her *uhadi* gourd bow,

> he knew right away that he'd better learn something about the real traditional Xhosa music before going any further... So, late in her life, *she was 'discovered,' as they say, and her group began to be invited to perform, close to home at first. But soon they were getting invitations much further afield, all over South Africa, then to Europe* several times, and [in 2001] I took them to Réunion, that was NoFinish's last trip [my emphasis].[9]

Dargie's 'chance meeting' with Mrs Dywili, therefore, became the foundation for the Ngqoko Cultural Group, as she became the focal point of the music of what was to become the Ngqoko Women's Ensemble and later the Ngqoko Cultural Group. As Tracey reports, Mrs Dywili was the group's *gravitas*, driving force, central figure or what would be called *isithunzi* amongst the Xhosa people. This account by Tracey coincides with a widely circulated official narrative by Dargie himself, ethnomusicology departments in South Africa and in some instances by members of the Ngqoko Cultural Group. Indeed, a large part of this official narrative is based on Dargie's written accounts, especially that of the early period (the early 1980s and 1990s), when the Ngqoko Cultural Group and the musical practices of Ngqoko had not yet garnered passable academic interest. As Kerryn-Ann Tracey (2008) puts it, 'Dargie's research is often consulted as the (only) authoritative source of

---

7   NoFinish Dywili was a prominent *uhadi* (a bow instrument with a calabash resonator) player from Ngqoko Village with whom David Dargie formed the Ngqoko Cultural Group in 1979/80.

8   'Lifetime Award for NoFinish'. *Arts and Culture Trust.* 15 October 2002. Found at: www.southafrica.info/about/arts/nofinish.htm, accessed on 4 March 2011.

9   Ibid.

information on them [the group], and while it is undeniably invaluable it is also by no means exhaustive or complete.' (2008:14). This official version, as given to me by the group leader and manager Mr Tsolwana Mpayipheli, and as recorded by Dargie, is a fairly consistent history of the way the Ngqoko Cultural Group came into being, and specifically lays claim to the 're-discovery' of two musical practices, the *uhadi* musical bow and *umngqokolo* singing, in Ngqoko Village/Lumko District.

In this narrative, the Ngqoko Cultural Group began in 1979, when as a Ph.D. student in ethnomusicology at Rhodes University, David Dargie moved to Lumko District to research Xhosa Christian hymnody. In the same year, Dargie began directing the music department at the Lumko Missiological Institute. According to Dargie (1986, 2007), while at the Institute he heard a girl playing what he then thought was a 'strange' musical instrument (*umrhube)* and at the same time singing in an unusual manner. As an ethnomusicologist, Dargie was inquisitive, and he set out on a mission to discover more about both the instrument and the type of singing. When Dargie subsequently decided to do research on 'traditional' music in the area around Lumko colleagues warned him not to expect to find any forms of such music, as over fifty years of missionary activity by the Lumko Institute would certainly have 'wiped them out'; the encounter with the young girl at Lumko (whistling with the *umrhube)* was to be regarded as a chanced upon rare case (Dargie 2007).[10] It was during this period in the same year that Dargie met Mr Tsolwana Mpayipheli, a catechist at the church and also a teacher from Ngqoko Village in Lady Frère, whom he asked about Xhosa musical bow instruments. Mpayipheli introduced Dargie to Mrs NoFinish Dywili, who according to Mpayipheli was the most famous *uhadi* player in Ngqoko. Dargie visited Dywili, who accompanied by her *umrhube*-playing daughter, Nongangekho (who later changed her name to Nothembisile Ndlokose), demonstrated to Dargie extraordinary *uhadi* playing skills (Dargie 1988, 2007). When Dargie sought to learn from Mpayipheli if there were other bow-instrument players in the village, she responded in the affirmative, that there were, in fact, far too many.[11]

---

10 The *umrhube* is a bow musical instrument (without a resonator) made of a piece of wood in the shape of a hunting bow. There are two techniques of playing this instrument, both of which involve rubbing the string/copper wire with a stick while using the mouth as a resonator. The second technique is a variation of this basic way of playing *umrhube* and involves whistling in such a way that the mouth resonator produces a melody higher than that produced by the stick and the wire/string. The girl that Dargie claims to have met in Lumko was playing the *umrhube* with *umlozi* (whistling).

11 Interview with Tsolwana Mpayipheli, 12 July 2010.

With the help of Mpayipheli, who from that point became his research assistant, Dargie decided to stand by the village paths, for several days, and randomly ask people to sing or play their instruments. According to Mrs Lungisa, the villagers at Ngqoko found this ridiculous, and advised Mpayipheli to bring Dargie to beer parties and other ceremonies where singing and dancing 'naturally occurs'.[12] This claim by Mrs Lungisa is particularly important in demonstrating that, at this point in Ngqoko, musical performances were highly contextualized and that these men and women had not yet begun to internalize 'out of context' performances. It was at one of the beer parties that one woman, Mrs Nowayilethi Mbizweni, claimed to do a kind of vocal imitation of beetles for which she had coined the name *umngqokolo ngomnqangi*.[13]

Up to this point, the history of the group seems coherent and 'neat', but a level of murkiness arises from the time *umngqokolo* enters the narrative. According to Mpayipheli, after several visits to Ngqoko, two other women, NoFirst Lungisa and NoSomething Ntese, followed Mbizweni's cue and mentioned to Dargie their expertise in another form of overtone singing, which he subsequently referred to as *ordinary umngqokolo*.[14] Indeed, this murkiness is worth teasing out, as it reflects the deeper inconsistencies in the larger narrative. On several occasions during research interviews with these two women (Mrs Lungisa and Mrs Ntese), they both gave me different answers to questions such as when they first sang in overtones, how they did it, from whom they first heard it, what they had learnt and how they became part of the Ngqoko Cultural Group. From these research interviews and from Dargie's own account of *umngqokolo* instances, two strands of the origins of *umngqokolo*, as a musical practice, are evident:

Mrs Lungisa claims to have first sung in overtones after listening to and imitating a specifically young-men's type of rough singing called *ukutshotsha*. She practised this as a young woman growing up in the neighbouring Ngcuka Village. However, in his account of Mrs Lungisa's overtone singing, Dargie claims that Lungisa learnt it from Nowayilethi Mbizweni (mentioned earlier) as recently as the early 1980s (Dargie 2007).

Nosomething Ntese claims to have first heard of overtone singing from Nowayilethi Mbizweni. Mrs Mbizweni's form of overtone singing, Mrs Ntese asserts, was an imitation of a sound originating in the Xhosa boys' habit of impaling a large flying beetle called *umqangi* on a thorn and then holding the desperately buzzing insect within their mouths. This account agrees with

---

12   Interview NoFirst Lungisa, 15 July 2010.
13   Ibid.
14   Interview Tsolwana Mpayipheli, 12 July 2010.

Dargie's relation of Mrs Ntese's entry into the group, but does not tally with Mr Mpayipheli's claim that Mrs Ntese and Mrs Lungisa had prior knowledge of *umngqokolo* in the infancy days of the Ngqoko Cultural Group. In a different interview, however, Mrs Ntese claims to have learnt *umngqokolo* from her mother. This account is also supported by Mrs Nogcinile Yekani, who, although not an overtone singer herself, claims to have heard her uncle's wife sing in overtones.[15]

From this illustration on the origins of *umngqokolo* amongst members of the Ngqoko Cultural Group, it is evident that although *umngqokolo* might have been a rare vocal practice, it existed pre-Dargie and prior to the formation of the Ngqoko Cultural Group. Although it is not clear whether *umngqokolo* was considered a musical practice *per se* in Thembu musical performance vocabulary, this vocal form began to be discussed alongside *ukuombela* (singing), *ukuxentsa* (dancing) and *ukukhalisa izixhobo* (playing instruments) upon Dargie's arrival in Ngqoko.[16] In the same year (1979) that Dargie began to take an obviously immense interest in *umngqokolo*, a chief diviner and leader of divination ritual in the village, Mrs Nokontoni (Nokoleji) Manisi, joined Dargie's project (Dargie 1988, 2007). Together with Mrs Manisi an apprentice diviner, Mrs Nofenitshala Mvotyo, joined the group. She played the friction drum (*umasengwane*) while Mrs Manisi took the role of lead singer in divination songs and dance. This new development in the early composition of the group introduced an interesting interplay between 'real life' and 'staged life'. Mrs Manisi and Mrs Mvotyo assumed the role of diviners (*amagqirha*) even in Dargie's project (Dargie 2007). Although Mrs Manisi and Mrs Mvotyo still maintained their divination roles in the community, they took with them into Dargie's project facets of this sacred ritual practice.

By 1980, Mpayipheli advised Dargie to limit the number of people that he was working with by concentrating on four categories of musical talent: vocalists, overtone singers, dancers and bow players. In 1981, the Ngqoko Ensemble was officially formed (comprising fifteen women and four men). In the same year, the group performed at Rhodes University in Grahamstown under Dargie. Between 1982 and 1988, Dargie alternated between lecturing in ethnomusicology at Rhodes University and the University of Fort Hare in Alice, and took the group to both universities to perform for his ethnomusicology students. During this time, Dargie recorded 'amateur' videos of the Ensemble for research and teaching purposes (the first in 1986 and then in 1988). In 1989, with Dargie's assistance, the Ngqoko Ensemble (by then reduced to nine members) made its first overseas trip to Paris, France, to perform at the

---

15   Interview with Nongcinile Yekani, 18 July 2010.
16   Interview with Mrs Nosomething Ntese, 16 July 2010.

Annual Autumn Festival.[17] On its return from Paris, the Ngqoko Ensemble
changed its name to Ngqoko Cultural Group, though Dargie was reluctant
and still preferred the Ngqoko Ensemble or the Ngqoko Traditional Music
Ensemble. After the name change, under the leadership of Mr Mpayipheli, the
group made its first attempt at using a concert performance format. This new
development within the group, Dargie argues in his later work, could be one
way through which 'traditional' music can be preserved, especially given the
increasing influence of modern musical styles. According to Dargie:

> The process [of losing 'traditional music'] can be reversed if a new reason
> for the music can be created. Since the late 1980s, they [the Ngqoko
> Cultural Group] have been earning money by their performances in South
> Africa and abroad, and in them the music has been kept alive. One of
> the first significant adaptations they made was to arrange their music for
> performance into a concert format.
>
> (Dargie 2007)

So, eight years after the official launching of the Ngqoko Cultural Group, it
made its first overseas trip and started earning money from performances. It is
not surprising, therefore, that in 1990 Mr Mpayipheli requested Dargie record
the group's music for sale, using an old recording machine at the University
of Fort Hare. In 1991, Dargie produced the first audio-tape recordings of the
group. According to Mr Mpayipheli, it is not clear if these tapes were already
being sold at that time, because Dargie first wanted to use them for his
research. In 1995, again with Dargie's assistance, the group made its second
overseas trip to Basel, Switzerland, where the group's live performance was
recorded by a friend of Dargie and then released later that year in Geneva
under the title *Afrique du Sud: Le chant des femmes Xhosa: The Ngqoko
Women's Ensemble*. This audio CD was, as Mpayipheli reports, the Ngqoko
Cultural Group's first commercial recording.[18]

On its return from Switzerland, in the same year, the Ngqoko Cultural
Group was commissioned by the government of the Republic of South Africa
to perform for the Queen of England on her first visit to the 'new' South Africa.

---

17   By this time most of the younger members who had started with Dargie (all of
     whom were relatives of older members of the group) had lost interest in the
     project and decided to withdraw their participation. At this point, there were
     only two men in the group – Mr Mpayipheli and Mr Sponono Klaas – and seven
     women – Nowayilethi Mbizweni, NoFinishi Dywili, Nosomething Ntese, NoFirst
     Lungisa, Nokontoni Manisi, Nofenitshala Mvotyo and Nolineti Ntese (who, as
     Dargie reports, is an excellent dancer).

18   Interview with Tsolwana Mpayipheli, 12 July 2010.

At this point, the Ngqoko Cultural Group entered, in addition to concerts and tours, larger discourses of heritage and representation as a government cultural project. By this time the popularity of the group was beginning to grow in South Africa, and in 1996 South African multi-instrumentalist musician and producer Pops Mohamed recorded several songs with the group in the album, *Yesterday, Today and Tomorrow*, which was released in the same year. In 1997, the group was invited (through Dargie's contacts) to perform at the Passover Festival in Jerusalem. Mr Mpayipheli is not certain about the proper name of the festival and it is not recorded in Dargie's work. Later in the year, the group made its first appearance at the Grahamstown Arts Festival alongside Pops Mohamed. In the same year, Dargie spoke at the Winter School (then part of the Grahamstown Festival) on 'Umngqokolo: the Xhosa art of two tones'. This talk, together with the performance with Mohamed, increased the popularity of the group amongst festival audiences and organizers. In the following year (1998), Dargie officially introduced the group to Andrew Tracey (then director of the International Library of African Music in Grahamstown), who began working towards 'preserving' their music. Towards the end of 1998, through Dargie's and Tracey's contacts, the Ngqoko Cultural Group performed at the opening ceremony of the International Society of Music Educators Conference in Pretoria. Later in the year Mr Sponono Klaas, the only other male member of the group besides Mr Mpayipheli, died, and the group temporarily reverted to being the Ngqoko Women's Ensemble. By this time, Mr Mpayipheli had reduced his stage appearances as a performer and instead accompanied the group as a leader and translator.

Between 1999 and 2000, the Ngqoko Women's Ensemble performed in Germany and in Sweden, invited by Dargie's networks, and on its return, once again performed for Queen Elizabeth II in South Africa. Also during this time, the Ngqoko Women's Ensemble signed a recording deal with one of Africa's biggest recording companies, GALLO, and the group's first studio recording, *The Ngqoko Women's Ensemble: Discography of CDs*, was released on 26 September 2000. With this recording, the group added to its other contexts of performance a studio context, highlighting the role of mediatization in the mediation of cultural processes: on a portable CD, the music of the Ngqoko Ensemble began to travel without necessarily having to be accompanied physically.

In 2002, lead singer and expert *uhadi* player NoFinish Dywili died and was posthumously awarded the Lifetime Achievement Award by the Department of Arts and Culture. This award to Mrs Dywili was proof of the South African government's position on 'traditional' music, and the Ngqoko Cultural Group began to enter into serious talks with it on the preservation of 'threatened traditional musical practices' and the role of culture in sustaining national

identity and ways of being South African. And so the Ngqoko Cultural
Group, alongside with other groups, became a site for the exploration of the
metaphors of 'nation', 'culture', 'heritage' and 'identity'.[19] In 2003, South African
composer and professor of music theory and composition at the University
of the Witwatersrand, Jeanne Zaidel-Rudolph, conducted an orchestral
concert entitled *Lifecycle*, in which music by the Ngqoko Cultural Group
was arranged alongside an ensemble of other orchestral instruments. With
Zaidel-Rudolph, the group toured many parts of the country including Cape
Town and Johannesburg.[20] Also between 2002 and 2005, Dargie recorded
more CDs with the group at the University of Fort Hare before he returned
to Germany in late 2007. During this period, Mpayipheli decided to have the
group play all the instruments together (something he claims is not done with
Xhosa instruments and of which Dargie and Tracey were sceptical) forming
an orchestra of its own. In the same year, lead overtone singer Nowayilethi
Mbizweni died of health complications that she had told Dargie (2007) were
her ancestors' punishment for not responding to their call to become a diviner
(*umbizo*).

In 2007, Dargie introduced the group to Ms Tandile Mandela, a newly
recruited lecturer in ethnomusicology at University of Fort Hare. With the
help of the group, Dargie and Mandela attempted teaching *umngqokolo* to
students at the University of Fort Hare with very little or no success. In 2008,
six members of the Ngqoko Cultural Group acted as the chorus in Yael Farber's
adaptation of Aeschylus' Greek Trilogy in the TRC-based play *Molora* (where
I first came into contact with them). As before with Zaidel-Rudolph's projects,
the group has been travelling with *Molora* since 2008 to the present. By 2009

---

19   When South Africa's Department of National Arts awarded grants relating to the
     'Indigenous Music and Oral History Project' (IMOHP) to the University of Fort
     Hare alongside the University of Venda and the University of Zululand in 2003,
     the music of the Ngqoko Cultural Group immediately took its place on archival
     shelves at the Music Department at the University of Fort Hare. According to
     the National Arts Department, this grant was geared towards 'conducting pilot
     projects on the state of Music and Oral History in each of the three provinces
     in which these universities [were] located' (Bleibinger 2008: 2). There was some
     urgency to conduct this research, according to the National Arts Department,
     as both indigenous music and oral history 'constituted key facets of the area of
     intangible heritage' (ibid.) and there was a particularly important need to 'preserve'
     cultural practices and goods often imagined as on the verge of extinction.
20   Since the *Lifecycle* project, the group has had numerous other projects with
     Zaidel-Rudolph including an NRF (National Research Funding) funded project
     on overtone singing. Part of this project was presented at the Gordon Institute
     of Performing and Creative Arts 'Emerging Modernities' Conference in February
     2011 at the University of Cape Town, South Africa.

the Ngqoko Cultural Group had established a strong working relationship with Ms Mandela and the University of Fort Hare, and in the same year the Eastern Cape Indigenous Orchestra was formed (comprising four different groups of which the Ngqoko Cultural Group was one) under the leadership of Ms Mandela, and first appeared at the Grahamstown National Arts Festival of that year. In 2010 the Orchestra reduced the number of its members from sixty-five to forty-five, following a request by the Department of Arts and Culture, but it still performs at the Grahamstown Festival alongside the only other group belonging to this Department, the Eastern Cape Cultural Ensemble.

My objective in providing such an elaborate historical timeline of the Ngqoko Cultural Group has been to draw attention to the various events and mediators that brought the group and its musical practices not only into 'heritage' but also into our present discussion of IP rights and claims within the framework of IKS in present-day South Africa. In the pages that follow, I will demonstrate how the group enters this discourse.

The Ngqoko Cultural Group and intellectual property rights: the cultural and legal problematic

Campaigns for intellectual property rights often argue for the need to protect 'indigenous communities' from exploitation in areas as diverse as bio-diversity, traditional medical/pharmaceutical know-how, useful plants, folktales and dances, so that these communities can gain economically from their own skills and knowledge. In the case of the Ngqoko Cultural Group, as is the case with similar other groups, the new contexts of performance provided by heritage projects, tourism and the media constantly oblige us to focus on changing ideas of ownership, and what it means for specific groups of people to draw from an assumed pool of musical knowledge. The Intellectual Property Laws Amendment Bill (IPLAB) of 2010 in South Africa is founded on these principles: protection and economic gain.

Because of the lack of legal instruments to address the protection or commercialization of collectively owned 'traditional knowledge' (Saurombe 2009:4), in 1999 the then Department of Arts, Culture, Science and Technology (DACST) approached the Cabinet to formulate a policy on 'indigenous knowledge'. The resulting policy – the Indigenous Knowledge Systems Policy – was adopted by Cabinet in November 2004. In subsequent years this policy was revised, due to difficulties that various departments had with developing legislative amendments to support its objectives. The result was a policy which encompassed a wide scope of actions and recommendations pertaining to IKS. A task team identified essentially two main concerns: first, while the current IP system allows individuals to protect their inventions and rights, communities cannot, as a collective, use it to protect their knowledge in all areas; and second, even in those areas where collective IP registration is possible, communities are not exercising their rights. As a result the South African government passed the Intellectual Property Laws Amendment Bill (IPLAB) in 2010 in order to allow collective ownership and protect local communities against exploitation.

Although the Department of Trade and Industry notes that the IP system has been protecting some 'traditional knowledge', for instance using geographical indications in the area of wines and spirits, exceedingly well, the same standards have not been successfully applied in dealing with folklore and 'traditional' music. One of the reasons for this difficulty is the fact that no definition for 'traditional knowledge' has been universally and/or locally accepted. This, as Saurombe (2009) explains, is because 'traditional knowledge may be perceived very differently by indigenous communities, governments, lawyers and international organizations' (2009:1).

The case of the Ngqoko Cultural Group is one in which a section of a perceived indigenous community's claims straddle the gamut of protection rights, ranging from IKS to legal copyright. It is clear that what the Ngqoko Cultural Group does is to selectively acquire IP rights for practices that emanate from a common repertoire of knowledge. In this way, the group gains, through copyright, ownership of the material manifestation of those practices in the form of CDs and DVDs, and is therefore entitled to claim such knowledge as artistic works (see Britz and Lipinski 2000, 2001). These works, as recordings, therefore cannot be considered communal property under current legislation, as they have become a 'new original' solely owned by the authors, the Ngqoko Cultural Group. In other words, while the group might not claim authorship of the repertoire of music as indigenous knowledge, as artists they do, however, have a claim to the music's mediatized form, such as the CDs and DVDs that bear the group's name. What is interesting, however, is what happens within the local communities from which these artistic works are drawn. Admittedly, members of the Ngqoko Cultural Group are in their own individual right members of this community and therefore entitled to protection as part of IKS. However, the remuneration that results from the performances and recordings of the Ngqoko Cultural Group is not ploughed back into the general community precisely because they, at the time of performance and recording, operate within the provisions of South Africa's Copyright laws. What is clearly emerging is a new way of understanding cultural performance in which 'authenticity' becomes central and this relationship, as Michael Brown states, is a form of metaphorical ownership (1998:194).

In order to unravel the complexities of the IPLAB and the case of the Ngqoko Cultural Group it is important to explore the continuum of legislation along which the group is situated, especially with the emergence and popularization of 'World Music'. In this regard, it is imperative that the IPLAB be read alongside copyright laws in South Africa. The Copyright Act 98 of 1978, which has been amended by several acts subsequently, governs all matters relating to copyright in South Africa and is based on the provisions of the Berne Convention for the Protection of Literary and Artistic Works of 1886 and the International Copyright Treaty of 1891, and expressly states in Section 41(4) that 'no copyright or right in the nature of copyright shall subsist otherwise than by virtue of this Act or of some other enactment in that behalf'.[21] Therefore no protection of copyright exists in terms of common law. Currently, the South African Copyright Act protects literary, musical and artistic works, sound recordings, cinematographic films, broadcasts, published editions and computer programs. The Copyright Act defines each of these works in Section 1. As soon as the two general requirements – originality and existence in a material form – are met, copyright emerges automatically as the South African Copyright Act does not specify formal procedures for its establishment and the duration of copyright varies for the different types of work (usually up to fifty years after the author's death).

As in most other countries that have over the years signed treaties on IP rights, the copyright law in force in South Africa today is based on a number of cultural presuppositions, some of which will be discussed further with respect to 'anonymity'. First, the law is based on the concept of individual creativity, that is, individuals' copyright products of their own creation. Second, it is based on the idea that an individual should receive compensation for a limited period of time, after which the idea may be used by anyone without paying a royalty. After the expiration of a copyright, music enters 'the public domain' and royalties may not be collected on it. Third, the law leaves unclear the status of arrangements of 'traditional' songs. Fourth, the musical item copyrighted is item-title-based (Seeger 1992:352–3). Anything that is not in copyright is regarded as in the 'public domain', which is, as McCann (2001:97) puts it, 'effectively infinity minus copyright'. Indeed, 'public domain' is synonymous with uninhibited exploitation of music or a song, and it reinforces the

---

21   For the origins of copyright in England following the introduction of the printing press and subsequent cases of plagiarism see Gasaway and Wiant 1994 or Mills 1996. The Statute of Anne (1710) considered a work the author's *personal property* for the first time, and to obtain protection under the statute, the work had to be officially registered with the Stationer's Company. Music was not treated as a separate art form until 1882 (see also Frith 1988; Seeger 1992; Gasaway and Wiant 1994; Mills 1996; and for the introduction of copyright to Africa Peukert in this volume). Some scholars argue, however, that the first form of protection for intellectual property arose in ancient Egypt; see, for example, Mendis 2003.

anonymous/authored dichotomy. Not only is a piece that 'sounds traditional' often assumed to be of unknown origin, but it is also therefore assumed to be open to all for free and unbridled commercial use. Both 'public domain' and 'copyright' have proven to be inadequate, especially in South Africa, as Feeny *et al.*, for example, point out, 'public domain often equates common property with open access' (1998:79). 'Public domain' is a concept that derives from the construction of copyright, and is, finally, nothing other than the 'space that is left over after all else has been parsed out' (McCann 2001).[22]

In addition to becoming technologically feasible and beneficial, 'world music' has garnered enormous interest, well-known examples of which are Paul Simon's *Graceland* (Erlmann 1998; Miller 1995), in 1986, and, in 1990, *Rhythm of the Saints*, drawing, respectively, on South African and Latin American (primarily Brazilian) music, and which together demonstrated the formidable profits that can result when Western pop stars incorporate non-Western music into their songs. Simon's *Graceland* is a particularly valid starting point for my analysis, as it has long been part of South African public discourse on copyright. According to Knoedelseder (1987), although Simon *hired* South African musicians, themselves already active recording artists in the country, and most of whom were represented by record companies, the copyright laws then current would not have prevented either unfair contracts or the blatant appropriation of the music of less 'powerful artists'. The enormous success of Simon's albums, however, revealed a tremendous market for non-Western sounds and certainly provided an incentive for other recording artists and companies to exploit the inadequate or absent legal protection for 'non-Western music'.

It is of special interest that one of the *Graceland* album's greatest hit, 'You can Call me Al', is not actually an original musical creation of either Ladysmith Black Mambazo (whose 'backup' was uncredited) or Paul Simon himself (considered its author), but rather a combination of a Zulu choral style known as *mbube* with aspects of *mbaqanga* and *kwela*, among other styles. Surprisingly, this fact did not seem to be worth considering in the case of *Graceland*.[23] In the next few pages, I will show how these kinds of recordings exemplify the futility of IP rights regimes, especially in the context of an assumed public domain.

---

22   For further discussion on the 'public domain' in the context of copyright, see Boyle 1996; Frow 1997 and Litman 1990.

23   See Louise Meintjes (1990) for an elaborate discussion of *Graceland* and the mediation of its meaning in South Africa. For similar cases, also based on *mbube*, see Veit Erlmann, this volume.

Ownership, mastery, control and the search for authenticity

This section of the chapter seeks to examine how the Ngqoko Cultural Group, with its numerous overarching narratives of preservation, heritage and national identity, introduces us to the intricacies of the implementation of IP and copyright laws in post-apartheid South Africa. It enquires into the extent that the 'search for authenticity' may become a 'new' form of 'natural' copyright.

If we discuss culture in the practitioners' own terms, we begin to understand how global forces often affect local ideas of culture and community. Admittedly, this is a daunting task because, as Karin Barber (2007) argues in *Anthropology of Texts, Persons and Publics*, societies do not often have concepts that can easily be translated into the terms that scholarship may allocate to them. As Madian notes regarding Egypt's musical heritage, in 'oral tradition' ownership of musical heritage is unclear: indeed, the very concept of *ownership* is often incongruent with the complex way in which oral culture is collectively held, developed and spread (2005:2). Indeed, evidence from Ngqoko, Isipongweni and Maseleni exemplifies this kind of misfit. It is also true, however, that notions of cultural ownership did not arise with the development of national IP systems, but rather had emerged in pre-colonial times, elaborated by local communities, as Ute Röschenthaler shows in her contribution to this volume.

According to Madian (2005), the oral nature of most African societies meant that over time the origins or contributors to popular folkloric materials such as folksongs were lost from the community's collective memory. Hence the view that expressive forms in 'traditional' African settings were rarely ascribed to individuals, but rather to cultural or ethnic communities in general (Amegatcher 2002; Githaiga 1998; Kawooya 2010). From this argument it follows that the IP system allocates anonymity to cultural expression only when an individual owner/author cannot be traced and accommodated within existing laws. This search for an owner/author is primarily based on three premises, the most significant of which is the concept of 'the individual' that copyright was designed to protect. Second, by ascribing the products of artistic practices to an individual, they can be conceptualized, legally, as intellectual goods; and finally, when an owner/author cannot be identified, the law resorts – depending on the interests involved – to the notion of an imaginary/imagined community that then can own such immaterial goods as property.

Cultural practices, however, exist for very specific reasons and serve various functions in the contexts within which they are exercised. The role of music amongst the Xhosa, and other communities in South Africa and beyond, cannot be overemphasized. Each and every song is performed for a specific occasion in a particular society. For example, one cannot sing a lullaby at an initiation ceremony. Although this does not mean that one must always sing on cue within fixed occasions of performance, Makuliwe (1995:8), quoting the great Xhosa scholar Samuel Edward Krune (popularly referred to as S.E.K.) Mqhayi, posits:

> A song is not sung solely for pleasure and happiness and peace, it is more than that ... there are songs for the declaration of war, lamentation and death. This shows that a song is a tool used by people in days of happiness, pleasure, lamentation and depression.

In its specific context music does, indeed, serve numerous functions and is vested with various, often immense, powers. As Mills (1996) observes, these powers can range from 'the power to heal sickness, create bountiful game, cause lightning to strike, kill, and, in one case, free a man from prison' (Mills 1996:57; see also Von Sturmer 1987). In the case of the Akamba people of Kenya, for instance, certain forms of music and beating of drums are intended to bring rain, and such music is only sung during an all-night ceremony in which a white goat is sacrificed and the ancestors are invited to commune with the rainmakers. Such music is therefore imbued with powerful connections to the spirit world, and although most people may be familiar with the lyrics and the particular drum beat, they may not actually perform the songs, which remain a preserve of the rainmakers. Although the rainmakers do not, and perhaps cannot, claim such music as theirs, there are rules governing such repertoires that are observed by the community at large. In his fundamental study of Africa's customary law and its protection of folklore and 'traditional' music, Kuruk (2002) argues that Africa's customary laws and practices do not necessarily address ownership, but rather the rights, obligations, responsibilities, duties or privileges assigned to individuals or groups. These obligations, however, do not constitute *private* ownership, but rather are a form of custodianship on behalf of the larger community.[24] Anthony Seeger (1992) makes a similar point in his study of the constitution of ownership amongst the Suyá Indians of Brazil. The owner/controller (*kandé*) of the song is the person who learns it and sings it aloud for the first time, Seeger reports. Using his own example as musician and ethnographer, Seeger argues that a song that he sang in the 1972 Mouse Ceremony was in this context *his* song, although a ritual specialist taught it to him. According to Seeger, '[t]he Suyá said I had become its "owner/controller" and if someone sang it badly I could complain' (1992:348). As Seeger himself admits, this case would have

---

24   For further examples see Barber 1991; Kuruk 2002 or Diawara in this volume.

been different if the song was performed or recorded by the Beatles rather than someone already acculturated within the performance responsibilities of Suyá music (like Seeger) or the last remaining Suyá musician who performs for posterity. The question then becomes where exactly would IPLAB and copyright fit in such varying ideas of ownership and performance rights?

Mr Mpumelelo Janda is a Xhosa healer/diviner (*iqirha*) from the Isipongweni area, just outside the small town of Idutywa in rural Eastern Cape. In an interview I held with him, Janda made reference to a now very common occurrence – not only in South Africa but across the world – whereby individuals and groups adopt material from a common 'traditional' practice for various other performance contexts. This co-opting of practices usually requires a setting that is different from the 'usual' one in which they functionally occur. That is, these are performances staged before an audience different from that for which they 'normally' occur. Although parts of the audience may be present at the staged performance, it is the dislocation of the practice from the initial 'performance' context that creates a disjuncture. Although a diviner himself, Janda does not claim ownership of diviner songs. He does, however, contest the *authenticity* in tourist performances by non-diviners, who, he says, *cannot* sing diviner songs *properly*.

As early as 1937, the Xhosa composer and scholar Tiyo Soga had already lamented the loss of authenticity in Xhosa music. Soga claims, and this is debatable, that at the time he was composing *Ulo Thixo Mkhulu*,[25] that there was not a single person who knew or could help researchers with 'original songs'. Soga writes:

> I, the writer of this book, have tried by all means humanly possible, although
> I have failed in my aim, the reason is that of the veterans who knew how
> Xhosa songs were sung long ago, there is not a single one left in these days
> of light and civilization.
>
> (Soga 1937:156, quoted in Dlepu 2009:55)

From Janda's contestation and Soga's lamentation, several claims can be derived which, although not translatable into ownership, highlight the various ways in which local actors in the Eastern Cape (to whom I have spoken) validate their relationship with music as original and authentic.

CRAFT ASSOCIATED WITH MUSIC

Diviner songs are a good example of how a particular musical repertoire can be claimed by sections of a community. From interviews I held with diviners in

---

25 The first Christian Xhosa hymnody.

both Isipongweni and Maseleni, it became clear that diviners have a repertoire – *iingoma zamagqirha* – that is specific to their practice and recognized within divination contexts. It is important to note that the Xhosa translation does not refer to such songs as 'divination' but rather as 'diviners' songs'. In an interview with a female diviner from Maseleni, Mrs Ndzuzo, it became evident that diviner songs have a spiritual aspect for the Xhosa people. One of the interesting revelations about music that Mrs Ndzuzo made is that before one can realize his or her calling as a diviner, the person becomes extremely sick. This episode of extreme physical and/or sometimes mental illness is called *ukuthwasa* and often lasts for as long as the 'chosen' diviner-to-be (*umkwetha*) is willing to go into seclusion for their installation as a diviner. It is during this period that the ancestors 'give' the apprentice a song that is meant to heal him or her, and this song then becomes their personal song once they are installed as a diviner. It is this song that diviners use when healing either other people or themselves. The song revealed this way, Mrs Ndzuzo told me, is not meant to be sung by other people because it becomes *ingoma yalogqirha yedwa* (that diviner's song only).

Nevertheless, on further probing, Mrs Ndzuzo expressed the need for diviner songs to be recorded for sale in music stores and archived in libraries. This, she says, would be a significant step towards showing other people that diviners can heal diseases such as AIDS and tuberculosis. This contradiction became particularly important to me in understanding how ambivalent and nuanced the Xhosa musical repertoire is in terms of its fluidity and appropriation for different reasons. Clearly, the rules that govern it are malleable and are either followed, misrepresented, bent or broken with clear objectives that aim at confirming, challenging or correcting ideas and notions of cultural practice.

METAPHORICAL RELATIONSHIPS WITH CULTURAL PRODUCTION

According to Michael Brown (1998), a group's relationship to its cultural productions constitutes a form of ownership. Mrs Nandi Phatayi, a member of the Ngqoko Cultural Group, contested, in an interview, the idea that some members of the Xhosa community claim the exclusive rights to certain dockets of indigenous knowledge. She asserted, for example, that although some praise poets compose their poems and songs for specific performances, once any other member of the community has mastered them, they are free to perform them in other contexts for as long as they constantly modify them through their personal creativity. According to Mrs Phatayi, part of the reason she loves Xhosa music is that it has immediate relevance to her life. The song 'Camagwini', for example, is for her a prayer to the ancestors, and it remains a prayer even when sung within a performance context. 'I am serious about every song I sing. I don't just sing for the sake of singing,' Mrs Phatayi tells me.

Mrs Phatayi's statement resonates with Mrs Nogcinile Yekani's (another member of the group), who argues that amongst the Thembu Xhosa:

Music is something that provokes each and everyone from all generations. Regardless of whether they are traditional or modernized people, whatever the mood, there is a song suitable for that.[26]

Although there are songs regarded as 'personal songs' (*amagwijo*), these are considered 'personal' not because they are attributed to a particular composer, but because, unlike other Thembu songs, they are performed solo rather than communally (see Hansen 1981). Individuals and groups are at liberty to modify the pieces. For example, 'Nondel'ekhaya' (literally 'married at home'), one of the most famous songs of the Ngqoko Cultural Group, has three versions within that group. One is an *umrhubhe* version, in which only overtones from the bow are heard, with the mouth cavity operating as the resonator. Another is an *umngqokolo*, in which the text becomes a chanting sound of complex hums. The third and most comprehensible version, at least acoustically, enunciates the complete lyrics, although often interjected with other song texts, producing a polyphony of sounds.

MODE OF TRANSMISSION AND INDUCTION

Depending on how the skill is acquired, anyone can perform Xhosa music. Musical practice is usually transmitted either through kinship – from older family members – or by apprenticeship. Some members of the Ngqoko Cultural Group claim that they learnt Xhosa music by observation, the younger ones watching and listening to their elders to learn the songs and how they were to be sung. They imitated singing the songs and some other techniques that were orally transmitted from father to son and mother to daughter.

One can also learn to perform Xhosa music through apprenticeship, gaining mastery through training by an 'expert' who was either born into a family of musicians or was also trained by someone else. Once trained, one may sing, dance or play a particular instrument depending on one's level of competence and the context of the performance. While teaching me how to play the *uhadi*, *umrhube* and the *inkinge*, my teachers NoSomething Ntese, NoFirst Lungisa and Nogcinile Yekani, all members of the Ngqoko Cultural Group, indicated that I could play the instruments anywhere, whenever I

---

26 See also Dlepu (2009).

wanted to. Mrs Ntese, for instance, told me I could do this even in Kenya because 'you are a daughter of the Xhosa'.

Mrs Ntese herself was not born into a particularly musical family, although she claims that part of being Xhosa is singing throughout one's life (*imgidini, umtshotshoeni* etc). However, after rigorous training by Mrs Nowayilethi Mbizweni and other women in Ngqoko, she is now one of two lead singers (*umhlabeli* or *iqela elihlabelayo*) in the Ngqoko Cultural Group. The role of lead singer is not an easy one, as she is responsible not only for initiating the song but also for controlling its speed, rhythm and the expression of its theme. Usually the leader starts the song by singing a line or verse that elicits a response from the rest of the group (*abalandeli*). This role is not confined to leading the song, but also means controlling the entire performance. For instance, if a verse is repeated numerous times (*ukuphindaphinda*) the *umhlabeli* has to decide when the song should move to the next part. This is called *ukujika ingoma* (turning the song), and just before *ukujikwa kwengoma* the leader will announce it to the rest of the group by saying, for example, *ndiyabuya* (I am turning or I am coming back). Dargie (1988:67) explains that usually *ukubuya* 'happens [when] a song is in two or more sections, this can be because in effect it becomes another song, or because it undergoes some rhythmic change and so on'.

MOMENTS OF INDIVIDUAL GENIUS

People can assert claims to certain forms of music as products of their individual genius. For instance, although the Ngqoko Cultural Group's *umngqokolo* often derives its overtones from bow instruments, especially the *umrhubhe* mouth bow, a special kind of *umngqokolo* (*Umngqokolo ngomqangi*) was 'discovered' in the village of Ngqoko by Dargie (1986). In this technique only two tones are audible (fundamental and overtone), and it is attributed to an individual, Mrs Nowayilethi Mbizweni, who explains its origin in the Xhosa boys' habit of impaling a large flying beetle (*umqangi*), as already recounted (Dargie 1991:39).[27] *Umqangi* is also an alternative name for the *umrhubhe* mouth bow, which produces similar overtones when placed within the mouth cavity, and it is suggested that the *umngqokolo ngomqangi* overtone technique and name were derived from the bow, either directly or through imitating the *umqangi* insect (ibid.). Although this particular kind of singing is associated with Mrs Mbizweni, other members of the group, such as NoFirst Lungisa and NoSomething Ntese, had learnt, before Mrs Mbizweni's death in 2002, how to *ukungqokola* the *umnqangi* style. Through mastery of the technique they

27 For a further discussion on the mechanical production of Ngqoko Cultural Group's *umngqokolo*, see Tracey 2008.

can therefore perform in this style but often acknowledging Mrs Mbizweni, in conversations, as its originator. However, Mrs Mbizweni does not *own* the particular technique, although she may well have been its 'author'. By acknowledging her, the 'community' reveres her genius, but nonetheless classifies the practice as communal knowledge.

In the complex interface of the different ways through which different actors stake their claims – or not – to modes of cultural production, and with respect to the ongoing concern about IKS, how then do we deal with the Ngqoko Cultural Group and the CD/DVD recordings of what is legally referred to as 'communal goods' or 'communal property'? Indeed, scholars of most African societies argue that the idea of collective *ownership* has been an avenue through which cohesive forces in cultural expressions are strengthened (Barz 2004; Cooke 2001). These scholars argue that collective *ownership*, or a sense of lack of *ownership*, has always been a significant element in what they consider traditional communities, as creative expressions in the form of cultural artefacts cement social cohesion through music and dance that emphasize community and group identity (Barz 2004; Kawooya 2010). Indeed, the World Intellectual Property Organization's (WIPO) Intergovernmental Committee on Intellectual Property, and Genetic Resources, Traditional Knowledge and Folklore (WIPO IGC) that was set up in 2000 asserts that what makes music 'traditional' has above all to do with the customary and intergenerational context within which it was created and disseminated (WIPO IGC 2001). What Dick Kawooya notes in his study of the Baganda and Busoga also applies to the Ngqoko Cultural Group, namely that 'the same customary laws, practices and protocols are at odds with some creative individuals in traditional communities, at least in the context of traditional music-making in the contemporary settings' (2010:5–6).

In a study entitled *Ethnicity, Inc.*, John and Jean Comaroff (2009) offer a significant account of how ethnicity in a neoliberal world becomes an industry relentlessly construed within discourses of copyright, intellectual products and the market. Although Comaroff and Comaroff's understanding of the relationship between ethnicity and neoliberalism seems overdone, it is clear that as 'traditional' music increasingly enters the commercial arena, collectors of these songs and tunes, at the source, and their performers, are personally claiming the 'copyright' to works presumed to be in the 'public domain'. Increasingly, however, many new compositions are assumed to be in the 'public domain', even though the composers can often be identified, and many of whom are still alive. As McCann notes with respect to a similar case in Ireland, 'the reluctance of traditional [Irish] composers to copyright their tunes, thus leaving their work vulnerable to piracy, stems from a complex web of social relationships, and a recognition of a "tradition" that incorporates past, present and future generations, and is often simply a case of offering a tune up to the possibility of future anonymity' (2001:9). McCann quotes one of the top musicians in the commercial scene in Ireland who admitted that 'there is no greater thrill than hearing one of her own tunes at a session with no-one knowing who composed it' (McCann 2001:10). In this case, authorship takes a backseat as a designation of respect and cultural capital rather than ownership.

Conclusion

In this chapter I have primarily done two things. First, I have attempted to establish a relationship between communal practice and IP, and identified the processes of transformation through which *communal* practices enter an emerging and contested realm of IP. The chapter presents the different levels of legislation through which the Ngqoko Cultural Group enters 1) the music industry within the various market conditions made available through heritage projects and tourism and 2) existing debates on IP and copyright laws in post-apartheid South Africa. Second, I have examined the various ways in which vernacular notions of *ownership*, responsibility, rights, obligations and custodianship of cultural practices are neither consistent among themselves nor, as a result, entirely compatible with regulations that seek to protect them.

IKS policy and other international regulations intended to safeguard cultural practices and knowledge are certainly 'well-meaning', especially given the various cases in which 'local' knowledge has been 'stolen' by multinational companies.[28] It is undeniably important that this knowledge be protected against exploitation and misappropriation. And yet the complexities of the local structures within which this knowledge is found often do not allow the conceptualization of practices as intellectual property. This is not primarily because these structures are inconsistent within themselves, but rather because the understanding of rights and ownership embedded in IP regimes does not coincide with local articulations. Completely different systems are thus seeking to regulate the same processes. The resulting discrepancies can perhaps be explained by the fact that while the IP system postulates the concept of communal property, the community itself often has modes in place that dictate privileges and responsibilities, but not rights or ownership, which are legal transplants. Even in cases where the origins of particular practices (such as songs, instruments, dances etc.) within a community cannot be traced to an individual author, this does not always grant every member of the particular community the right to perform them.

It can easily be presumptuous to apply legal terms to a community of practitioners and performers who seem oblivious to such jargon. However,

---

28   For example, the San hoodia (*Xhoba*) plant, see Comaroff and Comaroff 2009:89.

the implications of copyright laws across the world seem to be realized in other forms within local communities. There indeed exist norms parallel to emerging laws. There is a continued search for origins and claims to ownership. People want to be more closely linked with certain forms of their local knowledge. This is not an entirely new practice, as such communities' norms with respect to expertise, hereditary knowledge and performance practices were already in place before legal norms were introduced into the (post)colony. Although there exist silences on copyright and property – at least in the terminology – amongst members of the Ngqoko Cultural Group, the constant claim to origin and an unending search for authenticity is a result of the realization that Xhosa music is a *cultural good* marketable, saleable and consumable in various forms. This music, as the chapter has argued, becomes a *good* through transformation in existing normative orders.

Nevertheless, amongst the Xhosa people of Ngqoko, Isipongweni and Maseleni, as has been shown, there are conventions set by genre that have been, albeit with constant revision, passed from one generation to another. These conventions entail rules that govern music as a genre embedded within a larger cultural framework, and do not necessarily translate into ownership. While IP regimes concern themselves with translating these communal practices into property, and thus replacing the irreconcilable concept of authorship with anonymity, local actors are often much more concerned with posterity and the importance of cultural values and genre conventions. As a result, different sections of the local communities express concern with the possible loss of values embedded in certain practices, and as such seek to establish levels of 'authenticity' in out-of-local-context performances. Claims from other sections of the same communities, on the other hand, are nothing less than attempts to establish a form of copyright to these same practices by virtue of being members of the communities in question. These different claims cannot be entirely separated, however, as the music of the Ngqoko Cultural Group, for example, stretches along a continuum of cultural processes.

References

Amegatcher, Andrew. 2002. 'Protection of folklore by copyright: a contradiction in terms'. *Copyright Bulletin* 2(32):33–42.

Askew, Kelly. 2002. *Performing the Nation: Swahili Music and Cultural Politics in Tanzania*. Chicago: University of Chicago Press.

Barber, Karin. 1991. *I Could Speak Until Tomorrow: Oriki, Women and the Past in a Yoruba Town*. Edinburgh: Edinburgh University Press.

Barber, Karin. 2007. *The Anthropology of Texts, Persons and Publics: Oral and Written Culture in Africa and Beyond.* Cambridge: Cambridge University Press.

Barz, Gregory. 2004. *Music in East Africa: Experiencing Music, Expressing Culture.* New York: Oxford University Press.

Bleibinger, Bernhard. 2008. 'Rural backgrounds and academic strategies: higher education, the music department and the Indigenous Music and Oral History Project at the University of Fort Hare, South Africa.' *Proceedings of the 4ᵗʰ International Barcelona Conference on Higher Education, Vol. 4. Higher Education, Arts and Creativity.* Barcelona: GUNI, available at www.guni-rmies.net.

Britz, Johannes and Tomas Lipinski. 2000. 'Rethinking the ownership of information in the 21st century: ethical implications. *Ethics and Information Technology* 2(1):49–71.

——— 2001. 'Indigenous Knowledge: a moral reflection on current legal concepts of intellectual property.' *Libri* 51:234–46.

Brown, Michael. 1998. 'Can culture be copyrighted?' *Current Anthropology* 39(2):193–222.

Boyle, James. 1996. *Shamans, Software and Spleens: Law and the Construction of the Information Society.* Harvard: Harvard University Press.

Cooke, Peter. 2001. *Republic of Uganda.* Grove Music Online (ed. by L. Macy). Available at www.grovemusic.com, accessed 3 May 2010.

Comaroff, John and Jean Comaroff. 2009. *Ethnicity, Inc.* Chicago: University of Chicago Press.

Dargie, David. 1986. Techniques of Xhosa music: a study based on the music of the Lumko District. Ph.D. Thesis, Rhodes University, Grahamstown.

——— 1988. *Xhosa Music: Its Techniques and Instruments, with a Collection of Songs.* Cape Town: David Philip.

——— 1991. 'Umngqokolo: Xhosa overtone singing and the song Nondel'ekhaya.' *African Music* 7(1):33–47.

——— 2001. 'Magical musical bows.' *Talking Drum* 16:4–13.

——— 2007. 'Some recent developments in Xhosa music: activities of the Ngqoko Traditional Xhosa Music Ensemble, and at the University of Fort Hare.' Paper presented at the 16th Eurofinance Cash and Treasury Management Conference (ICTM) in *Vienna,* 18–20 September 2007. Available at tranquanghaisworld.blogspot.de/2008/01/dave-dargie-some-recent-developments-in.html, accessed 12 September 2015.

De Certeau, Michel. 1984. *The Practice of Everyday Life* (trans. Steven Rendall). Berkeley: University of California Press.

Dlamini, Sazi. 2004. 'The role of the *Umrhubhe* bow as transmitter of cultural knowledge among the AmaXhosa: an interview with Latozi "Madosini" Mpahleni'. *Journal of the Musical Arts in Africa* 1:138–60.

Dlepu, Siziwe. 2009. From song to literary texts: a study of the influence of IsiXhosa lyrics on selected IsiXhosa texts. Ph.D. Thesis, Nelson Mandela Metropolitan University.

Dontsa, Luvuyo. 2008. 'From the museum to the music classroom: teaching the *umrhubhe* as an ensemble instrument'. *International Journal of Music Education* 26(2):177–90.

Erlmann, Veit. 1998. 'How beautiful is small? Music, globalization and the aesthetics of the local'. *Yearbook for Traditional Music* 30:12–21.

Farber, Yael. 2009. *Molora*. London: Oberon Books.

Feeny, David, Fikret Berkes, Bonnie McCay and James Acheson 1998. 'The tragedy of the commons: twenty-two years later'. In: John Baden and Douglas Noonan (eds.). *Managing the Commons*. Bloomington: Indiana University Press, 76–94.

Frith, Simon. 1988. *Music for Pleasure: Essays in the Sociology of Pop*. New York: Routledge.

Frow, John. 1997. *Time and Commodity Culture: Essays in Cultural Theory and Postmodernity*. Oxford: Oxford University Press.

Gasaway, Laura and Sarah Wiant. 1994. *Libraries and Copyright: A Guide to Copyright Law in the 1990s*. Washington, DC: Special Libraries Association.

Githaiga, Joseph. 1998. 'Intellectual property law and the protection of indigenous folklore and knowledge'. *Current Developments* 5(2).

Hansen, Dierdre Doris. 1981. Music of the Xhosa speaking People. Unpublished Ph.D. Thesis. University of the Witwatersrand, Johannesburg.

Herbst, Anri, Meki Nzewi and Kofi Agawu (eds). 2002. *Musical Arts in Africa: Theory, Practice and Education*. Pretoria: UNISA Press.

Kawooya, Dick. 2010. Traditional Musician-Centered Perspectives on Ownership of Creative Expressions. Ph.D. dissertation, University of Tennessee.

Knoedelseder, Jr., William. 1987. 'Popping off: Simon and South Africa: why the fuss?' *Los Angeles Times* (18 January), Calendar section.

Kuruk, Paul. 2002. 'African customary law and the protection of folklore'. *Copyright Bulletin* 2(32):4–32.

Levine, Laurie. 2005. *The Drumcafé's Traditional Music of South Africa*. Johannesburg: Jacana.

Litman, Jessica. 1990. 'The public domain'. *Emory Law Journal* 39(4):1012–23.

Madian, Azza. 2005. 'The protection and promotion of Egypt's musical heritage'. www.iprsonline.org/unctadictsd/docs/Madian_ArabRD_music.pdf, accessed 17 May 2011.

Makuliwe, N.T.A. 1995. *Inkcubeko Yethu.* Pietermaritzburg: Shuter & Shooter (Pty)
    Ltd.

Meintjes, Louise. 1990. 'Paul Simon's *Graceland*, South Africa and the mediation of
    musical meaning'. *Ethnomusicology* 34(1):37–73.

Mendis, Dinusha. 2003. 'The historical development of exceptions to copyright
    and its application to copyright law in the twenty-first century'. *Electronic
    Journal of Comparative Law* 7(5). www.ejcl.org/ejcl/75/art75-8.html,
    accessed on 7 May 2010.

McCann, Anthony. 2001. 'All that is not given is lost: Irish traditional music,
    copyright, and common property'. *Ethnomusicology* 45(1):89–106.

Miller, Daniel (ed.). 1995. *Acknowledging Consumption: A Review of New Studies.*
    London: Routledge.

Mills, Sherylle. 1996. 'Indigenous music and the law: an analysis of national and
    international legislation'. *Yearbook for Traditional Music* 28:57–86.

Republic of South Africa. 2010. *Intellectual Property Law Amendment Bill.* www.ipo.
    org.za/IPO_docs/archive_2010/Intellectual Property Laws Amendment Bill,
    accessed 4 April 2011.

Saurombe, Amos. 2009. 'The protection of Indigenous Traditional Knowledge
    through the Intellectual Property System and the 2008 South African
    Intellectual Property Law Amendment Bill'. *Journal of International
    Commercial Law and Technology* 4(3):196–202.

Seeger, Anthony. 1992. 'Ethnomusicology and music law'. *Ethnomusicology*
    36(3):345–59.

Spencer, Jon Michael. 1991. 'The emergence of Black and the emergence of Rap'. *Black
    Sacred Music* 5: 1: 141–52.

Tracey, Kerryn Ann. 2008. Ngqoko Throat Singing: the Search for an Effective
    Music Notation. BMUS dissertation, University of the Witwatersrand,
    Johannesburg.

Truth and Reconciliation Commission. 1995. www.justice.gov.za/trc, accessed on 3
    December 2011.

Von Sturmer, John. 1987. 'Aboriginal singing and notions of power'. In: Margaret
    Clunies Ross, Tamsin Donaldson and Stephen Wild (eds). *Songs of
    Aboriginal Australia.* Sydney: University of Sydney, 63–76.

Wilmsen, Edwin. 1996. 'Premises of power in ethnic politics'. In: Edwin Wilmsen and
    Patrick McAllister (eds). *Politics of Difference: Ethnic Premises in a World of
    Power.* Chicago: University of Chicago Press, 1–24.

WIPO IGC. 2001. 'Needs and expectations of Traditional Knowledge holders'. WIPO
    publication no. 768(E). www.wipo.int/tk/en/tk/ffm/report, accessed 2 May
    2011.

Discography

Ezona Ngoma Zengqoko (Best new songs of Ngqoko, 2002). Dargie's Recording.

Afrique de Suid Le Chant des Femmes Xhosa: The Ngqoko Women's Ensemble (1995). Geneva.

Ngqoko Women's Ensemble: Discography of CDs (2002). GALLO Records.

Xhosa Music: Its Techniques and Instruments, with a Collection of Songs (1988). Dargie's Recording.

Umngqokolo: Xhosa Overtone Singing and the Song Nondel'ekhaya (1991). Dargie's Recording.

The Drumcafé's Traditional Music of South Africa (2005). Levine.

Eastern Cape Indigenous Orchestra: Grahamstown National Arts Festival (2009). Fieldwork recording.

CHAPTER 9

Breaking the contract?

Handling intangible cultural goods
among different generations in Mali[1]

☾☾☾☾☾☾☾☾☾☾

Mamadou Diawara

Mariam Bagayogo has been singing for more than half a century in her village, which is called Kolokani, in the land (*pays*) of Beledugu, which is situated in the district (*cercle*) of Kolokani, 125 km north of Bamako (interview 2010). She also performs in many other places in Mali, where she provides entertainment at all sorts of festivities. As a member of the Ensemble Instrumental National du Mali, she has already travelled the entire world. Reports of her performance in the Democratic Republic of Korea, for example, are breathtaking. The cheerful *'grande dame'* of small stature still dances with athletic dexterity on top of the balafon played by her instrumentalists. Vigorous as she is, she misses no opportunity to comment on her youth, her career and her relationship to those who are so dear to her: the people of her village that she has long since left behind, her family in Bamako and the orchestra members. With the quality of her performances, the density of her texts and the melody of her voice, she manages to gather around her people of all ages and backgrounds.

The songs of this perfect media woman are alive in her home, in the streets of Bamako and throughout the world. She has produced a repertoire of songs whose 'social life' is worth telling. Arjun Appadurai (1986), the originator of this concept, the social life of things, did not elaborate on many

1   I worked on this chapter during my stay as John G. Diefenbaker Award winner (2010–11) at the University of Québec. I am grateful to the Canadian Council for the Arts, the Département de Littératures de l'Université Laval, the Faculté des Lettres, and the Chaire de recherche du Canada en Littératures africaines et Francophonie for their support, which made it possible to carry out this research.

of its implications. I would like to show that the concept can be easily applied to the intangible goods of songs, lyrics and performance.

What does the 'social life' of this music and performance, and the knowledge it transmits, signify for the encounter between local media and electronic media, and for that between the normative orders that govern its local production and the urban framework in which it crosses a double threshold: circulation in the market and the resulting individual appropriation of heritage as merchandise?

This transformation takes place right in front of our eyes thanks to those players, among them Mariam Bagayogo, who have recourse to modern media. Important in this case is 'the cultural work of media technologies', to borrow a term that Brian Larkin (2008:2) has applied to urban cultures and media infrastructures in Nigeria.

In the following discussion I explore a triptych. First, the relationship between the creator and her original environment is described. This allows me to examine her debt towards the villagers from whom she learned before beginning to compose and entertain at festivities, and before she experienced how others duplicated parts of her repertoire. In a second step I contrast the singer from Beledugu, on the one hand, with some young women from Bamako who, with a full sense of entitlement, were busy in the 1980s and 1990s bringing out cassettes with all the benefits to be derived from them; and, on the other hand, with the Malian government, the pool of whose critics will never run dry. I attempt, thirdly, to locate the Malian example in African reality.

What resonates in this case are the protests of Algerians from Kabylia who, according to Jane E. Goodman (2002, 2005), distinguish between artists who appropriate outright local female heritage and those who continue to produce the artists at the margins of the market circuit. Can we speak of theft in Mali, as is done in Algeria? 'Theft' poses the delicate question of the ownership of intangible goods that, according to Western normative order, are part of the so-called public domain. This chapter explores the relationship between artists and the cultural heritage, the *commons* on which everybody draws in order to compose.

The 'romance of the public domain' (Chandler and Sunder 2004) is a classic issue in debates on the appropriation of cultural heritage from countries of the South by multinational corporations. What is this all about, and what ideas prevail among actors who are themselves engaged in the production and appropriation of intangible assets, particularly of music? The international context that has generated modern copyrights and 'pirates' in parts of the world such as Mali, where they had previously been unknown, will serve as a framework to make sense of Mariam Bagayogo's story.

Being a creator in the context of orality

The rich repertoire of Bagayogo comes from Beledugu in the district of Kolokani, and was familiar to her before she began her tireless travels (interview 2010). The long evenings that mark births, circumcisions, weddings and funerals were her preferred fields for collecting material. As a very young woman, she lost her heart to dancing and the passions of the *nkusunbala*, the great balafon of Beledugu, the largest of the Mande world. The songs of the women who crush the shea nuts, the songs that give rhythm to the hard work of these butter producers, did not escape her either. Her repertoire and singing style, the *nkusun*,[2] is the privilege of women. Let us keep in mind that Mariam Bagayogo is not a griot, one of those professional oral custodians of the past for a particular family or hero (Figure 9.1).

Mariam Bagayogo systematically collected songs from well-known singers. Then she began to sing herself at ceremonies in her own neighbourhood. Sometimes, she succeeded in performing her singing at more respectable places, and when she became more famous, she performed on the stage of her small town. She always had the humility to pay tribute to those (known or unknown) women to whom she owed her repertoire. This tribute is not simply a formality. This way of learning corresponds to the local modalities of the circulation of music. Traveling to acquire knowledge, learning on the spot and paying tribute to teachers are the unwritten rules governing apprenticeship in Beledugu and in most parts of the Mande world, except when sacred music is concerned. By sacred music we mean pieces produced by brotherhoods of hunters or other 'secret societies' such as the Komo (Dieterlen and Cissé 1972; Zahan 1970), an institution which goes far back into the past. Numerous authors have documented this phenomenon in medieval Mali or Ghana (Cissé 1994; Diawara 1990, 2011; Traoré 2000). As a student, she regularly went to the masters of the local scene to ask them to teach their songs and get permission to perform them. It is moreover in this way that she succeeded in entering into the good graces of the best singers and continued to extend her deep knowledge of the lyrics. She later used these lyrics as the ultimate source of inspiration when she herself began to compose, according to the local 'rules of the art'. With great regret, she later complained in radio broadcasts about the

---

2   *Nkusun* is a musicial genre typical of Beledugu. Sung by a woman who accompanies the lyrics to the sound of a large xylophone, *balaba* (the small one, called *jelibala*, the xylophone of the *jeliw*, characterizes the griots of the Mande). *Nkusun* also refers to the gourd containing pebbles which gives rhythm to the sound of the balafon mixed with the voice of the singer. However, contrary to the assertions of David Conrad (2002:61n.248), we know of no women who play the large xylophone, which is reserved for men.

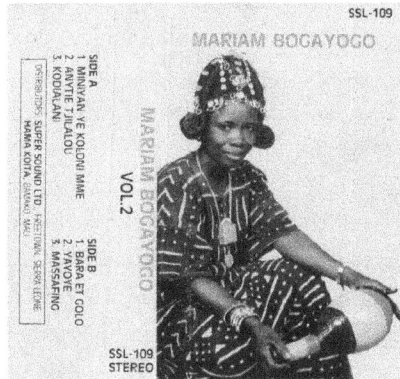

Figure 9.1   Mariam Bagayogo presents herself on the cover of a DVD in local outfit.

younger generation's refusal to undergo such aesthetic training before singing anything any way they pleased.

A true creator, Mariam Bagayogo grants herself the luxury of social criticism, even daring to turn against the village of Bassabougou, 150 km north of Bamako and 25 km from Kolokani, which became the subject of one of her best pieces. In the mid 1960s, Madame Bagayogo composed a song of rare quality which continues to make many tears flow. She sings of the fate of a woman who arrived at Bassabougou, a village of Bamana ancestral religion, when her husband died there. The lament of the widow relates the acts of a woman obliged to dig her husband's grave and bury him with the help of only one man, because the people of Bassabougou did not deign to touch the body of a Muslim, simply because of his faith. The singer set to music not only the plight of the widow but also the villagers' postures of refusal, buttressed by their intolerance. This song became a big hit at the time, enlivening the daily transmissions of the Radio Diffusion Nationale du Mali, the state radio, and the only one in the country at the time. Following the *coup d'état* of 1968, a complaint by the inhabitants of the denigrated village led to the censorship of the piece. According to the singer, the prohibition of its distribution followed from an unfortunate mixture of genres perpetrated by a griot who had permitted himself to combine this lamentation with a love song, and it was this that had provoked the outraged villagers to complain to the radio and obtain the banishment of the offending piece. However, according to independent sources, it was indeed the musician's criticism of the villagers that was at the origin of the prohibition, and nothing else.

What's essential here is the social criticism of intolerence with respect to a Muslim in a region of ancestral religion. One can hardly believe that this was still happening in the 1960s, as today the greater part of that region has been Islamicized, at least formally.

In addition to the example of Bassabougou, when the singer, in the mid 1960s, braved the opposition of a certain audience, she also had to confront the reprobation of the guardians of the art of *nkusun*, who deemed, not completely without grounds, that she had distorted not only the song, but also the dance. Why? If we are to believe A. Touré, a little girl growing up at the time, and Amita Sylla, a lady who lived in Kolokani during this period, the dynamic village singer was the object of heated criticism. Some accused her of mixing genres: songs for crushing nuts with nuptial songs, and the wedding repertory with airs intended for circumcisions. More seriously, according to them, was transforming this old home village repertoire into patriotic songs to celebrate Mali. Some were scandalized by her excessive tenancy of the scene of the spectacle. At over sixty years of age, she was still the outstanding dancer who spun to the four corners of the circle formed by dancers and spectators. A talented showperson, she continues today to take the liberty of springing up and down on top of the *nkusun bala*, the big xylophone of the Beledugu, while its player, drunk with delight, strikes at the blades of his instrument, which the irreverant call 'donkey ribs'. This dexterity, today much admired, was in those days execrated. For the orthodox of the *nkusun*, the song must be calm and deep, the singer serene. The attitude of Mariam Bagayogo, a singer and dancer who springs up and down while the drums and other instruments are playing, is the opposite of this. What a gaffe the singer makes in dancing in a way that might unsettle the principal instrumentalist focused on playing his xylophone…

Let us return to the learning of songs, which Mariam Bagayogo says is laborious and slow. The highly local circulation of musical knowledge, and possibilities of what to do with it, did not last long, as the French Sudan, which included in its territory part of contemporary Mali, was occupied by France in 1880. The colonial government turned Kolokani into the headquarters of a subdivision in the middle of the twentieth century. As its successor, the Malian state, confirmed this choice in 1960. Kolokani remained the governmental seat of a so-called district (*cercle*). The local authorities were in charge of the cultural activities of the *cercle*, of which the small town had become the administrative centre. When independence was obtained in 1960, the socialist regime of the first President of the Republic made one of its goals the highlighting and valorizing of the cultural and artistic heritage of the young nation by drawing on traditional songs, dances, stories and other cultural treasures, both tangible and intangible. Like neighbouring Guinea, a pioneer in such matters, the Malian state undertook an active campaign for the revival of cultural heritage that soon had effects in the countryside, Kolokani included (Diawara 1996, 2003:179f.; Schulz 2001:169f.).[3]

In addition to performing at the usual occasions (life-cycle ceremonies of name-giving, of circumcision, of mariage and of death, or calendar festivals, such as those of the harvest), Mariam Bagayogo became the authorized host of welcoming ceremonies for officials. She recalls with emotion the great consideration accorded her by the late Monsieur Lakami Sylla, vice-head of the district of Kolokani. When she advanced from a village and very modest semi-urban audience to that of the entire Republic via national radio broadcasts, she passed on to a new phase. While the young singer made her country proud, listening to its own music on the radio for the first time, she also created jealousy. Bagayogo was no longer engaged only to entertain at occasional commemorations of annual festivities or at the arrival of guests in Kolokani. Much sought after, she joined the local theatre troupe consisting of singers, choristers, soloists and dancers. This is how she made it to Bamako in order to represent her district at the annual regional competition that took place in the capital. She now had to compete with the representatives of seven other districts from throughout the region of Bamako.[4] Her presence in Bamako was not limited to her songs on the radio, from this point onwards she also performed at competitions in the capital. These competitions opened up a new career for her and for her repertoire, which was now no longer hers alone but rather represented the district and the entire region of Bamako. How was this metamorphosis accomplished?

In Kolokani, the songs no longer remained in the state in which they were collected in the villages. We have mentioned that the purists of the *nkusun* criticized Bagayogo for transforming local songs into tunes celebrating Mali or Africa, topics completely foreign to the *nkusun* and to Beledugu (Diawara 1996).[5] In each district, the state had selected skilled teachers to conduct research on cultural heritage (among other aspects, art, oral narrative, dance, song, performance) in their respective constituencies. They were in charge of advising the youth in these domains and on sport. The task of these so-called '*animateurs de jeunesse*' was, among others, to look for the best songs and singers to entrust with representing the district in the annual cultural competitions. Some of these advisers were trained in the Soviet Union

---

3   Other interesting cases in this regard are Guinea (Charry 2000; van der Wiele 2010) and Congo (White 2008).

4   The seven regions are: Bamako, Banamba, Dioïla, Kangaba, Kati, Koulikoro and Nara.

5   Dorothea Schulz (2001:174, see particularly footnote 20) provides relevant indications about the process of transformation of the songs.

or Czechoslovakia, or had sojourned in other socialist countries. The 'local annual youth arts and sport week' (*semaine locale de la jeunesse*) was held in each administrative centre of the district during the Christmas school holidays so as to prepare for the 'regional annual youth arts and sport week' during Easter break in the regional capital (*semaine régionale de la jeunesse*). The latter, in turn, prepared for the 'annual youth arts and sport week' (*semaine nationale de la jeunesse*) scheduled for July in Bamako.[6] The scene was set. The songs were now reviewed and re-composed to correspond to different audiences, nationally or even internationally.

The further removed they were from the villages, the more the songs were transformed. Neither their form nor their content escaped intact; they had to become patriotic and serve to educate the masses, according to the socialist jargon of that time. The combination of radio- and media-savvy women (such as Bagayogo) aimed and aims at creating a new type of 'social subject', to use the expression of Brian Larkin (2008:3). Indeed, as in the USA and Europe at the time, the radio served to promote the interests of the state. Larkin mentions that the intention of the British colonialist was to educate and develop the Nigerians into 'modern' colonial citizens. Modernization was and is key in independent Mali as well. People who refused to send their relatives, sons and daughters to the 'youth arts and sports week' were often coerced (Arnoldi 2006:60; Diawara 2003:185–6; Schulz 2001:169, 172). By replacing the colonial radio station with a national one, and by introducing the 'youth arts and sports weeks' (*semaines de la jeunesse*), the independent Malian government aimed at the creation of national identity.

The songs which had inspired singers in the rural areas celebrated female cultivators, i.e. the champions of the millet fields of Beledugu. In Kolokani, they were refurbished by Mariam Bagayoko and her mentors, who replaced the cultivators with women of independent Mali, and their fields with those of the nation. Later, the songs were dedicated to the revolutionary women not only of Mali but of Africa or indeed of the world. This trend has even increased since 1984, which was declared the International Year of Women. The songs in the villages celebrated local heroes, but when transformed in the 1960s, they

---

6   *La semaine de la jeunesse* (annual youth arts and sports week) has met with various fates between its creation in 1962 to the present day. From 1962 to 1968, the Socialist regime founded and ran the event, but the military *coup d'état* of 1968 interrupted its organization and progress. The week or festival resumed, however, in 1970, under the name *Biennale artistique, culturelle et sportive*, until 1990. The revolution of 1991, which put an end to the military dictatorship, also kept the Biennale from functioning, until it resumed once again, in 2000, as the *Semaine nationale des arts et la culture* (for further details see Arnoldi 2006).

had to eulogize the heroes of Mali's and Africa's independence. From a certain point of view, this restructuring follows the rules of the art, as this kind of repertoire of popular songs was originally malleable. Even in the past singers always transformed their repertoires according to the circumstances. But suddenly, an unprecedented player, the state, represented by politicians and functionaries, appeared after independence in 1960 and claimed the right to recompose songs and select topics apt to promote a national patriotic culture.

This type of alteration was not unique to Mali. The most famous example of this kind of textual manipulation is that of Guinea and its national anthem (Van der Wiele 2010).[7] Many other countries, including Zaire/Congo (Stewart 2000; White 2008) and Cameroon (see Tcheuyap in this volume) followed the example set by Guinea.

To push forward the new songs and chosen singers, the national radio was called upon. The ministry in charge of culture and youth created a system of competition at all levels among the songs and singers of the country. The various competitive festivities – the 'local annual youth arts and sports week', the 'regional annual youth arts and sports week' and the 'national annual youth arts and sports week', in addition to the unofficial competitions that were held in the villages to prepare for the local 'week' – held the country in suspense every year. What was included? In the artistic part, the youths competed in such diverse domains as solo singing, choirs, instrumental ensembles, ballet and theatre. In sports, they competed against each other in track and field, football, basketball, handball, volleyball, table tennis, cycling and wrestling (see Ibrahima Wane in this volume). On each day of the week, the best in each discipline were selected. The national week was held under the patronage of the President of the Republic, who ceremonially opened the competitions. All of the national week's events were broadcast live on national radio, the Radio Diffusion Nationale du Mali, the only radio station in the country until the late 1980s. The end of the week was marked by an official closing ceremony during which the competition's official results were announced in an ambience reminiscent of the Olympic Games.

In addition, a special programme, the *concert des auditeurs* ('request time'), hosted by popular radio personalities, was broadcast every Sunday on the airwaves of Radio Diffusion Nationale du Mali. In return for a fixed sum, the listeners could ask for a piece to be dedicated to their parents, friends or acquaintances. They could request and listen to any of their favourite songs, completely unaware that some pieces had been historically destined

---

7   In Guinea, the government transformed the song from a Maninka griot and adapted it to the life history of a Peul king in order to celebrate the nation of Guinea (Diawara 1996, 2003; van der Wiele 2010).

for specific families only (cf. Cissé and Kamissoko 1988, 1991; Diawara 1990, 1996; Traoré 2000). As was only to be expected, a harsh competition took place among the artists, among the most requested songs and among the patrons who were celebrated the most in the pieces. In this context a radio programme, *Les Étoiles de la Musique* ('The Stars of Music'), ranked the songs and artists based on the votes of listeners. M'Baye Boubacar Diarra (Figure 9.2), the founder of the show, recalls its popularity and the cheating it inspired. The principle was simple. Whoever was in favour of one artist sent a letter to the showmakers at the Radio Diffusion Nationale du Mali in Bamako. Officials went through the mail manually to rank the most requested song, which implies the most requested artist. To position their favourite artist among the first, some of the fans, especially in Bamako, voted for the same person several times, a well-known tactic in show business (Diarra M.B., interview 2009). The most requested song was distributed, published and became famous. A global market hitherto unknown for music (which extends far beyond Mali) was born.

The role of the media in stimulating a new aesthetic in the urban context is striking, as Brian Larkin has also observed (2008:5). Larkin shows how this aesthetic borrows from the old in order to generate new forms through adaptation, creation and recreation. This is certainly also the case in Mali. I would even go further by adding that the new compositions, due to Mariam Bagayogo and many others who migrated from the countryside, are now presented in the city as ancient heritage. The city, a reference point for emigrants from the villages, became the most fertile environment for faux archaisms, to borrow Lévi-Strauss' formulation (1952), presented as genuine, an observation which particularly applies to the pieces by Mariam Bagayogo.

Until the 1980s, according to Malian radio and culture professionals and the artists themselves, they sang for the country (B. Traoré, interview 2009; see also Schulz 2001:174). Nothing was paid to the artist. They were accomodated at the government's expense during the festivals. For the artists, to hear their names, or the names of their city or village, was sufficient. The symbolic capital generated by radio waves fulfilled everyone's expectations: those of the singer, the listeners and the people of the region. The songs were taken up in chorus throughout the country and the sub-region.

Meanwhile, musicians, mediated by the radio, began to construct a musical and artistic national heritage in its shadow. A phenomenal shift in the country's mediated landscape took place before our eyes. The singers saw their national careers take shape as radio hosts went to seek them out in the most remote villages. Once it became known that an individual was particularly good at singing or playing an instrument, the host, ever on the lookout, did everything possible to recruit the person for the local, then the regional and

Figure 9.2 M'Baye Boubacar Diarra and his young assistant preparing the programme of his famous concert 'Africa Show' broadcast on the television network Africable in 2010 (photo by M. Diawara).

finally the national troupe. Now the voice embodied that of the country, the district, the region and eventually the nation, as the National Instrumental Ensemble was established to bring together the best elements of this competition. It was a matter of constituting a troupe of professionals at the national level charged with representing the nation at the international level. In 1961, a body of artists employed by the state, living and working in Bamako in the service of art, was born (Ba Konaré 1993:244; Diawara 2003:183). The appeal of foreign horizons materialized at the end of careers initially intended only to be national.

Boubacar Traoré (interview in Bamako 2009), a senior radio personality, certainly the most experienced of all sound technicians and someone who contributed to the careers of top Malian singers, told me that between 1960 and 1970 piracy was not an issue at all. 'I was the only one to take care of the sound,' Traoré said. 'I knew each and every artist. I recorded them to my liking, and tapes were safe.' When I was privileged to meet the radio pioneers who had worked as journalists or sound technicians, they told me that formerly everything was done for the country. No one demanded further gratification. Of course, in the 1960s, some black sheep were already duplicating tapes illegally and selling them to the emigrant community in France. Traoré still rails against this practice, which flourished undercover despite an order issued to all, including the sound technicians, prohibiting them from meddling with any tape whatsoever. Undoubtedly, this was the era of the cassette (see also Tcheuyap in this volume).

This statement deserves elaboration. Music was virtually a monopoly of the radio. It was not yet the time of tape recorders, and phonographs were rare and expensive. In the context of increasingly austere socialist Mali (1960–8), young people quenched their thirst for Western music with the sound of the Voice of America (VOA), the BBC and France Inter, later Radio France International. No fee was paid by Radio Mali and no one was affected by this. What's more, records of the National Instrumental Ensemble were pressed by the state, but nothing impacted on the situation regarding the rights of the arts corporation that the colonial and post-colonial state had created.[8] The most notable of these newcomers, the artists of the Ensemble Instrumental National (EIN), were just employees of the state ensuring that pieces were published.

What can be concluded from this? A group of professional musicians and dancers with knowledge of what is going on in foreign countries emerged slowly but surely from the 1960s onward. Then songs were gradually transformed into a commodity which came to be recognized as such. From the village, where it was carried by many voices, music reached the town where 'the rules of art' were different (Bourdieu 1992). However, at this time, neither musicians nor the state raised any question regarding the payment of rights, for the simple reason that mechanical reproduction, still quite rare, was not perceived as a threat to art or the artists. Bagayogo, like all her colleagues from the same background, composed and sung by vocation, for pleasure, out of social obligation and patriotism. They contented themselves with the fruits of their art and the symbolic capital that it represented at the time. Everyone was aware that this was converted into toppling mounds of coins and banknotes. The more her art was valued, the greater the popularity of the singer became and, with it, her income. The coexistence of two media represented, on the one hand, by the singers, who are mostly female,[9] the 'megaphones' of their

---

8   The Malian government had published in 1971 the first anthology of Malian music, in four volumes, issued by Bärenreiter (Musicaphon 30L.2504). Sydoni SA and Mali K7 SA, founded respectively in 2001 and 2002, constituted the first two enterprises for the commercial reproduction of musical cassettes in the country. At the time they counted between them sixty employees. See www.mali-music. com/Mag/Press/Press2005/independanto50316A.htm, accessed 15 May 2012, and www.africalabel.com/files/WHO_S_WHO_-_version_15_mars.pdf, accessed 8 July 2015.

9   Most has been written about them. See Diawara 2003; Duràn 1995; Hale 1998; Hoffman 2001; Schulz 2001.

colleagues, and on the other by the radio, seemed harmonious until the emergence of the tape recorder generation.

The tape-recorder generation

This cohabitation, which at first seemed to function in relative harmony, began to deteriorate in the late 1970s. In effect, the singer who had made it to town, who introduced her people and held their banner high, was no longer necessarily the same. The advent of the tape recorder and the acceleration of the 'mechanical reproduction' of sound carriers placed stress on the relations between those from the villages, who serve as the source, and the youth who go to the city and put their music on the airwaves, or more.

By 'mechanical reproduction' I refer to Walter Benjamin's concept of the 1930s, which highlights the disenchantment of the original work by duplicating it under market pressure. What happens in Africa is far from Benjamin, both in time and space. Benjamin (1980) based his assessment for the most part on writing and painting; the following lines apply his theory to the field of intangible culture.

In this light, the case of Bagayogo is illuminating for several reasons. First and foremost, Bagayogo is a singer from the village. She cultivated this image by getting herself regularly invited to host the festivities of people from her country, Beledugu, who had resettled in Bamako. Now living in Bamako herself, her modest home swarms with people from the deep countryside. She composes her lyrics and sings them, mixing choreography and local songs with what she has learned under the guidance of the organizers of youth festivals, some of whom had been trained in the USSR. Back when she was still living in Kolokani, she was even more present in the village ceremonies, going from village to village, from weddings to name-giving and circumcision ceremonies. As is usually the case with public figures, especially artists, many rumors have circulated around her. It's pointless to seek their origins, nor, for deontological reasons will I try, all the less so because the narrative I tell is related in several milieus of the Malian capital and is perfectly well known to showpeople.

The local FM stations that proliferated in Mali with democratization in the 1990s made Bagayogo their idol. The FM stations from the Kolokani district and its environs recorded Bagayogo free of charge and without her permission, so as to liven up their shows intended for the neighbouring countryside, i.e. to the country of the singer who brought happiness to her admirers, who no longer had to travel to her village to hear her. Her voice was even more appreciated when she sang unreleased songs, songs rooted in the land with which she expressly and impassionedly identified when addressing her compatriots. When setting foot in all parts of her country, as she did, she composed lyrics praising her hosts, providing a rare opportunity for the elect to enter the local pantheon, at least for the time a celebration lasted.

In the joy shared by radio professionals and the listeners, however, a man (whose name I will not mention) from Bamako bustled about. He also had only ears for the great voice wooed by everyone. He was aware of the diva's movements and knew when the sound hunters (people searching to record music) would return. Without necessarily following the sound technicians on the ground, he quietly re-recorded the field cassettes of the radio professionals in the village and then took them along with him on his travels back to the capital.

He delivered these products to a young lady (whom I also cannot name), who found in them the source of inspiration for her own repertoire. This straw singer learned these songs without referring to a teacher and without troubling to go to the source of her knowledge. She did not burden herself with becoming the apprentice of an authority, to whom she would then, for her entire life, owe the respect rightly due to a teacher. Had she taken this formal step, she would have had to perform a number of symbolic gestures of deference towards her source of knowledge. Nothing could have been further from the mind of this young singer, however, who abridged the process of apprenticeship by finding a unique and original source, recording it and, finally, exploiting it without making payments to anyone. She is one of the artists of what I call the tape-recorder generation. One easily learns the repertoire of others recorded on tapes that are listened to and rehearsed until one knows how to sing it. On this basis, one revises the songs by adding bits and pieces to them, such as the names of one's patrons on one or the other occasion (Bazin 1979:591–2; Diawara 1996).

What did the young lady make of these songs? The attractive young 'tape-recorder' artist with a beautiful voice built herself a repertoire that she did not content herself with only singing. She also found producers to publish cassettes in her name, quickly putting several on the market. Even better, by making herself known everywhere, she created a large audience and found a wide circle of people ready to invite her to host public concerts and recreational soirees. Her pieces made the rounds, not just of small country radio stations, but rather of the big stations in the capital and beyond, making her renowned in certain particular circles of power.

Mariam Bagayogo was confronted by another even more crucial case. Another young artist, coming from the same country as herself, contested her supremacy – even seeming monopoly – on the *nkusun*. I do not give any further details on this point.

This story, which is obviously not limited to Mariam Bagayogo and these young ladies, raises the questions of apprenticeship and of a singer's relationship to the community that originally created the music. To listen to both protagonists of this affair, some intellectuals up-to-date with the debates on authors' rights believe that the young lady has as great a claim to the songs of her country as Mariam Bagayogo. Both come from the same village, so it goes without saying that both have the right to the songs. But what is to be done once the younger generation has broken with the preceding one? We can catch a whiff of failed management of the commons, to which I will return later.

We are in the context of upheavals that deeply anger the proponents of the normative order with respect to the circulation of intellectual goods and to a certain sense of ethics that should govern borrowing in a fair way. The singer considered, like the village, the guardian of the repertoire, appears not to be entitled to any respect. On the contrary, the relations between the old singer of Kolokani and the young singer of Bamako can be characterized in two words: invective and contempt. The first is convinced that she is abused by the second and harshly criticizes her. The second artist is also disdainful of her rival. A situation of latent conflict prevails that cannot be regulated by usage and custom, and even less by modern law, as neither protagonists will dare sue the other.

The harshest critics' vision of the young singer strongly recalls the biting reproach that Martin Luther addressed to the plagiarist, who is 'a thief of work' (quoted Edelman 2004:147). Erasmus dealt the plagiarist the death blow: 'No one understands his own interests better than the person who publishes under his own name someone else's works.' (trans. Nolhac 1992 in Edelman 2004:148; see Diawara 2011). The critics' argument against the young singers is that they insolently arrogate to themselves knowledge they have not in any way earned. Moreover, in defiance of all the rules of propriety, they lay claim to rights or to a body of knowledge of which they know nothing, with the obvious intent of deriving profit and, in addition, making an exhibition of it. One can hardly speak of 'piracy' in this case, but the basis of the conflict becomes clear when one focuses on the violation of an anchored local law that managed and still manages the transmission of knowledge and the circulation of songs.

The mechanical reproduction of music allows some of the younger generation to break the tacit contract that exists between teacher and student in the countryside. Reproducing songs, does not seem to be the major problem; what is, is the breaking all the rules that govern the production of knowledge. While some stigmatize the tendency of the elders to keep knowledge to themselves, opponents condemn the laziness and lack of creativity that feeds the nonchalant copying of them.

The crisis of the commons in Mali

In the mid 1960s, the troupe of Kolokani was distinguished at the 'youth week' in Bamako, its solo performance winning first place. The award-winning song, titled 'Bambo', celebrated the new family and guardianship law (*code de la famille et de la tutelle*) of the young Republic of Mali, issued in 1962, which instituted a civil marriage to be concluded between two partners free to accept the contract, or not (Info Prodej 2006). One had to choose the matrimonial regime, i.e. either polygamy or monogamy. For the first time, a woman could refuse a marriage whose regime she did not accept, and even better, refuse an arranged marriage. The solo was sung by the young Mariam Bagayogo. In this context, she caused a sensation both in Kolokani and in the city of Bamako. The urban residents of Bamako, many of whom had broken links with the village, were literally seduced by what might be called 'the hymn to chosen marriage'.

The musical ensemble of Bamako chose the song to be presented at the 'annual youth arts and sports week' – a meteoric rise! To make it fit for the occasion, the organizers of the festival in the capital rearranged the piece by introducing, among other names, that of the President of the Republic, who himself became, in the song, the official who handed over the marriage certificate to the model young couple that had decided to get married under the new law. His pronouncement was a key sentence that differentiated this version from that of the Kolokani. In addition, the framers from Bamako decided to have the piece sung by a girl who was barely seven years old, named Fatoumata Kouyaté, known as Tata. The instant success earned her the nickname 'Bambo' forever. 'Bambo' is not meant to be danced to, but for new couples of the time, its success was comparable to that of the 'Blue Danube' waltz of Strauss. It was requested for thousands of couples on the radio.

Few people know the prehistory of the song 'Bambo'. Clearly subject to the mediatic sway of Radio Mali, it was discovered, in Mali and places beyond, through the voice of Tata Bambo. During 'Request Time' (*concert des auditeurs*) on the Sunday radio, people who asked for the song to celebrate weddings or to wish happiness to new couples always heard: 'Bambo by Tata Bambo'. This formula – coined by the journalists presenting the piece – remained eternally fixed. The discography of the national radio recognizes only the young singer. Broadcast interviews with Tata Bambo reinforced the identification, offending people who knew the whole story. Journalists, among others propagating this myth, consider her as the composer and interpreter of the song (Koné 2010).

Without Bagayogo, the young singer would obviously never have intoned this song, because she would not have known it. Here, as in the two cases discussed above, one witnesses a breach of the tacit oral contract that customarily binds the singer with the person to whom she owes her repertoire. The famous singer, although she certainly owes her career to her own great talent, does not any less owe the piece that earned her name and her fame to a humble village woman, Mariam Bagayoko. The state never considered the question of authorship, preferring Tata Bambo Kouyaté, the end performer of the song, to Mariam Bagayoko, who had created it. The young singer, an urbanite, as in the preceding case, ascribes the reason for her success to herself and herself alone, as does the Romantic author (Edelman 2004:211–4).[10] This injustice could only produce frustration and bitterness in the social relations which linked the two implicated artists. The price of success was bitter for Mariam Bagayogo, even though she never expresses herself in that tone.

Initially, when songs passed between artists, no one protested, since there was no individual, or selfish, advantage to be gained. It was only later, with the advent of the mechanical reproduction of works by individuals for commercial purposes that the question of who held the rights to a song was asked in a hitherto unknown context.

There are many cases, however, in which the relationship between the renowned musician, present on Western stages, and his local source is marked by harmony. The world music star Salif Kéïta, whose custom it was to sing songs of the hunters, a secret brotherhood, got along well with his principal source Bala Djimba Diakité. In his book on Salif Kéïta, Chérif Kéïta (2009:30, 99) refers to this teacher-student relationship and publishes a photo of the blind bard Diakité, who lived in Babala, a tiny Mande village.[11] It is also known that Youssou N'Dour, inspired by the repertory of the Malian singer Fanta Damba Numéro 2 in composing his piece called 'Wareff', visited her in Bamako to pay her homage (Duràn 1989:282). Other less well-known musicians did the same, calling attention to a capital oversight on the part of a state, which creates copyrights but fails to define, in any satisfactory way, the status of pieces composed by troupes underwritten by the state.

A news item of 2010 eloquently illustrates the situation and at the same time sheds new light on the relationship between the two protagonists of the 'hymn to chosen marriage'. Word of a legal proceeding concerning plagiarism spread through the streets of Bamako. According to the rumour, Assa Kida – a

---

10   Foucault (1994) analyses the emergence of the Romantic author in the European context and pertinently remarks on the moment in which he frees himself from the influences of the court and from the privileges and the yoke of publishers. Edelman (2004) paints out this itinerary, which he solemnly calls the 'The consecration of the author', the title of his masterwork. An analogous phenomenon unrolls before our eyes with these musicians in an unusual context (see Diawara 2011).

11   Bala Djimba sings and plays an instrument called *simbi*. About this musicial genius, see Charry (2000:70, 84–9).

Figure 9.3   *'Café des Arts' is a popular place where international African musicians perform (photo by M. Diawara).*

well-known local singer who is currently presenting 'Sumu Kura', the famous singer's show on the private television network Africable – was accused of having 'stolen' a piece from the Biton National, the orchestra from her home town Ségou, which had filed suit. On the evening of 6 June 2010, in the course of a musical programme called 'Top Étoile', broadcast on the national television of Mali (ORTM), the host presented this singer and opened a debate on the subject. She had just returned from a tour in Italy and was shocked to find the answering machine of her mobile phone overloaded with messages from friends and admirers worried by the trial. Invited by 'Top Étoile', she took the opportunity to inform the public face-to-face with Mamadou Coulibaly, called 'the Cuban', the lead singer of Biton in the 1970s. The rumor was about the song 'Sike Nyenanba', which Assa Kida had taken up. 'The Cuban' explained that since Biton was a national orchestra, its entire repertoire was state property. Any work funded by the state and performed as such falls within the public domain, making anyone entitled to sing it without risk of being called a thief or plagiarist. Taking the accused under his wing on national television, Coulibaly expressed all his respect for the falsely accused singer. He strongly emphasized the benefits he received from the singer, and her own respect for the orchestra. Proud to have been exonerated by the very person – also invited to appear on the same show – from whom she had been accused of having stolen, she and her defender sung together the piece in question in the most

Figure 9.4   The 'Café des Arts': a view from the stage (photo by M. Diawara).

beautiful way. Meanwhile, the originator of 'Top Etoile', M'Baye Boubacar Diarra, one of Mariam Bagayogo promotors, founded a new place to organize concerts called 'Café des Arts' and continues to create and to compete as private entrepreneur against the state-owned entreprise. (Figures 9.3 and 9.4).

Accusations of theft or plagiarism are of course not unique to Bamako, and even less to Mali. Jane E. Goodman (2002:85–97) devoted a well-known article to women's folksongs in Algeria that had been the object of a complaint of 'theft of heritage' coming from both Algerian circles in Paris and the local Algerian public. She mentions the case of a teacher who was furious to see singers with international careers seize for themselves what in fact belonged to the feminine heritage of the country. The problem took on such proportions that the matter was referred to the courts (Goodman 2002:85–86). A female singer of advanced age, a long-time acquaintance of Goodman, speaking of the young people who confiscated her repertoire, observed that they disguised her songs. Listening to their songs taken up by young people, the old women singers find it confusing that they are unable to repeat them. We can understand Mariam Bagayogo's adding scathingly: 'They [the young people] do not even know what they are talking about!'

Song has entered another phase of its life, marked this time by the young wolves, as the critics might say. These youths monopolize the songs and, disdaining the rules for the transmission of knowledge, transform them and sell them like any other vulgar merchandise. The songs leave their customary context, and invade the stages of the Malian capital and of the world, bringing fame, and perhaps wealth, to their new singers. The singer empties the field of its sacred terrain. The song of Salif Kéïta, the world-music star, is quite far from the secret society of the hunters' brotherhood. Kéïta has liberated this modern song from a particular religion, just as other singers had done with other songs, long ago, vis-a-vis the churches of Europe. The song has been freed from the relations of exchange and reciprocity that were based upon it, from the hierarchical relations between teacher and student it had symbolized. Song abandoned the 'social world', as European music had in the nineteenth century (Goehr 1992:191). However, by breaking its anchorage, it seems to me it forms another one that conforms more to the expectations of neo-urbanites, of world citizens and of the artist him or herself.

Goodman (2002:86) raises the issue of morality, precisely the point on which the duped seniors insist, although for the most part tacitly. On the other hand, they rail against the shameless way – with disdain for the rules of propriety and for work well done – in which the young intrude into a domain which is far from being theirs. They speak of their impertinence, even personal rudeness, towards the rights holders according to the local normative order they scoff. To be sure, morality maintains its full strength among the elders, but it is no longer sufficient, no more in Algeria than in Mali, when society has had a taste of the substantive law and the market. The attitude of older people is remiscent of what Bernard Edelman (2004:147–48) teaches us about France before the inauguration of and respect for copyright. There, it was public opinion, instituted as a court of honour, which stigmatized the stealing of authors' glory and renown.

The tone is obviously different when one looks at the Malian press. Here the terms are identical to those in Algeria. The press talks about theft and plagiarism. The Malian and Algerian realities raise the question of the consequences of the private appropriation of oral heritage and of the intrusion of money. In fact, who has the right to appropriate what, and where does heritage begin?

In Mali, the public domain is the black hole of public debates on copyright. Few people are aware of it, and when they evoke it they confuse it with the right to sing without the risk of being accused of plagiarism. Speaking as seldom as artists about it, apart from the scandal recounted above, officials of the Malian copyright office appear to give it little heed. It is only really evoked when one speaks of foreigners (Diakité, interview 2009). Obviously the law talks about it the way it should, but to what good if the concerned actors take no heed?

When the socialist state (1960–8) systematically took Malian youth in hand and invested heavily in artistic production, individual copyrights were not on the agenda; neither was the danger of mechanical reproduction. The military regime that followed the socialists in 1968 largely continued the same system, although reducing support for the youth. A Malian copyright did not exist by name before 1978. Applying the French copyright law was not a priority. If the notion of 'national heritage' seems to have been acquired under the socialists, what happened to it under military rule before the penetration of copyright law?

Section 107 of Title Two of 'the Law 024 of 23 July 2008 defining the regime of literary and artistic property in the Republic of Mali' stipulates that 'expressions of folklore whose *individual authors* are unknown, but are most likely nationals of the Republic of Mali, belong to the *national heritage*' (Présidence de la République 2008:23, emphases added). Since we know that most Malians do not declare their works, are they automatically national heritage? What about all the works that are registered and desposited at the radio or television without a declaration by identified and identifiable creators?

We may even go one step further. With respect to the fate of singers who shamelessly exploit heritage and its owners, what are we say when these singers are exploited in turn by what they call pirates, in particular traders, shady producers, owners of cybercafés or bars? Those given to moralistic judgments suggest that these singers have been hoisted by their own petard. Although, obviously, this observation in no way justifies the crime of piracy, it may lead some complainants, who feel that they need to protect their rights, to reflect on the ones they themselves flout.

Conclusion

Mariam Bagayogo is regarded in her country as a great voice. She is a creator and an author in the sense that I have defined elsewhere (Diawara 2011; see also Barber 1999). She created a show each and every time she appeared on stage. There is a chasm between creators who openly share their work and those of a new generation marked by the Western stamp of exclusive possession. This Western point of view, which merges with that of the Romantic author, is a source of exclusion, even of works' sources, as in the case of the Algerian women analysed by Jane E. Goodman (2002:92).

By looking at the life of a woman from the village, I have illustrated the various forms that the relation between local and electronic media can assume. I wanted to illustrate how what was part of a common heritage, governed by known and respected rules, gradually became reified, and thus merchandise. These changes, which result from political, social and economic transformations, are perceived differently by the actors, whose generational affiliations play a major role. The tape-recorder generation confiscates for profit the heritage it reduces to goods of its own. At the same time, more cunning and better connected actors grab hold of the appropriated heritage, and confiscate it once again. Meanwhile, the material and its creators inexorably detach themselves from the universe that engendered them.

My aim here was to show that the material concerned (singing, text, choreography) has become more complex over the years. The intervention of the independent state of Mali, urbanization, the appearance of the radio and electronic media contribute to this complexity. Mariam Bagayogo herself, and a host of artists before and after her who act on the local and international scenes, played and still play a central role in this transformation. We are far from so-called tradition being abused by a modernity claiming to emerge ex nihilo. Mariam Bagayogo, labelled as a 'traditional' singer, is a highly modern one.[12] Cultural intermediaries have sprouted in large numbers and reduced the territory of a singer who formerly dominated the scene with her orchestra. Thanks to technology, these players from the city have stolen her show. Operative here is the social and cultural 'work' of media technology, to refer once again to Larkin (2008:3). One woman and her works illustrate this perfectly: from guardian of the temple, to the flame bearer of local culture, dumbfounded by the appetite of the young wolves.

---

12   This recalls the article 'Our tradition is a very modern tradition' by Christopher Waterman (1995).

References

Appadurai, Arjun (ed.). 1986. *The Social Life of Things: Commodities in Cultural Perspective.* Cambridge: Cambridge University Press.

Arnoldi, Mary Jo. 2006. 'Youth festivals and museums: the cultural politics of public memory in postcolonial Mali'. *Africa Today* 52(4):55–76.

Ba Konaré, Adam. 1993. *Dictionnaire des femmes célèbres du Mali (des temps mythico-légendaires au 26 mars 1991) précédé d'une analyse sur le rôle et l'image de la femme dans l'histoire du Mali.* Bamako: Editions Jamana.

Barber, Karin. 1999. 'Quotation in the constitution of Yorùbá oral texts'. *Research in African Literatures* 30, 2:17–41.

Bazin, Jean. 1979. 'La production d'un récit historique'. *Cahiers d'Études africaines* XIX(73–6), 1-4:435–83.

Benjamin, Walter. 1980. 'Das Kunstwerk im Zeitalter seiner technischen Reproduzierbarkeit'. In his: *Gesammelte Schriften* (ed. by Rolf Tiedermann and Hermann Schweppenhäuser). Frankfurt/Main: Suhrkamp, vol. 1(2):471–508.

Bourdieu, Pierre. 1992. *Les regles de l'art: Genèse et structure du champ littéraire.* Paris: Seuil.

Chandler, Anupam and Madhavi Sunder. 2004. 'The romance of the public domain'. *California Law Review* 92:1331–73.

Charry, Eric. 2000. *Mande Music: Traditional and Modern Music of the Maninka and Mandinka of Western Africa.* Chicago: University of Chicago Press.

Cissé, Youssouf Tata and Wa Kamissoko. 1988. *La grande geste du Mali.* Vol. 1, *Des origines à la fondation de l'empire.* Paris: Karthala.

——— 1991. *Soundjata, la gloire du Mali.* Paris: Karthala-Arsan.

Cissé, Youssouf Tata. 1994. *La confrérie des chasseurs Malinké et Bambara: mythes, rites et récits initiatiques.* Paris: Editions Nouvelles du Sud.

Conrad, David. 2002. *Somono Bala of the Upper Niger: River People, Charismatic Bards, and Mischievous Music in a West African Culture.* Leiden: Brill.

Diawara, Mamadou. 1990. *La graine de la parole.* Stuttgart: Franz Steiner Verlag.

——— 1996. 'Traditions orales, chanson et média: le griot et l'artiste de l'aire culturelle mande'. *Cahiers d'Études africaines* XXXVI (144), 4:591–612.

——— 2003. *L'empire du verbe – l'éloquence du silence: vers une anthropologie du discours dans les groupes dits dominés au Sahel.* Köln: Rüdiger Köppe Verlag.

——— 2011. 'Comment peut-on être auteur? De la création dans un contexte de tradition orale en Afrique subsaharienne'. In: Justin Bisanswa and Kasereka Kavwahirehi (eds). *Dire le social dans le roman francophone contemporain.* Paris: Honoré Champion, 33–52.

Dieterlen, Germaine and Youssouf Cissé. 1972. *Les fondements de la société d'initiation du Komo.* Paris: Mouton.

Duràn, Lucy. 1989. 'Key to N'Dour: roots of the Senegalese star'. *Popular Music* 8(3):275–84.

——— 1995. 'Jelimusow: the superwoman of Malian music'. In: Graham Furniss/Liz Gunner (eds). *Power, Marginality, and African Oral Literature*. Cambridge: Cambridge University Press, 197–207.

Edelman, Bernard. 2004. *Le sacre de l'auteur*. Paris: Seuil.

Erasmus, Desiderius. 1992. *Eloge de la folie* (trans. Pierre de Nolhac). Flammarion: Paris.

Foucault, Michel. 1994. 'Qu'est-ce qu'un auteur'. In: *Dits et écrits*, Paris, Gallimard.

Goehr, Lydia. 1992. 'Writing music history'. *History and Theory* 31:182–99.

Goodman, Jane. 2002. '"Stealing our heritage?": women's folksongs, copyright law, and the public domain in Algeria'. *Africa Today* 49(1):85–97.

——— 2005. *Berber Culture on the World Stage: From Village to Video*. Bloomington: Indiana University Press.

Hale, Thomas. 1998. *Griots and Griottes*. Bloomington/Indianapolis: Indiana University Press.

Hoffman, Barbara. 2001. *Griots at War: Conflict, Conciliation, and Caste in Mande*. Bloomington/Indianapolis: Indiana University Press.

Info Prodej. 2006. 'La réforme de la justice au Mali: Prodej 2000–2006: Les partenaires apprécient le bilan', found at www.justicemali.org/www.justicemali.org/bulletin07.htm, accessed 28 March 2012.

Kéïta, Cheick Chérif. 2009. *L'ambassadeur de la musique au Mali*. Paris: Grandvaux.

Koné, Assane. 2010. 'Tata Bambo, une carrière au fil des cinquante ans du Mali'. *Le Républicain*, 19 August 2010, found at www.journaldumali.com/article.php?aid=1901, accessed 8 July 2015.

Larkin, Brian. 2008. *Signal and Noise: Media, Infrastructure, and Urban Culture in Nigeria*. Durham/London: Duke University Press.

Lévi-Strauss, Claude. 1952. 'La notion d'archaïsme en ethnologie'. *Cahiers internationaux de sociologie* XII:3–25.

Présidence de la République. 2008. Loi N° 08-024 du 23 juillet 2008 fixant le régime de la propriété littéraire et artistique en république du Mali. Coulouba, Bamako, Mali.

Schulz, Dorothea. 2001. *Perpetuating the Politics of Praise*. Köln: Rüdiger Köppe Verlag.

Stewart, Gary. 2000. *Rumba on the River: A History of the Popular Music of the Two Congos*. London: Verso.

Traoré, Karim. 2000. *Le jeu et le sérieux: essai d'anthropologie littéraire sur la poésie épique des chasseurs du Mande (Afrique de l'Ouest)*. Köln: Rüdiger Köppe Verlag.

Van der Wiele, Brieuc. 2010. 'L'impact du NON sur la politique culturelle guinéenne: indépendance politique et "décolonisation" culturelle'. In: Odile Goerg, Céline Pauthier and Abdoulaye Diallo (eds). *Le NON de la Guinée (1958): Entre mythe, relecture historique et résonances contemporaines*. Paris: l'Harmattan, 159–78.

Waterman, Christopher. 1995. 'Our tradition is a very modern tradition: popular music and the construction of pan-Yoruba identity'. *Ethnomusicology* 34(3):367–79.

White, Bob. 2008. *Rumba Rules: The Politics of Dance Music in Mobutu's Zaire*. Durham: Duke University Press.

Zahan, Dominique. 1970. *Religion, spiritualité et pensée africaines*. Paris: Payot.

INTERVIEWS

With Mariam Bagayogo in March 2010; she is a famous singer leaving now in Bamako. She is more than 70 years old but still performs with amazing dexterity. I interviewed her in Bamako in March 2010. *Bassabougou* and *Ciwara* are among her most famous pieces.

With Mandé Moussa Diakité in 2009; he is deputy to the director of the Bureau malien des droits d'auteurs, very knowledgeable, and was until his promotion a few months earlier, chief of the department of documentation. He is author of an MA entitled *La piraterie des œuvres musicales dans le district de Bamako: cas du Dabanani*. *Mémoire de maîtrise*, Institut national de la jeunesse et des sports (Bamako), 2006.

With Diarra M'Baye Boubacar in March 2009, a retired producer of the Office de Radiodiffusion Télévision du Mali who created the programme *Etoiles du Mali* in December 1992.

With Aïssé Touré in April 2010, who grew up in Kolokani, Mariam Bagayogo's town, and whose grandfather, Lakamy Sylla, was a District Commissioner and one of Bagayogo's promoters..

With Bounèye Traoré in 2009; he was the most experienced sound technician of the National Radio of Mali. He started in the colonial times as sound specialist at Radio Soudan and carried out training sessions, among other countries, in Germany. He retired in the 1980s.

CHAPTER 10

Music for everyone

The dynamics of piracy in Cameroon

©©©©©©©©©©

ALEXIE TCHEUYAP

Rapid developments in information technology drastically transformed the entertainment industry and made access to music exceptionally cheap, easy and, at the same time, massively fraudulent during the past couple of decades. With the arrival of the internet, US courts had to step in, in response to an epidemic of illegal file sharing, which, with Napster in 1999, had become a simple pastime for music lovers. When Steve Jobs came up with iTunes, it appeared to be the best workable solution for reconciling culture and technology. The reconstruction of business models in the music industry has had a huge impact on the sales of CDs, which, before the invention of iTunes, MP3 players and the storage of music in hard-drives, were the most efficient way of storing songs. Songs began to be sold incredibly cheaply. This change of the business model of the music industry has completely transformed popular cultures and has greatly increased the accessibility of music to consumers, especially in developed countries. However, Ben Sisario of the *New York Times* quotes an astounding statistic from the International Federation of the Phonographic Industry: between 2003 and 2010, after the advent of iTunes, overall music sales declined by 32 per cent (Sisario 2011). The music industry has therefore undergone a drastic shift with implications, above all, for musicians in the Global South, whose work remains more vulnerable to piracy than that of artists in the developed world. Cameroon is a notable example.

In an interview with *Le Messager* newspaper, Richard Bona, a world-famous Cameroonian jazz musician, made an unexpected statement about music piracy in his home country: 'There is no music distributor in Cameroon. When there is a good distributor, you will have original CDs. In the meantime, as far as non-original (i.e. fake) CDs are concerned, we must do with what we have. *I am not against piracy.*' In the same interview, in order to solve the problem, Bona pleads for what may be called 'selective' or 'strategic' piracy in the following terms:

> For those local artists who only have access to the local market, solutions need to be found. You cannot make piracy disappear just like that. This is what I propose. One can tell people: 'Please preserve local artists from piracy and leave them alone. Rather copy and loot people like Richard Bona and Manu Dibango.' We must find solutions like these, and not just going after pirated CD sellers in the streets.[1]

Bona perceives piracy not only as a survival strategy for those who generate fake CDs, but also as the direct consequence of an infrastructural and economic impediment. A desperate complaint by Longuè Longuè, another Cameroonian musician, echoes Richard Bona's plea for 'strategic piracy' that would help protect local artists, confirming Bona's point that local artists are extremely vulnerable to this practice. Before the official release of his new album *Child of God*, several of its tracks were already circulating in Cameroonian cities and were played in nightclubs. But piracy is a problem because 'production cost me 20,000 Euros [ca. £17,000]. I released thousands of CDs I am not even sure to sell because the market is already inundated with counterfeit copies of this album.'[2]

What Longuè Longuè describes is all too notorious in Cameroon and elsewhere in the Global South, where struggles for cultural appropriation in times of persistent economic hardship have diluted the need or, worse, the ability to distinguish between what is legal or not, what is an original and what is a copy. Ravi Sundaram in his influential *Pirate Modernity* (2010) even argues that modern technology and piracy are like the two sides of the same coin, and that one cannot appear without the other (see also Jedlowski in this volume).

Longuè Longuè complains about piracy and Richard Bona pleads for selective piracy only. Bona suggests that piracy has made artists better known to Cameroonian music lovers, although it has also endangered the profitability of their profession, especially as finding a reliable producer has become more

---

1   Interview with Richard Bona by Richard Tamba in *Le Messager*, 30 December 2008, found at: www.cameroon-info.net/stories/0,24258,@,richard-bona-se-confie-laquo-piratez-les-richard-bona-manu-dibango-et-laissez-le.html, accessed 27 August 2011.
2   'Album: Longuè Longuè lynche la justice populaire', www.cameroon-info.net/stories/0,29032,@,album-longue-longue-lynche-la-justice-populaire.html, accessed 11 July 2011

and more difficult, to the point that several musicians are their own producers. According to a document prepared by the *Groupement Inter-Patronal du Cameroun* – GICAM, the national association incorporating most influential businesses – on illegal commerce from 2006 to 2009, more than 90 per cent of artworks circulating in Cameroon derive from piracy, which represents fiscal and customs loss of about 8.4 billion FCFA for the government (GICAM 2009).

In this chapter, I wish to argue that the piracy crisis in the recorded music sector is the consequence of an immense technological transformation. This transformation of music began with the technical possibilities of storing music on electronic media and the introduction of the international copyright law, which protects individual artists and their work. It is important to keep in mind this historical situation provided the basis for the emergence of electronic music piracy. Copyright laws have existed in Cameroon since colonial times, but they only became of considerable relevance with the exposure of music to new technologies. This situation has altered the sense of music ownership by privileging the rights of the individual artist, and has contributed to the emergence of new norms in the of distribution of music.

Creative individuals quickly saw the production of copies of music on these media as an entrepreneurial opportunity. Musicians, producers and pirates are the main actors in this scenario. As soon as the new media had become accessible, reproduction of music proliferated for financial reasons. Some were distributed legally by their owners, or by producers of music that had acquired the copyrights; others, illegally, by pirates who had not acquired these rights. Piracy is by definition an activity which undermines established norms, and in states that are reluctant to prosecute pirates, sooner or later piracy itself becomes the new normality.

This chapter has two sections. The first is a historical approach to the practice of musical reproduction and performance in Cameroon as I experienced it in the 1980s and 1990s. At that time, copying music was tolerated by both state officials and artists. Artists were still paid royalties by a company existing since colonial times. I have confirmed these findings with several cultural leaders as well as with a Cameroonian musician, André Marie Tala, whose insights help better understand the usages of piracy. The situation changed recently with the turbulence encountered by the copyright management companies, from and with the introduction of new technologies of copying, which created a piracy crisis in Cameroon. The second section focuses on the operating modes of piracy and is based on data gathered through interviews with music retailers in Yaounde. It is based on personal observations in the field, interviews with a veteran Cameroonian musician and with sellers of pirated music in Yaounde, the capital of Cameroon.

Performance and public copying as social practices

Copyright is no less the product of historical development in Africa than it is anywhere else in the world. In the Cameroon Grassfields, for example, some of the music and popular dances were free to perform for everybody, without financial reward attached to them. Others belonged to specific groups of people, who were compensated for their performance (see Röschenthaler 2011). The choreography and the music accompanying the dances were transmitted through weekly or monthly practices that used to take place on Sundays afternoon.[3] Examples are dances like the Ndangji, the Mbaya, the Ndimassale, the Mandjong or even the very secret Kounga of the Western Region in Cameroon.[4] Such music and dances were performed for specific events, such as death, birth, war, coronations, meetings or official ceremonies. Members of cult associations or cultural groups trained regularly, and the dancing steps, as well as the musical beats and tones were 'reproduced' this way, that is, *by practice and repetition.* These groups had the right to claim compensation when invited to perform at various occasions. This generally consisted of fixed quantities of cooked food and drink, live animals such as goats and, at times, a negotiable amount of money. Dance groups and cult associations were recognizable as coming from a specific community or area in the Western Region of Cameroon. Dance and music were not owned by an individual but by the cult association or dance group, or in other cases by the community in general. Until the 1980s, the technology to record music and dances on a large scale was not available, and copyright was not a big issue (for the ownership and local forms of rights in performances, see Röschenthaler in this volume).

In this context, artwork was reproduced by means of memory, rehearsal and practice, not mechanically. Payment was made directly to the artists and not by an institution in charge of centrally collecting and redistributing royalties to its members. During performances, an exceptionally talented dancer could be 'sprayed' with money, because of his/her performance, by people the dancer personally knew that wanted to signal their presence at the ceremony. Monetary compensation has become more important over the years, and cultural groups have been created with the aim of using performance (music and dance) to make money. This is the case with Bend

---

3   The examples I quote here are from personal experience in the Western Region of Cameroon in the 1990s.

4   For illustrations and descriptions of Bamileke dances in the Western Region, see, for example, Harter 1986 or Perrois 1993.

Skin, a very popular dance from the Western Region.[5] Bend Skin groups can require payments amounting to more than £155 in order to perform at parties or death ceremonies. Although many members of these groups make a living from this activity, they do not actually 'own' these rhythms, as the same songs and dances are performed by different groups at different locations for the same purpose. The 'rights' to ownership here are not the 'private' rights of an individual. With the introduction of the technical means, these groups began to record and sell their performances on DVDs.

Moreover, during the second half of the twentieth century, Cameroonian (and other African) musicians have systematically borrowed folk performances and transformed them into songs, a process that has made them individual copyright holders of collective cultural heritage. In Cameroon, the most notable cases are André Marie Tala, Manu Dibango, Pierre Didy Tchakounte and all the Bikutsi musicians. The majority of the repertoire of Jacques Yams, a Toronto-based musician, consists of easily recognisable Bamileke songs. In other words, by using technology to reproduce and play popular collective music that used to belong to vast communities, musicians have transformed themselves into *individual copyright holders* (for a similar discussion of Algeria see Goodman 2005). Technological means of reproduction have not only successfully transformed performances, but also made them more popular and at the same time exposed to piracy, which has meanwhile reached an endemic proportion in Cameroon.

The copying of music and performances is nothing unusual. But the norms of what is considered an acceptable activity or an illegitimate practice have changed with time. The concept of copyright and the illegality of the multiplication of recorded music only emerged in a specific historical constellation. Walter Benjamin in his seminal essay 'The work of art in the age of mechanical reproduction' rightly indicates that

> *[in] principle a work of art has always been reproducible.* Man-made artifacts could always be imitated by men. Replicas were made by pupils in practice of their craft, by masters for diffusing their works, and, finally, by third parties in the pursuit of gain. *Mechanical reproduction of a work of art, however, represents something new. Historically, it advanced intermittently and in leaps at long intervals, but with accelerated intensity.* The Greeks

---

5   André Marie Tala has brought Bend Skin music and dance to the popular scene and made it a virtually national rhythm, known to a much wider public. It was the very popular tune 'Bend Skin' that brought the style to the attention of the public. From that point on, many other musicians and groups playing in that genre began to emerge.

knew only two procedures of technically reproducing works of art: founding and stamping.... The enormous changes which printing, the mechanical reproduction of writing, has brought about in literature are a familiar story.

(Benjamin 1970:219, emphases added)

What Benjamin (1970) foresaw remains essential to the history and development of cultural productions. He mainly focuses on the copying of art and the printing of literary work. He basically indicates that reproductions have democratized arts and provided it with a much needed emancipation because

for the first time in world history, mechanical reproduction emancipates the work of art from its parasitical dependence on ritual. *To an ever greater degree the work of art reproduced becomes the work of art designed for reproducibility.* From a photographic negative, for example, one can make any number of prints; *to ask for the 'authentic' print makes no sense. But the instant the criterion of authenticity ceases to be applicable to artistic production, the total function of art is reversed.* Instead of being based on ritual, it begins to be based on another practice – politics.

(Benjamin 1970:254, emphases added).

Interesting in Benjamin's observation is that fakes are handmade copies declared as originals, but that the mechanical copy is not a fake. He compares the copying of art with the mechanical reproduction by print, but he does not discuss the question of ownership or the right to make copies. While Benjamin is fascinated by the opportunities of mechanical copying as a feature of modernity, Michel Foucault situates the increasingly endemic forms of copying in post-modernity. The dissolution of the original, the first-time and faithfulness is typical of a (post)modern age of 'simulacrum' (Foucault 1977:172) in which the copy and the original can no longer be differentiated. Moreover, Gilles Deleuze argues in *The Logic of Sense* that imitation is now viewed with indecent admiration, for 'The simulacrum is not a degraded copy. It harbours a positive power which denies the original and the copy, the model and the reproduction.' (1992:262). What he describes is in a way central to the Cameroonian context, where (pirate) copies, and copies of copies, triumph and infest the market, to the point where originals have become suspicious, if not useless.

In his book *On the Postcolony*, Achille Mbembe (2001) argues that because of the success of the local authoritarian regime in crushing most popular uprisings, cultural strategies for challenging and resisting the state have generated a situation where 'Everything has gone underground. Everything now has a reverse side.' (2001:147). The distribution of music in Cameroon comes with a few intriguing paradoxes. This alternative economic production system derives from a political culture fraught with a complete lack of authenticity, with historical and social ramifications. This political context has cultural and economic implications in that, on the one hand, the political experience of 'going underground' was a necessary strategy to avoid censorship and government brutality. In the music sector, the black market of piracy deprives artists of their revenues while allowing consumers to have better access to music, albeit of poor quality, hence making counterfeiters the economic beneficiaries of someone else's work. Pirated music CDs are openly sold to a public that has little ability or willingness to determine its 'underground source'. The source does not always matter to the consumer at the receiving end of the cultural and economic delinquency which, for Bona, is tolerable as long as the pirated work is that of a world-famous artist like him.

The public has reacted in a similar way to other illegally traded products. In the 1990s, Cameroonians were used to using smuggled petrol or '*zouazoua*', which was imported through specific circuits from Nigeria and even from other parts of Cameroon. Like CDs, *zouazoua* was openly sold in streets, and there was 'real', that is, authentic and good quality, as well as 'well-mixed' *zouazoua*, to which water or diesel oil had been added. Interestingly, the state was able to put an end to the commercialization of *zouazoua*, petrol being a more profitable tax-generating commodity than, for example, music.

Before the 1990s, copying music already flourished in Cameroon. It started with tape recordings, which were sold in stores called *discothèques*. These were fully legal. They paid taxes and specialized in transferring recorded music from LPs to audio tapes. Copyright had existed since colonial times, but it was not of much concern in daily life either for artists or for state officials. Whenever a new album was released, owners of these stores would buy *a single copy* of it and then record it to a near infinite number of tapes, until the LP was completely scratched. There were 60- and 90-minute tapes, which cost between 1,000–1,500 CFA (about £1.25–£1.85) to be recorded. These shopkeepers did not need to be 'underground' in order to perform an activity that, for the Cameroonian artist André Marie Tala, was equivalent to piracy. However, it is difficult to determine exactly how much money was ever paid to artists; according to André Marie Tala it was absolutely nothing.

In a conversation held on 10 September 2011, André Marie Tala explained that before the creation of the *Société Camerounaise des Droits d'Auteurs* (SOCADRA) on 22 September 1979 by former President Ahmadou Ahidjo, copyright fees were paid in Cameroon by the French *Société des Auteurs, Compositeurs et Editeurs de Musique* (SACEM). Every quarter (January, April, July and October) SACEM paid royalties to artists. SACEM had a French delegate who came to Cameroon in order to administer these rights. Because *all* LPs were produced in France, and before releasing a new record the producer had to pay any copyright fees, the exact number of LPs produced was known, and because it was not possible for individuals to engage in fraudulent activities that would saturate the market with music, compensation was never a problem. Moreover, in each radio station, whenever there was a programme, journalists would give the name of the technicians and also mention the person in charge of copyrights, who took note of all the songs played during the programme. The French administrator of the SACEM would generate reports from these notes and make sure that all artists were paid.

SACEM ran copyright matters from colonial times till after independence, when SOCADRA was created. Subsequently, over the next three decades, Cameroonian musicians' financial interests were served, with more or less success, by several companies: the *Société Camerounaise des Droits d'auteurs* (SOCADRA), the *Société Civile Nationale des Droits d'Auteurs* (SOCINADA), Cameroon Music Corporation and then, until 7 September 2011, by the *Société Civile Camerounaise de l'Art Musical* (SOCAM), which has been recently dissolved.[6]

6 The history of music copyrights in Cameroon is similar to that of local political upheavals. Former President Ahmadou Ahidjo (in power from 1960–82) created SOCADRA to take over the copyright business from the French. In the early 1990s, Augustin Kontchou Kouomegni, then Minister of Information and Culture, helped create the SOCINADA, which was then run by one of Cameroon's most renowned legal experts, Professor Stanislas Melone. The company became the site for all kinds of conflicts, with rival groups of musicians claiming legitimacy to run it and several elections cancelled or fraught with fraud. It was succeeded by the Cameroon Music Corporation (CMC), which, contrary to previous companies which included all creators, was specifically concerned with musical productions, and, for the first time, run by a musician, Sam Mbende. After several conflicts and court cases, Manu Dibango was elected its director. He had so many problems with the administration and, especially, with the Minister of Culture, who wanted to control the financial resources of the company, that he had to give up. His replacement was Odile Ngaska, a local religious singer whose election was said to be so exceptionally fraudulent that the Minister of Culture arbitrarily dissolved CMC to create SOCAM. This new company was run until 7 September 2011 by the same Odile Ngaska. After a court case filed by Sam Mbende (former president of CMC), challenging the legality of the creation of SOCAM and the dissolution of CMC by Ama Tutu Muna, Cameroon's Minister of Culture, Cameroon's Supreme Court ruled on 7 September 2011 to dissolve SOCAM. There are now talks about merging the two rival entities, SOCAM and CMC, and given the volatility and sluggishness of anything that happens in Cameroon, no one can predict what will happen.

According to Tala, the 'official' and public piracy by *discothèques* remained very 'rudimentary', and artists received some money from the government and SACEM anyway. Artists also derived 'extra' money by driving from city to city to sell copies of their own album to the owners of these music shops, who occasionally would keep a few extra copies on hand for the privileged individuals who could afford one. Although these *discothèque* owners did not – and could not either, because there was no legal framework – pay local artists, it should be mentioned that foreign musicians were also victims of this 'open' piracy, as the recorded tapes often contained music from all over the world. Differently put, both local and foreign artists were duplicated with neither restriction nor control in these stores, and the tax paid was generally so meagre (about £6.50 per year) that one is left to wonder what kind of royalties, if any, could ever be paid to artists by the government. Foreign artists like Michael Jackson, ABBA or Michel Sardou, to name just a few, probably never imagined that their work was being enjoyed almost freely in remote countries.

French musicians were certainly paid by SACEM, but authors of records not produced in France and reproduced in Cameroon probably did not get any cheques from its Cameroonian branch. This is also true for the world-famous musicians such as Bob Marley, James Brown or Jimmy Cliff who were very popular in Cameroon. Like Richard Bona, they probably did not need money from Cameroon to live. Nevertheless, in 1986 the British Phonographic Industry (BPI) suggested that a blank tape sold is a record not sold. In the same year, the IFPI, the International Federation of Phonogram and Videogram Producers, even wanted to impose a levy on the sale of blank tapes and recording equipment.

In the times of SACEM, when copyrights were paid, the more talented artists were able to survive with their music, although none became rich from it. Additional income came from concerts, which people still attended, and the proceeds were paid directly to them in cash, without intermediaries apart from the concert promoter/organizer. Artists also could experience – what has become rare these days – the pleasure of interacting with the public that came to enjoy their music. Improved technology, wider audiences and changing questions of ownership have since that time made issues of copyright much more important.

In his article 'Copyright and the music business', Simon Frith (1988:61–2) indicates that in the 1980s piracy constituted a modest 30 per cent of the tape and record market in Africa, compared to a ballooning 66 per cent in Asia. Since the year 2000, Cameroon has been witnessing resurgence in the trade of pirated music DVDs and CDs. In 2008, the Music Committee against Piracy (MCAP) reported that counterfeiting and piracy costs Cameroon over ten billion FCFA per year, and hundreds of billions of dollars worldwide. The Committee initiated an anti-piracy awareness week in 2008, during which it distributed a flyer stating that the counterfeiting of artistic works is linked to a multitude of factors, including the economic dynamics of the black market, weak anti-piracy enforcement, globalization, the technological boom and the invasion of Cameroonian markets by Asian products (Sony, Amstech etc.).[7] As predicted by Frith, piracy is growing exponentially, to the point that the quantity of counterfeit CDs dumped on the market is larger than that of lawfully manufactured CDs. The following section is based on conversations with sellers and field research undertaken in Yaounde in April and May 2011.[8]

Piracy at work: supply, production and distribution

In his *The Practice of Everyday Life*, Michel de Certeau (2002) describes and interprets the tactical strategies of the everyday and its alternative productivity, characterized by ruses, fragmentation (the result of circumstances), clandestine nature and quasi-invisibility (2002:31). Piracy belongs in this domain, and is by itself a 'cultural activity', because it makes commodities available to a larger public. Brian Larkin (2004) talks of a sort of 'creative aesthetics' when analysing the Nigerian video industry, giving credit to 'cultural creativity' such as piracy. In Cameroon, piracy has become one of the major avenues for the economic survival of youth who have no other occupation.[9] In the interview quoted above, Bona considers piracy an economic necessity for those who otherwise would have absolutely nothing to live on. As he puts it, 'Look at it carefully. A small boy calls me in the street "Hey Boss", and shows me four or five of my CDs for sale. Well, these CDs provide food for a few children in

---

7　Pamphlet: 'Anti-piracy awareness week' (6–24 May 2008).

8　Preliminary research was carried out by my assistant, Ms Marie-Nadège Tchogo Momo. I later met with the same and several other CD sellers in June 2011. It was extremely difficult to make an appointment or get any of them to speak. Although they considered our investigation as an opportunity for them to earn extra income for an activity where competition is high and no revenue guaranteed, they needed to make sure we were not working for the police.

9　Many of the sellers consulted for this research were twenty-six years old or younger. Some held university degrees in various disciplines. Others were students selling fake CDs as a summer job. According to a 2009 World Bank report, unemployment and poverty are particularly severe among Cameroonian youth, with some 60 per cent living on less than £1.25 a day in rural areas. 50 per cent are 'out of labour force' (those who have given up searching for a job) and only 7 per cent are considered 'unemployed' (people actively looking for a job). In urban areas, the 'out of labour force' statistic is almost 60 per cent, and 41 per cent in rural areas. 12 per cent are 'unemployed' in cities, and 3 per cent in villages. The underemployment rate is 31 per cent. For more, see World Bank 2009.

homes.' The only objection to these sales that Bona has is that these deprived citizens should feed only on world stars such as him. Such alternative strategies, gone 'underground', with public exposure and displays of its products, are a variation of what Mbembe calls 'revenge from below'. That is, 'subaltern populations' have no choice but to develop ways to resist a vampire state (1991). In a context in which the corrupt post-colonial government has left citizens, many of whom are university graduates, with no job opportunities, and where it is well-known that when paid, tax money is misspent, then the piracy industry, as well as the open display of its counterfeit products, appears to be nothing less than another resistance strategy. Although counterfeiting is illegal, the open sale of fakes, right in government buildings, is a clear rejection of state legislation. According to Sundaram, piracy becomes a superstructure, an industry with its own networks:

> For urban populations long used to more stable sites like the cinema hall, piracy's decentralized proliferation induced a narcotic disorientation of the senses. Populations conceived by state media policy as an abstract public now entered piracy's landscape of infinite attractions, where images, sounds, objects, moved rapidly through networks of proliferation, small shops, bazaars, video theaters, friends. Piracy escapes the boundaries of space, of particular networks, of form, a before and after, a *limit.* Although it has complex strategies of deployment and movement, piracy is like no other form of expression, respecting no formal barriers. The lines between the surface and the inside, original and copy, which transfixed the Western modernist archive and its postmodern reformulations, are called into question in piracy.
>
> (2010:112, original emphasis)

It is within a comparable technology and superstructure that piracy in Cameroon can be understood. The following sections address the 'piracy chain' as observed during fieldwork in Yaounde. The 'piracy chain' may be divided into two main categories, one of which is 'individual' and 'small-scale', and a second which is much broader, organized and truly 'industrial'.

As a student in the 1990s, I recalled that most bedrooms in student's dormitories had radio-cassettes,[10] which were used to dub tapes for friends. This practice was routine and perceived as very legitimate, since most could not afford to purchase an original tape. With the advent and, later, affordability

---

10   The models then used (from Kenwood, JVC, Sharp, Sansui, Sony) have completely disappeared from the market, which now only rarely carries tape recorders.

of computers as well as cheaper CD and DVD players or iPods, also came the ability to copy more easily for free and easy access to an almost unlimited supply of music. This stage is generally 'personal', in that the music lover interacts within a very limited network. In these instances, an individual goes to a music shop or to an internet café with a blank CD, an MP3 player or a USB memory stick. She or he either downloads music from various websites or just pays a shopkeeper to obtain the music desired online. This practice is even more difficult to quantify. But most importantly, piracy here is generally for *individual consumption*, as the music lover either cannot afford the original or is unwilling to pay for it. Those who are a little more computer or internet savvy do it themselves.

Another example of individual and small-scale piracy is the traffic and exchange of music files among relatives and friends. The people we interviewed confessed that it is a very common, if not routine, practice to simply share audio files between music lovers, who genuinely believe they are doing nothing wrong. They have pirated works from both local and foreign musicians. Many simply want the music, and are not necessarily bothered about knowing the titles of songs, or having a case or pictures of the musician, which on pirate CDs are of extremely poor quality anyway. In addition, copies can be either partial or total, depending on what is available. Both works of single authors and playlists are very common. The size of the selection does not really matter, as huge music collections can cost very little or be free.

'Industrial piracy' operates a little differently and involves several parties: suppliers, publishers, distributors, vendors and consumers. The publishers (or pirates) need suppliers, who furnish them with 'raw materials' required for counterfeiting and piracy. These materials comprise, among others, blank CDs, CD writers/burners, computers equipped with mastering software, CD covers and holsters. Importers and business persons engage in the sale of these electronics and computer equipment. Their activity is legal and recognized, but they supply the potential pirates with materials. Suppliers interviewed in Yaounde admit that their biggest customers are pirate publishers, who they know very well and with whom they maintain good relationships. Referring to these publishers, Mr Onana, a supplier, acknowledges that: 'they earn us much money and promote the development of our activity'.[11] He says they (the suppliers) are very familiar with the pirate publishers, but cannot denounce them because such a move would end their lucrative business and render themselves unemployed. Another supplier, Mr Mballa, voices his concerns via

---

11   Onana, 38, an electronics retailer at the Yaounde central market, Yaounde, 20 April 2011.

the following question: 'If we denounce the pirates, with what shall we feed our poor families. It is a matter of survival.'[12]

Suppliers fall into four categories: first, those who provide publishers with blank CDs, cases, writers/burners, mastering software, computers, etc. They are usually vendors of appliances, electronic equipment and computers. Second, those who provide publishers with genuine and promotional CDs. These are in fact distributors, artists who want to promote their own music or film, TV and radio hosts, and relatives of artists. The latter sometimes steal the album masters of musicians and sell them to publishers. For example, the Bikutsi artist Lady Ponce admitted that the master of her third album, *Atomic Bomb*, had been stolen during a burglary of her home and was later sold to pirates.[13] Third, those who provide pirate publishers with the most popular or trendy CDs or VCDs. These are studio technicians from radio and television stations. Henry Tedongmo Teko claims that 85 per cent of videos available on the black market come from television channels. 'That's why the images of these videos always have the logo of a television channel.' (Teko 2008:53). Fourth, IT professionals who install and maintain mastering software in the computers of pirate publishers.

The various suppliers mentioned above are attracted to the business because it is lucrative. For them, the viability of their business hinges on the efficiency of the market for pirated music and films. They have much to lose if the market disappears. That is why they sustain its network and have no qualms about bribing law enforcement agents whenever their interests are at stake. Publishers also play an important part in cultural looting.

Publishers are people who are responsible for publishing artistic works. Under Article 42 of Law No. 2000/011 relating to copyright and adjacent rights, the publishing contract is an agreement by which the copyright holder authorizes a person called the publisher, under defined conditions, to produce a fixed number of copies of a work and to ensure their publication.[14] A pirate publisher is anyone who produces copies of artistic works without a publishing contract, that is to say, without permission from the copyright holder. Pirate publishers are at the second level of the piracy chain, next to the suppliers with whom they work. Admittedly, pirate publishers carry out the most delicate activity within the piracy chain. In the jargon of the trade, they are called 'copiers', because they are responsible for producing copies of CDs, DVDs and VCDs. They use purchased original products to manufacture fake

---

12   Mballa, 36, an electronics and computer retailer at the Mokolo market, Yaounde, 19 April 2011.
13   See www.thegoducamer.cm, accessed 15 December 2011.
14   Law No. 2000/011. This law exists since 2000.

ones without having the right to produce them. In other words, they purchase one 'authentic' copy of a CD or DVD and proceed, through sophisticated technology, to make multiple copies of the same work. The materials used are none other than the raw materials purchased from suppliers: blank and genuine CDs, DVDs and VCDs; writers/burners;[15] computers equipped with Nero, Power DVD and Roxio burning software; cases; printers; scanners etc. Unlike suppliers, publishers are not easily detected, because their offices, called 'labs', are located in their homes. Teko gives a very accurate description of these labs in the following excerpt:

> There are always in the corner of the room hundreds and often thousands of CDs, VCDs, DVDs already burned and ready for delivery. On the floor, you can see bits of paper which contain photographs of musicians and the titles of their songs. On the table is the purchase order register which is a large notebook in which all orders are registered.
>
> (Teko 2008:63)

Pirate publishers have transformed the copying of artistic works into a major activity. For Jérôme, a pirate publisher for two years, 'one must be a professional to successfully burn and present the titles'. He admits that he owes his success to his IT knowledge, because 'you cannot make it if you do not master IT'.[16] In an unpublished Master's dissertation 'Piraterie ou contrefaçon des œuvres musicales: facteurs explicatifs, modes opératoires et impacts sur les artistes-musiciens à Yaoundé', Joël Christian Nkeng à Nkeng describes a pirate industrial facility with the capacity to produce 100 CDs in fifteen minutes (2010:55). The production is packed and shipped nightly to big cities in Cameroon. With such a capability, if the shop works only one hour a day, it will flood the market with 400 copies. Even taking into account the various costs, it is clear just how many CDs or DVDs can be placed on the market from this production site alone.

In this case just mentioned, having some start-up funds and, especially, technology are key to running the business. Jérôme says he embraced the business on the advice of a friend with whom he had trained in computer science. For him, it was the best way to escape unemployment and use his computer skills. He confessed that at the outset it was not easy, because he had no capital. He had, nonetheless, a computer and some burning software. With the loan obtained from his friend, he could start the business in his room. He

---

15   These devices, in the jargon of the milieu, are called 'layers'.
16   Jérôme, 33, a computer specialist (publisher), Mendong-Yaounde, 19 April 2011.

bought some blank CDs, DVDs and VCDs, cases, a scanner, a printer and genuine CDs, DVDs and VCDs.[17]

To justify their actions, some publishers claim that they contribute to the promotion of the artistic works of authors. Some even contend that certain musicians owe their fame to them, and that for that reason publishers deserve some praise. This way of thinking suggests that publishers are conscious of the consequences of their actions on the nation's music and film industry. In 2011, however, Andé Marie Tala reported to me that music piracy was a major causal factor in the decline of artistic production in Cameroon, because it 'kills' artistic works. Many music producers have either gone out of business for lack of profit or are facing bankruptcy. The production company Ebobolofio that was the pride of Bikutsi artists is no longer in business.[18] Others such as Nkuli Nnam and Angoula Angoula have also disappeared. MC Pop music and Mendy Show left the sector to pursue other activities. Today, artists walk around with their album demos in hand seeking courageous producers who can survive piracy. However, neither publishers nor suppliers are solely responsible for this fiasco. It is the distributors who form the other class of counterfeiter.

Publishers deliver the fruits of their labour to distributors, who in turn make these counterfeited CDs, DVDs and VCDs available to vendors. They thus serve as intermediaries between the publisher and the vendor, who generally do not know each other. The distribution of counterfeit films and music is a risky business, because distributors are often betrayed by vendors when they are pressed by the police. In other words, when a vendor is caught, he may be forced to disclose where he gets his commodity. In addition, distributors always maintain storage spaces in specific locations, close to their homes, where thousands of pirated CDs, DVDs and VCDs are amassed, ready for delivery. Our research has revealed that, given the risk involved in the business, distributors generally operate on an interim basis while searching for a safer activity.

The distributors are mostly small operators who hire and manage a number of vendors, with whom they establish oral contracts. These contracts stipulate that the vendor must pay them a certain amount at the end of each day. Some vendors confess they were recruited by their boss (distributor) through an intermediary who connected them. Clotel admits that 'it is thanks to my cousin Achille, who is older than me, that I got recruited by the boss Mr Jérôme'.[19] A recruitment policy based on certain affinities is not accidental; it

17   Ibid.
18   Pascal Nguiamba, see www.journalducameroun.com, accessed 22 May 2011.
19   Clotel 28, a vendor of pirated works, 5 May 2011.

is part of the precautionary measures taken by distributors to hire people they can trust. For nearly all the pirate distributors contacted for the purpose of this research, the distribution business is highly risky, but very profitable, and does not require an enormous amount of effort. This explains the ever-growing number of vendors recruited to expand the business. The distribution sector owes its success to the active involvement of numerous actors who work to ensure that their products are everywhere. According to one Cameroonian artist, their distribution policy is incredibly aggressive, and has succeeded at putting lawful record stores and distributors out of business. The illicit network has thus outperformed the officially authorized one. The distributor owes his activity to vendors strategically chosen to make products available to the larger public.

Pirate vendors are individuals who are responsible for selling pirated products on the streets, and in markets, restaurants, government departments, newsstands, bars, hotels etc. There are two categories of vendors, itinerant and non-itinerant. The former are the most vulnerable, because they and their products are visible. One sees them everywhere, during the day and at night. They are young people, with bags and CDs in hand. They visit places in search of potential customers. From time to time, a passers-by stops and approaches them to enquire about a specific product. The customer may buy a product if the price is acceptable. In either case, the vendor just moves on. Achille, an itinerant vendor who ironically goes by the nickname 'Sam Mbende' (the name of a Cameroonian musician and president of Cameroon Music Corporation, which protected copyrights and tried to fight piracy), describes his working day as follows:

> When I go out every morning, I go out with a huge amount of CDs, DVDs and VCDs that I put in my backpack. With the most requested CDs in hand, I go out to attack. I usually choose a neighbourhood I know well. But before entering the neighbourhood, I present my products in cafeterias and roadside bars. Then I go into the neighbourhood and I present my products to passersby that I meet. I also go to film clubs in popular areas to present trendy movies. If business is not good, I change neighbourhoods. When it is noon, I sit somewhere to rest. I chose a popular corner; in so doing, I will continue to display my products even when I am taking a rest. After my rest, I resume my business and visits in the streets and road intersections till 6 or 7 pm. At the end of the month, I may end up with a profit of over 20,000 FCFA.[20]

---

20 Achille, 28, a vendor of counterfeit CDs, DVDs and VCDs, Acacia-Yaounde, 18 April 2011.

Unlike Achille, Célestin, another vendor, says he starts at 7 p.m. and continues until early morning. He visits bistros, bars and other areas where people dance and listen to music. At these places he presents products to DJs and customers.[21] According to these two vendors, the holiday periods (December, June–August) are good times for business. This makes sense, considering that during the holidays people are looking to have fun; they are freer and want to enjoy themselves listening to music or watching a good film.

Non-itinerant vendors set up their products on the ground or in stalls. The behaviour of these vendors is comparable to that of vendors of other products. When they see a customer approaching, they present their products to them using phrases like: 'Baby, you want the latest CD from Lady Ponce', 'Big Bro, I have the latest Richard Bona', 'Dad, there is music of your era', 'Madam, I have the latest tunes by El Diablo' etc. At midday, like all the other vendors, they take a break and resume business one hour later. Just like the vendors of other products, they, paradoxically, pay taxes for the temporary occupation of public roads (TOPR) in order to sell fake music.

At the Central Post Office area, the Central and the Mokolo Markets in Yaounde, at Mboppi and Ndokoti Markets in Douala, a number of vendors often set up their businesses next to each other. For them, the strategy of operating as a group helps them to defend themselves if attacked. At some stalls, pirated CDs are placed next to the original CDs. The individuals found at these record stalls taking customer orders are either illegal publishers or their customers. Vendors rely on customer segmentation criteria to fix prices. Depending on the customer, they would offer a given CD for 300, 500 or sometimes even 1,000 FCFA. DVD prices also vary. Depending on the customer, the same DVD would sell for 400, 500, 800 or 1,000 FCFA.

The task of non-itinerant vendors is not limited to sales. They also convey market and customer data to distributors, who in turn transmit them to the publishers. When prices drop, publishers minimize costs and losses by marketing low-quality products. When prices go up, they place on the market expensive high-quality products. In this market, competition is fairly administered and the situation of each publisher, distributor or vendor depends on his or her ability to adapt to customer needs and current developments. In any case, this business is driven by a crude law of supply and demand, with quality given little or no consideration. The following table gives a sample list of prices of CDs by various artists. Prices listed below (in CFA Francs) are *average* because the discrepancies among them were at times very sharp. Some sellers had two versions of the same CD, one more expensive than

---

21   Célestin, 29, a vendor of counterfeit CDs, DVDs and VCDs, Mendong-Yaounde, 18 April 2011.

the other because, they say, the CD or software used to copy it was of better quality and the manufacturing costs were more.[22]

Title of Album	Artist	Original copy (FCFA)	Pirated copy (FCFA)	Difference (FCFA)
Best of André Marie Tala	André Marie Tala	4,500	1,000	3,500
Bombe A	Lady Ponce	5,000	500	4,500
Graceland	Paul Simon	2,500	400	2,100
Konkai Makossa	Charlotte Mbango	4,500	400	4,000
La Bible du Makossa	Medley	3,500	500	3,000
Levez les doigts	Aî-Jo Mamadou	4,700	450	4,250
Reverence	Richard Bona	7,500	750	6,250
Saphir	Ben Decca	5,000	600	4,400
Sergeo Polo	Lili	5,000	450	4,250
Thriller	Michael Jackson	3,000	300	2,700
Tiki	Richard Bona	7,500	750	6,250
Wakafrica	Manu Dibango	6,000	500	5,500
Yi Décembre	Bisso Solo	4,000	350	3,650

Table 10.1   List of prices of CDs in Yaounde (2011).[23]

It should be noted that people selling originals are generally 'established', in that they have a spot where they may be located at any time. They also have a vast variety of CDs from many artists to sell, and sophisticated equipment to play albums in which customers are interested. In any case, merchants who sell originals have products of visibly higher quality: the labels, fonts, pictures and sounds of originals are the best. They get these CDs either from artists themselves or from official (read, legal) production companies. These merchants are the real partners in the protection of copyrights and except in one isolated case, not a single pirate copy was found on their stalls. They consider street vendors enemies (of culture).

In such a context, understanding the table above is pretty straightforward. Unless he or she feels a strong cultural patriotism or, alternatively, the need to support artists whose working conditions and difficulties are often unknown, the average Cameroonian would not easily purchase an original CD. This is even truer in times of economic constraint, especially as the counterfeit options are so many. The price gap is far too large to be disregarded. One can easily understand why piracy is the cause of such concern for Cameroonian artists, and the motivation behind Richard Bona's plea for 'selective' piracy.

---

22   This turned out true in the case of Richard Bona's Munia (*The Tale*, 2009) which had two versions at respectively FCFA 250 and 500. The less expensive had a terrible sound and, after some time, stopped working. The more expensive one is still playing.

23   £1 was approximately 790 FCFA Francs in 2012.

What the table also tells us is that CDs by foreign musicians are much less expensive than those of, say, Bona or Manu Dibango. In the perverted cultural and industrial chain, there is only one loser: the artist who cannot enjoy the fruits of his creativity (although he gains popularity). The winners are the producers and the consumers at the beginning and end, respectively, of the piracy chain.

Consumers are those who buy counterfeit music and films. The price list above suggests that a vast majority of Cameroonian music lovers are inclined to consume counterfeit CDs. Women, men and young people approached for the purpose of this chapter welcomed piracy as a phenomenon, because it allows them to watch the movies and listen to the music they like, whenever they want to, at low prices. The fact that CD prices have dropped from 15,000 FCFA to 300 FCFA can only make them happy. Furthermore, it has been observed that expatriates supply themselves with pirated media when they are about to return to their homelands. For them, pirated CDs, DVDs and VCDs are a boon to be taken advantage of. French students have been spotted stocking up on hundreds of CDs, DVDs and VCDs of famous artists like Michael Jackson, Whitney Houston, Rihanna and many others. They acknowledge that in their home countries these CDs are much more expensive.[24] The bottom line is that the piracy market is driven by supply and demand. The cheaper the CD and the more accessible the technology, the greater the vulnerability of artists. Differently put, if people cannot afford to buy legally produced music, it is very likely that this pervasive situation will reproduce itself indefinitely. Artists will continue to work hard, and consumers will continue to enjoy music for almost nothing. The lack of state control and oversight of market dynamics (not to mention a clear and active cultural-political strategy) does not help either, and needs to be addressed accordingly.

Conclusion

The purpose of this chapter has been to explore the dynamics of piracy and the distribution of counterfeit music in Cameroon. It is so widespread that Longuè Longuè complains desperately about it, and Richard Bona makes the case for 'selective appropriation'. Despite legal regulations that guarantee the moral and patrimonial rights of musicians (Law No 2000.11 on Copyright and Neighbouring Rights, Chapter II, Section 13), field research provides ample evidence that consumers care little about these rights. They love local artists, but are not prepared to support them by purchasing original CDs. The main reason is affordability.

---

24 Guillaume, 25, a student at Catholic University, Yaounde, 20 April 2011.

In Cameroon, the sale of counterfeit works is tolerated by the consumers, who consider pirate vendors not as outlaws, but rather as resourceful individuals. People even view them as saviours, because they allow customers to listen to their favourite music or watch movies of their choice at low prices. That is the reason why some people shield or defend itinerant CD vendors when they are hunted by the police. In addition, the lack of political will also accounts for the generalization of the counterfeit. While the Cameroonian state was able to eliminate the illegal trade in Nigerian petrol in the 1990s, it does not appear to devote much energy to fighting piracy in the music sector. This is quite different from the US, where courts make concerted efforts to eliminate piracy and have forced even big companies such as Napster to shut down their illegal free music file-sharing operations. One question remains: why is the Cameroonian state reluctant to fight piracy, while keen to control so many other things, such petrol and, especially, the media? In my view, such lack of interest can only be explained by the fact that politicians have not yet realized that music, in particular, and culture, in general, can be easily transformed into an enormously successful business industry. They have yet to catch on to the huge potential represented by music, the performing arts and cultural tourism.

In the course of the past two decades, business models and technological developments have completely transformed media consumption around the world. Each form of media use has brought about its own forms of piracy and distribution networks. It is interesting to observe that some states are more eager or successful to fight media piracy than others, but globally, the practice contributes to democratize media consumption, it makes artists more widely known and it also enables many people to earn a living – at the expense of the artists who experience hardship and have problems making a livelihood with their music.

The exploration of pirated music in Cameroon revealed some interesting theoretical and practical considerations that would make strict copyright laws difficult to enforce. Cameroonian expertise in piracy comes with a rather unexpected variety of what Brian Larkin (2004) called 'creative aesthetics'. It has to do with the fact that counterfeiters 'create' albums that cannot, legally speaking, be traced or related to a specific producer. All vendors had albums with titles no artist would recognize. For example, *Richard Bona Special, The Best of Lady Ponce, Tala André Marie Ben Skin Special* or *Archeology of Makossa* are names of albums that these artists never produced. What counterfeiters do, in such cases, is simply search through the repertoire of a successful musician and come up with a compilation of his or her most popular songs. In addition, they select the artist's picture from anywhere, making the new 'creation' somehow original. There is no single company that can claim ownership of these discs. In this way, the counterfeit industry transforms itself into a creation machine, leaving the artists to complain in a vacuum. The fight against this phenomenon has been hard, and largely unsuccessful. Occasionally CDs are seized and burnt in public. But the following statement by a CD vendor in the newspaper *Mutations* makes us wonder if any solution can be found:

> At any time when counterfeit CDs are seized and burned, there will always be hundreds of copies (left or made). Each time they come and chase us out of the Central Market, they will come back and find us here. We will see who gets tired first. Instead of coming here to arrest us, they should first go after our suppliers and places where these CDs are pressed. Everyone knows where that is and who they are.
>
> (*Quotidien Mutations*, 25 August 2005)

This confirms Ravi Sundaram's statement that piracy is an intrinsic part of the electronic media boom. Although this sound pessimistic, it is crucial to address and solve the issue of copyright in Cameroon. Perhaps when governments finally consider culture as an irreplaceable asset, Richard Bona and Longuè Longuè will find different reactions to artistic delinquency.

References

Benjamin, Walter. 1970 [1936] 'The work of art in the age of mechanical reproduction'. In his: *Illuminations* (ed. Hannah Arendt, trans. Harry Zohn). London: Jonathan Cape, 219–254.

de Certeau, Michel. 2002. *The Practice of Everyday Life* (trans. Timothy Tomasik). Berkerley: University of California Press.

Deleuze, Gille. 1992. *The Logic of Sense.* New York: Continuum Books.

Foucault, Michel. 1977. *Discipline and Punish: The Birth of the Prison.* New York: Vintage Books.

Frith, Simon. 1988. 'Copyrights and the music business'. *Popular Music* 7(1):57–75.

GICAM. 2009. 'Synthèse des actions de la cellule de lutte contre le commerce illicite en 2006, 2007, 2008 et 2009'; www.legicam.org/index2.php?option=com_docman&task=doc_view&gid=171&Itemid=98, accessed 10 August 2011.

Gigi Durham, Meenakshi and Douglas Kellner. 2006. *Media and Cultural Studies: Keywords.* Malden, MA: Blackwell.

Goodman, Jane. 2005. *Berber Culture on the World Stage: From Village to Video.* Bloomington: Indiana University Press.

Harter, Pierre. 1986. *Arts anciens du Cameroun.* Arnouville: Arts d'Afrique noire.

Larkin, Brian. 2004. 'Degraded images, distorted sounds: Nigerian video and the infrastructure of piracy'. *Public Culture* 16(2):289–314.

Mbembe, Achille. 1991. *Le politique par le bas: Contribution à une problématique de la démocratie en Afrique noire.* Paris: Karthala.

——— 2001. *On the Postcolony.* Berkeley: University of California Press.

Nkeng à Nkeng, Joël Christian. 2010. Piraterie ou contrefaçon des œuvres musicales: facteurs explicatifs, modes opératoires et impacts sur les artistes-musiciens à Yaoundé. Unpublished Master's Thesis, Department of Sociology, University of Yaoundé I.

Perrois, Louis. 1993. *Les rois sculptuers: art et pouvoir dans le Grasland Camerounais.* Paris: Editions de la réunion des musées nationaux.

Röschenthaler, Ute. 2011. *Purchasing Culture: The Dissemination of Associations in the Cross River Region of Cameroon and Nigeria.* Trenton: Africa World Press.

Sisario, Ben. 2011. 'Master of the media marketplace, and its demanding gatekeeper'. *New York Times*, 6 October 2011.

Sundaram, Ravi. 2010. *Pirate Modernity: Delhi's Media Urbanism.* New York: Routledge.

Teko, Henri Tedongmo. 2008. The Socio-economic Dynamics of the Emergence of Black Market Music in Douala's New Economy. Master's thesis, Department of Sociology, University of Douala.

World Bank. 2009. 'Youth and unemployment in Africa: the potential, the problem, the promise'. Washington, DC (Africa Development Indicators 2008/09); siteresources.worldbank.org/INTSTATINAFR/Resources/ADI-200809-essay-EN.pdf, accessed 15 December 2011.

CHAPTER 11

Regulating mobility, reshaping accessibility

Nollywood and the piracy scapegoat[1]

ⒸⒸⒸⒸⒸⒸⒸⒸⒸⒸ

Alessandro Jedlowski

With the introduction of new media technologies in the 1980s and 1990s, the African continent has witnessed an exponential growth in media production and circulation. The affordability, portability and technological accessibility of new analogue and digital recording and editing devices have opened unexpected highways of communication for people that had previously been relegated to the political and economic margins of society. The emergence and the progressive consolidation of the Nigerian video phenomenon in the past twenty years are largely the result of these factors. Low budgets, inexpensive technological equipment and informal networks of production and distribution have combined in transforming videos, intended for local consumption, into continentally successful cultural products. But, as I have argued elsewhere (Jedlowski 2013), the video industry's economy, which since its beginnings has been characterized by a high level of volatility, has faced over the past few years an economic crisis that may radically transform the nature of the video phenomenon itself.

The video industry in Nigeria developed within a largely informal economic environment in which the illicit reproduction and circulation of goods were the rule rather than the exception. The informality of circulation has played a particularly influential role in both the history of the video

---

1   This chapter is the result of a research funded by the University of Naples 'L'Orientale' and conducted in Lagos in 2010 and 2011. The research focuses on the southern Nigerian section of the video industry and particularly on the one producing videos in English.

industry and the genesis of the present crisis. While, on the one hand, it has made videos available all over the African continent and within the diaspora, creating the basis for Nollywood's[2] international success; it has, on the other hand, weakened the industry's economy, exposing it to consecutive cycles of saturation and collapse. For this reason, the production crisis that emerged over the past few years has crystallized numerous controversies concerning the structure of the video economy and the rules that regulate it. The informality on which the video economy has been based since its inception is today often considered a threat to its very survival. While the industry has achieved global recognition, the economic fragility of its success has provoked growing anxiety. This anxiety has been progressively concentrated, by both media and video entrepreneurs, on issues of piracy and copyright protection.

The aim of this chapter is to investigate the causes of this anxiety and the role that piracy and transformations in copyright legislation have had in crystallizing it, while shaping the economy of the industry. Throughout this chapter I will argue that when the uncontrolled circulation of goods begins to undermine the economic basis of the industry that produces them, the rhetoric of piracy is mobilized to restore the control over the accessibility to the economy of both the production and the distribution of the goods themselves. This allows some of the entrepreneurs involved in the production process to gain exclusive control over it and the capital it generates. Within the Nigerian context, the rhetorical construction of piracy and the legal and economic consequences of this construction are the result of specific conflicts among different segments of the Nigerian video industry and, more precisely, different models of economic entrepreneurship. As the history of the Nigerian video phenomenon shows, a loose copyright regime seems to have positive consequences for the emergence and early development of a creative industry; but once the industry seeks to attain higher levels of profitability, it tends to become problematic, and the rhetoric of piracy can become a tool to orient processes of restructuration of the cultural industry's economy. In relation to this dynamic, I analyse the way in which the normative orders that regulate the reproduction and circulation of images and contents developed within the Nigerian context, and I discuss how their introduction and implementation

---

2   The term Nollywood was introduced ten years after the beginning of the Nigerian video phenomenon by a *New York Times* article (Onishi 2002). The term was initially rejected, but progressively local fans and media adopted it. It is often used to refer to the entirety of Nigerian video production, but many critics prefer today to limit its use, employing it only to define the Nigerian videos in English or Pidgin produced in southern Nigeria, in order to differentiate them from local-language productions that take place in other regions of Nigeria.

progressively shaped people's perception of legal and illegal practices in the field of local cultural production.

This chapter is the result of in-depth field research in southern Nigeria between 2009 and 2011, mainly focused on the video industry's economic structure. The data on which this analysis is based were collected through direct interviews with industry practitioners (directors, producers, marketers, retail vendors), government functionaries (Censors Board and Copyright Commission officers) and local experts (intellectual property lawyers, university professors and journalists), through archival research (in newspaper and institutional archives) and through direct observation of the production and distribution processes of videos. The chapter is divided into four sections. The first defines the use of the term 'piracy', differentiating it from 'informality' within the Nigerian video industry's economy, and, by briefly outlining the history of copyright regulation in Nigeria, traces the use of this term in the Nigerian public sphere. The second discusses the relationship between the media piracy economy and that of the video industry, highlighting the continuity between them and defining the role that informal and pirated modes of operation have had in Nollywood's popular success. The third analyses the recent anti-piracy campaigns in Nigeria and the institutional actions adopted to solve Nollywood's production crisis (up to 2011). I will show that while these measures did not achieve major results, they did bring the issue of piracy to the centre of the debate about the future of the video industry in local newspapers and television. The last section describes the anti-piracy anxiety that has developed in Nigeria as a result of these debates, and interprets it in relation to the structural transformations the industry has faced after the eruption of the economic crisis mentioned above.

Between informality and piracy: defining the video industry's economic and legal environment

Within the debate about the Nigerian video industry's economy, the terms of informality and piracy have often been used interchangeably. This has created a problematic confusion in the current stage of the debate, which I will discuss in more detail in the last section of this chapter. A first basic distinction to be made, however, is that while not everything related to informal economic activity is the result of piracy, everything pirated travels within the regime of informality. While the idea of informality mainly relates to the unregulated and unmonitored production and circulation of goods, the idea of piracy is principally connected to the unauthorized reproduction of specific goods, which can then travel along the networks provided by the informal economy. As I will discuss below in detail, the connection between informality and piracy within the context of the video economy is particularly complex. As we shall see, the legitimate, but informal, economy of the video industry originated directly from its illegitimate, and also informal, counterpart: the economy of media piracy (cf. Larkin 2004).

Both terms, 'informality' and 'piracy', have become common in the media debate of the past few years, and the exponential increase of their use has blurred their contextual definitions. The term 'piracy' is generally charged with moral connotations and connected with illicit practices. But, as highlighted by Ramon Lobato (2009), the term has taken on at least six profoundly different meanings in the international debate: first, in the understanding predominant in Western media industries, it is simply 'theft': the appropriation of someone else's intellectual property (IP); second, from the perspective explicitly espoused by emerging industrial economies (such as those of China, India and Brazil) trying to compete with the West in sectors locked by a strong copyright regime, it is considered 'free enterprise', an extreme manifestation of the capitalist economic model; third, in the position prevalent among those 'affiliated with the open-source movement' (Lobato 2009:24), it is considered as 'free speech', a guarantee of free expression and of the free circulation of knowledge; fourth, for post-modern critics who suggest that every text and every artwork are combinations of pre-existing materials (Barthes 1977; Foucault 1984), and for whom, therefore, either everything or nothing is piracy, it is a form of 'authorship'; fifth, it is seen as anti-capitalistic 'resistance' by those who perceive copyright as a 'strategy of property regulation and market colonization' (Lobato 2009:28) that serves the interests of capitalist hegemony; and sixth, within post-colonial studies looking at non-Western societies largely excluded from the global circulation of copyrighted material (Liang 2005; Sundaram 1999, 2010), it is often considered the only way to access specific cultural and material products, including 'knowledge'.[3]

As these examples – and numerous articles, including chapters that comprise this book – demonstrate, 'piracy' is anything but a fixed and circumscribed term. It is, rather, a fluctuating quality whose attribution to an object or a process depends on specific political, social and economic conditions.[4]

---

3 Each of these different understandings of piracy is grounded in a specific body of literature. For a wider discussion of this fascinating topic see Coombe (1998), Karaganis (2011) and, specifically in relation to non-Western film industries, Lobato (2012).

4 See Peukert in this volume. As Philip Altbach has stressed, 'copyright as a world issue is of recent origin. Nations have used copyright for their own purposes for a very long period of time. The United States ... was one of the world's major "pirates" until it had securely developed its own cultural industry in the late nineteenth century.' (1986:1644).

It is, furthermore, important to note this distinction: what is considered illicit is not the object itself but rather the process through which it is made available on the market. An object is thus considered 'pirated' only as the result of specific (unauthorized) conditions of reproduction and sale – one of the most striking ambiguities of the phenomenon. While, for example, certain drugs are always illegal regardless of what process made them available on the market, a DVD is illegal only under specific circumstances. This means that two DVDs that look exactly alike, are reproduced by the same person and sold in the same place, can potentially stand on the opposite sides of the line that divides legality from illegality. The person who reproduced them might in fact have had an authorization to do so, but limited to a certain number of copies, so that he can obtain profit from any additional copy only by selling it on the pirate market. This is in many cases what happens within the context of the Nigerian video industry, where two copies of a video can be reproduced in the same replicating plant, sold in the same video shop (even if at different prices) and at the same time occupy opposite positions in the moral and legal structure that regulates the society.

So what piracy actually is, and with what moral value it is endowed, varies profoundly from place to place, and depends entirely on the moral and political orientation of the person defining it. Within the Nigerian context, a concern with phenomena that can be defined in 'modern' terms as 'piracy' only entered the public sphere when the first copyright law was promulgated – which was, as in most Commonwealth countries, during colonial times, through the 1911 extension of the English Copyright Act intended to protect the interests of British firms in the colonies (see Altbach 1986; Peukert in this volume; Sodipo 1997).

As Bankole Sodipo underscores,

> whatever form of writing, art or music prevailed in British colonies at that time, it appears that 'local piracy' never became an issue.... It therefore follows that the 1911 Act was not initially aimed at protecting local publishers or other local copyright interests from piracy ... rather [it] was primarily aimed at protecting the trade in British books, art, music, films and broadcasts, which constituted reasonable trade interests in [the colonies] as a result of the assimilated British culture.
>
> (Sodipo 1997:26)

Hence, for many years after the introduction of copyright in Nigeria, the violation of copyright law was associated with the circulation of foreign products. Most local cultural production was not industrialized at that time and its informal circulation was hardly conceptualized as piracy.[5] As suggested in general terms by Bankole Sodipo (1997), and confirmed by the in-depth anthropological fieldwork conducted in the Nigerian and Cameroonian Cross River region by Ute Röschenthaler (2011), forms of regulation of the circulation of immaterial cultural goods already existed in pre-colonial Nigeria and continued to exist parallel to modern Western-inspired copyright laws (see also Röschenthaler in this volume). Until significant local cultural industries began to emerge, local concerns about modern forms of copyright laws and piracy were relatively few. Within this framework, piracy was often conceived as a form of appropriation and redistribution of foreign cultural products that would otherwise be unavailable on the local market.[6]

An entirely different situation materialized, however, when local cultural industries began to consolidate throughout the 1970s and 1980s, with the boom of the music industry, the phenomenon of Onitsha market literature[7] and the progressive development of cinema and television. According to the IP lawyers that I interviewed during my fieldwork (Oyewunmi 2011; Sodipo 2011), it is around this period that public concern about copyright and piracy started to grow. The first court case related to IP rights in the field of cultural production took place in 1972, just after a new Copyright Act was approved, but the discussion gained momentum in the mid 1980s, when the first IP-related court case got to the Supreme Court (1986) and artists (particularly musicians) began to demonstrate publicly for better enforcement of their rights.[8] The intense lobbying conducted by the numerous artists' associations existing in

---

5   The newspaper industry might be considered an exception here. As discussed by Karin Barber in this volume, the newspaper industry in English and in local languages was very well developed in early-1920s Lagos, and forms of plagiarism and illicit reproduction of already published material did occur. However, these phenomena were hardly conceptualized and discussed in terms of piracy.

6   According to Uche Ewelukwa-Ofodile, this legacy is still particularly influential in the debates around IP laws and copyright today in Nigeria: 'the question is how to effectively protect the creative works of ordinary Nigerians in a cultural climate that largely views intellectual property rights as a Western concept viable only in developed countries and exported to developing countries to further Western interests' (2010).

7   A pamphlet-literature phenomenon emerged in Eastern Nigeria in the 1950s – cf. Obiechina 1971.

8   The law approved in 1970 had in fact many weaknesses and did not offer a strong framework to protect artists and producers from the growth of piracy that followed the boom of the music and book industries in the late 1970s. As underlined by Babafemi (2006:5–6), the 1970 Act did not create any administrative structure to deal with IP rights, but rather only established minimal criminal sanctions for the infringer and did not even allow police to intervene to enforce the law.

Nigeria resulted, in 1987, in the institution of a National Planning Committee for the revision of the Copyright Act. A new law was therefore approved at the end of 1988, just a few weeks after a nationwide protest march organized by artists' associations. The approval of this law shows the peculiarity of the Nigerian case. In fact 'the genesis of the 1988 Act ... was not driven by pressure from foreign governments or trade associations. Rather, it developed out of the lobbying of the indigenous copyright industry.' (Sodipo 1997:27). Since the approval of this law, however, piracy has not been consistently reduced. On the contrary, it has mushroomed, becoming an important element in the evolution of the Nigerian media environment.

This historical overview shows how, within the Nigerian context, modern copyright law developed along the line that divides old colonial interests and emerging local forms of cultural entrepreneurship. This liminal position often made the debate about copyright and piracy confused and politically problematic. As underlined by Bruce Carruthers and Laura Ariovich, the respect of IP laws is related to how legitimate a specific legal regime is considered to be: 'Voluntary compliance [to copyright] depends on the perceived legitimacy of the rules, and without legitimacy enforcement is difficult.' (2004:29). Even if, as just mentioned, the recent modifications of the Nigerian copyright law resulted from the lobbying of indigenous cultural industries, people generally connect the introduction of IP laws to the violence of the colonial authority. This association inevitably weakened the legitimacy of Western-inspired copyright laws in Nigeria, and made their acceptance slow. As suggested by Uche Ewelukwa-Ofodile, a central question in this context becomes the following: 'How can countries in Africa deal with the growing internal demand for stronger IP protection.' and at the same time maintain their opposition to attempts by developed countries to coerce them to adopt Western-style law?' (2010). The complexity of this situation has generated a diffuse atmosphere of indeterminacy within which the definition of the line that divides informality from piracy, unmonitored from illegal transactions, is hard to draw. As I will show in the last section of this chapter, it is precisely around such distinctions that most of the conflicts that emerged from the production crisis revolve.

The Nigerian video industry and the infrastructures of piracy

As I suggested in the introduction, piracy has had ambiguous effects on the economy of the video industry. While, on the one hand, it has eroded Nigerian producers' revenues, it has, on the other, undoubtedly helped to transform Nigerian videos into an internationally successful cultural product. As Amaka Igwe has emphasized, 'piracy made our films very popular ... [as] pirates are bringing the films where we are not bringing them. As a matter of fact piracy is a multiplier. Whether it is sold legitimately or not, the film travels!' (2010). Piracy has also had a key function in shaping the media environment within which the industry could grow and the infrastructures of circulation upon which its economy depended during the first days of the industry's existence.

Following Brian Larkin's (2004) analysis of the development of the VHS cassettes business in Kano, it is possible to point out three main factors in the evolution of film piracy in Nigeria. First of all, the suspension, in 1981, by the Motion Picture Association of America (MPAA) of the distribution of Hollywood films in Nigeria, in response to the nationalistic cultural policy assumed by the Nigerian government; second, the effects of the oil boom on the consumption of media products, which allowed 'the mass dissemination of cassette-based technologies' (Larkin 2004:294); finally, the century-old centrality of Nigeria in trans-continental trading networks, which facilitated the exploitation of new digital technologies in the development of the commercial possibilities that depended on them.

The combination of these elements rapidly pushed Nigeria into the global network of pirated goods, providing Nigerians with 'a vast array of world media at a speed they could never imagine, hooking them up to the accelerated circuit of global media flows' (Larkin 2004:297). Until the beginning of the 1980s, Hollywood, Bollywood[9] and Hong Kong films were, in fact, available in Nigeria only a long time after their official release, and then only in badly damaged celluloid copies. Complex networks of media piracy, which often touched the Emirates (Dubai, Abu-Dhabi) or the Southeast Asian metropolises (Singapore, Kuala Lumpur), however, suddenly made them available to a larger audience in far shorter time. The availability of these media products increasingly influenced the imagination of video makers, who created a creole aesthetic formula in which local and transnational elements converged.

Piracy also influenced Nigerian video aesthetics by shaping their technical quality. The interferences and breakdowns typical of the reproduction process became, in fact, a constitutive feature of the first Nollywood videos, as they had been for all pirated media circulating in Nigeria since the end of the 1970s. As Brian Larkin (2008) has pointed out, the failures of infrastructures profoundly affect the way media are produced and circulated. Nigerian audiences experienced global media through the filter of piracy, and thus never appreciated their full technical and aesthetic quality. The framework of their enjoyment became, instead, what Yuri Tsivian has defined as a 'semiotic

---

9   The term Bollywood is generally used to refer to the Bombay-based Indian film industry producing films in Hindi and English. For a discussion of the genesis of the term see Prasad (2008), while for an analysis of Indian films' circulation in Nigeria see Larkin (1997).

of interference' (1994, quoted in Larkin 2004), a semiotic according to which scratches on the film, background noise recorded during the shooting and unpredicted breakdowns of recording equipment become 'part of the "message" of films themselves' (Larkin 2004:308). Already accustomed to this kind of viewing experience, Nigerian audiences showed no intolerance for the initial technical deficiencies of Nollywood videos. Piracy thus created a media environment that enabled the emergence and acceptance of these videos within a market dominated by foreign products which, in their original but not pirated versions, were of much higher technical quality (see also Adejunmobi 2007).

Apart from influencing the aesthetics and narratives of the video industry and creating the environment for the reception of its products, piracy also provided the infrastructures that allowed media goods to circulate. Media piracy in fact established the production modes and the distribution networks along which the local video industry developed. Most of the traders that invested in video production and distribution in the early days of the industry developed their business through the commerce of pirated VHS cassettes of foreign films. The places where Nigerian videos were duplicated, as well as the venues where they were sold, initially served as reproduction and distribution points for pirated goods. The video industry thus grew and became established as a branch of a business whose position between legality and illegality was ambiguous.

In the years that preceded the emergence of the Nigerian video industry, piracy of foreign media products was largely tolerated and, when local video productions began to emerge, legitimate copies of locally produced films were distributed and sold together with pirated copies of foreign productions. As soon as the local industry started to become economically successful this became a problematic issue, because of the confusion created by the overlap between legal and illegal circulation of media products.[10] How to distinguish legitimate from pirated copies in a system in which most often they are reproduced in the same replicating plant, shipped in the same package, and eventually sold in the same place? The difficulty in distinguishing between original and fake products, legitimate and illegitimate copies, pirates and legal

---

10   It is important to stress that piracy began affecting the local industry very early in its history, as testified to by Haynes and Okome in one of the first academic articles written on the video industry. As the two authors underline, '[t]he main constraint on the market is piracy... Popular videos are rapidly pirated, sometimes by the marketer entrusted with distributing the film. But the greatest problem is piracy by video rental clubs, which rent out films with no mechanism for paying royalties to the producer. There are said to be two thousand such video clubs in Lagos alone.' (1998:115).

distributors, became one of the principal reasons for the anxiety that began traversing the Nigerian video industry a few years after the onset of the video boom. Before analysing this further, however, it is necessary to explore a few more elements fundamental to the continuity between the economies of media piracy and the video industry.

As suggested earlier in this chapter, the business of media piracy, like most of the Nigerian economy, is part of what is normally defined as 'informal' (grey, shadow, submerged) economy. It is structured according to 'rhizomatic' networks comprised by a series of small segments.[11] In most cases these segments do not respond to a central ordering authority but are instead connected through a largely flexible system of relations in which cooperation and competition coexist. Within this framework, transactions are not monitored by financial authorities, but happen in cash and are often characterized by unwritten deals based on reciprocal (mis)trust. Being constitutively deregulated, this kind of economy is open to a large degree of imitation and to an exponential level of competition. When a product is successful, many slightly different variations of it appear on the market, eventually resulting in its saturation. In a context like the Nigerian one, in which the copyright regime was, and still partly is, very weak, the quick imitation and reproduction of products that are particularly successful on the market drives the economy towards consecutive cycles of saturation and collapse.

If we look at the history of the Nigerian video industry's economy, its continuity with the economy that I have just described is evident. Comprised by constellations of small production companies, the video industry still relies on the 'rhizomatic' and segmented networks of pirated media distribution to connect to its widespread audience. No contract or insurance is ever signed, deals are rarely written and transactions happen mostly in cash. Consequently, the industry does not produce any figures, and the size of its economy, the number of monetary transactions occurring within it, as well as the profits it generates, cannot be measured. When the industry's business seems to be going well, it attracts newcomers. The exponential growth of films leads to the saturation of the market that consequently brings on a period of recession.

This kind of dynamic has affected the industry since its earliest days, and each cycle of saturation and collapse has been harder to overcome. Headlines like 'Video: farewell to a year of pain and penury' (Aihe 1997), 'Before the video

---

11   I borrow the concept of 'rhizome' from Deleuze and Guattari (1988). According to their definition, 'unlike trees or their roots, the rhizome connects any point to any other point, and its traits are not necessarily linked to traits of the same nature … the rhizome is reducible neither to the One nor to the multiple… it constitutes linear multiplicities with n dimensions having neither subject nor object.' (1988:21).

eclipse' (Onoko 2001), 'Nollywood is sinking' (Sowole 2005) and 'Nollywood is dying' (Njoku 2009) have appeared cyclically in Nigerian newspapers, testifying to the vulnerability of the video industry's economy. Since 2006–7 the crisis seems to have reached an almost irreversible level. It is during this period that the anxiety over piracy and copyright infringement peaked, and it is also in this period that some of the most important measures to contain these phenomena were adopted.

Regulating videos' mobility: the growth of anti-piracy enforcement

As Eyinaya Nwauche, head of the Nigerian Copyright Commission in the early 2000s, emphasized, 'a weak system breeds a culture of piracy. An enormous amount of resources would have to be spent to change this attitude when the country decides to institute a stronger level of protection.' (2003). As mentioned, piracy of foreign films was generally tolerated because there was almost no other way to access them. But when piracy started to consistently affect the local film industry and the need to put a stop to this phenomenon became a priority, it was too late to separate the infrastructures of piracy from the legitimate industry's economy.

One of the most structured interventions introduced to tackle the problem is the new distribution framework authorized by the Nigerian Censors Board (cf. Bud 2014; Obiaya 2013). As shown in the previous section, the continuity between the economies of media piracy and of the video industry played an important role in the industry's initial success, but it has also generated a profound economic fragility which makes it difficult to further develop the industry today. Within this context, distribution seemed to be the key problem, the one that needed to be urgently addressed in order to revive the industry's economy, long affected in many ways by the absence of a structured distribution system. It made it impossible for the authorities to pursue pirates, because in an informal system no distributor is officially licensed and no official number of copies released is published.[12] VCDs[13] are not encoded, so they do

---

12 As Emeka Mba, Director General of the Nigerian Censors Board, says, 'we don't know who is distributing for you … so you can't come and say they've pirated my movie. Who [sic] do I chase?' (Ajeluorou 2009).

13 VCD stands for Video Compact Disc. According to Darrel Davis 'VCDs first caught on in Hong Kong when Japanese serial dramas, or *dorama*, were circulated in the mid-1990s.' (2003:166). Since then, thanks to their low cost of manufacturing, their versatility and their disposability, they have become extremely popular in most non-Western countries. Within the Nigerian industry they replaced VHS in around 1999/2000. Apparently they were introduced thanks to the initiative of marketers who decided to pioneer in the business of selling Chinese VCD readers

not have any digital protection, and illicit copies can easily be duplicated and sold on the market. No video shop or video club is licensed either, so anyone can decide to start to sell videos without authorization. Furthermore, the lack of an organized structure made it impossible to produce official figures about the industry's economy, discouraging external investment from banks or other private corporations.

The Censors Board's new distribution framework was approved in 2006. It imposes the acquisition of a license on all distributors, video shops and video clubs. It also insists on the marking of every VCD placed on the market with official stamps of the Censors Board. In this way the Board can know the number of official copies released and bought, and can also have the information needed to pursue all vendors selling unauthorized copies. The framework distinguishes between five different categories of distributors and imposes on them a number of financial rules that have the aim of regulating access to the industry's economy and discouraging tax evasion.[14] This last point created profound tension between the Censors Board and numerous video entrepreneurs. In the first months after the framework was approved a violent clash took place, leading to the arrest of some marketers and, in response, to legal proceeding against the Censors Board (Akpovi-Esade 2008, 2009). The violence of the collision was both literal and extreme: two members of the Censors Board staff were killed, one in Makurdi and the other in Niger State, and others were stabbed and injured (Ajeluorou 2009).

Just previously, the Nigerian Copyright Commission had begun to enforce a new anti-piracy campaign, the Strategic Action Against Piracy (STRAP), approved in 2005. As its name clearly states, the objective of this campaign was to reduce the incidence of piracy in order to create a healthier environment for media entrepreneurship in the country. Compared to earlier governmental initiatives with respect to IP protection, the STRAP stands out for its insistence on police actions. Numerous anti-piracy raids were in fact carried out once the campaign was set in motion. According to a World Intellectual Property Organization report, 115 operations were executed, 373 suspects arrested and 15 cases brought to trial between May 2005 and May 2007.[15] At the same time, a number of administrative measures were taken, amongst the most influential of which are the Video Rental Scheme and the

---

and subsequently also invested in distributing Nigerian videos in this format (Ajirire 2000).

14 Data from the text of the Distribution Framework, National Film and Video Censors Board (2007, accessible at the Nigerian Censors Board headquarter in Abuja).

15 Data from the WIPO official website: www.wipo.int/wipo_magazine/en/2008/05/ article_0009.html, accessed 18 May 2011.

Optical Discs Plant Regulation, according to which all video rental shops and all replicating plants have to register with the Copyright Commission and are obliged to keep an inspection-ready register of all their economic transactions.

Once the STRAP began to be enforced, anti-piracy raids were highly mediatized, increasing the general anxiety about piracy. The number of newspaper articles discussing the issue grew exponentially, as testified to by the fact that in 2007 one of the most influential Nigerian newspapers, *The Guardian*, dedicated a section of its archive to piracy and copyright in order to give coherent archival order to the debate ongoing in Nigerian newspaper columns. This mediatization, however, did more to serve the interests of governmental propaganda than those of the video industry. It did not reduce the incidence of piracy in the video economy in any consistent way, and the production crisis, far from being solved, reached its most dramatic pinnacle. As demonstrated, the economy of the industry remains tightly interrelated with the pre-existing economy of media piracy. For this reason, the attempt to tackle piracy inevitably affected the entire organization of the video industry, producing a progressive structural transformation. The anti-piracy anxiety that has become so pervasive over the past few years can be read as – ironically – resulting from the tensions created by this transformation.

Mobility, accessibility and the piracy scapegoat

In Nigeria issues concerning piracy and copyright infringements often crystallized nodal controversies. For instance, the continuity/discontinuity between pre-colonial, colonial and post-colonial forms of IP regimes generated intricate debates concerning the definition of communal and individual ownership of intangible goods and the legitimacy of the application of modern IP rights to the Nigerian context. Furthermore, as in many other non-Western countries, the fact that IP laws have often been used to protect Western capitalist interests created an atmosphere of widespread suspicion towards the protection of copyright. This generated debates centring on the position of Nigeria within a global framework dictated by Western capitalism and imperialism. The combination of these factors has often created multiple obstacles for Nigerian cultural industries attempting to assert their rights and have them respected.

Piracy has also been the highway for the participation of Nigerian society in technological globalization. The rapid introduction of new technologies and the participation in global networks of the informal circulation of media generated, however, both positive and negative effects for local cultural industries. As observed throughout this chapter, new technologies shaped the modes of operation of cultural industries, giving them a high degree of flexibility, but also imposing on them a high level of vulnerability.

Each of these controversies revolved around complex issues, such as the articulation of local and foreign conceptualizations of ownership, the position of Nigeria within the framework of global capitalism, and the role played by new technologies in both the accessibility of knowledge and in the development of non-Western cultural industries. Within this context, the recent increment of anti-piracy anxiety can be read as the expression of another nodal controversy that sees the Nigerian video industry's economy suspended between diverging economic strategies. This controversy also reflects the competition between conflicting paradigms of economic entrepreneurship, opposing both different segments of Nigerian society and different groups of interest.

It is possible to identify two diverging orientations emerging within the video industry's environment. While inevitably an act of conceptual simplification, defining them is useful to understanding the ways in which the industry is transforming. It is in fact within the field defined by these opposite poles that Nollywood's future is going to be shaped.

On the one hand, a section of the video industry is pushing towards a formalization of the industry's economic structure. This section would like the industry to have limited accessibility, high-entry investments, a highly regulated system of circulation and an effective copyright regime. As transpires from the materials collected during my fieldwork, the members of this section are mainly established independent directors and producers, interested in producing high-budget films capable of targeting both the international and the local markets. To do so, they need to rely on a solid and formal industrial infrastructure that can guarantee that the money they invest will not be lost to piracy and informal circulation. The other section would like the industry maintain a more horizontal structure, with high accessibility, low-entry investments, a weak copyright regime and porous legality. The members of this section are mostly small marketers, video-rental shop operators and all those who fear that a transition to formality will push them out of business.

The anxiety growing around issues of piracy and copyright infringement is thus a symptom of the battle being waged within Nigerian cultural industries. Those who are lobbying for the implementation of the new distribution framework and for the enforcement of the NCC's anti-piracy campaign are those who see economic opportunities arising from the formalization of the system, while those opposing the transformation are those who have scarce opportunities to keep a foot in the industry's business if anything changes. Within this framework, piracy plays the role of scapegoat. It is an accusation that can highlight the tensions traversing Nigerian society at many levels, tensions that oppose different models of economic entrepreneurship and different spheres of interest. The debate on piracy and the anxiety surrounding it have attracted the attention of the media and the public sphere, displacing the discussion from the field of economics to the field of legality. The use of moral arguments (good vs. evil, legal vs. illegal, legitimate vs. pirated) has radicalized the positions of many actors involved in the debate and contributed to concealing more problematic issues related to the economic accessibility of both the production and the consumption of videos.

An example will make this point clearer and move this chapter towards a conclusion. When speaking at the opening ceremony of the 2010 edition of the Eko International Film Festival in Lagos, the former Governor of Lagos State, Babatunde Raji Fashola, suggested looking for a constructive solution to the issue of piracy. If the pirates could be actively introduced into the legal business, 'they would become your distributors, marketers and agents and everybody will have a win-win situation', suggested Fashola (Abodunrin 2010). With this statement, Fashola tried to move the focus from legality to economic sustainability, suggesting that a solution can be found if 'pirates' can be integrated into a new formalized economy of the video industry. But the radicalization of the debate around piracy that has developed in recent years has made a solution of this kind harder to achieve. The reaction of the audience to Fashola's statement was in fact cold, if not hostile, as exemplified by one of the many comments that his statement provoked online:

> Governor Fashola seems to be losing the plot. How on earth can he advise
> film producers to befriend pirates who reap where they have not sown?
> He could as well ask us to befriend armed robbers for both are criminal
> behaviours. If Mr Fashola has forgotten his responsibility let me remind him
> here. It is the duty of the State to prosecute criminals and to ensure that
> appropriate sanctions are meted [out] to anyone found guilty to serve as a
> deterrent to others. Asking film producers to befriend pirates is tantamount
> to abdication of responsibility.[16]

As the title of an article by Majid Yar rightly puts it, we need to ask if 'the global "epidemic" of movie "piracy" [is a] crime-wave or [a] social construction' (2005). As discussed in previous sections, patterns of legality and illegality move according to the transformations of local and global spheres of interests and social balances. Piracy is a construction whose definition varies according to these parameters. The economy of the Nigerian video industry is rapidly transforming and this transformation needs to be addressed openly, while the anxiety surrounding the issue of piracy risks orienting the focus of the debate

---

16   Comment on Fashola's intervention published on the *Next* newspaper's website by
     Odiri Oghre: 234next.com/csp/cms/sites/Next/News/Metro/Politics/5645190-146/
     befriend_pirates_fashola_tells_filmmakers.csp, accessed 12 February 2011.

elsewhere. At this point of its history, the future of the video phenomenon is an open question, and the way the anxiety toward piracy is handled may well determine the path of the industry's evolution.

Conclusion

As this chapter has shown, piracy is a central issue within the debate that concerns the circulation and consumption of Nigerian videos. However, as I have also tried to demonstrate, a deeper analysis of the role that piracy has played in shaping the economy of the Nigerian video industry and the mobility of Nollywood videos shows that the debate around piracy, because of its moral and legal connotations, often tends to hide other, in my view more relevant, issues, in particular the growing tension concerning both the production and consumption of local media products.

As we can learn from the recent history of the Nigerian video industry, a high degree of informality and a low level of copyright enforcement tend to create a suitable economic environment for the emergence of new cultural industries, particularly in non-Western countries. However, when a cultural industry becomes sizeable, as in the case of Nollywood, it tends to orient itself towards processes of formalization that protect the interests of those who control the largest part of the industry's capital. As Lawrence Liang (2005) has shown with respect to the music industry in India, those who have benefited most from the economy of media piracy can become, in some cases, the most aggressive supporters and enforcers of stronger copyright regimes. Finally, then, the rhetoric of piracy and the paranoia it generates can become tools to protect and further specific interests.

As I have shown throughout this chapter, a similar process has taken place within the Nigerian video industry. Over the past few years, those who, thanks to the high initial accessibility of the industry's economic structure, managed to accumulate important economic and professional capital are today among the most vocal proponents of a restructuration of the industry's economy, which would imply a regulation and limitation of its economic accessibility. In this respect, the instrumental use of discourses concerning piracy has an impact on the way both institutions and private actors relate to the production and the distribution of media contents. By mobilizing moral and legal arguments, such discourses generate interventions that tend to modify the economic accessibility of the video industry. The economic structure that results from this process favours specific interests, allowing for the accumulation of greater capital that can then be spent in developing the cultural industry's profitability. The result of this dynamic cannot but be ambivalent: in the coming years Nollywood may well become one of the leading film industries in the world, but most likely only at the cost of a radical reduction of its economic and social accessibility.

References

Abodunrin, Akintayo. 2010. 'Befriend pirates, Fashola tells filmmakers'. *Next*: 23
        November.

Adejunmobi, Moradewun. 2007. 'Nigerian video film as minor transnational
        practice'. *Postcolonial Text* 3(2):1–16; postcolonial.org/index.php/pct/article/
        download/548/405.

Akpovi-Esade, Justin. 2008. 'Film marketers seek legal succour against censors board's
        policy'. *The Guardian Nigeria*: 7 August.

——— 2009. 'Movie marketers shelve picketing, to dialogue with censors' board'. *The
        Guardian Nigeria*: 4 February.

Ajeluorou, Anote. 2009. 'Emeka Mba: we need institutional structure to move
        Nollywood forward: interview with Emeka Mba'. *The Guardian Nigeria*: 29
        August.

Ajirire, Tosin. 2000. 'How I pioneered video CD in Nigeria: Ken Hero'. *National
        Concord*: 15 July.

Aihe, Okoh. 1997. 'Video: farewell to a year of pain and penury'. *The Vanguard*: 25
        January.

Altbach, Philip. 1986. 'Knowledge enigma: copyright in the Third World'. *Economic
        and Political Weekly* 21(37):1643–50.

Babafemi, Jide. 2006. *Intellectual Property: The Law and Practice of Copyright, Trade
        Marks, Patents and Industrial Designs in Nigeria*. Ibadan: Justinian Books
        Limited.

Barthes, Roland. 1977. 'The death of the author'. In his: *Image-Music-Text* (select and
        trans. Stephen Heath). London: Fontana, 142–9.

Bud, Alexander, 2014. 'The end of Nollywood's guilded age? Marketers, the State and
        the struggle for distribution'. *Critical African Studies* 6(1):91–121.

Carruthers, Bruce and Laura Ariovich. 2004. 'The sociology of property rights'.
        Annual Review of Sociology 30:23–46.

Coombe, Rosemary. 1998. *The Cultural Life of Intellectual Properties: Authorship,
        Appropriation and the Law*. Durham: Duke University Press.

Davis, Darrel William. 2003. 'Compact generation: VCD markets in Asia'. *Historical
        Journal of Film, Radio and Television* 23(2):165–76.

Deleuze, Gilles and Félix Guattari. 1988 [1987]. *A Thousand Plateaus: Capitalism and
        Schizophrenia*. London: Athlone Press.

Ewelukwa-Ofodile, Uche. 2010. 'Intellectual property rights: time for an honest
        debate'. *The Guardian Nigeria*: 9 April.

Foucault, Michel. 1984. 'What is an author?'. In: Paul Rabinow (ed.). *The Foucault
        Reader*. New York: Pantheon Books, 101–20.

Haynes, Jonathan and Onokoome Okome. 1998. 'Evolving popular media: Nigerian
        video films'. *Research in African Literatures* 29(3):106–28.

Igwe, Amaka. 2010. Personal communication, Lagos, 25 January.

Jedlowski, Alessandro. 2013. 'From Nollywood to Nollyworld: processes of transnationalization in the Nigerian video industry'. In: Matthias Krings and Onookome Okome (eds). *Global Nollywood: Transnational Dimensions of an African Video Film Industry*. Bloomington: Indiana University Press, 25–45.

Karaganis, Joe (ed.). 2011. *Media Piracy in Emerging Economies*. New York: Social Sciences Research Council.

Larkin, Brian. 1997. 'Indian films and Nigerian lovers: media and the creation of parallel modernities'. *Africa* 67(3):406–40.

——— 2004. 'Degraded images, distorted sounds: Nigerian video and the infrastructure of piracy'. *Public Culture* 16(2):289–314.

——— 2008. *Signal and Noise: Media, Infrastructure and Urban Culture in Northern Nigeria*. Chapel Hill: Duke University Press.

Liang, Lawrence. 2005. 'Porous legalities and avenues of participation'. In: Monica Narula, Shuddhabrata Sengupta and Jebesh Bagchi (eds). *The Sarai Reader 2005*. Delhi: Sarai Media Lab, 6–17.

Lobato, Ramon. 2009. 'The six faces of piracy: global media distribution from below'. In: Robert Sickels (ed.). *The Business of Entertainment*. Westport: Greenwood Press, 16–36.

——— 2012. *Shadow Economies of Cinema*. London: British Film Institute.

Nigerian Film and Video Censors Board. 2007. *Comprehensive Policy on the Distribution, Exhibition and Marketing of Films and Video Works in Nigeria*. Abuja: NFVCB.

Njoku, Benjamin. 2009. 'Nollywood is dying: interview with Francis Onwochei'. *The Vanguard*: 21 February.

Nwauche, Eyinaya. 2003. 'Intellectual property rights, copyright and development policy in a developing country: options for sub-Saharan African countries'. Paper presented to the Copyright Workshop at Zimbabwe International Book Fair, 30 July.

Obiaya, Ikechukwu. 2013. 'Taking Nigeria to the movies: The innovative regulatory role of the National Film and Video Censors Board'. *Journal of African Media Studies* 5(3):261–74.

Obiechina, Emmanuel. 1971. *An African Popular Literature: A Study of Onitsha Market Pamphlet*. Cambridge: Cambridge University Press.

Onishi, Norimitsu. 2002. 'Step aside, L.A. and Bombay, for Nollywood'. *New York Times*: 16 September.

Onoko, Oji. 2001. 'Before the video eclipse'. *Thisday*: 19 January.

Oyewunmi, Adejoke. 2011. Personal Communication, Lagos, 9 February.

Prasad, Madhava. 2008. 'Surviving Bollywood'. In: Anandam Kavoori and Aswin Punathanbekar (eds). *Global Bollywood*. New York: New York University Press, 41–51.

Röschenthaler, Ute. 2011. *Purchasing Culture: The Dissemination of Associations in the Cross River Region of Cameroon and Nigeria.* Trenton: Africa World Press.

Sodipo, Bankole. 1997. *Piracy and Counterfeiting: GATT, TRIPS and Developing Countries.* London: Kluwer Law International.

——— 2011. Personal communication, Lagos, 13 January.

Sowole, Tajudeen. 2005. 'Nollywood is sinking'. *The Guardian Nigeria*: 19 February.

Sundaram, Ravi. 1999. 'Recycling modernity: pirate electronic cultures in India'. *Third Text* 13(47):59–65.

——— 2010. *Pirate Modernity: Delhi's Media Urbanism.* London: Routledge.

Tsivian, Yuri. 1994. *Early Cinema in Russia and its Cultural Reception.* New York: Routledge.

Yar, Majid. 2005. 'The global "epidemic" of movie "piracy": crime-wave or social construction?'. *Media, Culture and Society* 27(5):677–96.

IV

MARKETING CULTURE AND THE BODY:

PERFORMANCE, COMPETITION

AND IDENTITY PRACTICES

CHAPTER 12

Between transnational and local aesthetic standards

Beauty pageants in Mali

☾☾☾☾☾☾☾☾☾☾

DOROTHEA E. SCHULZ

Introduction

This chapter explores shifting standards of female beauty that are staged during national beauty pageants[1] in Mali, and the controversies that emerge around these standards. Of particular interest is the extent to which these standards are recognized and accepted by spectators of these events as representative of 'Malian' notions of beauty and womanhood. To this end, the chapter examines what aesthetic standards and what frameworks of evaluation audiences articulate, and possibly reformulate, during the staging and judging of national feminine beauty.[2]

---

1   Following Cohen *et al.* (1996:11), I distinguish beauty 'contests' from 'pageants', in that the former term refers to an event of competition and judging alone, while 'pageant' refers to an event that combines the contest with other forms of entertainment.

2   The analysis is based on research in urban southern Mali in the period between 1994 and 1999, 2001 and 2006 and in 2010. A major focus of this research was on the responses of listeners and spectators to the national beauty pageants broadcasts of Malian national radio and television. In addition to quantitative data collected in 1995, 1996, 1999, 2001 and 2010, in-depth interviews were conducted. Additional information on responses to the beauty pageants in and around the northern towns of Gao and Kidal was collected through qualitative interviews with residents from these towns who at that time were living in Bamako.

For forty years now, Mali's national beauty pageant 'Miss ORTM'[3] has been organized by the national broadcast station in Bamako. Initiated first by the workers' syndicate of the national broadcasting station on the occasion of their annual New Year's ball, the pageant gradually expanded in publicity and national relevance, along with its move from a radio-mediated to a televised national event.[4] Starting in 1985, that is, shortly after the creation of Malian national television, this event was broadcast annually on television, where it is followed attentively by those urbanites in a position to watch it. Days before, and still weeks after the event, the pageant constitutes an important subject of debate among friends and neighbours, especially among certain (primarily female) segments of the urban population. Young women who have emerged as the winners of the different regional contests come to Bamako to compete for the prize of 'the country's most beautiful woman'. Their allure, glamorous costumes, hairstyles, enticing smiles and evocative manner of walking are noted and commented upon in great detail by female spectators as well as in numerous press publications and also on talk radio programmes.

But each year, the event also generates a host of controversial reactions. Social conservatives, such as Muslim groups, but also many older television viewers vociferously disparage the national broadcast station for setting up the event; they also level harsh criticisms at the contestants and their parents for publicly displaying women's bodies and for instigating in women a desire for money, material things and public flattery. The fact that the event is broadcast to a national audience only reinforces the resentment of these critics of the stress on outer appearance popularized by the beauty contest.[5] Other critical responses, some of them publicized in the written

---

3   The name of the national radio station 'Radio Mali' changed into 'Radio et Télévision du Mali' (RTM) when national television was established in Bamako in 1983. On 1 January 1993, following its reorganization into a publicly financed, independently run entity (an 'Établissement Public à Caractère Administratif' [EPA]), the broadcast station was renamed 'Office de Radiodiffusion et Télévision du Mali' (ORTM).

4   As several former employees of national radio recalled in 1994 and 1995, their initial motivation to stage a beauty contest had been to create an attractive side event for their annual ball. As they explained to me, it was only in response to the enthusiastic reactions they received from radio listeners who followed the broadcasting of the event on national radio, that they came to view the contest as a platform to celebrate 'Malian beauty'. After 1985 the television coverage of the pageant was summarized on national radio, to ensure a more inclusive national public for the event.

5   Still, it is important to note that parents' initial opposition to the 'corrupting' effects of the beauty contests was in many cases overcome by their realization of the financial advantages generated by their daughters' participation in the contest.

press, others conveyed in letters sent to the broadcast station, target the type of female beauty on display, arguing that the contestants promulgate ideals of femininity at variance with 'African' values and preferences (see Schulz 2000).

The critical reactions to the televised national pageant have also led to the invention of 'alternative' formats. For instance, in 1998, in reaction to many spectators' criticism of the 'wire girls' presented on stage, an alternative contest was integrated into the Miss ORTM event: the competition over the 'Prix Yansafarin', the prize for the most beautiful bulky woman. Initially designed as 'mere amusement to entertain people',[6] the organizers repeated the contest in subsequent years, responding to the enthusiastic reactions by spectators, men and women, who expressed their satisfaction at finally seeing on stage a woman whose bodily build represented 'the real Malian woman'. Other alternative formats include regional contests designed to promote 'truly local' ideals of female beauty and mock contests accompanying the ORTM pageant that parody, among other things, the inability of certain contestants to present themselves and their home region in a convincing introductory speech.

Although these alternative formats have not subverted the dominant position of the 'mainstream' Miss ORTM, they, like the controversies that surround the staging of 'Malian' beauty at regional and national levels, illustrate that the event itself, that is, the public staging of 'Malian female beauty', enjoys great interest, even popularity among some segments of the television audience. The Miss ORTM beauty pageant and the controversial reactions it prompts, offer an entry point to explore two important questions raised in the introduction to this edited volume. First, how do people develop their immaterial local goods to enable their participation and dissemination in global networks? And secondly, how are the cultural goods transformed in this process, in part through their transposition on mass media? Finally, to add to these questions, what happens to the social conventions and framework of evaluation in which these cultural forms are – or become – embedded? And what changing meanings are ascribed to the cultural forms in this process?

National beauty pageants offer a good occasion to address these questions. As events that stage female beauty as political and cultural projects of the nation-state, and also as tokens of the country's integration into an international order of political modernity and consumerist lifestyles, beauty pageants put into relief tensions between cultural globalization and

---

6   This expression classifies the Yansafarin contest as part of the side programme and hence disclaims its potentially high significance to spectators.

national identity; between local aesthetic perceptions and globalizing beauty standards; and between various understandings of adequate cultural and aesthetic representations of local or national identity and pride. Moreover, as Cohen, Wilk and Stoeltje (1996) point out, the ubiquitous format of beauty pageants at local, regional, national and international levels makes these events into 'places where cultural meanings are produced, consumed, and rejected'. In a situation in which some global pageants in Asia and Africa, such as the 1996 pageant in Bangalore and the 2001 pageant in Nigeria, have recently become arenas for 'protest against Western imperialism and global capitalism' (Parameswaran 2005:419), these controversies and contestations feed back into debates at national and local levels, generating new occasions for reflection on one's own criteria of evaluation, and for revising and reworking them. In short, beauty pageants reflect the dynamic, malleable nature of cultural forms as they travel back and forth along local, national, and international vectors of circulation.

Scholarship that interprets beauty contests along these lines is growing fast. The studies differ with respect to the kinds of contests they treat, such as national beauty contests as opposed to international ones; beauty contests devised for a particular 'ethnic' or 'immigrant' community within diasporic settings; and contests that stage marginalized ideals of male beauty, such as gay beauty contests, or that counter the dominant norms of masculinity or femininity in other ways. Because of the great variety of contests these studies cover, they come to different conclusions regarding the dynamics and ultimate significance of the contests in their function as sites for the production and celebration of beauty standards. Still, in spite of the diversity of perspectives and conclusions, much of the literature on beauty contests can be roughly grouped along a continuum of opposed interpretations.

On one side of the continuum are studies that read national and international beauty pageants, and the standards of female beauty they promote, along the lines of a cultural homogenization paradigm. Beauty contests, so the argument goes, exemplify the standardizing effects of a Western culture industry that increasingly imposes the white middle-class ideals of female beauty on a global scale. This line of reasoning finds a strong echo, and indeed considerable substantiation, in the literature on the global spread of skin lighteners, driven by a highly diverse and immensely powerful cosmetics industry that has a vested interest in promoting light skin as symbolic capital. According to this argument, multiple links between beauty pageants and an international beauty industry contribute to the thriving of 'colourism', understood as the 'preference for and privileging of lighter skin and discrimination against those with darker skin' (Glenn 2008:281).

The opposite end of the continuum is occupied by studies that seek to discover instances of resistance in the 'hybrid' local appropriations of cultural forms that, associated with 'capitalist forms, subjectivities, embodiments and attachments' (Hoad 2004:57), circulate internationally. These studies stress the diversity of local aesthetic norms and evaluations, and submit that these locally diverse standards effectively counter the global spread of white middle-class femininity. An obvious question raised by these studies is whether and where to situate national beauty pageants in Mali in these opposed interpretative schemes. Another, perhaps more productive perspective is to ask not whether the Malian example fits the 'cultural homogenization' or the 'globalization' paradigm, but instead to explore how questions of female beauty, about typical features of 'the Malian woman', are being framed, and how the ways these questions have been posed have shifted over the last two decades. Also, the controversies surrounding the ORTM beauty contest, and the notions of 'inner' and physical beauty it is said to promote, call for a closer analysis of the processes that further the emergence of, and struggles over, new ideals of femininity.

The 'Miss ORTM' beauty pageant

Since 1994, the year in which I started following the yearly pageants and the debates emerging around it, this event of national importance has undergone considerable transformations. These transformations can only be understood through consideration of the intertwining of local, national and international developments and influences.

In an earlier article on Mali's annual beauty pageant during the mid and late 1990s, I highlighted its role in official attempts to evoke a diverse yet harmoniously integrated 'cultural essence' of the Malian nation (Schulz 2000). Prior to the 1990s, the pageant already provided an occasion for the relatively young nation-state to stage the government's view of the nation as a national community with a common cultural heritage. After all, the event was closely associated with the state and depended on its funding. In addition, the aesthetic dimension inherent in the public display of female beauty facilitated the representation of women as icons of national identity and pride (see Kandiyoti 1993; Moghadam 1994).

The strong alignment of the pageant with a nationalist discourse fitted already established patterns of promoting 'Malian' culture on national radio: whatever was promoted on Radio Mali as an instance of Malian 'national' culture mostly reflected the cultural traditions of certain groups of Mali's southern populations, that is, of people who speak the two closely related languages of Bamana and Maninka. Comparatively less time was devoted to the musical and oral traditions of other peoples, most notably of the Tuareg,

Sonrai and Fulbe populations dwelling in Mali's northern regions.[7] The first democratically elected government under Alpha Konaré (1992–2002) slightly revised this unequal representation on national media, yet for years (and always justified with organizational and technical reasons), the predominance of southern cultures, languages and musicians on national media, and on the popular-music market continued (Schulz 1997, 2000). A similarly skewed view of Malian identity, and of what type of woman should represent it, was evident in the beauty pageants of these years: the majority of the contestants came from the southern regions, and the few women who did come from the north were often derided for the kind of beauty they embodied.

I also explored the event as a site for the claims and contestation of this nationalist discourse by various groups of spectators and listeners. Moreover, I argued that the pageant, by staging certain beauty standards, but also by displaying a particular view of the Malian nation as being based on a uniform image of nationhood, generated new disagreements about the 'essence' of Malian culture, about what characterizes national identity, and about which particular region-based or ethnic groups are considered to embody the typical features of 'the' Malian woman. Drawing on a detailed analysis of the responses by different audience segments, and of the controversies around individual contestants and winners of the Miss ORTM beauty pageant in the years between 1994 and 1999, I showed that, while the event itself adopts a globalized convention of celebrating female beauty as an expression of individual success and consumerist orientation, the event also provides an arena for the articulation and display of specifically national or local notions of beauty; in this sense, I argued, the pageants also offer a platform for assertions of local, national or, in the case of some spectators, 'African' distinctiveness (Schulz 2000). In this process, a sense of a shared 'northern' identity,[8] exemplified in distinctive standards of feminine beauty, was claimed,

---

7   This partial representation of 'national' cultural traditions also affected ethnic groups which form minorities within Mali's south, such as the Soninke, Dogon, Bozo and Senufo. Still, because these ethnic groups partake to a greater extent of the politically and economically privileged position of southern populations, their unequal cultural representation does not correspond to the one experienced by wide segments of Mali's northern population. Thus, rather than positing a simple North-South divide, it is more appropriate to view official cultural policy as generating a 'nested' hierarchy among Mali's different ethnic and cultural traditions, a hierarchy that not only opposes Mali's northern and southern populations but also reproduces divisions among Mali's southern peoples.

8   This identity cannot even be adequately rendered as a 'northern Malian' identity because, as Lecoq (2002) illustrates in the case of Kel Tamasheq, many of them question their belonging to the Malian nation and formulate instead the vision of

attributed and thus newly reified, in contradistinction to the identity and beauty ideals of 'southerners'.

With this argument, I followed studies that account for the great popularity of beauty pageants in countries of the post-colonial south in the context of new articulations of particularistic identities, in contrast to the official discourse of nationalist identity and moral community. These expressions of particularity, it is argued, support trends of the objectification, folklorization and commoditization of 'tradition' and of 'cultural authenticity' (e.g. Schackt 2005).

I also argued that the association of the pageant with the national broadcast station, although seemingly coincidental, points to a crucial dimension of the pageant's broader significance: mass-mediation processes are instrumental in generating 'structures of common difference' (Wilk 1995:111) because they draw spectators from different localities within the nation-state, and from different countries, into larger audiences. These audiences may gradually privilege one particular standard of female beauty; at the same time, once the pageant is broadcast to a large, highly stratified and heterogeneous audience, it offers ample opportunity to emphasize cultural difference from national or Western standards (Cohen *et al.* 1996:11). I therefore stressed that pageants cannot be read as structures that facilitate the homogenizing tendencies of globalizing Western aesthetic standards in any straightforward way, because they offer room for disagreement, resentment and outright refusal to participate in and endorse it. Nevertheless, in my concluding reflections, I also surmised that one possible direction into which the Miss ORTM contest would develop in the near future was a gradual (even though not totally uniform or consistent) move towards crowning as Miss ORTM a candidate who, in terms of body shape, complexion and hair style, corresponds to the beauty standards of international fashion and beauty industry, and thus embodies something close to a 'global Barbie' (Xu and Feiner 2007). In this respect, I identified Mali's participation in the West African Economic Community beauty pageant, Miss CEDEAO, since 1996, as an important motor of transformation of beauty standards. Here, my analysis came close to interpretations of beauty pageants as furthering a worldwide adaptation to Western standards of beauty (e.g. Xu and Feiner 2007).

The purpose of this chapter is to embark on a rereading of my earlier argument to probe – and possibly refine – the narrative of a steady trend toward the global imposition of Western beauty standards. Questioning the 'cultural homogenization argument' implicit in this interpretation means to

---

a Tamasheq nation. Recent political developments, most notably the attempt to establish an autonomous Azawad, support this view.

take a closer look at how the beauty ideals promoted during pageants actually resonate with spectators' and consumers' understandings and aesthetic preferences. Even if a trend towards homogenization and towards the adoption of Western beauty standards seems evident in the case of beauty pageants, what does this development imply for actual practices 'on the ground'? What is the relationship between the mass-mediated and hence publicly promoted beauty standards and people's actual perceptions and judgments? Or, to adopt Holy and Stuchlik's (1983) conception of norms: what is the relationship between representations, norms and practices? Response to these questions requires a critical consideration of the reach and efficacy of 'globally' imposed beauty standards and of their implications for the transformation of local norms. We need to examine the extent to which norms and aesthetic preferences are altered by the globally 'imposed' beauty standards and by the pressure exerted under the conditions of an expanding Western-oriented consumer taste. This means that we should investigate, rather than posit, the internalization of Western standards of beauty by Malian consumers of the beauty pageants and related events.

Staging Malian beauty: the formal set-up of the Miss ORTM pageant

Still today, the organization of the Miss ORTM beauty pageants is in the hands of the steering committee of ORTM workers' syndicate. The pageants take place at public venues, such as hotels or concert halls in the capital Bamako, and are introduced and directed by one to two announcers from the national broadcast station. They start at about 8 p.m., stretching over several tours or rounds and an additional music and entertainment programme, and lasting into the early morning. The principal rationale for integrating an entertainment side-programme into the pageant is to maintain suspense and a festive atmosphere during the often lengthy periods during which contestants need to change into the next outfit. But depending on the popularity of the musicians who are invited to the music programme, the entertainment may be as important a reason to attend the event, or to follow it on national television, as the beauty contest proper. The jury of the contest is composed of well-known personalities of public life, and of a few members taken from the audience.[9] The contest itself consists of one introductory and three competitive tours during which the contestants are asked to present themselves in different outfits. Whereas dress cut and fabric for the first costume follow a clearly prescribed standard, contestants can display imagination and variety in the

---

9   The selection of jury members from among the audience was introduced for the
    first time during the 1996 Miss ORTM pageant.

following two outfits, the 'traditional' or 'ethnic' costume and the 'modern' outfit.[10] One implication of the rule that contestants should present themselves in a 'traditional costume' (*tenue traditionelle*) representative of their region is that this supports a trend towards the folklorization of ethnic tradition and the representation of ethnic identity through material culture. Making the display of regional and ethnic diversity part of the national pageant also fits a long-standing official policy of celebrating the Malian nation as a 'community-in-diversity' and of invoking in spectators a pride in their 'authentic cultural roots' (Schulz 2007a). Slogans written on billboards and on banners hanging across the showroom, and also the ways in which the announcers introduce the different contestants, illustrate how the pageant is presented and perceived as a celebration of Malian womanhood. However, the portrayal of contestants as representatives of 'the Malian woman' implies a significant slippage. Among other things, selection criteria stipulate that a contestant be unmarried and under the age of twenty-five. There are also implicit criteria, such as height, body shape, weight and demeanour that determine that contestants are drawn from the age-status category of girls, not of married women. Last but not least, most contestants come from urban areas. As a consequence, to represent contestants as representatives of the dignity and beauty of Malian womanhood blurs the socially relevant distinction between girlhood and womanhood, and also obscures the disproportionate participation of urban contestants in the pageant.

Although it would be far-fetched to argue that their statements amount to a coherent official discourse on the essence of Malian culture (or, for that matter, on the intent of the pageant), the announcers clearly play an important role in presenting the contestants as emblematic figures of an essence of Malian culture, and of the beauty and dignity of Malian traditions. In this way, the Miss ORTM beauty pageant helps naturalize the arbitrary relationship between (select) women's physical appearances and the values of a national culture; they also posit the representativeness of the slender girl (whose body size and shape conform to Western 'skinny' fashion models) for Malian womanhood.

Announcers also link the *misis'* pleasing appearance to their moral excellence and 'inner beauty', all of which they claim to be illustrative of Malian womanhood *tout court*. Thus, whereas the ethnic costumes put on display Mali's cultural diversity, repeated references by the announcers to 'the' Malian woman and her 'natural beauty and elegance' gloss over regional differences in appearance and ideals of beauty, and blur the earlier mentioned divisions between Mali's different ethnic traditions and regional cultures, divisions that do not simply map onto a north-south divide, but also structure relations

---

10 For a detailed description of the different forms of female dress, see Schulz 2007b.

among different ethnic groups within a region.[11] Inherent in these official celebrations of Malian feminine beauty is therefore a tension between the claim to cohesion and unity on one side, and a celebration of diversity and difference on the other.

The presentation of the candidates in the different costumes alternates with musical and comedy performances, such as the earlier mentioned 'Misi' mock contest. In some years the event also comprised longer periods of dance music during which audience members were invited to dance and entertain themselves. During these musical 'breaks' (which are also covered by national television), members of the audience often make an effort to move to a highly visible position to be easily spotted by the ORTM camera team so that their participation in the general dance is broadcast live on national television and followed by family members and friends back home. The entire Miss ORTM event is therefore not just about the staging and celebrating of national female beauty and about consumerist lifestyles, but it offers a multifaceted evening of entertainment during which members of the audience engage in their individual pursuit of greater public renown.

Performing and contesting Malian womanhood: dynamics of the early 1990s

Until the mid 1990s, the discourse of 'Malian' female beauty formulated by the organizers of the Miss ORTM beauty pageant glossed over the fact that the contestants did not reflect the cultural diversity of Malian peoples. While doing research on the pageants in the mid 1990s, I found particularly striking that members of the organizational committee were generally reticent to reflect on the reasons and implications of the unequal representation of Mali's diverse regional populations in the pageant. Prompted by my questions, organizers offered purely technical explanations for the strong participation of the southern regions and the capital at the expense of the north, arguing that logistical impediments were the only reason why the pre-selection procedures systematically disadvantaged contestants from the northern regions.[12] However, whenever I discussed this argument with people involved

---

11   The extent to which these divisions and hierarchies are acknowledged by speakers varies with their regional origins and political and economic positions. Television spectators from one of the regions in Mali's far north are more likely to pinpoint these hierarchies – and to stress their own position of marginality – than are spectators who live in southern urban areas.

12   Until the mid 1990s each region was asked to make a pre-selection of women and to send them to Bamako, yet more than fifty per cent of the finalists usually came from the capital, Bamako.

in the pre-selection process in the regions under question, I was told that a sufficient number of candidates had been sent for the finals in Bamako, and that it was the application of certain selection criteria, not logistical considerations, that had excluded northern contestants from participating in the contest. What these critics maintained, then, was that those in charge of making the final selection preceding the pageant proper were partial in the sense that they championed standards of beauty in line with the taste and expectations of southern, urban audiences.

This situation of de facto marginalization of the northern regions has changed to a certain degree over the last ten years. A greater representativeness of the regional diversity of Malian culture has been ensured, mostly by integrating a greater number of finalists from the northern regions into the contest in Bamako. Still, these efforts at greater inclusivity have not led to an equitable representation of northern regions at the national level. Also, the 'all-inclusive' official rhetoric of the Miss ORTM beauty pageant conceals that during the final contest, it is those markers and criteria of female beauty that correspond to the preferences by peoples from the country's southern regions which take on prominence. In the late 1990s and early 2000s I witnessed several occasions on which the television audience in Bamako derided the bodily demeanour of certain Tuareg and Moor contestants as 'plump' and as 'walking like a cow', contrasting them explicitly to contestants from their southern home regions whom they described as 'gracious' and 'charming' (see Schulz 2000). Several Tuareg friends who resided in Bamako and with whom I subsequently discussed these derogatory comments simply snorted and countered this mockery by praising 'their' contestants as 'nicely rounded' women who represented the beauty of 'their own' women. As dissonant as these assessments of the different contestants are, they reveal that spectators consider a woman's complexion to be only one among several 'typical' features of a Malian woman, such as her body shape, height, facial expression and her way of walking.

There was also a marked disjuncture between official celebrations of Malian womanhood and the ways in which spectators from different regions judge the kind of beauty displayed on stage and the criteria applied by the jury. The most frequent point of criticism was that the ideal of the slender girl displayed on stage did not correspond to people's actual preferences for 'nicely rounded' women. Contestants were mockingly referred to as 'dry girls' whose body shape made them look like 'wire girls'[13] and clearly indicated the imposition of Western beauty standards on an event officially dedicated to

---

13   In French, this nickname is an alliteration: *'filles de fer'*. The Bamana term is *pegelen*.

the celebration of authentic Malian womanhood. To be sure, this criticism is based on the somewhat erroneous assumption that individuals' preference for slender women might be taken as an indication of their aping of Western beauty standards. Still, what these comments perform is a simple opposition between 'African' (or 'Malian') beauty standards and Western beauty ideals, an opposition that leaves little room for the considerable diversity of local Malian beauty standards and for the possibility that different spectators from the same locality and ethnic group may in fact favour very diverse beauty standards.

Dress prescriptions became another issue of debate among spectators, and a reason for some of them to take issue with the pageant. The debate opposed those in favour of 'Malian' dress codes and those in favour of Western-style skirts and dresses. This controversy over the appropriate skirt length was set up as an opposition between a Western and an 'authentically Malian' length, an opposition that was somehow ironic because what the critics of the 'Westernized' dress codes tended to ignore was that girls are 'traditionally' allowed to wear knee-length skirts.

Perhaps the most hotly contested issue for spectators was the question of whether the preference of jury members for contestants with a light complexion was proof of an 'aping' of international beauty standards or not. Many spectators tended to present a light skin as something 'authentically Malian', by which they referred to the widespread conventional preferences for Fulbe female beauties famed for their light complexion, as well as to the light-skinned women among the Moors and Tuareg in Mali's northern regions. In these comments by spectators, then, a light complexion had a connotation different from the one it is generally given in the Euro-American West, or that of the literature discussed earlier in this chapter, where skin colour indexes 'race' or 'ethnicity', and a preference for a light complexion is taken as a sign of an imitation of the hegemonic Caucasian phenotype. What was at stake in spectators' assessments of the appearance and complexion of individual contestants was not the light skin colour per se, but whether a woman's complexion was 'genuine' or 'fake', that is, achieved with the help of skin lighteners. Only an artificial change of skin colour was considered an undignified imitation of Western ideals of femininity. Spectators who articulated this view justified their preference for light-skinned contestants by referring to 'authentic' and long-standing cultural conventions that endorse similar preferences. That is, spectators explain their predilection for contestants with a light complexion by representing this aesthetic preference as an at once modern and authentically Malian one, and as an attitude that does not indicate an adoption of Western beauty ideals. What we witness here is a process of 'indigenization' of an international beauty marker, a process that goes along with a reinterpretation of light skin as a marker of one's attachment to 'authentic' Malian preferences.

This interpretation contributes to a critical reflection on the limits of the cultural homogenization narrative, and thus to 'contest theories of popular culture that argue for the homogenizing effects of the culture industry' (Hoad 2004:57; also see Balogun 2009). However, spectators' repeated references to 'our light-skinned beauties' are somewhat ironic, because many women with a light complexion come from the country's northern regions, where the Tuareg, Moors and Fulbe live, and thus from the very regions that were for a long time underrepresented in the national beauty pageant and whose contestants were sometimes considered 'unattractive' by southerners because of their body size, shape and postures.

Transformations of the Miss ORTM pageants: changing formats and significances

How has the formal set-up of the Miss ORTM event transformed since the mid 1990s, and what changing significance of the pageant do these transformations reflect?

A changing political and economic context, most notably the new administrative decentralization programme and the increasing commercialization of the pageant fundamentally affected its formats and protocols of presentation. Mirroring the new politics of decentralization and its attendant recognition of regional and cultural heterogeneity, there was a notable effort on the part of the organizers to ensure a stronger representation of the country's northern regions in the competition over crowning 'the nation's most beautiful woman'. Secondly, following the loss in state sponsorship of the event, the commercial character of the Miss ORTM beauty contest and the growing importance of private sponsors for the pageant became more and more manifest in the iconography of the event.

The event is still organized under the aegis of the Ministry of Communication, but its evolution towards an event in which substantial commercial interests are involved makes it less able to provide a platform for the staging of nationalist claims.

Private enterprises have a vested interest in competing with each other to become sponsors of the event: the national broadcasting station grants each sponsor air-time for advertisements during the live broadcasting of the pageant and in forms of posters and banners that comprise part of the material infrastructure of the pageant. Because the pageant has become closely tied to entrepreneurs in the national and international fashion and beauty-products industries, it is now set up as a mix between a fashion show and a public concert. The provision, free of charge, of dresses and accessories by several

Figure 12.1   Title page of the 1998 Miss CEDEAO beauty-contest booklet.

dressmakers and beauty salons has gradually transformed the pageant into a televised show in which new fashion trends are promoted. Because their costumes become ever more elaborate and daring, more than before, the contestants figure as objects onto which some spectators, many of them girls and younger women, project their desires to purchase particular fabrics, costumes and jewellery. Whereas formerly being selected as a finalist for the Miss ORTM pageant offered a point of entry for a potential career as a fashion model, it is now already during the pageant itself that contestants act as models for Mali's fashion-related industries.

Another development that substantially altered the outcome and significance of the event was Mali's joining, in 1996, of the West African

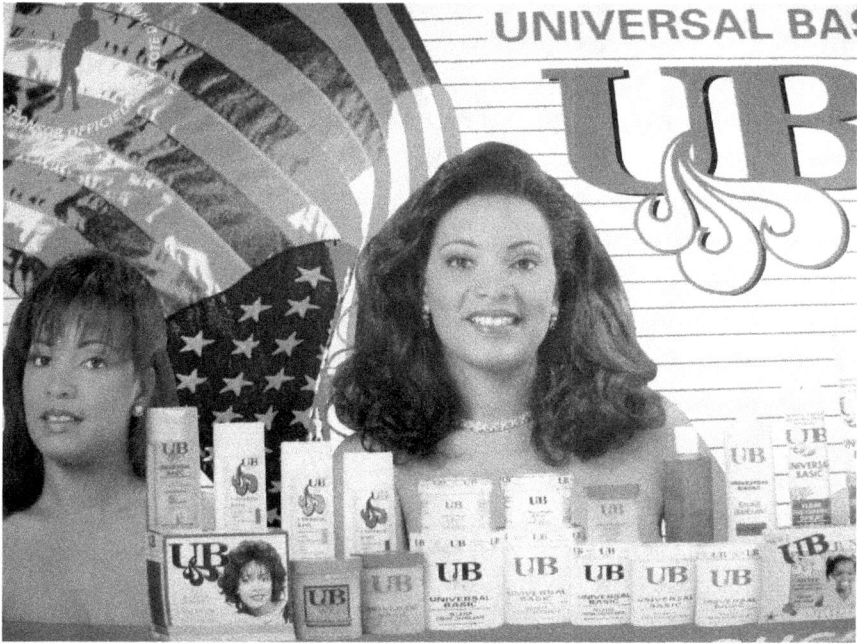

Figure 12.2   Advertisement for the beauty-product line 'Universal Basic', contained in the Miss CEDEAO beauty-contest booklet.

international beauty competition organized by the West African Economic Community, CEDEAO. Mali's participation in this regional event has supported a trend toward the routinization and standardization of the national beauty contest. The organizational committee has established a number of procedures that bring the Miss ORTM pageant in line with the global formats of beauty pageants, mainly with regard to its criteria and selection procedures (Figures 12.1–4).

As part of the routinization process, before being admitted to the pre-selection process, all contestants are examined by a dermatologist, whose task it is to verify that contestants have not been using skin-lightening products. Also, since 1998, the contestants' rhetorical skills and 'education' have been added as criteria of evaluation. This measure signalled not merely the organization committee's efforts to emulate international beauty pageant conventions, but also an effort to continue with the official narrative that the triumphant *misi* of the pageant should act as the nation's 'cultural ambassador'. That this official narrative is widely shared by spectators became evident in the widespread criticism of the *misi* who, when the Miss CEDEAO contest took place in Bamako in 1998, did not win the prize. It was mostly male spectators who were extremely disappointed about the failure of Miss Mali to present herself in a consistent way to the international public, and who severely

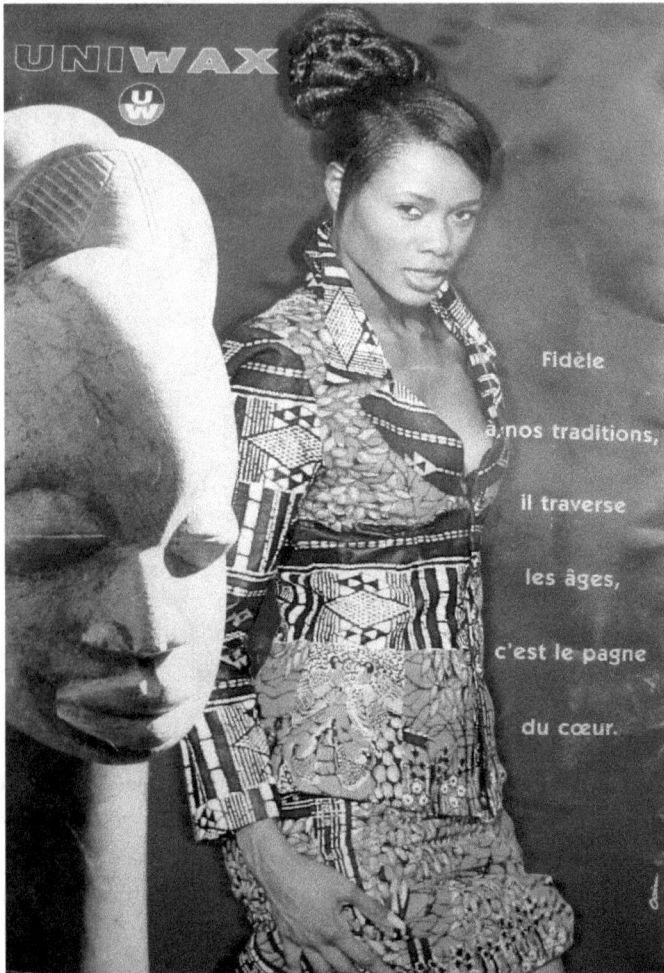

Figure 12.3 Light-skinned fashion model posing for an advertisement of the textile company UNIWAX (back page of the Miss CEDEAO beauty-contest booklet).

criticized her for her failure to 'speak proper French'. This development suggests that Mali's participation in the international, West African beauty contest supports, rather than undermines, official efforts to make the winner stand for the dignified beauty of Malian national culture.

Mali's participation in the Miss CEDEAO contest has not only encouraged the standardization of the criteria of beauty on the basis of which the jury selects the contestants; it has also fundamentally reset the criteria for selection. Winners of the Miss CEDAO award are young women whose appearance, especially bodily measurements, comes closer to the ideal of the slender, young woman that dominates the Western beauty and fashion industries.

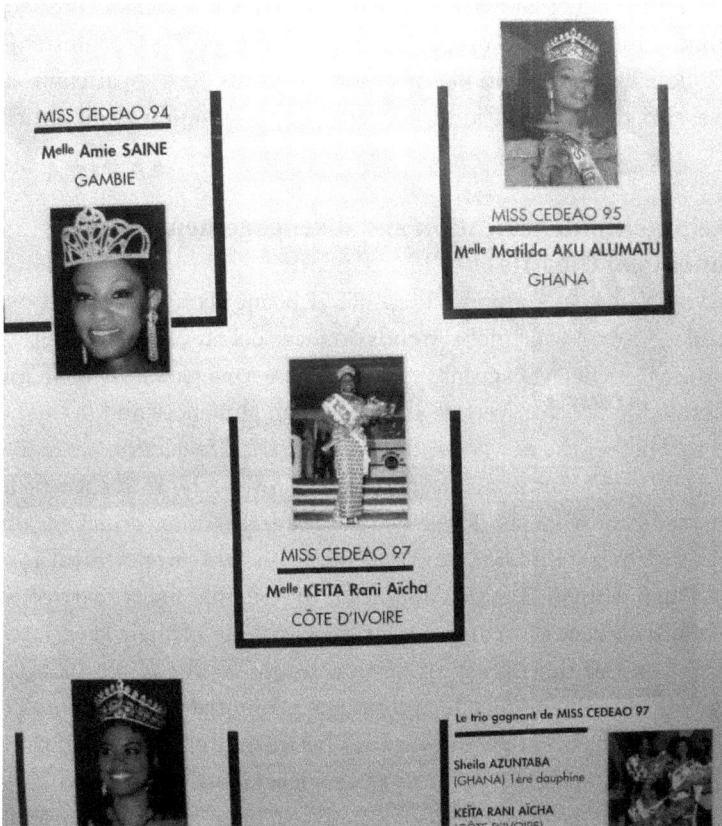

Figure 12.4 Page of a beauty-pageant booklet featuring different Miss CEDEAO beauty queens.

Decisions by the Miss ORTM jury have revealed a clear effort to conform to these international trends, so as to heighten the chances of the Malian *misi* at the international level. As a consequence, Malian television viewers and the broader public have witnessed a gradual shift in the appearance of the finalists towards a 'global Barbie' femininity (see Xu and Feiner 2007). In 1998 and 1999, two of the three costumes had to be Western-style dresses. Participants were asked to appear during one tour in knee-length or shorter skirts and in a second tour in combinations of a thigh-length skirt and a bikini-shaped top. The contestants have become more skilled in exhibiting their bodies, and their efforts to direct spectators' attention to breasts and buttocks have clearly become more routinized. Contestants, even if they do not wholeheartedly adopt the presentation style of Western beauty contests, seek to exhibit their bodies in a way that no longer conforms with conventional, everyday standards of female conduct. With this, contestants seek to adopt globalized forms of self-presentation, such as an evocative walking style and provocative smiles and dress cuts that markedly go against conventional local conceptions of youthful femininity and proper conduct. In this process, contestants have adapted globalized conventions of beauty pageants to a local environment, but have also transformed local conceptions of femininity and appropriate conduct.

Entertainment, identification and disengagement: popular assessments of the Miss ORTM pageant

How have debates surrounding the ORTM beauty contest evolved over the last decade? And on what global trends do these debates reflect? The tendency to turn the Miss ORTM pageant into a showcase for a global Barbie femininity has generated new controversies among Malian audiences and in the popular press as to whether the newly standardized criteria of selection are in line with 'genuinely Malian' standards or, in contrast, reveal the influence of foreign and imposed beauty ideals. These debates reiterate earlier criticisms directed mainly at the contestants' body size and shape, and at their portrayal as models of 'the' Malian woman. It is also important to note that many married women who watch the event on national television, in spite of their keen interest in the contest and in the display of fashion trends by the contestants, do not identify with the type of female appearance promoted by the event. They, as well as many men, stress the discrepancy between the beauty ideal celebrated on stage and their actual, lived ideals and preferences. Girls and young women, in contrast, often keenly identify with the slender and girl-like femininity presented on stage, yet perhaps not (or not only) because of the beauty ideal per se, but because of the world of glitzy consumerism the models represent, with their exquisite dresses, accessories and evocative ways of presenting themselves.

In contrast to these diverging positions taken by different groups of women, men's views were more unanimous. Many men in town do not show a great interest in the event, even if many of them follow it on television. When asked about how they felt about the outcome of the contest, they asserted that the model's physical appearance had little to do with what they themselves considered a beautiful woman. Among intellectuals, there was also a stronger tendency to complain about contestants' lack of rhetorical skills and hence inability to 'coherently present themselves or their region of origin'. This complaint not only hints at a conventional, widespread tendency to value highly those who, through rhetorical sophistication, properly represent the individuals or collectivity they are called to speak for. It also, along with the responses cited above, illustrates that official attempts to turn the pageant into a platform for individual identification with an evoked essence of national identity and pride intersects with, and is reworked by, what different segments of the Malian public consider to be constitutive elements of their own or of 'Malian' identity.

By staging women as icons of the nation, the Miss ORTM beauty pageant promotes the urban-based ideal of the slender girl as a standard of 'national' womanhood. The Miss ORTM pageant celebrates women as the embodiment of authentic Malian culture and thus supports a process in which a nationalist narrative centred on female inner and external beauty is broadcast to a nationwide audience. The pageant thus appears to have a strongly normalizing effect on people's perceptions of female beauty. Here we can detect certain parallels to the normalizing effects that beauty pageants, and the entire beauty commodity industry in which they are embedded, have on viewers' – and consumers' – perceptions. At the same time, the political context in which this normalizing process unfolds generates historically and socially specific effects. That is, the disparity between the symbolic qualities that officials and spectators attribute to the pageant shows that this annual event, situated at the nexus of local and international conceptions of female beauty, commercial networks and media images, constitutes a prism that reflects and refracts competing claims to membership in regional, national and international communities.

Many spectators challenge the official claim that there is a national consensus about what makes a woman beautiful. Spectators from the city, the southern triangle and the northern regions disagree, albeit for different reasons, with the current standard of female beauty that is promoted on national television. While many older spectators from the south have strong reservations about the lowering of moral standards, for a number of men and women the major point of criticism is that the pageant promotes an ideal of female perfection that is based exclusively on women's physical appearance. On the one hand, they appreciate the beauty pageant as an entertaining event of national importance, and, in some cases, as an indicator of being modern and 'up to date'. On the other hand, many spectators distance themselves, at least rhetorically, from the Western preoccupation with the female body and the fetishization of the slim young woman.

Spectators who followed the beauty contests on national television from their locations in the northern towns of Mali had other reasons to challenge the official narrative. Their references to the contestants' alleged lack of morality reflected their disappointment with the nationalist discourse that dominates the sphere of the media[14] and become a justification for them to distance

---

14 It is likely that different audience segments of the northern population have very divergent views of the beauty pageant and the standards it promotes. Detailed research is necessary to account for these views, which is beyond the scope of this chapter.

themselves from the political apparatus in Bamako, the administrative politics of which, they feel, has led to their own systematic marginalization within the national body politic.

Viewers' criticisms[15] of the 'wire girls' have also led to new initiatives at the regional level to organize their own beauty contests, and to promote what regional audiences consider their authentic ideal of female beauty, the well-rounded woman. These contests are organized by the administration and by local relay stations of national radio. The ways they are presented to and appreciated by the local public attest to the great popularity of these contests, to their entertainment value, but also to their role as a foil onto which spectators can project their diverse understandings of female beauty and of who represents 'the' Malian woman.

Although these regional contests promote, to a certain extent, standards of beauty that are more palatable to local tastes and expectations, it is unlikely that the regional contests will counterbalance the trends set by the national and CEDEAO pageants. That is to say, the jury of regional contests may favour contestants who represent the local preference for heavier women, but they will still select slender girls as contestants for the national pageant to increase their chances of winning it.[16] Jury members often do so by justifying their selection of light-skinned women as finalists by reference to a 'traditional' and 'authentically Malian' preference for this type of woman. This line of reasoning reflects a naturalization and indigenization of the global beauty ideal of fair complexion as a 'genuinely and naturally Malian' – or 'African' – aesthetic choice.

Considering these developments, one could argue that the alignment of the national Miss ORTM contest with international standards, exemplified by the Miss CEDEAO contest, has led to a certain levelling of the different conceptions of beauty held by rural and urban Malians, and by the country's different regional populations. Still, it seems that Malian audiences remain divided about the Miss CEDEAO contest and about the beauty ideal it promotes. Spectators express a strong awareness of the discrepancy between the beauty ideals displayed on stage and their 'real' aesthetic preferences.

---

15   They were voiced in phone calls and letters, and are also reported upon in popular press publications.

16   The alternative ORTM contest, 'Prix Yansafarin' (an award for the most beautiful bulky woman), has not been successful in establishing an 'alternative' model of beauty at the national level. Although a lack of funding opportunities has been given as the official reason for eliminating the prize from the programme of the Miss ORTM event, there are reasons to assume that it was suppressed because it could not be exploited by the national and international beauty industries.

Many people also articulate their concerns that the international contest exerts a strong pressure to screen out heavier women and those of a darker complexion, as well as others who do not conform to the Western fashion model type. While some spectators support Mali's participation in the event because of the opportunities for international publicity this grants, others remain suspicious of the contest because of the Western standards it promulgates at the West African, national and ultimately also regional levels.

Regardless of these ambivalences expressed vis-à-vis the national and the West African beauty contests, it is important to stress that people may be at once critical of beauty ideals presented on stage and of the rhetoric accompanying the presentation, and at the same time derive great pleasure from watching the contestants, and their provocative exhibition of their bodies and dresses.

Conclusion

The Miss ORTM beauty pageant and recent transformations in its format and significance illustrate how local and national aesthetic standards are changed through their mediation via international institutions and structures (see Hin-Yuk Wong and McDonogh 1991).

As we have seen, the national beauty pageant has undergone a marked process of adaptation to Western beauty standards, in an effort by organizers to heighten the nation's chance to emerge as the winner of the West African beauty contest and thus ultimately to move on to the global stage of beauty pageants. Simultaneously, however, there is a noticeable, and perhaps growing, gap between beauty ideals displayed on stage and 'lived' beauty ideals. Therefore, the evolution of the Miss ORTM pageant demonstrates how national beauty contests *simultaneously* promote the proliferation of Western styles and values, and the highlighting of contrasts between local and globalized standards of feminine beauty (see Cohen *et al.* 1996). Moreover, the adoption of certain global criteria of female beauty, such as a fair complexion, also opens new opportunities to ascribe different meanings to these developments.

The Miss ORTM contest has turned from a state-orchestrated celebration of national culture into a commercialized event that, since 1997, has served as a springboard for Mali's participation in international pageants. National television broadcasts the pageant to a nationwide audience and mediates a field in which global forces and images of consumer culture intersect and interact with both state-orchestrated processes of nation building and regional and local assertions of a particular and distinctive cultural tradition in a multicultural nation-state. Beauty pageants broadcast on television thus provide a window onto the complex and contradictory dynamics that shape official discourses of nationhood and the emergence of new local identities.

The ramifications of the local attempts to claim a particular culture – and disagreements about the nature of these locally particular identities – can only be understood if we recognize that these dynamics are embedded in, and reflect, a field of transnational (often global) influences and the effects of Western consumer culture.

In Mali, one of the implications of a stronger influence of Western consumerist lifestyles on local practices and aesthetic perceptions is that it feeds into the relatively new dynamics of assertions of regional and local identities, dynamics that were initiated with the political liberalization process of the early 1990s. These are shaped by long-standing tension between the hegemonic cultural politics of the government (which are rooted in the urban centres and rural areas of the south) and the political aspirations of peoples who live in the northern triangle of Mali. Although these people have very diverse cultures and political traditions, their shared experience of marginalization in the national arena motivates them to adopt a common position of opposition to the dominant culture of the south. As international consumer culture supports the concurrent 'Bamananization' and standardization of national beauty, people from different areas of the north claim a uniform 'northern' identity.

Positions taken by different spectators follow the divisions between urban and rural segments of the television audience, between the north and the south, between an allegedly authentic Malian culture and Western influences. One and the same spectator may make multiple, contingent claims about her own position, taste and the significance of the pageant as a celebration of 'national' identity, 'local' culture and even 'African beauty'.

The particular line along which beauty pageants in Mali have evolved over the past fifteen years points to the open ended and contested nature of standards of female beauty, and to the contingent ways in which women's inner and outer beauty is variously associated with the nation's 'cultural essence'. Nevertheless, competition at both national and international levels supports the process of alignment of heterogeneous Malian standards of beauty with one particular female appearance, the slender, light-skinned girl.

The new technology of visual broadcasting has been instrumental to this development. While national radio gave the official narrative of the beautiful woman as an emblem of national pride and dignity a wider reach and special appeal, it was national television that prompted a decisive move towards the standardization of images of 'the' ideal Malian woman. The visual representation, more than the aural rendering of the contest, served as a driving force in the creation of consumer desires that are mapped onto the bodies of the contestants. Visual broadcasting supports a process in which a woman's body is turned into a commodity that can be consumed independently from her qualities as a social and moral being. Television, in combination with a trend towards the commodification of women's physical appearance that is strongly driven by an international cosmetics industry, constitutes a driving force in this process. In its double role as a state institution and a technology of mediation, television substantially impinges upon the ways in which people conceive of themselves, of their place in a social environment, and of the consumer orientation they adopt to identify themselves with modern life in the city.

At the same time, broadcasting opens up a field of contestation, because it offers ample opportunity to spectators to disagree with the official definitions of the features of nationhood and national identity. Although national television and radio broadcast an increasingly standardized ideal of femininity to a nationwide audience, they have not created an uncontested norm of female beauty. Nor did these state institutions ensure a common agreement about the elements of 'authentic culture' and 'Malianness'.

Beauty contests thus illustrate both the attempts of urban Malian people to establish their own consumer orientations as 'modern' subjects and the limitations of these attempts, because by the very adoption of the conventions of globalizing pageants, Malians are drawn into an international market of consumer capitalism that has normalizing and limiting effects on their cultural production and inventiveness.

References

Balogun, Oluwakemi. 2009. 'The cultural politics of beauty pageants: new representations of Miss World Nigeria'. Paper presented at the Annual Meeting of the American Sociological Association, San Francisco, August 2009.

Cohen, Colleen, Richard Wilk and Beverly Stoeltje. 1996. 'Introduction: beauty queens on the global stage'. In: Colleen Cohen, Richard Wilk and Beverly Stoeltje (eds). *Beauty Queens on the Global Stage: Gender, Contests and Power*. New York and London: Routledge, 1–12.

Glenn, Evelyn Nakano. 2008. 'Yearning for lightness: transnational circuits in the marketing and consumption of skin lighteners'. *Gender and Society* 22(3):281–302.

Hin-Yuk Wong, Cindy and Gary McDonogh. 2001. 'The mediated metropolis: anthropological issues in cities and mass communication'. *American Anthropologist* 103(1):96–111.

Hoad, Neville. 2004. 'World piece: what the Miss World Pageant can teach us about globalization'. *Cultural Critique* 58:56–81.

Holy, Ladislas and Milan Stuchlik. 1983. *Actions, Norms and Representations: Foundations of Anthropological Inquiry.* Cambridge: Cambridge University Press.

Kandiyoti, Deniz. 1993 [1991]. 'Identity and its discontents: women and the nation'. In: Patrick Williams and Laura Chrisman (eds). *Colonial Discourse and Post-Colonial Theory.* Cambridge: Cambridge University Press, 376–91.

Lecoq, Jean Sebastian. 2002. 'That desert is our country': Tuareg rebellions and competing nationalisms in contemporary Mali (1946–1996). Ph.D. Thesis, Dept. of History, University of Amsterdam.

Moghadam, Valentine (ed.). 1994. *Gender and National Identity: Women and Politics in Muslim Societies.* London and Atlantic Highlands, NJ: Zed Books.

Parameswaran, Radhika. 2005. 'Global beauty queens in post-liberalization India'. *Peace Review: A Journal of Social Justice* 17:419–26.

Schackt, John. 2005. 'Mayahood through beauty: Indian beauty pageants in Guatemala'. *Bulletin for Latin American Research* 24(3):269–87.

Schulz, Dorothea. 1997. 'Praise without enchantment: griots, broadcast media, and the politics of tradition in Mali'. *Africa Today* 44(4):443–64.

——— 'Morals of praise: broadcast media and the commoditization of Jeli praise performances in Mali'. *Research in Economic Anthropology* 19:117–33.

——— 2000. 'Mesmerizing "Missis", nationalist musings: beauty pageants and the public debate on "Malian" womanhood'. *Paideuma* 46:111–35.

——— 2007a. 'From a glorious past to the lands of origin: media consumption and changing narratives of cultural belonging in Mali'. In: Michael Rowlands and Ferdinand de Jong (eds). *Reclaiming Heritage: Alternative Imaginaries of Memory in West Africa.* Walnut Creek, CA: Westcoast Press, 184–213.

——— 2007b. 'Competing sartorial assertions of femininity and Muslim identity in Mali'. *Fashion Theory* 11(2/3):253–80.

Wilk, Richard. 1995. 'Learning to be local in Belize: global systems of common difference'. In: Daniel Miller (ed.). *Worlds Apart: Modernity Through the Prism of the Local.* London and New York: Routledge, 110–33.

Xu, Gary and Susan Feiner. 2007. 'Meinü Jingji – China's beauty economy: buying looks, shifting value, and changing place'. *Feminist Economics* 13(3–4):307–23.

CHAPTER 13

Wrestling, the media and marketing

When folklore meets show business

◎◎◎◎◎◎◎◎◎◎

IBRAHIMA WANE

Introduction

In West African societies the production of music and poetry penetrates all sectors of life, and imparts a rhythm to the most diverse activities. It accompanies virtually all events, from religious ritual to leisure-time distractions, and everything in between, including the combat of warriors and the exercise of trade. Sport competitions are particularly enhanced by artistic side programmes, to which regattas and horse races, for example, owe, in large part, their attraction. These occasions put on display, in addition to the athletic prowess of their principal protgonists, the artistic expertise of diverse constituents of the community, as reflected in the skillfully tailored ceremonial dress of the rowers, the decoration of the pirogues and paddles, the panoplies of the jockeys, and the way the steeds are bedecked. But, among all these disciplines in Senegal, it is beyond all doubt wrestling that makes the most extensive use of the resources of cultural heritage.

Wrestling has two basic forms: 'simple wrestling' and wrestling in which blows are struck, combining traditional wrestling with boxing. While in rural zones only the first form is practised, the second is more popular in urban centres, where simple wrestling also remains important. Wrestling competitions have always harmoniously blended the fierce confrontations characteristic of combat sports with the delights of a spectacle, a particularity not foreign to the dimension that wrestling has now taken on: the sport that rallies most public attention, even (or especially) in Senegal's big cities. The questions which follow from this observation, and the ones I examine here, are what process led to its supremacy, and what problems were created by its rise.

In fact, among the sport activities imported to Africa with its colonization, it was football (soccer) that, after the First World War, benefited from large-scale promotion by the political authorities. Introduced into the athletic programmes of schools and increasingly cultivated through the creation of clubs, by the 1950s it had become the reigning sport in the cities and towns of French West Africa (Houedakor 2010:172). During the same period, 'traditional games' – local sport activities such as wrestling – were deliberately ignored (Gouda 2010:158). Immediately upon achieving independence, however, the Senagalese government pronounced its desire to establish local wrestling as the national sport. Nevertheless, despite this stated intention, football remained far and away the most favoured discipline, the sport to which the country's principal infrastructures continued to be dedicated, and whose championships were still the most prestigious (Deville-Danthu 1997:114). And alongside the championship of the elite there has existed, since 1969, a 'popular national championship', a competition among neighbourhood teams organized during school vacations, and which still stokes the ardour of its followers. Today, however, in Senegal's cities, wrestling has become no less of a craze, and this without the active support of public officialdom. Its extraordinary appeal to youth and the powerful mediatization its major contests inspire would have been unimaginable just a few years ago.

To define and understand the shifts that have occurred, I will, first of all, describe the world of wrestling as it functioned until the end of the 1980s, taking a look at its various actors and the roles they played. I will then focus on the current countenance of this 'home-grown sport'.[1] In this part I will primarily be interested in the innovations contributed by the new masters of the circuit, and the impact these have had on the configuration and orchestration of the production spaces, the arenas. The space of the confrontation itself retains its traditional circular shape; even if the combat takes place in a stadium, the wrestlers' circle is delimited by barriers such as sacks of sand. The third part treats the problem of intellectual property, which has arisen from the use of wrestlers' songs by professional musicians. This analysis will enable us to form an even more complete idea of what this game has become due to the far-reaching consequences of the interests at stake at the end of the 1980s.

In Senegal wrestling was always an activity closely linked to social life. In many communities it functioned at once as a framework for leisurely diversion and as a test of physical prowess and strength that, according to the context, enabled the authority (the king, the head of a clan etc.) to identify the able-bodied men, and young women to select their ideal spouse (Faye 2002:316). In

---

1   '*Sport de chez nous*' is an expression which reporters and other commentators are fond of repeating to call attention to the particularity of Senegalese wrestling.

Senegal it is still one of the principal festivities celebrated in the public squares of villages following the harvests. At the beginning of the twentieth century it spread, as a sport alone, to the cities (Faye 2002:318). There the contests were at first organized in the derelict wastelands of neighbourhoods. By the 1920s spaces exclusively reserved for wrestling began to appear.

The pioneer of this 'revolution' was the French impresario Maurice Jacquin, who, in 1927, conceived the idea of organizing wrestling matches in the cinema he owned in the city centre of Dakar. For the first time, wrestling took place in a closed space and became a spectacle to which people had to pay admittance. The wrestlers were remunerated from the entrance fees, which had been negotiated in advance. When the cinema became too cramped for the public attracted by this innovation, Jacquin acquired an empty lot, which he closed off to turn into the first Senagelese wrestling arena. The success of this initiative inspired many Dakar entrepreneurs, leading to the multiplication of arenas (Bidiar 1990:18–19). Then, from the 1950s, the great wrestling matches were staged in the Municipal Sports Park of Dakar. And then, since the early 1970s, only the newly built Demba Diop, with 25,000 seats, could accomodate the crowds drawn to witness the major combats. Today these three spaces co-exist (the public squares of villages, urban arenas and stadiums). They are graduated, by the wrestler who aspires to a professional career, like a staircase: the village square or the open spaces of popular neighbourhoods constitute places of apprenticeship; the urban arenes are the circuits that allow the athlete to be discovered by the great promoters; and the grand stadiums are the spaces which offer fame and riches.

The numerous studies of sport in Africa have so far primarily concerned track and field, football, basketball and the like. Wrestling, probably as a result of its local dimension, has not yet attracted anything like the same level of attention (Faouzi 1978; Melik-Chakhnazarov 1970). It is, however, abundantly referred to in colonial ethnographic literature. The travel notebooks that describe the customs of Senegalese populations devote much space to wrestling shows. Louis Moreau de Chambonneau, an explorer and French administrator who made frequent stays in Senegal between 1674 and 1693, recounts in one of his manuscripts ('A treatise on the origin of Negroes of Senegal, on the African coast, about their country, religion, customs and habits') the performances he had attended in the following terms. As this is the earliest description of Senegalese wrestling known to me, I cite it at length:

> When everyone is gathered together the leader of the band of guriots has a
> space cleared and announces that the Folgar is going to begin with wrestling
> and combats between men, that only the strongest and those who may be
> able to endure are to come forward so that the Folgar and the sport may

be better and also so that they may not have the shame of being overcome. When this has been done the music passes to seven or eight drums of different sizes which are used in different combinations for the different parts of the music. Men and lads enter into the circle of the Folgar. They are naked to the waist, and stripped of everything that might harm them or scratch them in the struggle. They dance in a slow movement till they have chosen their men, whom they take hold of and hug by the head or other part of the body so as to throw them down, if the other does not do it to them first. When one of the two is beaten, by being thrown down by the other, all the guriots and those who are friends go to fetch the victors. They put dust on their own heads, and throw their clothes on the ground, so that the conqueror may be honoured by passing over them.

(quoted in Ritchie 1967:91–2)[2]

The text goes on to say that the wrestlers then presented gifts to the griots, a gesture that did not, however, mark the end of the matches; these generally lasted for some two hours, until the victors were too tired to continue. Following the fights, men armed with spears performed, then girls danced, and then young men danced on until the early morning. This early description of a wrestling event in a village square mentions that the fights themselves were accompanied by the music of griots, and that the event was part of a larger celebration, but focuses on its agonistic dimension.

The first work devoted to this discipline was not, however, published until 1990: *Manuel de lutte africaine*. As its title indicates, this text, published by the Conférence des Ministres de la Jeunesse et des Sports de la Francophonie (Conference of Ministers of Youth and Sports of Francophone Countries), is a guide intended for the use of practitioners, and inventories the principal combat techniques and suggests training methods.

With respect to wrestling in Niger, another country in which it is among the most important sports, a few studies are cited in the literature. One of the best known is the biography of the famous griot Sagalo, who specialized in the recitation of praises of the wrestlers before matches: *Sagalo, le maître des arènes* (Sidi 2002). Another study concerns the role played by wrestling in the consolidation of national unity and social cohesion (Sériba 2005).

---

2   Louis Moreau de Chambonneau uses the term 'guriots', properly 'guiriots', which is an obsolete French term for 'griots', the praise singers of the Mande world, see also Diawara in this volume. 'Folgar' is an obsolete term of Portuguese origin indicating 'merry-making', 'entertainment' or 'diversion' (and a cognate of Spanish 'holgar', still current in the sense 'to be idle').

In Senegal, the essential corpus of literature on wrestling is constituted by the theses presented to obtain a Master's degree in 'Sciences et techniques de l'activité physique et sportive' at the Institut National Supérieur de l'Education Populaire et du Sport (INSEPS) of Dakar. These studies are primarily dedicated to technical aspects of the sport (the rules of the game, wrestling techniques etc.). Only a handful of scholars have, to date, looked into the subject. Raphael Ndiaye, one of the first, wrote an article exploring the origins and functions of wrestling among the Serer[3] (Ndiaye 1996). The historian Ousseynou Faye has studied the evolution of wrestling in the urban world, dwelling on the ways in which combat is staged (Faye 2002). In a more recent and expansive study, Abdoulaye Keïta concentrates on its artistic and literary aspects, analyzing the poetic discourse of the wrestlers (Keïta 2008).

In this chapter I examine the interaction between the different actors who are involved in the world of Senegalese wrestling. A chronological approach enables me to observe the transformations that have occurred over time. This study has its primary basis in my position as a spectator who has observed the practice of wrestling over some thirty years in various contexts – competitions in villages organized in the framework of festivals; wrestling tournaments in neighbourhoods of the city of Mbour,[4] where I passed my youth; the major matches that take place at least once a month in the great stadium Demba Diop of Dakar; and the live broadcasts of wrestling galas on television. To this field experience are to be added the testimonies and information gathered from interviews I conducted with both retired and active wrestlers, members of the National Management Committee of Wrestling, and representatives of the Senagalese Office of Author's Rights (BSDA) in 2010 and 2011, for the purposes of this chapter.

The arena, a space of cultural production

This section describes the proceedings and the ambience of wrestling sessions from their origins until the 1980s, when, as we shall see, the arena underwent a series of important changes. Wrestling has doubtlessly evolved in a number of ways throughout the course of its history, but here I focus specifically on the countenance it assumed during the two decades preceding the 1980s and – by way of contrast – during the two decades which followed them. Some nuances do exist among various ethnic groups concerning the manner of organizing matches, and I have chosen to concentrate on the Wolof model.

---

3   The Serer are the third largest ethnic group in Senegal, after the Wolof and the Peuls.
4   The city of Mbour, situated 80 km from Dakar, is surrounded by villages where wrestling is particularly important.

Practised by the ethnic majority of Senegal, this was the model imposed on the urban arenas.

Wrestling events have always provided the setting for different segments of society to converge. As Ndiaye points out (1996:111), wrestling – as opposed to other social manifestations which are selective with respect to age, gender or socio-professional categories – constitutes one of the rare vehicles which bring together the entire social body, in this case as witnesses to the strength and prowess of opponents who share an ambition to emerge from a contest as victor and champion.

In rural space, wrestling spectacles may be staged by the village chief or a youth association. In town, the promoters are most often businessmen or former wrestlers who founded enterprises for the purpose. These encounters – whether urban or rural – bring on stage, side-by-side with the contestants, other actors whose scripts are an integral part of the game: the singers (female) and drummers. This alchemy (or fusion) creates an ambience punctuated by coordinated performances reflecting the aesthetics or moral code of the social group.

THE CHOIR OF WOMEN

In the virile confrontation that wrestling is, women have been in the foreground since pre-colonial times.[5] This positioning is not coincidental. It is, in fact, the women – usually between two and ten – who sound the notes which define and complete the scenario. Their voices are the first to be raised together in song, even before the wrestlers arrive. For certain spectators they are the 'call to the arena', signaling the event that they delineate, and they accompany all the matches that ensue. Their tonality has sufficient range both to underscore the festive character of the entire representation and to express the ferocity of the competition. Their refrains, raised at the very moment of the face-off, resonate – and reverberate – like a summons. The singers leave the antagonists without options when they intone the hymn to masculine power beginning '*Bëre baaxu gòor la*': 'Wrestling is the privilege of men.' These chants create a solemn atmosphere that stimulates the athletes.

Formerly interpreted by the wrestlers' sisters or aunts, these incantations – which possess the gift of 'pushing men to surpass their limits' (Cissé 2009:137) – have passed into the repertoires of professional singers, who have become the 'institutional' (no longer family-linked) mistresses of ceremonies in the arenas. Their couplets provide the rhythm of the matches, push each of

---

5   Wrestling is the privilege of men, except among the Diola, an ethnic group whose majority is situated in the south of Senegal, and in which women also devote themselves to this sport (Badji 1982).

the adversaries to give the best they have within themselves to vanquish their opponents or at least preserve their own honour, the arenas becoming, while the combat lasts, a place in which the 'moral and social ideals of the group' (Ly 1967:43) can be realized.

THE RHYTHM OF THE GRIOTS

The arrival of a wrestler in the arena never goes unnoticed. The singers pause, tallowing the wrestler to make the public aware of his powerful presence on stage. His entry on scene is marked by the rhythm of the griot drummers.

For a wrestler to enter the scene the right conditions must be created. It is for this reason that the companionship of the griot is essential. These drummers, who are the griots of his family, or (as is often the case today) griots who come from the same neighbourhood, village or town, are auxiliaries (or partners) indispensable to the wrestler. By their mastery of the secrets of drumming, they possess the gift of 'creating in him an enthusiasm, a determination propitious for performing exploits' (Marone 1969:797). Accompanied by the sounds of the drums, he presents himself to the arena with an impetus that communicates his energy and self-assuredness.

This prelude to the exercise of the wrestler's skill will be completed moments later by a performance carried out in good and proper form, still under the orchestration of the griot-drummer, who will touch even more deeply the sensitive fibre of his champion by playing the rhythm that constitutes his 'device', his identity. Through this drummed message he sets his wrestler apart and invites him to take true possession of the arena. The wrestler cannot but respond to the irresistible appeal of the drumming that compels him into action. A dialogue between him and the drummer follows which confirms their complicity, as 'his "signature-rhythm" never fails to have the effect of rendering the person intensely present to himself, and thus impel him into a paroxysm of exaltation that lifts him to his highest capability, summons him to incorporate the most authentic part of himself' (Seydou 1977:199).

THE PARADE OF THE ATHLETE

The wrestler reacts to the solicitation of his drummer with a choreography that serves to heat him up yet further. In displaying his talents as a dancer, he exhibits his muscles and unveils (or lets everyone admire) his physical condition. His body language is emphasized and rendered more majestic by a ceremonial gown, primarily consisting of length of woven loincloth,

Figure 13.1   Wrestlers of the 1970s, in performance costume (photographer unknown).

attached to his waist and reaching to his feet (Figure 13.1).[6] This display is a demonstration of his power and his suppleness.

Through this ritual action, the wrestler communes with his public. He attempts in this way to reassure his unconditional suppporters, attract the sympathy of other spectators and cast doubt on the adversary camp. And, beyond this, he 'tacitly launches a challenge to the other protagonists present' (Mbuub 1985:54).

The champion's poetry

The champion is obliged to wed his words to his gestures (not his gestures to his words, the usual concept). Having let his body speak, he clears his voice to sing his own praises (Figure 13.2). Drawing on the epic chants and other symbolic repertoires, his models, the wrestler elaborates a composition built

---

6   These pieces of loincloth – given to the wrestler by his female patrons (who can be female cousins or neighbours, businesswomen or women politicians) and their women friends – are symbolic and generous gifts. As the loincloth properly belongs to women, it is women who have to see to the attire of their wrestler, and they do their utmost to make it as beautiful as possible. Like his garb of display, the *ngemb* – his combat attire – is also owed to women. The loincloth with which the wrestler girds himself to compete is offered by his grandmother, mother, sister or fiancée (Faye 1984:29). At the moment of encounter it is the only garment retained by the wrestler, whose naked torso is adorned only by *gris-gris* (amulets).

Figure 13.2 The wrestler Mame Gorgui Ndiaye, one of the greatest poets in the field of wrestling in the 1970s, preparing for his bàkku (praise song) (photographer unknown).

around his genealogy and the awards he has won. In this discourse he intones all the factors which permit him to claim or confirm his status: his origins, his religious references, his physical assets and even his diet (Mbaye 2003:306). In the course of this verbal performance, the wrestler galvanizes himself while also seeking to gain a psychological advantage over his opponent and win the favour of the spectators. The efficacy of this declamation depends to a large extent on his skill at improvisation. Spellbound by his poetic inspiration, his supporters often leap from their seats to barge into the arena and shower the virtuoso with banknotes.[7]

History has shown, by the way, that many wrestlers owe their popularity more to their eloquence than to their physical exploits. Some great champions are absent from the 'pantheon' of wrestling – i.e. from collective memory – because they did not bestow posterity with an ode rendering their feats

---

7   This practice developped with the birth of urban arenas and the monetization of wrestling that began in the 1920s.

Figure 13.3   Two wrestlers fighting, Dakar, Stade Demba Diop, 2009 (photo by Louis Dasylva).

unforgettable.[8] Conversely, other wrestlers have sometimes known how to reap from defeat a moral victory through the magic of the word, by ridiculing their conquerors, for example, or by skillfully justifying their loss (Keïta 2008:49). Its strong poetical and musical dimension makes wrestling a total spectacle, of which the physical combat is only one element.

When the referee blows his whistle, the two wrestlers are already standing face to face. The hand-to-hand fighting begins with both protagonists swaying their arms, each attempting, with various techniques, to throw his opponent

8   Barabara, a wrestler who arrived from Fouladou, in the south of Senegal, in the 1960s, defeated almost all his adversaries in the arenas of Dakar. He is, nonetheless, never named by journalists and other commentators in their historical memoirs of the sport nor in other comparisons of the champions of different generations – interview with Bocar Ly, lawyer and researcher, and the author of two works on sport in Senegal and West Africa: *Football: histoire de la coupe d'AOF* (1992) and *Allou: l'âme d'un peuple?* (2005).

off-balance and make him fall (Figure 13.3). A wrestler is declared defeated when he is knocked on his back, buttucks, belly or side – if his head touches the ground – or if he finds himself with four supports at once, that is with both hands and both knees on the ground. The rules vary according to the type of wrestling practised. While in traditional or 'simple wrestling' punches, for example, are forbidden, 'wrestling with blows' joins the techniques of traditional wrestling with those of English boxing. This second form of wrestling, which is no less old than the first but was first developed on a large scale in cities at the beginning of the twentieth century, is the more financially rewarding of the two, and today has become an unprecedented craze. Youths flood to the arenas from both the countryside and other cities. For several decades, wrestling has been filling the stadiums formerly reserved for football, as the audience for the great matches can no longer be accommodated by the arenas.[9] Wrestling came into its own as a trade with the professionalism inaugurated at the end of the 1980s by a new generation of sport enthusiasts.

Wrestling, like all traditional sports, was a recreational activity. Even for the great champions of the urban arenas between the 1950s and the 1980s, and who fought as much for the enjoyment and honour it accorded as for financial gain, it remained a part-time occupation. But as a result of its mediatization and a significant rise in its profitability it became a profession. Increasing numbers of youths now abandon school or their trades to devote themselves exclusively to wrestling. The figureheads of this revolution are Moustapha Guèye and Mohamed Ndao 'Tyson', who showed, by personal example, that wrestling is no longer a matter of interest only to rural folk, illiterates or the unemployed. The profile and style of these two wrestlers attract youths and intellectuals alike, and has enormously widened the popular base for urban wrestling. From this period onwards the arenas have undergone many transformations and modifications.

Wrestling, a commercial product

Wrestling no longer leaves anyone in Senegal indifferent. The major matches organized in Dakar or in other, regional capitals are transmitted live by the television channels who own the rights to do so. Millions of spectators remain glued to their small screens, both in Senegal and foreign countries, during these contests.

Its sponsors, entranced by the large public following of these matches, compete in the creation of enticing advertising posters. The ranks of producers

---

9   The State has been promising for twenty years to construct a national arena in Dakar.

Figure 13.4   The wrestler Modou Lô (left) enters the stage, accompanied by his followers, Dakar, Stade Demba Diop, 2010 (photo by Louis Dasylva).

and promoters of spectacles grow incessantly larger.[10] Wrestling stables and schools proliferate.[11] The admittance fees divided among the wrestlers who reign over the urban arenas constantly increase and have become the stuff of dreams.[12]

---

10   The promoter's license is acquired, at the cost of 300,000 FCFA (457 €), at the opening of each season from the *Comité national de gestion de la lutte* (CNG), an entity created by the Sports Ministry. For each wrestling gala, the promoter also pays the CNG, to offset 'organizational costs', a sum which varies between one million (1,524 €) and five million FCFA (7,624 €) according to the size of the event. Until the beginning of the 1980s, the organization of wrestling matches had been a matter for the performance associations officially recognized by the state (Faye 2002: 319) which had been set up by some personalities of the world of sport or by dignitaries. Football clubs and other structures have also attempted to gather funds by similar means. Since the 1990s, however, wrestling has become a goldmine for businessmen arriving from diverse sectors, and, as a result, for the ministries too.

11   Tens of thousands of young men train every day on beaches or open spaces, dreaming of enthralling 'tomorrows'. According to estimates, the CNG registered over 8000 licenses in 2010.

12   Attaining hardly a million FCFA (1,524 €) in the 1970s, the remuneration of today's great stars of the arena is measured in tens of millions. A wrestler can earn, today, up to 100 million FCFA (152,000 €) for a single match. These 'admittance fees' are negotiated in advance and their amount depends on the market value of the wrestlers in question. We are very far from the days in which the take was destined only for the victors and consisted of sheep, cows, horses and other animals.

Figure 13.5   Modou Lô, one of the most popular Senegalese wrestlers, preparing for the battle in his own mysterious way, Dakar, Stade Demba Diop, 2010 (photo by Louis Dasylva).

If everyone in Senegal is convinced of their obligation to accord ever greater value to a national sport so deeply anchored in the country's cultural heritage, the ways in which its principal actors handle it are, however, far from uniform and unamimous. Indeed, the obsession with 'modernizing', promoting and making financially profitable this Senegalese speciality often leads to controversial initiatives and innovations.

AN OVERLOADED SPECTACLE

If the wrestler was once the only one to dance to the beat of the griot's drum, today he is accompanied in the ring by at least fifteen members of his entourage (or partners) (Figure 13.4), and the choreography performed by this group is, in addition, fully the equal of that of any ballet or other professional dance company. This show has assumed such an important place in the entire ritual that the wrestlers systematically rehearse, alongside their combat training, and under the guidance of a choreographer, the dance steps which they are now expected to offer their public. The aim is to present the most spectacular performance possible by blending combat dances with the dance steps most in fashion in nightclubs and on dance floors.

Creativity and originality do not, however, extend to vestimentary style. The choreographies are no longer performed in any particular costume, wearing outer clothing advertising the official sponsor of the event being the only requirement. On this level nothing distinguishes wrestling stables from football or basketball teams (Figure 13.5). A kind of 'uniformization' has occurred, to the detriment of tradition.

Moreover, the performance of the wrestler has increasingly become subject to competition from other performers. Sometimes he is even eclipsed by popular singers who perform live or in playback to 'enhance the ambience'. Concerts now often serve as preludes to wrestling galas, and comedians participate in the event to entertain the audience with parodies of the matches. To be added to these various scripts is that of arriving fans armed with drums to spur on their hero from the crowd. The images of youths noisily encouraging their teams that we see at football and basketball matches, among others, are now also part of the landscape of wrestling. What these young people have long been doing for their neighbourhood, city or country teams, they now also do for their favourite wrestler.

All of this reflects the multiplicity of interests, and in part explains the fixation of the organizers with presenting wrestling to a foreign public – both the tourists who increasingly flock to the stadiums and the foreign television channels interested in this sport – as the cultural showcase of Senegal. The quest for originality at any price often also leads, moreoever, to 'innovations' whose relevance is highly dubious: the presence of 'pompom girls' in the arena, fireworks, smoke grenades etc. Such initiatives on the part of the promoters do not contribute anything to the arena, and those mentioned are nothing more than imitations of practices that can easily be observed in football stadiums. Wrestling has become a catch-all pretext for engaging in diverse publicity schemes and experiments.

CONFRONTATIONS FROM A DISTANCE

The arena is no longer the terrain of confrontation of official contestants only. It rather puts into direct or indirect confrontation all the actors who have vested interests in it: promoters, television stations, sponsors etc. (Gaye 2007:38).

The promoters compete ruthlessly with each other. Each one tries to make the difference, and their inventions are more often than not in direct conflict with each other and with everything else. It would often be easy to believe that we are watching some kind of American 'reality show'.[13] The promoter is no longer the project manager who arrives the first thing in the morning at the place where the event will take place and directly supervises everything from beginning to end. He appears nowadays as a 'star' who wants to be perceived as the true hero of the day. He does not even show up in the arena until all is finished and done, and his grandiose entry is often yet one more crude scenario.[14] He then offers himelf a victor's lap of honour before taking up position beside the television reporters to benefit from screen time, comment on his event and pass along his messsages. Every prominent promoter proudly wears all the titles and superlatives which the self-interested reporters have come up with for him.[15]

The television stations also push the rivalry between them to its limits. And these 'fights' are not always, by the way, purely figurative.[16] The television station which has clinched the exclusive rights to broadcast the event makes much ado about this as an 'event' in itself, and its reporters even go so far as to harangue the public. The contracts between the television stations and the promoters are fat commercial transactions entirely based on high audience ratings. The annoucers constantly shove each other aside throughout the days of the broadcast,[17] and the deluge of commercials sometimes keep television viewers from seeing very much of the matches themselves.[18]

And as to the commercial sponsors, they fully occupy the space with their billboards, streamers and other attention-getting props. The leaders in the domain of wrestling are currently (in the first decade of the 2000s) the major

---

13 In 2003 the promoter Alioune 'Petit' Mbaye installed a ring in the middle of the stadium to referee the preview of the fight between 'Yékini' and 'Tyson', who were the two biggest stars of the arenas. In 2010 another promoter, Luc Nicolaï, awarded the victor of the match he had organized a boxing belt as his trophy.

14 For example, standing in the open top of a convertible, or even landing by parachute.

15 Gaston Mbengue has himself called 'the Don King of the arena' or 'the people's promoter'. His rival Luc Nicolaï wants to be known as 'the promoter of the continent'. Serigne Modou Niang prided himself on being 'the alternative's promoter'.

16 In February 2011 a President-General Manager of television and the lawyer of a wrestling promoter came to blows in a fist-fight on the platform during a televised debate.

17 The advertising receipts are split between the promoter and his television partners.

18 In 2010 the Commercial Director of *Radiotélévision sénégalaise* (RTS) was obliged, the day following a gala, to offer his apologies to the television viewers who could hardly see the programmed matches because of the relentless pace at which commercial spots had been broadcast.

multinational mobile-phone operators,[19] which employ their large advertising budgets to finance particularly aggressive marketing styles.

But the personal patrons cannot easily be outdone. They have become full actors in the game. During the colonial period, there were only a few official sponsorships, and these concerned only the great tournaments at the completion of which the political authorities arrived to bestow the victor with the trophy of the game: the flag of Cap-Vert (the current region of Dakar) or the flag of the AOF (Afrique occidentale française), which might also be accompanied by a cup or other gifts. After independence, this became the flag of the Fédération du Mali and, later on, the flag of the Chief of State (of Senegal). But beginning in the 2000s, such patronage became almost a rule; every wrestling gala is dedicated by the promoter to a political authority, to a businessman or businesswoman, or to another associate, and these arrive at the head of large delegations to bathe in the adulation of the crowd.

In this full-fledged carnival of 'interests', the male and female singers are less concerned with stimulating the wrestlers than with spotting and flattering the promoter, the sponsors, the political authorities or other public personalities seated at the platform of honour.

Thus everyone puts on his or her own show in this space, which has become the High Meeting Place, the rallying point for diverse layers of society, the arena transformed into the personal springboard of each actor. The wrestler is, finally, in the midst of this cacophony, the least talkative of all in the very place where his declamations alone had once been the privileged centre of attention.

A RECONFIGURED DISCOURSE

The wrestler of the new generation is not capable of a verbal performance that would be equal to his physical prowess. Poetical declamation is no longer an integral part of the ritual. It has ceded to set phrases and verbal tics borrowed from boxers or from American rappers.[20] The adversaries settle for exchanging some short sentences in the form of taunts or threats during the ceremonial signing of contracts or as asides in the course of interviews they accord the press.

---

19   Orange, Tigo and Expresso.

20   Mohamed Ndao 'Tyson', who has been one of the greatest attractions of the Senegalese arenas since his baptism of fire in 1995, manifests in various ways his identification with the black American boxer Mike Tyson; he is, for example, immediately recognizable by ceremonial regalia made from the American flag. In their hairstyles and dress, a large percentage of Senagalese wrestlers, and not just Mohamed Ndao, express their identification with black American stars.

When the match ends, the victor does not avail himself of the radio and television microphones assaulting him to do anything more than recite a litany of the names of the innumerable persons to whom he owes his gratitude, which range from members of his technical staff to his religious guide and include, along the way, his parents, his friends and the political leaders of his locality. In this recitation, not only does he endow with value all the people around him, but also emigrants (Senegalese living in Europe or the US) and politicians in search of fame who have given him material or financial support in the hope of being cited. It is not uncommon, by the way, to see someone in his entourage whisper to the wrestler names he has forgotten.

Preoccupied by these acknowledgements, the victor does not linger when describing the action that took place, rarely yielding to the pressure of journalists eager to review the technico-tactical sequences of the match. Perceiving himself as less eloquent and evocative than the images abundantly served up on television and the snapshots of photographers in the newspapers, he says little about his feats.[21] The only commentary that a number of wrestlers are quick to add – as if they had somehow overlooked it – is intended to enlighten us with respect to their interest in financial gain: 'All my efforts and sacrifices have been made with only one thought in mind: to lighten my parents' burdens and provide for the necessities of my family.'

The numerous platforms provided them by the ceremonies of signature, previews of the contest and special broadcasts finally serve only to underscore the decline of 'beautiful speech'. The arena is less and less a space of literary creation in which poetry takes on the aura of music and whose movement is stimulated by rhythm. It has, however, inspired other actors who know how to derive benefit from this passion for the *làmb*.[22]

Wrestling, music and authors' rights

While the tradition of gymnastic poetry (*bàkku*) is itself defunct, it has been, like traditional chants, taken up by modern music: *mbalax* (Senegalese popular music), reggae, rap etc. The artists who appear onstage in show business (in orchestras, concerts, CDs, video-clips) update the verbal creations of yester-year's wrestlers, inserting the rhythms and choreographies of the new figures

---

21   The wrestler's reading of his fight, as communicated through his *bàkku*, had been an important source of information when radio reporting and the photos appearing in the next day's press were the only ways to experience, or relive, the contest. At that time, there was only one daily newspaper with general information, *Paris-Dakar* (1933–61), which became *Dakar-Matin* (1961–70) before it was renamed *Le Soleil* (from 1970 onward).

22   'Wrestling' in Wolof.

of the arena and, at the same time, assign themselves the role of praising the champions. In this way, the verses of the wrestlers are incorporated into the works of professional musicians. These productions that have been created for the arenas are found on new media and enter into previously unknown circuits.

The artists' products, intended for sale, do not fail to pose the problem of intellectual property, giving rise to quarrels and litigation. The success of these pieces of popular music allows us an immediate glimpse of the financial stakes involved in creation. This is why paternity disputes are so common.[23]

In fact, the modern singers often register these works that are adaptations of *bàkku* in their own names, and the ancient wrestlers who are the 'true' authors, rarely being informed about questions concerning authors' rights, are not aware of any revenues resulting from the exploitation of their works (for similar cases see Diawara in this volume).[24]

The way in which chants and rythms of the world of wrestling have been gathered and distributed has, until now, deprived them of appropriate treatment. Exclusively performed in the space of wrestlers, they arrived on the airwaves following their live recording by reporters; consequently, they are often incorporated as interludes or theme tunes in broadcasts dedicated to wrestling, without, however, being accorded the same dignity as works drawn from an album or recorded in the studios of the same radio stations that play

------

23   The *bàkku* documented by Pathé Diop on a record in the 1930s are attributed by certain old timers to another wrestler of the same generation, Ousmane Sène. Some couplets of '*Kaaro yalla*', a chant of exhortation to combat made famous by the diva Khar Mbaye Madiaga, whose voice has rung out in the arenas since the 1960s, are also claimed by Ndèye Ngom Mbambilor, a woman author of traditional songs. In 1997 an authorship dispute opposed the percussionist Oumar Thiam to his partner Bada Seck, who had just published on a cassette the title 'Génération Boul Falé', a hommage to Mohamed Ndao. '*Boul Falé*' is a slogan originating in a title of the first Senegalese rap group, Positive Black Soul, which came out in 1992. The expression, which in urban Wolof means 'don't worry about it', 'take it easy, don't let it get to you', connotes repudiation and fatality, fixing one's boundaries with respect to the established order, and, in a word, self-reliance. Mohamed Ndao 'Tyson', who does not come from the traditional milieu of wrestling, appropriated this set phrase, which accords special value to success achieved by individual effort. By his origins, itinerary and awards, he established himself in the mid 1990s as the figurehead of the 'Génération Boul Falé'.

24   Among the performers, only the former wrestlers Mame Gorgui Ndiaye and Ndiouga Tine, and the female singer Ndèye Ngom Mbambilor have been registered with their songs, to date, by the Bureau sénégalais du droit d'auteur (BSDA) – interview with M. Sène, representative of the *Service de la Documentation Générale et de l'Automatisation du Fichier* of the BSDA.

them. The nature of these creations (seen as informal) and the status of the composers (who are not the classical actors of show business) explain this kind of neglect and exclusion from the 'market' or art business. The musicians also consider these works (the *bàkku* and other wrestling songs), which are hardly ever registered by their authors at the Bureau Sénégalais du Droit d'Auteur (BSDA), simply as a kind of raw material that they reappropriate and reshape to their liking and their own profit.

Meanwhile, with the new juridical environment of artistic and literary creation and the scope the phenomenon of wrestling has assumed, we are progressively moving towards further changes.[25] The development of wrestling and the place that business has taken in it has given rise to new reactions that motivate people to search for profit in this large 'fair'. The onslaught of singers towards the world of the arenas in search of both inspiration and a new audience has occasioned a tight competition in which originality alone allows one to get ahead of the pack. The example of Ndèye Kassé gives us an idea of this ambience. This female singer, attempting to add a particular touch, invited an 'old glory' of wrestling, Papa Kane, to participate in the recording of her title 'Làmbi góor'[26] (the arena of men); the guest star, however, declaiming his *bàkku*, quite obviously became both co-author and co-interpreter of the song. This experience of direct involvement of the producer of the *bàkku* provides the wrestlers and poets of long-since forgotten arenas, whom the show business has meanwhile replaced, with new perspectives for successful careers.

Conclusion

Senegalese wrestling, which, like all traditional sport, was a means of distraction, has become an attractive profession completely embedded in a commercial milieu. In the course of these past twenty years, it has produced

---

25   In 2008 Senegal acquired a new 'Law on authors' and related rights' which takes into account developments linked to technologies of information and communication, the protection of folklore, the phenomenon of counterfeiting, among other subjects of recent debate (see République du Sénégal 2008). In April 2011 the Senegalese Office of Authors' Rights (BSDA) began taking steps directed towards the *Comité national de gestion de la lutte* (CNG) and promoters so that the question of authors' rights will henceforth be taken into consideration with respect to the organization of wrestling matches, which had become a privileged framework for the public performance of artistic works (as the General Director of the Senegalese Office of Authors' Rights stated in an interview, broadcast in May 2011 by the television station 2STV in *Bantamba*, a weekly programme devoted to wrestling).

26   CD *Teggil say bët*, 2009.

new high-profile figures and behaviours revealing the speed at which the social patchwork can be rearranged. The arenas, invaded by a new type of clientele, are the receptacles for contents ever less drawn from traditional resources. The intineraries and frames of reference of today's wrestlers are often the polar opposites of those of their predecessors. Their vestimentary manners, their hair styles, their choreographies and their discourses are only some of the signs of this rupture. The current masters of the game, who are the promoters and the sponsors, have placed their bets on the spectacular and the sensational to sell their product. This new format strongly privileges the wrestling show and favours the professionals of popular music whose manner of elaboration and exploitation necessarily raises the question of intellectual property. The enhanced mediatization not only amplifies the performance or the production (the sequence of actions in the matches, the chants, the dances etc.), but also reorients and reformats them, making them subject to exogenous norms. Senegalese wrestling, after centuries of evolvement, is approaching a critical turning point. At an intersection where diverse stakes merge, it is seeking its path between anchourage in the cultural values which nourished it and opening out to innovations aimed at increasing its audience and financial profitability.

References

Badji, Abdou. 1982. La lutte traditionnelle joola: étude et perspectives. Mémoire de
        maîtrise (MA thesis), Dakar: INSEPS.

Bidiar, Ithiar. 1990. La lutte traditionnelle avec frappe à Dakar: quelles perspectives?
        Mémoire de maîtrise (M.A. thesis), Dakar: INSEPS.

Cissé, Momar. 2009. *Parole chantée et communication sociale chez les Wolof du
        Sénégal.* Paris: L'Harmattan.

Conférence des Ministres de la Jeunesse et des Sports de la Francophonie
        (CONFEJES). 1990. *Manuel de lutte africaine.* Dakar: CONFEJES.

Deville-Danthu, Bernadette. 1997. 'Le sport support de l'idée de nation'. *Quasimodo*
        3(4):109–15.

Faouzi, Mahjoub. 1978. *Le sport africain.* Paris: ABC.

Faye, Ousseynou. 2002. 'Sport, argent et politique: la lutte libre à Dakar (1800–2000)'.
        In: Momar-Coumba Diop (ed.). *Le Sénégal contemporain.* Paris: Karthala,
        309–40.

Faye, Joseph-Victor. 1984. La lutte traditionnelle: son importance, sa signification
        en fonction des éthos et des habitus ethniques au Sénégal. Mémoire de
        maîtrise (M.A. thesis). Dakar: INSEPS.

Gaye, Mor-Talla. 2007. 'Business de la lutte: les millions de la suspicion'. *Weekend
        Magazine* 11:30–46.

Gouda, Souaïbou. 2010. 'Sports, identités culturelles et développement dans l'espace francophone: France, Bénin, Congo, Niger et Sénégal'. *Journal Of Global Business Administration* 2(2):150–62.

Houedakor, Eteh Koissi. 2010. L'action sportive organisée au Togo: réalité nationale, contraintes et perspectives de développement: Essai d'analyse comparée avec le Sénégal et le Bénin. Ph.D. Dissertation, Bordeaux, Université Victor Segalen.

Keïta, Abdoulaye. 2008. La poésie orale d'exhortation: l'exemple des *bàkku*, des lutteurs wolof (Sénégal). Ph.D. Dissertation, Paris, INALCO.

Ly, Boubakar. 1967. 'L'honneur chez les Toucouleurs et les Ouolofs'. *Présence africaine* 61:32–67.

Ly, Bocar. 1992. *Football: histoire de la coupe d'AOF.* Dakar: Nouvelles Editions africaines.

——— 2005. *Allou: l'âme d'un peuple?* Dakar: PUD.

Marone, Oumar. 1969. 'Essai sur les fondements de la littérature sénégalaise à la lumière des métaphores aqueuses de la langue wolof'. *Bulletin de l'IFAN* 31(3):787–852.

Mbaye, Lamane. 2003. Rôle et statut du griot dans la littérature wolof. Ph.D. Dissertation, Dakar, Université Cheikh Anta Diop, Faculté des Lettres et Sciences Humaines.

Mbuub, Sàmba. 1985. 'Défi, bravade et antagonisme: aspects dans la littérature d'expression wolof'. *Bulletin des études africaines de l'INALCO* 5(9):53–85.

Melik-Chakhnazarov, Achôt. 1970. *Le sport en Afrique*, Paris: Présence Africaine.

Ndiaye, Alphonse-Raphaël. 1996. 'De la lutte traditionnelle chez les Sérère: fondements mythiques, techniques et langages gestuels'. In: *Peuples du Sénégal*. Paris: Sepia, 109–38.

République du Sénégal. 2008. *Loi sur le droit d'auteur et les droits voisins*. Dakar.

Ritchie, Carson. 1967. 'Impressions on Senegal on the seventeenth century'. *African studies* 26, 2:59–93.

Seydou, Christiane. 1977. 'La devise dans la culture peule: évocation et invocation de la personne. In: Geneviéve Calame-Griaule (ed.). *Langage et cultures africaines: essais d'ethnolinguistique.* Paris: Maspéro, 187–264.

Sériba, Mahaman-L. 2005. 'La lutte traditionnelle au Niger: entre volontarisme étatique et symbolisme ancestral'. *Tydskrif Vir Letterkunde* 42, 2:239–53.

Sidi, Zakari. 2002. *Sagalo, le maître des arènes,* Niamey: NIN.

CHAPTER 14

Who owns the vuvuzela?

Local interests, intellectual property and

the football World Cup in South Africa

ⒸⒸⒸⒸⒸⒸⒸⒸⒸⒸ

Matthias Gruber

Kick-off

In the run-up to the World Cup in South Africa, every Friday was 'Football Friday'. The government and its commissioned agencies launched this campaign to rally South Africans behind the event. To show their support, South Africans were expected to wear the colours of the national team, Bafana Bafana, on Fridays. In schools, offices, shops or on the street many people were dressed in yellow-and-green T-shirts, most of them replicas of the team shirt. It was, of course, optional for South Africans to wear the 'colours'. But an obligation to be part of 'Football Friday' was in the air. I learnt that schoolteachers put pressure on parents if their kids' Friday outfit wasn't green and yellow, and not every company who expected their employees to be in the Friday uniform was willing to provide the T-shirts. Aside from those drafted into the Football Friday campaign, many others were eager to show their national pride and their commitment to the World Cup. Bafana Bafana shirts were not the only items multiplying with the World Cup around the corner.

9 June 2010 was the 'Vuvuzela Moment' (Figures 14.1–3). Two days before the tournament, people gathered on the streets at noon and blew their vuvuzelas as loud as they could. Vuvuzelas are long plastic trumpets which became both famous and notorious in 2009/2010, although they had been in use in South African football stadiums for nearly a decade. The sound of the vuvuzela provides overwhelming background noise during matches, and the instrument is the standard equipment of most football supporters. Another prominent item in South African stadiums is the *makarapa:* a construction helmet with carved-out figurative designs and paintings. Replica shirts,

Figure 14.1   'Vuvuzela Moment', 9 June 2010 in Newtown, Johannesburg (photo by M. Gruber).

vuvuzelas and *makarapas*, which constitute South African football fan regalia, attracted global attention during the World Cup as images transported in media coverage. Although used for the same purpose, they differ greatly with respect to intellectual property (IP) rights. Football shirts, especially those used by professional and national teams, are produced by big corporations. In the case of the World Cup it was Adidas, Nike and Puma who provided the shirts for the teams and campaigned to sell replicas to fans.[1] The replicas are expensive, so countless fake copies are sold on the street. Vuvuzela are cheap to produce and are not related to specific brands. The *makarapa* was invented in the late 1970s by a football aficionado who is still producing them, and attracted some attention for his creation during the World Cup.

The World Cup provided unique opportunities to research the dissemination and transformation of norms. Because of the importance of the event the host country had to accept significant foreign interventions in legislation, budgeting and other aspects. The World Cup also opened a space for South African debates, innovative ideas, and negotiations of lifestyle and of the country's position in the world. In this chapter I will discuss the impact

---

1   The exception is North Korea, playing in shirts made by Legea, an Italian company that also provided for Iran, Zimbabwe and Belarus among others. Found at: www. sportspromedia.com/news/north_korea_agrees_kit_deal_in_time_for_world_cup_ return; www.handelsblatt.com/sport/fussball/nachrichten/wm-ausruestervertraege-ladenhueter-nordkorea-seite-2/3451564-2.html, accessed 17 April 2012.

Figure 14.2   'Vuvuzela Moment', 9 June 2010 in Newtown, Johannesburg (photo by M. Gruber).

Figure 14.3   Traffic cone used as vuvuzela on 'Vuvuzela Moment', 9 June 2010 in Newtown, Johannesburg (photo by M. Gruber).

of the IP rights regime on the local context in Johannesburg, the justifications for infringements, the emerging of a public discourse and the 'unfairness' of a legal construction under the impact of a so-called global 'mega event'.

The three examples – the vuvuzela, the *makarapa* and sport shirts – differ in terms of the legal basis, i.e. their relevance for the judicial system, the kind of actors involved and their economic, social and cultural dimensions. Producers of sportswear protect their products with trademarks, industrial design rights and/or patents on technical innovations. The *makarapa* can be related to copyright, and the vuvuzela might have a case in terms of trademarks. Why certain goods fall under IP rights protection and others not, even if they are clearly more original than others, has much to do with historical, cultural and social constellations. The examples show how norms are constructed and transformed, and I will follow the traces of these processes on the ground, including their justification and embedment in the local normative framework. This chapter is based on ethnographic research carried out during the World Cup[2] in Johannesburg among fans and traders and producers of the items. Moreover, a diachronic perspective was applied to understand the entanglement and transformation of norms in daily action and economic practice.

Intellectual property and the World Cup

Although World Cups were used in advertisements from the very beginnings in the 1930s, FIFA was only sporadically involved in the marketing business until the mid 1970s (Eisenberg *et al.* 2004; Tumblety 2008). When in 1974 the Brazilian official and manager João Havelange took over the presidency from Sir Stanley Rous, the politics of FIFA changed profoundly. Havelange ended the era of old-school dignitaries who regarded the entanglement with business partners as an impertinence, and made the Federation into a global economic player (Eisenberg *et al.* 2004:245). Under the aegis of Havelange and his successor Sepp Blatter the World Cup became a valuable brand whose revenues rocketed from 1.8 million Swiss francs in 1958 to *c.*2,100 million in 2010. While in 1958 income depended on ticket sales, in 2010 two-thirds of the money was generated from broadcasts and almost another third from marketing rights.[3] This development went hand in hand with

---

2   Fieldwork was carried out in 2009 and 2010 with the support of the Cluster of Excellence 'The Formation of Normative Orders' at the Goethe University Frankfurt.

3   Figure of 1958 in Eisenberg *et al.* (2004). Figures are published in the FIFA Financial Report 2010 (FIFA 2011). Ticket sales (around 300 million Swiss francs) were only a minor part of the 2010 receipts, went to the local organization committee and are not included in the 2010 figures. In 1958, 1.8 million Swiss francs were *c.*£150,000; 2,100 million Swiss francs were *c.*£1.750 million sterling in 2012.

efforts to promote international property rights within the framework of increasingly neoliberal capitalism. It is not a coincidence that when the global homogenization of IP rights reached a peak with the TRIPS agreements in the 1990s a new level of commercialization was attained. In football the big European leagues and federations developed elaborate marketing strategies and intensified their efforts to win sponsors. Economically, the protection of IP rights is one of the Federation's main concerns. Until the 1990s the issues of copyright infringements, ambush marketing and combating counterfeits were not prominent on FIFA's agenda. That they became so may have to do with the increase of revenue generated through the event, but it also almost certainly reflects the increasing attention paid to IP rights in public discourse and the omnipresent presence of trademarks, brands and their symbols. The large investment in marketing had to pay off for the sport-equipment manufacturers. The selling of team shirts became an important factor in sport economics. The manufacture of shoes and the development of new fabrics are not the reason for the outstanding position of these companies.[4] Logos and marketing are their main assets (see also LaFeber 1999).

FIFA itself released a 'Rights Protection Programme' (FIFA n.d.) containing 'Do's and Don'ts' and a FAQ section so as to provide businesses and customers with guidelines on how to behave and how to shop. This programme is in accordance with international and national IP law, but it also tried to deflect the impression that FIFA was taking over the country. World Cup critics has that suspicion, and pointed to the creation of exclusion zones[5] that resulted in alleged forced displacement and restrictions for the local poor. Formulations such as: 'In implementing the Rights Protection Programme, FIFA has adopted a policy of business as usual', meaning that business in the respective areas may continue 'as usual' (FIFA n.d.:7), reflect the hubris of an international institution that considers its own rules as above those of any given state. Friends and interview partners, random conversations on the streets or in taxis, gave me the impression that everyone was certain that a 'takeover' was underway.

The local perception of FIFA as a superpower was further boosted by the implementation of temporary World Cup laws at federal and provincial

---

4   Information about patents can be retrieved publicly, notably via the web. Everybody can see that even minor innovations like the shape of particular plastic parts can be the content of a patent. Chinese counterfeiters are able to copy new products and so-called technological innovations as soon as they leave the factory (Lin 2011).

5   'Exclusion zone' refers to a perimeter around the stadium with special trade regulations during World Cup matches.

levels, years before the event, beginning shortly after the successful bid (Republic of South Africa 2006a, 2006b). While most sections of these laws grant temporary work permits to those involved in the World Cup (broadcast personnel, official players, team doctors etc.), other parts were designed to facilitate the importation of pharmaceutical products and other equipment used by the football teams, or regulated alcohol consumption in the stadiums (usually prohibited). The section dealing with property rights declared the World Cup a 'protected event'.[6] However, there was no need to fill potential gaps in the South African civil code with an additional legislation. The country's IP law is particularly strong and dates back to 1916, long before most Northern countries implemented their corresponding acts (Kaplan 2009:1). When South Africa signed the TRIPS agreements in 1995 only minor changes were needed to bring the law into compliance with it (Wolson 2007:353).

Special Courts (Republic of South Africa 2010) were introduced in South Africa, a country where the justice system is often perceived as slow and overstretched. Fifty-six courts in the nine host cities, i.e. every city where matches were played, were open from 7:45 a.m. to 11 p.m. and were responsible for World Cup-related crimes.[7] In the Johannesburg magistrates' court a signpost with the inscription 'FIFA World Cup Courts' pointed the way to the right tribunal. These courts, manned with South African magistrates, and not run by the FIFA as the name might suggest, became well known when a case was opened in Johannesburg against two Dutch women who had organized an ambush-marketing stunt during the Netherlands vs. Denmark match in Soccer City on 14 June 2010.[8] The ladies were dressed in orange with a little Bavaria Beer tag on their dresses. After their passports were confiscated

---

6   The 'protected event' status was of such far-reaching importance for FIFA that the Federal Court of Justice of Germany, the highest court of ordinary jurisdiction, decided that the term 'World Cup 2006' could not be protected as a trademark. The court found that the name of the event is generally intelligible and therefore not protectable (BGH GRUR 2006, 850 [854 f.] – FUSSBALL WM 2006; BGH, I ZB 97/05, Rn. 20 f. – WM 2006).

7   Until 13 July 2010, the courts had dealt with a total number of 205 cases. Most were related to theft and robbery followed by the illegal selling of World Cup tickets (Demana 2010).

8   A group of thirty-six young Dutch women were ejected from the stadium during the Denmark vs. Netherlands game in Johannesburg. They wore the orange dresses which were sold with beer packs by the Dutch brewer Bavaria. The action was the follow-up to a stunt in Germany four years earlier, when a group of Dutch fans was forced to doff their Bavaria-branded coverall trousers (so called '*leeuwenhosen*') and watch the match in their underwear. The Bavaria case is now a textbook example for successful guerilla marketing.

and the payment of bail had been extracted, the two were threatened with jail sentences of up to six months.[9]

The vuvuzela

When the World Cup was awarded to South Africa, it was often pointed out that the world's biggest sporting event was now to be staged for the first time in Africa. Until 2002, when the Cup was held in Japan/South Korea, the event had always taken place either in the Americas or in Europe. Africans have played football almost as long as Europeans and South Americans, the game having been introduced to the world by English soldiers, missionaries and merchants (Alegi 2004; Eisenberg 1997; Guilanotti Armstrong 2004; Martin 1995). Egypt was the first African team to play in the World Cup, as early as 1934, the second time the tournament took place. Fifty years later Zaire was the first team from sub-Saharan Africa to participate. Today the total number of World Cup berths for African teams is still limited to six, while the European countries have thirteen (Darby 2005). That Africa came to host the World Cup was the result of negotiations and power struggles within FIFA.[10]

Unlike World Cups in European or American countries which were staged in and by a nation-state, 2010 was the 'the African World Cup'. Cornelissen (2004) has shown how the bid for the World Cup was accompanied with legitimating narratives. One was of South Africa's equal place on the global stage and its ability to host such an event, with benefits for the continent as a whole. A strong argument to justify the event to the public, with its enormous cost, was the 'development' narrative. With the help of the tournament 'Africa stands tall and resolutely turns the tide on centuries of poverty and conflict' as the former South African president Thabo Mbeki was repeatedly quoted as saying. Other politicians such as Jacob Zuma stressed the economic benefit for the continent. High expectations were fuelled. These ranged from individual profits to the implementation of modern transport systems (Van der Westhuizen 2007), nation-building (Ndlovu-Gatsheni 2011) and the end of 'Afro-pessimism' (Czeglédy 2009; Tomlinson 2009).

In fact, much of the success of football depends on local identification with club teams, but only to a certain extent with national teams. Narratives of economic development, nation-building or the end of Afro-pessimism do not provide a basis for an emotional identification with the tournament.

---

9   This inappropriately long sentence was made possible through the World Cup 2010 amendment to the Merchandise Marks Act (Republic of South Africa 2006c). The case was dropped after FIFA and the brewery negotiated a settlement out of court.

10 See for example Desai and Vahed 2010.

Bromberger (1998) pointed out the analogies between ritual performances and great football matches. The formal characteristics are spatial configurations and behaviours grounded in local customs around the game, such as the performances of European Ultra groups led by a so-called *'capo'*, or the singing, dancing and masquerade in the Seisa Ramabodu Stadium in Rocklands, when Celtic Bloemfontein is playing.[11] International tournaments lack some of the elements of club football. But as international tournaments are as much media- as stadium-spectacles, a local flavour has to be added to make them attractive. South Africa's football was not on global display until 1996, when the national team Bafana Bafana won the African Cup of Nations, a competition that attracts only little attention outside the continent. Two years later, Bafana Bafana qualified for the World Cup in France, and then in 2002 for the tournament in Japan/South Korea, but without leaving a strong impression on the international stage. In the advertising of the South African World Cup, only the political dimension of local football heritage, notably the anti-apartheid struggle, was exploitable. Consequently, in 2004 a unique South African fan item entered the global arena: the vuvuzela.

The vuvuzela, a plastic trumpet, emerged as a mass phenomenon in South African stadiums around 2000. The instrument appeared on the global stage in 2004, when the World Cup was awarded to South Africa in Zurich. Nelson Mandela brought the 'truly South African' vuvuzela to the FIFA congress as a piece of African culture. Culture and identity were used as symbolic capital in the bid campaign. In 2009, during the Confederation Cup,[12] the final rehearsal for the World Cup, the vuvuzela was at the centre of a fierce debate among football players, TV professionals, worldwide football supporters and the South African public. European and to a lesser degree South American audiences and players were annoyed by the waves of sound from the vuvuzelas, declaiming the end of football supporter culture and possible damage to the game. European media, especially, fostered an anti-vuvuzela campaign with the support of certain internet groups. Dislike for the vuvuzela became an emotional factor in the European public debate concerning South Africa's

---

11   Celtic Bloemfontein has a particularly colourful example of South African fan culture. Other clubs in the country could also be mentioned in this respect.

12   The Confederations Cup is a FIFA competition held every four years. Since 2001 it has served as a trial run for the host country of the World Cup. Participants are the holders of the continental championships, the reigning world champion and the team of the host country. The esteem of this tournament is limited.

ability to host the World Cup.[13] It did not take long for a countermovement to form, and the responses to the critiques from abroad were furious.

The vuvuzela debate in the Western public was understood as an attack on the cultural integrity of the country, an example of the arrogance of the established football nations, especially those from Europe. The vuvuzela suddenly became the quintessence of South African culture and FIFA's Sepp Blatter was urged on more than one occasion to lay down the law in favour of the vuvuzela. Indeed, vuvuzelas are loud. An average vuvuzela player can produce a limited number of tones; more sophisticated musicians are able to play simple melodies. As stadium audiences are not often in tune, the sound of the vuvuzelas can be disturbing.[14] To understand the idea of the vuvuzela, one has to visit a big match in South Africa such as the Soweto Derby,[15] when thousands of spectators produce a loud rhythm that has the entire stadium vibrating. The vuvuzela itself is cheap, everyone can handle it and it can be personalized with colours and flags, or by adding plastic pipes to extend it. The vuvuzela is mass-produced, at first only in South Africa; later Chinese copycats entered the market. Vuvuzelas are usually distributed by informal traders in front of the stadiums. At the time of the World Cup the instrument was available almost everywhere and in many different forms, from give-aways with company logos to expensive airport-art versions with beadwork of various qualities.

Now a national symbol, the vuvuzela needed a biography, and a discussion of ownership and origin arose. To give the vuvuzela some historical credibility, the South African National Parks Administration (SANParks) used the similarity to the kudu horn to present a predecessor, and created the *kuduzela*. Horns of the kudu antelope were used to transmit signals over

---

13   The debate took place in the media and on the web. German tabloids in particular speculated on the failure of South Africa, imagining a second German 'Summer Night's Dream' following the World Cup of 2006. The doubts as to South Africa's capability were further fuelled when Togo's national football team was attacked in January 2010 in Cabinda, Angola. The fact that thousands of kilometres separate Cabinda from South Africa did not count in Eurocentric news coverage.

14   The vuvuzela are even made responsible for serious ear diseases (Swanepoel and Hall III 2011).

15   The Soweto Derby refers to matches between the Orlando Pirates and Kaizer Chiefs, two of the biggest clubs in the country, also known as the Soweto Giants. Both teams have their roots in Soweto but have supporters everywhere in South Africa. According to informants, violence among spectators had been the norm. In 2001 a disaster occurred at Ellis Park Stadium, Johannesburg. Forty-three people died in a stampede (Alegi 2005). Fans of the Pirates and the Chiefs entered the dialogue which followed the disaster. Today the Derby stands out for its peaceful atmosphere.

distances in southern Africa. SANParks launched the *kuduzela* in cooperation with a South African plastics manufacturer to collect money for one of its programmes. It was introduced as 'Truly African Heritage'.[16] The media picked this up enthusiastically, but the South African fan scene rejected the idea. One informant, a long-time follower of South African football since the early 1960s, was furious about this 'invented tradition' (interview 2009a). For him the kudu horn is related to 'serious matters'. It was blown in remote areas to gather the people together, often for funerals, sometimes for war. In contrast, football is related to joy, excitement and pleasure.[17] Others were less emotional, but stressed that there is no connection between the kudu horn and the vuvuzela.

Another historical derivation is the claim made by the Shembe Church. According to his followers, the founder of the Church, Isaiah Shembe, created the vuvuzela in 1910; it was first made out of cane, later of iron sheet. In fact trumpets in the shape of the vuvuzela are used during services of the Church. Media reports during the World Cup said that Neil van Schalkwyk, manufacturer of vuvuzelas in Cape Town, was willing to pay compensation to the Church for the appropriation of Shembe's invention.[18] Van Schalkwyk, who had been successful in selling vuvuzelas since 2001, filed a claim to it with the South African Registrar of Trademarks, as did various other persons (Van Rooyen 2010). No one can use the word vuvuzela exclusively, as it is a generic term and as such cannot be registered as a trademark.[19] Nor can it be registered as a functional design or patent because a trumpet, even when made out of plastic, is not an invention. The rumour that a manufacturer of vuvuzelas was willing to pay the Shembe Church compensation was most probably a hoax. It was obvious that the topic was fuelled by the media. Interestingly, all articles about property rights and vuvuzelas in the press and on the web were more or less based on a statement by a South African attorney which made clear that the vuvuzela is in the public domain (Van Rooyen 2010).

Within football, it is Saddam Maake who claims to be the creator of the vuvuzela. A celebrity in South African professional football, he is a die-hard supporter of one of the biggest local football clubs in the country, the Kaizer Chiefs. Saddam, living in Tembisa, a township east of Johannesburg, made himself a name by creating the institution of Fan Number One. Usually the Fan Number One plays an important role in football fan clubs and acts as voice and face of the fans. These outstanding fans are not necessarily elected,

---

16   www.sanparks.org/about/news/2009/july/kuduzela.php, accessed 17 April 2012.
17   In other contexts there is clearly an analogy between football and war; see Armstrong and Giulianotti 2001; Kuper 2003 [1994].
18   See Madlala and Foss 2010 and N.N. 2010.
19   The derivation of the term vuvuzela is unclear.

but rather earn their prestige by merit. Like players and coaches they appear
in the media and give interviews. They follow their teams to all the matches,
and some of them sell merchandise products among their fellows. During
my field research a Fan Number One was trying to influence his fellows not
to buy fake shirts or other sports fashions, but instead to buy the officially
licensed ones. His club was sponsored by Adidas, and the company not only
provided shirts but also shorts, tracksuits and caps. He was arguing that only
money spent on official fan-gear would benefit the club. Sometimes a sponsor
like South African Breweries (SAB) provided tickets for international games
or small compensations for these PR activities.[20] You could call these fans
small entrepreneurs or entertainers in the football business, but the income
they generate through their activities is not their main motivation, which is
their passion for their club or, during the World Cup, national team. Most
of the professional clubs do have a Fan Number One, but only a handful of
them describe their position as a full-time job or attach importance to this
'title' (interview 2009b). The position and the institution are disputed among
South African fans. Some younger fans feel patronized; others appreciate
the commitment of the Fans Number One, or enjoy the entertainment they
provide.

During the World Cup a group of 'Number Ones' travelled as 'Castle
Superfans' through South Africa.[21] Saddam Maake was not among them.
Hence, he had to follow another strategy to be visible at the World Cup. He
claimed that he invented the vuvuzela in the late 1960s or 1970s (depending on
different statements), and brought it back again onto the football stage in the
late 1990s. Saddam told this story to various international TV stations covering
the World Cup and to print journalists (Moyo 2010). His claim is denied by
other long-time followers of South African football (interview 2009c), for
whom the vuvuzela developed gradually from small rubber hooters, in the
late 1960s, to larger instruments. Two of my informants recalled a now
deceased Kaizer Chiefs fan who first came up with a metal vuvuzela, its shape
later transformed into that of the plastic vuvuzela we now know. The last
noteworthy 'myth of origin' comes from China. It was reported that Mr Wu
Yijun invented the vuvuzela. According to a major German broadcaster and an

20 SAB also supported Neil Van Schalkwyk, who was honoured with the Kickstart
    Award in 2001. Later SAB announced that the company would support Van
    Schalkwyk's attempts to protect his product (SABC News, 19 May 2004, found at:
    196.35.74.234/south_africa/general/0,2172,80078,00.html, accessed 16 March 2012.
21 The 'Castle Super Fan' campaign was launched by SAB. With the help of a public-
    relation agency, the fans went 'on tour' and were featured in TV commercials, on
    posters and on beer bottles and cans.

important soccer monthly, Mr Wu saw the instrument, made out of bamboo, in a South African comic strip (Freyeisen 2010; Hollmann 2010). He said that he changed the material and exported the first vuvuzela to South Africa.

The vuvuzela is an example of the dissemination of an idea. In all of the attempts to account for its origin, with perhaps the exception of the fantastic story of Mr Wu, who is in some respects out of the competition, claims to the 'ownership' of the vuvuzela are regarded as a means to earn money, whether the rights implied belong to an individual (Saddam, Van Schalkwyk) or to a group (SANParks, Shembe). In each case, the claim to ownership of the idea is economically motivated. In a kind of countermovement, the public domain is defended by those of my informants who trace the vuvuzela back to small rubber hooters. I suggest that without the World Cup the concept of IP would not have been applied to the vuvuzela, in the debate about which economic value is at the forefront of the question of ownership of an idea.

The *makarapa*

In contrast to the vuvuzela, it is easy to trace the origin of the *makarapa*, first designed by Alfred Baloyi in the late 1970s or early 1980s (Figure 14.4). According to Baloyi, the modified hard hats originally had two purposes. They were meant to protect their wearers from missiles (such as bottles) in the stadium while also serving as striking parts of their match-day costumes. Beyond the 'ordinary' outfit, consisting of replica shirts or T-shirts with prints, fans vie with each other in donning fanciful dress: South African stadiums are populated with *sangomas* (traditional healers), bishops, cowboys, transvestites and people with oversized glasses, masks and *makarapas* of all varieties.[22] To give a *makarapa* its shape a profile is carved out of the plastic with a hot knife, and then modelled over a kerosene stove.[23] Various extensions can be added, and that the size of the *makarapa* is limited only by the practical ability to wear it. Following this process the hard hats are painted and finished with varnish. Baloyi also produces *makarapas* in small editions for companies, for marketing or corporate-identity purposes. His customers are football supporters of various local clubs. Many fans use different *makarapas* for different occasions, such as cup competitions or league games. As sponsors and names of the competition change, the designs of the helmets have to change too. *Makarapas* often feature trademark logos. The idea is not to

---

22 Kaminju and Ndlovu (2011) describe specific performance personas of some popular fans to illustrate the creativity of supporting football in South Africa.

23 Some manufacturers alter the production process and use more sophisticated devices to cut and heat the raw hard hats, see www.designboom.com/weblog/cat/8/view/11164/making-the-makarapa.html, accessed 28 March 2012.

Figure 14.4   Alfred Baloyi in front of his Primrose Workshop, August 2009 (photo
by M. Gruber).

advertise, but rather to relate the *makarapa* to the particular event. A very
popular design, for example, displayed two Nokia cell phones of a popular type
for the Vodacom Challenge.[24] *Makarapas* for the World Cup featured flags,
vuvuzelas, mascots, badges, Coke bottles,[25] prominent players and even Sepp
Blatter himself. When Baloyi came up with his first *makarapa*, protecting
his idea in terms of IP rights was beyond his reach. The access to 'white'
jurisdiction and administration was very limited for black South Africans and
was avoided. Not only were IP rights little known among the black labour
force, but also IP played a minor role in sport in general. As described above,
even the FIFA had barely begun to explore the advantages of IP rights in order
to protect their own interests in the late 1970s. With the end of apartheid,
Baloyi undertook several attempts to protect his idea. But by then it was
simply too late. The IP rights regime subsequently targeted him. Some years
ago 'his' club banned him from selling *makarapas* in front of the stadium with
the explanation that this would violate copyright laws by the appropriation

---

24 The Vodacom Challenge is a pre-season tournament featuring the two Soweto
    Giants and two teams from Europe. Other Cup tournaments are also named after
    their respective sponsors.
25 Coke bottles were very visible during the World Cup as the company is an official
    FIFA sponsor and advertised everywhere.

Figure 14.5 *'Home of the Baloyi Makarapa studio' Wynberg, between Sandton and Alexandra, Johannesburg, June 2010 (photo by M. Gruber).*

of trademarks and designs. Baloyi is perfectly aware that promoting his own artistic creations does not violate any laws, but he nonetheless stopped selling them in the stadium to avoid further trouble (interview 2009/2010).

Even without formal recognition of his status as creator, Baloyi and his *makarapas* are a 'brand'. For the World Cup he associated himself with a company producing the 'original' *makarapas* in Johannesburg. The man, who until 2010 had worked in a shack in an informal settlement in Johannesburg, was featured larger than life on the front of a commercial building close to Sandton, the business centre of the city. Next to his picture one can read: 'Home of the Baloyi Makarapa studio' (Figure 14.5). His portrait in oil could be found in the nearby posh shopping mall to add some credibility to the World Cup adornment. Dozens of cutters and painters worked for 'Baloyis Makarapas' (Figure 14.6). All this was made possible by diverse business partners, who were at home in the business world of South Africa. His story attracted media coverage concerning the World Cup. The media told the story of an artist from the shacks who would benefit from his idea. In fact, the *makarapa* business was fiercely competitive. Massive numbers of *makarapas* were produced by various copycats, both in factory-like conditions and by one-man businesses. Baloyi himself is deflated about the possibilities of using IP rights for his own benefit. He did not worry that *makarapa* was not protected and that it was copied by many others trying to grab their share of the cash generated by the

Figure 14.6   Baloyi working in the 'Home of the Baloyi Makarapa studio' Wynberg, Johannesburg, June 2010 (photo by M. Gruber).

World Cup. His main concern during the World Cup was that of an artist and gifted craftsman: the poor quality of the *makarapas* often distributed under his name.

No one would deny Baloyi's creatorship, as he is the undisputed inventor of the *makarapa*. But IP rights are of no use to him. In legal terms he was simply too late to protect his invention. Reasons for this can be found in the specific historical circumstances of South Africa, including unawareness of the possibilities to protect designs in informal settlements in the South Africa of the 1970s.[26] *Makarapas* were first used in a cultural sphere in which the state was regarded as dangerous and not as a protector of rights. The irony is that the IP laws in South Africa, which date back to 1916 when they were adopted to protect European right holders, today, nearly two decades after the democratization, still serve the interests of the big and powerful multinational corporations.

---

26   Informal settlements are unplanned, unauthorized residential areas. Dwellings consist of simple shacks, usually without water supply and sewage systems or electricity. They occur on farmland, in townships and in the urban periphery.

Replica Shirts

The third fan item that I want to discuss is the shirt. Most South Africans and World Cup tourists were not involved in IP issues like Baloyi or the protagonists of the vuvuzela question, but many did have to make up their minds as to whether to buy a fake/copy shirt or not. Shirts in club colours or from the national team are basic equipment for many soccer fans.[27] The 'Football Friday' campaign contributed to the high demand as well as to the desire of many South Africans to be part of the event. In addition to Bafana Bafana shirts, there was also a demand for shirts of other nations. If people were able to attend matches, they wanted to be dressed or costumed appropriately to support their favoured team. Replicas of the team shirts are expensive. An 'original' Bafana Bafana cost between 500 and 600 Rand (around £40–50), whereas fake copies are considerably cheaper (about 55 Rand). For weeks before the kick-off and during the first two weeks of the tournament, the pavements of the bustling fashion quarter in Johannesburg's Central Business District (CBD) were packed. Dealers could barely meet the dramatic spike in demand. People were asking for national symbols such as flags, so-called 'car-mirror socks' (fabrics to cover car mirrors in national colours), caps and scarfs. But the best-selling goods were the replicas of the Bafana Bafana shirt. Hardly one of the shirts was an original from Adidas, just as none of the Levi jeans and Gucci bags offered on the street are 'real'.[28] According to the traders, all the fakes were imported from China. According to a local Customs officer, however, the counterfeits were made in South Africa (interview 2010a).

Fake copies are locally known as 'Fong Kong', a term that conflates 'fake' with 'Hong Kong', the commonly alleged source of the fakes. The traders' version of their origin is much more likely. In 1992 China advocated an open-market strategy. This was not only a substantial change for billions of Chinese but also profoundly affected the world economy. The market and production facilities for counterfeit goods expanded. In China, large wholesale markets for counterfeits opened their gates (Lin 2011). This increased the availability of affordable consumer goods in South Africa. The success of the Football Friday campaign created a paradoxical situation. The World Cup was at least

---

27 European Ultra groups refuse to buy team shirts or other licensed products to express their resistance to the commercialization of their sport and their clubs. In South Africa, as in other African countries, shirts of the national team, local or international club teams are a common way to dress.

28 This leads to the question of what makes a commodity like blue jeans original or not. They look the same, the labels are copied one to one and sometimes – as in case of high-priced blue jeans labels or football shirts – they even have fake price tags with the amount in Euro. Often, the materials used are a distinctive feature (originals do have more elaborate and different chemical fibres or special prints).

rhetorically advertised as a tool for nation-building and development, and as belonging to all (South) Africans regardless of class, colour or religious affiliation. The country was promoted as investor friendly, capable of running mega-events featuring up-to-date infrastructure, and the Johannesburg City Council used every opportunity to promote Johannesburg as a 'World Class City'. Yet, the demand for Bafana Bafana shirts led to a lively trade in fakes. A trade associated with the informal and illegal, possible through smuggling and often carried out by migrants with unclear residence permit status. Obviously not the well-administrated state that the official rhetoric wanted to create. In the case of Johannesburg, where my fieldwork was carried out, the epicentre of the trade was the fashion district in the inner city, also known as 'Little Addis'. This part of Johannesburg's CBD is close to the exclusion zone around the Ellis Park Stadium.[29] If you ask traders where they get their goods, they sometimes point, with a good measure of irony, to the China Mall next to Ellis Park. In fact, none of them is keen to reveal the routes of distribution. Once they reach Johannesburg, the counterfeits were usually stored in warehouses, then parcelled out in smaller quantities to retail shops and stalls on the street. This happens in the garages and houses of the CBD. There is obviously a hierarchy in this trading business. At the top, are businessmen who can afford to own or rent whole buildings. Storage rooms, garages, cafés (as spaces for negotiation or just the exchange of ideas), shops and stalls are subleased to petty entrepreneurs. At the 'bottom' of the trade are street vendors who run around trying to sell their goods to pedestrians and car drivers. In the shirt trade they played only a minor role in the CBD, where the main business was established in the shops and street stalls.

The inner city has undergone a radical change since the 1980s (Beavon 2004; Chipkin 2008). It was once the unchallenged centre of the South African economy. The area accommodated the country's wealthiest corporations and displayed the latest developments in city planning and architecture until the late 1970s (Chipkin 2008; Murray 2011). What once had the 'reputation as the quintessential apartheid city' (Murray 2011:xi) has become a 'global' African city. Most of the formal businesses left to create a new CBD in Sandton. Others were not willing to move, either because they had invested large sums in real estate and were not willing to abandon their investments, or because they insisted on maintaining their old dignified addresses, especially large mining enterprises, banks and insurance companies. These major economic players created a kind of segregated space within the CBD by taking strong security measures.

---

29 'Exclusion zone' refers to a perimeter around the stadium with special trade regulations during World Cup matches.

Figure 14.7   Jeppe street scene, the banner reads: 'Ethiopian & Eritrean Community – World Cup 2010 in Support of Bafana Bafana', July 2010 (photo by M. Gruber).

With the arrival of new residents from all parts of Africa the nature of business changed. The pavements and buildings outside this corporate world are now overflowing with countless small shops, street hawkers and all kinds of informal and formal trading. Storehouses that were once reserved for 'Whites Only' are now controlled by Indian entrepreneurs or Ethiopian businessman (Figure 14.7). Buildings that hosted offices and apartments are now the home of countless small shops selling clothes, but also of internet cafés, music shops and restaurants. The CBD is, depending on one's perspective, in a process of degeneration or vitalization. In the 1990s parts of the CBD, and some of the surrounding areas like Yeoville and Hillbrow which accommodate many people involved in trade in the CBD, became partly ungovernable. Houses were no longer maintained; slum landlords hijacked entire blocks and rented out rooms to whoever was able to pay. Often the 'decline' and transformation of the inner city is attributed to the end of apartheid and the migration of people from various African countries. But these views do not consider the fact that areas like Hillbrow, Doornfontein and Berea were always populated by newcomers, and for the same reason the CBD has also the reputation of being a dangerous place. Well-known novelist H. Rider Haggard wrote in his diary almost one century ago: 'It [Johannesburg] is a huge tumultuous city rather more evil and menacing than most and fearfully expensive to live in, that is all.' (Haggard and Coan 2001 [1914]:132). Haggard did not tell us what made Johannesburg so menacing and tumultuous. Today the discrepancy between the architecture, city planning and social engineering efforts of modernity, and the way the space is actually used by individuals, is striking. Simone (2004) showed how people manoeuvred in this environment, where almost nothing is stable, the idea of community is ephemeral and people of various cultural backgrounds live together in very limited space. He introduced the notion 'people as infrastructure' (2004:407) to describe the mobility and flexibility people have to develop to constitute economic options.

Local responses to intellectual property rights and the World Cup

The capacity of the state to stop the trade in counterfeit goods is usually limited (cf. Sundaram 2010). The World Cup brought the legal norms of intellectual property into the spotlight and police responded to violations, such as the sale of Bafana Bafana shirts, with daily raids. Police appeared in larger numbers, arrested traders and confiscated the shirts from traders and customers alike. Usually the trade halted for the duration of the action, and then moved to another street. Those who were arrested were set free after paying a fine.[30] Traders and clients perceived the actions as unjust. Even if they knew about the violation of property and trademark rights and so on, it had no meaning for them. They did not regard violating these legal norms as unethical. In fact, not all of the traders are fully aware that the trade in Fong Kong is an infringement. Others take the risk. The claim of a global corporation like Adidas is abstract and remote for the people on the streets of the CBD. If you ask people directly why they buy Fong Kong, they answer that it is affordable and that it looks like the real brand stuff.

As Peukert has shown, the notion of right and wrong in the context of IP rights entails 'an inherent conflict with basic norms rooted in our emotionally and intuitively grounded sense of justice' (2012:166). Even though he draws this conclusion from discussions on copyright violation by millions of German Internet users, there is an analogy with the trade in shirts at the time of the World Cup. In his article Peukert argues that law-abiding Germans who would never steal a tangible good such as a CD, copy music (illegally) via the net en masse. A shared music file primarily used in the private realm of one's own home does not take anything tangible away from somebody else, and by using the internet, a medium ideologically charged with the free circulation of ideas, the infringement of copyright laws does not feel like theft. Germany

---

30 While police officers didn't want to talk about the issue, traders told me that they pay a bribe to get out of the police cars and an additional fee if they want their goods back.

is not the Johannesburg CBD, and team shirts are much more tangible than songs consisting of bytes, but when shirts are 'sold' on the streets, there is no idea of stealing goods. Indeed, those who pirate the shirts take great pains to camouflage what they are doing. Prints and labels hardly differ from the originals. Price tags are reproduced in detail. For occasional consumers of sport shirts it is not easy to detect the fake. There were no Fong Kongs on the market with spelling mistakes or other obvious markers.[31] But for the traders the shirts are tangible, their value arising from their materiality. Asked for the right or wrong of his action one of the many Ethiopian migrant traders answered: 'I don't steal from nobody; I buy 200 or 400 Bafana shirts, twenty-five [in the colours of] Brazil, twenty-five [in those of] Germany [and of] Spain; I pay money for it and I sell it. So what is wrong?' (interview 2010b). Of course traders were aware that their action could be sanctioned.

For customers buying Fong Kong means buying a tangible good rather than stealing an IP owned by a company. Furthermore, as argued above, there was the feeling that if the World Cup is supposed to be for all, the shirt of the home team should be accessible to everybody. Here the norms of the IP rights are in contradiction with the right all Africans have to be part of the World Cup. In China, the presumable source of most of the counterfeit shirts, a 'copycat culture' (Lin 2011:59) has developed as an expression of a subculture reflecting everyday experience with faked commodities. In South Africa, there is no such popular culture around Fong Kong. Copies are regarded as inferior to brand-name products, but also as affordable and justifiable alternatives and therefore as a way to participate in mainstream culture. This view highlights the injustices in South Africa, based on the unequal distribution of wealth on both the local and on the global stage. From this simplistic perspective, there is an 'imperative to break the law'. If people could not buy fake shirts, a large part of the population would be excluded from Football Friday and from the football dress code and therefore from 'their' Football World Cup.

The penalization of Fong Kong was perceived by retailers and their customers as an arbitrary measure on the part of authorities, a marker of inequality. This argument is appealing, as it justifies the action of many people I like and who granted hospitality and support to me. Trading and buying Fong Kong becomes a subversive act against an unfair 'world system'. In the case of the counterfeit market in Johannesburg's CBD this argument is indeed tempting, but it is not the only aspect to trading counterfeits during the time

---

31 Modern football shirts consist of special, so-called performance fabrics, that are also protected as trademarks, and somebody familiar with the matter can easily distinguish these. Counterfeit Bafana Bafana shirts were made out of a different fabric.

of the World Cup. There is another dimension behind trading and policing activities grounded in the social structure of the CBD, where most of the customers and all of the law-enforcement officers are South Africans, and the traders are from Somalia, Ethiopia, Nigeria and other African countries. These traders work and live in South Africa as asylum seekers, refugees and naturalized South Africans. Compared with European countries, the South African state is very open with regard to the right of asylum. But migrants are still in a marginalized position and have to develop strategies to meet the challenges of a foreign, and as they often perceive, a hostile environment. One of the most pressing problems is a person's need for security, and Johannesburg's inner city with its migrant community can provide this to at least a certain extent. In Hillbrow, Berea and Yeoville, residential areas preferred by the migrant communities, housing space is very expensive. Apartments have to be rented or owned by people either with South African citizenship or with a residence permit. It often happens that a system of sub-leases is at work. Of course the rent rises as a function of the number of people who are engaged, i.e. one rents the apartment from someone else who rents from someone else in turn. At the end one pays, depending on the standard, up to 4000 Rand (*c.*£300) a month for a single room in an apartment shared with two other families, as I observed in 2010. For the same money you could have a nice cottage in the suburbs, if you were white or somehow established in the South African middle class. The networks among migrants are less stable, as one might assume, and often limited to direct mutual help with the possibility of immediate reciprocity (interviews 2010c; see also Masden 2004). The main reason for the instability of these networks is the high mobility of the migrants (Landau 2009:201). Almost none of the Ethiopians and Eritreans I know in Johannesburg see the city as a final destination. South Africa is difficult to reach, but not as impossible or dangerous as the route to Europe. Xenophobic attacks are a serious problem for migrants, especially if they are involved in informal trade.[32] Although the CBD of Johannesburg is relatively safe, traders there are still affected. The attacks usually occur in townships and informal settlements outside the big cities. During the attacks foreigners that live in the communities are violently forced to leave the area. In many cases people are killed and severely injured. Reasons for the attacks are various: offenders justify their behaviour with arguments like 'they [the victims] betrayed us, they took away our women, and they are exploiting the scarce resources'. The fact is that migrant traders are among the first targets in the communities.

---

32   The nature of 'xenophobia' is a matter of serious debate in the humanities and
     social sciences in South Africa. Important contributions are those of Dodson 2010;
     Hassim *et al.* 2008; Nyamnjoh 2006.

They maintain small shops for goods of daily use, such as soap, soft drinks, staple foods, etc. The attacks on them often take the form of simple looting. Offenders not only steal their goods, but also, by driving these tradesmen off, escape from any debts they may have accumulated to them. In addition to the economic risk for migrants, there is a much more menacing threat of physical and sexual violence. The seriousness of the problem is shown by the fact that the fashion district was closed on the Monday immediately after the World Cup final. Rumours, disseminated via the media and '*radio trottoir*' migrant networks were talking about the flare-up of attacks that had paused only as long as the World Cup lasted. Although no such attacks had occurred in the inner city, many traders had experiences of them in rural areas outside the city.

During the tournament an increase of police activity challenged the fragile system that maintains order and security in the fashion district. Landau (2009:203) concludes that 'the police have also capitalized on foreigners' unpopularity to bolster their reputation and bank accounts'.[33] Dealing with the police is a day-to-day business for the traders and the possibility of getting arrested is calculated. The reason for the arrest plays a minor role in the whole affair. Only a minority of the migrant traders are in the possession of proper papers. Migrant traders spend a good deal of time with all kinds of administrative work. One of my Ethiopian 'informants' is a specialist in something he calls 'processing'. He spends a good share of his time filling in forms, securing documents and finding innovative answers when important documents are missing. In addition to this cleverness in dealing with executive authorities, money does help to speed up the system or to compensate for the lack of certain unavailable documents. The whole arrangement can be described as an alternative normative order, where norm deviations are necessary and justifiable. Hornberger (2004) pointed to the gap between the norms of policing and the actual patterns of behaviour in the interaction of migrants and representatives of the state. While norms are expressed in laws, they are a matter of negotiation on a face-to-face basis. This means that people in the CBD usually know their counterparts and that they have policemen they can trust and others they don't know. During the World Cup the system of 'mutual agreements' between police and those who make their living in the inner city was unbalanced. Many traders blamed the police for going after bribes without offering something in return, i.e. a secure environment to trade in counterfeit goods.

33　I don't want to suggest that the South African Police is rotten to the core, but corruption is decidedly a problem. Most South Africans have an ambivalent relation to the police. This ambivalence is described in Hornberger 2009.

Street trade was affected by the City of Johannesburg World Cup by-laws.[34] Their purpose was to regulate advertisements, ambush marketing, the access to World Cup-relevant areas like fan parks and stadiums, traffic control and the street trade. Trading prohibitions were restricted to exclusion zones, the immediate perimeter around the stadiums and 'controlled access sites' (training grounds, team hotels, FIFA Fan Parks, accreditation centres). While most regulations did not introduce anything new or contrary to common sense, for example: 'A street trader shall not dispose litter in a manhole or storm water drain' (by-law 6.2.1.2), they were still problematic. They allowed the municipality to identify and demarcate as restricted any area 'it deems appropriate' (by-laws. 6.4.2), a formulation that raised serious concerns among human-rights activists (interviews 2010d).

The police were overtaxed by the special situation of the World Cup and the FIFA requirements.[35] My request for an official interview with a spokesperson of the Johannesburg Metropolitan Police has remained unanswered. My conversations with policemen have been serendipitous and never structured. Unsurprisingly, most Metrocops were not willing to talk about their actions. On one occasion I talked to a policewoman standing to the side of colleagues that were busy arguing with street traders. She pretended not to know what would happen to the arrested traders in the police car. Asked for the reason of the police action she just mumbled: 'FIFA wants it.' How 'FIFA wants it' justified the practices of the local police action is unclear. Cops certainly do not get orders from the local organization committee or FIFA, but of course FIFA is interested in protecting its own rights to branding and logos and the rights of their sponsors. I was unable to discover if FIFA or its partners actually sued anyone for selling counterfeits or misusing logos. Direct questions were answered with general remarks on the problematic of piracy.[36]

Conclusion

Coombe and Herman (2004:562) state that: 'Through intellectual property law, symbolic practice is transformed into symbolic capital – a "strange" sort of alchemy that even Marx couldn't imagine.' The Football World Cup relies on

---

34 The Province of Gauteng. 2009. Local Government: Municipal Systems Act (32/2000): City of Johannesburg Metropolitan Municipality: 20/10 FIFA World Cup South Africa By-laws: Provincial Gazette Extraordinary. URL: www.joburg-archive.co.za/bylaws/2010_bylaws.pdf, accessed 14 December 2011.

35 Beside its actual duty to maintain order and fight crime in the country, the South African Police was also made responsible for stadium security after a private security company had failed to assure this.

36 Email exchange with FIFA and Adidas, August/September 2009.

symbolic capital and definitely has an alchemy of its own. Instead of turning lead into gold, it seems that it turns a game into development, nation-building, global approval of a whole continent and money. The way IP was discussed on the ground by most actors followed, with few exceptions, the money argument. The ownership question of the vuvuzela revolved around issues of economic exploitability and the moral right to be recognized as the inventor (Saddam Maake) or the attempt to claim rights for 'traditional knowledge' or 'traditional cultural expression' (Shembe).[37] In the case of Baloyi's *makarapa*, common-sense justice should concede him the copyright for his creation and the right to make money from it. All this highlights how IP rights have depended on historical constellations and personal circumstances in South Africa, and unawareness of the possibilities to protect designs and make use of these rights for one's own purposes. Under the 1970s apartheid conditions a modified hard hat was not part of the capitalistic system and the idea of the commodification of intellectual inventions was absent in the political economics of black South African football supporters.[38]

In the case of the counterfeit trade in Johannesburg's CBD, the 'regime' of rights challenged the tenuous balance of relation between migrants and the state.[39] To be sure, arrangements between traders and police officers often violate legal norms. On the other hand, this arrangement offers ways to achieve justifiable goals, which are officially denied to migrants. In this case, copyright legislation not only entails further risk in the lives of migrant traders. It also reveals a paradoxical situation for the state. The availability of copies of shirts was of national importance, as the World Cup was seen as a showcase for the country and South Africans had to rally behind the event to make it a success in nation- and identity-building. The Bafana Bafana shirt was a visible symbol of this inclusive aspect of the World Cup. More intensive prosecution would have meant relinquishing the broad-based local support for the cup that was expressed by the wearing of the Bafana Bafana shirt.

---

37 South African IP legislation is currently without corresponding regulations. Attempts to introduce traditional knowledge or traditional cultural expression have failed (Monika Bruss, 'Intellectual Property as a legal transplant', unpublished paper presented at the conference 'Intellectual Property, Normative Orders and Globalization', Bad Homburg, 2–4 June 2011).

38 I don't want to suggest here that there was no commercialization of black sports during that time. Television started in South Africa in 1976 and the first football matches were shown as early as 1977. Consequently the sport was more and more in the focus of companies sponsoring the teams (Alegi 2004:142).

39 Of course the World Cup was also an important business opportunity for successful traders.

FIFA did not literally take over power in South Africa, but the federation's focus on reserving exclusive rights for itself and its partners created an atmosphere in which ownership became a major issue. Space was contested in exclusion zones, stadiums and traffic regulation; ideologies and ownership were contested by the question of participation and appropriation of the World Cup or special rights for the Football Federation. Immaterial culture and its tangible output (like *makarapas* and vuvuzelas) were reduced to marketable property. This expresses the true ambivalence of the World Cup. On the one hand the tournament is imagined as a global event, bringing people together, benefitting the host country and even the continent. On the other hand, it's a global business enterprise, following the rules of neoliberal economy. Here different orders are at work and often clash. The examples discussed show that normative orders such as IP rights can only be accepted as valid in particular frameworks. If they are in conflict with historical experiences or current life situations they require justification beyond mere legal regulations.

References

Alegi, Peter. 2004. *Laduma!: Soccer, Politics and Society in South Africa*. Pietermaritzburg: University of Kwazulu-Natal Press.

——— 2005. "'Like cows driven to a dip': the 2001 Ellis Park stadium disaster in South Africa'. In: Paul Darby, Martin Johnes and Gavin Mellor (eds). *Soccer and Disaster*. London: Routledge, 109–23.

Armstrong, Gary and Richard Giulianotti (eds). 1997. *Entering the Field: New Perspectives on World Football*. Oxford: Berg.

——— 2001. *Fear and loathing in World Football*. Oxford: Berg.

Beavon, Keith. 2004. *Johannesburg: The Making and Shaping of the City*. Leiden: Brill and University of South Africa Press.

Bromberger, Christian. 1998. 'Fussball als Weltsicht und Ritual'. In: Andréa Belliger and David Krieger (eds). *Ritualtheorien. Ein einführendes Handbuch*. Opladen: Westdeutscher Verlag, 285–302.

Chipkin, Clive. 2008. *Johannesburg Transition: Architecture & Society from 1950*. Johannesburg: Ste Publishers.

Coombe, Rosemary and Andrew Herman. 2004. 'Rhetorical virtues: property, speech, and the commons on the world-wide web'. *Anthropological Quarterly* 77(3):559–74.

Cornelissen, Scarlett. 2004. "'It's Africa's turn!" The narratives and legitimations surrounding the Moroccan and South African bids for the 2006 and 2010 FIFA finals'. *Third World Quarterly* 25(7):1293–309.

Czeglédy, André. 2009. 'Urban dreams: the 2010 Football World Cup and expectations of benefit in Johannesburg'. In: Udesh Pillay, Richard Tomlinson and Orli Bass (eds). *Development and Dreams: The Urban Legacy of the 2010 Football World Cup.* Cape Town South Africa: HSRC Press, 225–45.

Darby, Paul. 2005. 'Africa and the "World" Cup: FIFA politics, eurocentrism and resistance'. *The International Journal of the History of Sport* 22(5):883–905.

Demana, Neliswa. 2010. 'Dedicated courts deliver swift justice'. *Justice Today – Official Newsletter of the Department of Justice & Constitutional Development* 3:4–5.

Desai, Ashwin and Goolam Vahed. 2010. 'World Cup 2010: Africa's turn or the turn on Africa?' *Soccer & Society* 11(1):154–67.

Dodson, Belinda. 2010. 'Locating xenophobia: debate, discourse, and everyday experience in Cape Town, South Africa'. *Africa Today* 56(3):2–22.

Eisenberg, Christiane. 1997. *Fußball, soccer, calcio: Ein englischer Sport auf seinem Weg um die Welt.* München: Dt. Taschenbuch-Verlag.

Eisenberg, Christiane, Pierre Lanfrachi, Tony Mason and Alfred Wahl. 2004. *FIFA 1904–2004: 100 Jahre Weltfußball.* Göttingen: Verlag Die Werkstatt.

FIFA. n.d. 'The FIFA Rights Protection Programme at the 2010 FIFA World Cup South Africa™'. Fédération Internationale de Football Association; found at: es.fifa.com/mm/document/affederation/marketing/01/18/98/99/march2010rightsprotectiona520100308.pdf, accessed 14 March 2012.

——— 2011. 'FIFA-Finanzbericht 2010'. Zürich; found at: de.fifa.com/mm/document/affederation/administration/01/39/20/45/webfifafr2010ger.pdf, accessed 14 March 2012.

Freyeisen, Astrid. 2010. 'Vuvzelas made in China'. Radio broadcast, ARD Hörfunkstudio Schanghai, 1 July 2010.

Giulianotti, Richard and Roland Robertson. 2004. 'The globalization of football: a study in the glocalization of the "serious life"'. *The British Journal of Sociology* 55(4):545–68.

Haggard, Rider and Stephen Coan (eds). 2001 (1914). *Diary of an African Journey.* London: Hurst.

Hassim, Shireen. Tawana Kupe and Eric Worby (eds). 2008. *Go Home or Die Here: Violence, Xenophobia and the Reinvention of Difference in South Africa.* Johannesburg: Wits University Press.

Hollmann, Frank. 2010. 'Handarbeit aus der Badewanne. Ortsbesuch im Vuvuzela-Geburtsort'; found at: www.11freunde.de/international/131257, accessed 30 August 2011.

Hornberger, Julia. 2004. '"My police – your police": the informal privatisation of the police in the inner city of Johannesburg'. *African Studies* 63(2):213–30.

—— 2009. 'Ma-slaan-pa dockets: negotiatians at the boundary between the private and the public'. In: Giorgio Blundo and Pierre-Yves Le Meur (eds). *The Governance of Daily Life in Africa: Ethnographic Explorations of Public and Collective Services.* Leiden: Brill (African Social Studies Series 19), 171–204.

Kaminju, Anthony and Tabisani Ndlovu. 2011. 'Playing from the terraces: notes on expressions of football fandom in South Africa'. *African Identities* 9(3):307–21.

Kaplan, David. 2009. 'Intellectual property rights and innovation in South Africa: a framework'. In: *The Economics of Intellectual Property in South Africa.* Geneva: World Intellectual Property Organization, 1–17.

Kuper, Simon. 2003 (1994). *Football Against the Enemy.* London: Orion.

LaFeber, Walter. 1999. *Michael Jordan and the New Global Capitalism.* New York: W.W. Norton.

Landau, Loren. 2009. 'Living within and beyond Johannesburg: exclusion, religion, and emerging forms of being'. *African Studies* 68(2):197–214.

Lin, Yi-Chieh Jessica. 2011. *Fake Stuff: China and the Rise of Counterfeit Goods.* London: Routledge.

Madlala, Mpume and Kanina Foss. 2010. *Vuvuzela deal for Shembe church*; found at: www.iol.co.za/news/south-africa/vuvuzela-deal-for-shembe-church-1.487721, accessed 14 March 2012.

Madsen, Morten. 2004. 'Living for home: policing immorality among undocumented migrants in Johannesburg'. *African Studies* 63(2):173–92.

Martin, Phyllis. 1995: *Leisure and Society in Colonial Brazzaville.* Cambridge, New York: Cambridge University Press.

Moyo, Phathisani. 2010. 'Vuvuzela creator blown off?' *Mail & Guardian*, 8 January; found at: www.mg.co.za/article/2010-01-08-vuvuzela-creator-blown-off, accessed 8 January 2010.

Murray, Martin. 2011. *City of Extremes: The Spatial Politics of Johannesburg.* Durham: Duke University Press.

N.N. 2010. 'Shembe Church wins vuvzela battle'; found at: www.gospellife.co.za/shembe-church-wins-vuvuzela-battle, accessed 14 March 2012.

Ndlovu-Gatsheni, Sabelo. 2011. 'The World Cup, vuvuzelas, flag-waving patriots and the burden of building South Africa'. *Third World Quarterly* 32(2):279–93.

Nyamnjoh, Francis. 2006. *Insiders and Outsiders: Citizenship and Xenophobia in Contemporary Southern Africa.* London: Zed Books.

Peukert, Alexander. 2011. 'Intellectual property'. In: Jürgen Basedow, Klaus Hopt and Reinhard Zimmermann (eds). *Max Planck Encyclopedia of European Private Law.* Oxford: Oxford University Press, 926–30.

————— 2012. 'Why do "good people" disregard copyright on the internet?' In: Christophe Geiger (ed.): *Criminal Enforcement of Intellectual Property: A Handbook of of Contemporary Research.* Cheltenham/Northampton: Edward Elgar Publishing, 151–67

Republic of South Africa. 2006a. '2010 FIFA World Cup South Africa Special Measures Act, 2006'.*Government Gazette* 495(29198):2–8.

————— 2006b. 'Second 2010 FIFA World Cup South Africa Special Measures Act, 2006'. *Government Gazette* 495(29199):2–8.

————— 2006c. 'Designation of 2010 FIFA World Cup as a protected event in terms of section 15a of the Merchandise Marks Act, 1941'. *Government Gazette* 91(28877):3–7.

————— 2010. 'Magistrate's Courts Act (32/1944): Annexure of certain districts to other districts for the duration of the 2010 FIFA World cup Tournament'. *Government Gazette* 539(33208): 3–5.

Simone, Abdou Maliq. 2004. 'People as Infrastructure: Intersecting Fragments in Johannesburg'. *Public Culture* 16(3):407–29.

Sundaram, Ravi. 2010. *Pirate Modernity: Delhi's Media Urbanism.* London: Routledge.

Swanepoel, Wet de and James W. Hall III. 2010. 'Football match spectator sound exposure and effect on hearing: a pretest-post-test study'. *South African Medical Journal* 100:239–42.

Tomlinson, Richard (ed.). 2003. *Emerging Johannesburg: Perspectives on the Postapartheid City.* New York: Routledge.

————— 2009. 'Anticipating 2011'. In: Udesh Pillay, Richard Tomlinson and Orli Bass (eds). *Development and Dreams: The Urban Legacy of the 2010 Football World Cup.* Cape Town South Africa: HSRC Press, 94–113.

Tumblety, Joan. 2008. 'The Soccer World Cup of 1938: politics, spectacles, and la culture physique in interwar France'. *French Historical Studies* 31(1):77–116.

Van der Westhuizen, Janis. 2007. 'Glitz, glamour and the Gautrain: mega-projects as political symbols'. *Politikon* 34(3):333–51.

Van Rooyen, Carl. 2010. 'Doubts raised over vuvuzela trade mark: managing intellectual property'; found at: www.managingip.com/article/2477715/ Doubts-raised-over-vuvuzela-trade-mark.html, accessed 16 March 2012.

Wolson, Rosemary. 2007. 'The role of technology transfer offices in building the South African biotechnology sector: an assessment of policies, practices and impact'. *The Journal of Technology Transfer* 32(4):343–65.

LIST OF INTERVIEWS

Interview 2009a: with a male, 60-year-old football supporter in Sebokeng, South Africa, August 2009.

Interview 2009b: with a 34-year-old, male football supporter in Braamfontein, Johannesburg, September 2009.

Interview 2009c: with two football supporters in their early 60s in Primrose Squatter
        Camp, Johannesburg, September 2009.

Interview 2009/2010: several interviews and talks with Alfred Baloyi, Johannesburg,
        September and October 2009 and June 2010.

Interview 2010a: with a customs officer in CBD, Johannesburg, June 2010.

Interview 2010b: with a *c.*25-year-old Ethiopian trader in CBD, Johannesburg, July
        2010.

Interviews 2010c: with Ethiopian and Eritrean migrants in the CBD and Yeoville
        Johannesburg, July 2010.

Interviews 2010d: with human right activists, male and female, in Braamfontein and
        CBD Johannesburg, June 2010.

INDEX

www.ingramcontent.com/pod-product-compliance
Lightning Source LLC
Chambersburg PA
CBHW060020030426
42334CB00019B/2115